Air Fryer Cookbook

The Ultimate Guide to Mastering your Air Fryer with Many Tasty and Healthy Recipes. Step by Step Instruction to Prepare Easy and Delicious Meals Without Fat.

PATTON TREVIS

Table of Contents

Introduction

The air fryer is a countertop convection oven with more power. An air fryer is almost like a convection oven that uses no oil to simulate deep frying. A high-speed fan circulates hot air, forming a crisp layer by browning surfaces. Regular convection toaster ovens or convection ovens, according to some reviews, show outstanding performance. In virtually every kitchen, the counter room is in high demand. And if you have a number of it, it's simple to overcrowd it and fill it with the new kitchen gadgets. However, you'll want to find space for an air fryer.

Another advantage of air frying is the ease with which it can be cleaned. The majority of air fryer buckets and racks can be washed in the dishwasher. We recommend a decent dish brush, such as one from Casabella, for those who aren't dishwasher resistant. It'll get all of the crannies — which help to circulate air! — Without making you crazy.

Air fryers cook food that would have otherwise been immersed in oil by circulating heated air. The cooking chamber of an air fryer radiates heat from just a heating element above the food, and a fan circulates hot air.

Cooking vegetables in an air fryer, just a brilliant idea. Your vegetables can tan and crisp up with a gentle spritz of olive oil or avocado oil. Crawford claims that most vegetables can be prepared in under 10 minutes. Green beans, broccoli, and mushrooms are among her favorites, and she claims that asparagus & baked potatoes both work well in the air fryer.

Air fryers do not really fry. Instead, the food is placed in a perforated basket and then cooked through blowing hot air circulated by the device. The air force creates a convection effect, which cooks and browns that foods exterior in the basket. Breaded meats, such as frozen chicken tenders, and unbraided starchy foods, such as tater tots or French fries or, can turn brown if the air temperature rises over 320 F.

An air fryer functions similarly to a countertop convection oven. It's a compact electric cooker with a heating element as well as a fan that circulates air in the cooking chamber. In an air fryer, though, the air is swirled quite rapidly in a circular pattern, which allows it to cover all of the food's surfaces to provide a crisp crust. Furthermore, the food is placed in a perforated basket, which raises the amount of time it is in touch with the hot flowing air.

Anything that creates a significant difference? Since there isn't any room between the chamber's walls and the basket, the heat is amplified.

Many families use the air fryer for cooking canned, frozen snacks like tater tots, French fries, and chicken nuggets, yet many parents appreciate that their children can easily prepare a meal in the air fryer when they get home from school. That isn't what it can do, however.

"You can cook something in an air fryer that you can roast — chicken breasts, sandwiches, fish, lamb chops — and they don't have to be breaded.

"The air fryer prepares them to the right temperature — they're juicy and tender."

Chapter 1: Air Fryer – A Handy Equipment

The air fryer is basically a countertop convection oven with more power. An air fryer is a kind of convection oven that simulates deep frying without the use of oil. A high-speed fan circulates hot air, forming a crisp layer by browning reactions like the Maillard reaction. Regular convection toaster ovens or convection ovens, according to some reviews, show outstanding performance.

In the way that it roasts and bakes, an air fryer is identical to an oven, but the distinction is that the heating elements are just on top & accompanied by a powerful, strong fan, resulted in food that is super crispy in almost no time — and, most importantly, with less oil, unlike deep-fried equivalents. Because of the use of a distributed heat source, the size and positioning of the fan, air fryers usually heat up efficiently and cook food quickly and evenly.

According to the market analysis company NPD Group, almost 40% of homes in the United States had one as of August 2020. Anything from frozen chicken wings to organic French fries and roasted veggies and fresh-baked cookies can be air-fried.

In virtually every kitchen, the counter room is in high demand. And if you have a number of it, it's simple to overcrowd it and fill it with the new kitchen gadgets. However, you'll want to find space for an air fryer.

Another advantage of air frying is the ease with which it can be cleaned. The majority of air fryer buckets and racks can be washed in the dishwasher. We recommend a decent dish brush, such as this one from Casabella, for those who aren't dishwasher resistant. It'll get all of the crannies — which help to circulate air! — Without making you crazy.

Air fryers cook food that would have otherwise been immersed in oil by circulating heated air. The cooking chamber of an air fryer radiates heat from just a heating element above the food, and a fan circulates hot air. Depending on the model, temperatures will reach 250 °C (482 °F). In an air fryer, there isn't a lot of cooking oil included. When opposed to non-convection ovens, the cooking time in the air fryer can be shortened by up to 20%.

By totally submerging food in hot oil just past the boiling point of water, traditional frying methods cause the Maillard effect to temperatures ranging from 140 – 165 °C (284 - 329 °F). The air fryer operates by wrapping the target food in a thinner layer of oil, applying heat, and initiating the reaction with circulation air heated to 200 °C (392 °F). Consequently, the gadget can brown foods such as potato chips, shrimp, seafood, beef, cheeseburgers, French fries, or pastries by utilizing 70% – 80% less oil than from a conventional deep fryer.

Temperature and timer variations are available on most air fryers, allowing for more accurate cooking. Usually, food is cooked in a basket on a drip plate. The basket must be agitated on a regular basis, either manually or with the aid of an automated food agitator. Convection ovens & air fryers cook food in identical ways, but air fryers are often smaller and produce less heat.

Since the more significant amount of oil used in conventional frying penetrates the food (or the coating batter, whether it is used) and contributes its own color, the texture and consistency of food cooked using traditional fried approaches and air fried techniques are not similar.

Additional attachments for various types of cooking, such as pie pans, grilling trays, skewer racks, and cake barrels, are available for specific air fryers.

Air fryers, like traditional convection ovens, can roast, steam, and also dry food.

Chapter 2: How Do Air fryers Works?

Air fryers use a high-powered fan for baking foods at a high temperature, whereas deep fryers cook the food in a container of oil which has been heated to a particular temperature. Both cook food fast, although an air fryer takes almost no time to preheat, while a deep fryer will take up to 10 minutes. Air fryers use little or no oil, while deep fryers use a lot of oil that absorbs into the foods. Food in both machines comes out crispy & juicy, but they don't taste the same because deep-fried foods are covered in batter that cooks distinctly in an air fryer than a deep fryer. In an air fryer, sprayed foods need to be sprayed by oil before frying to make them flavor and crisp up, while in a deep fryer, the heating oil soaks into the batter. Wet batters and flour-based batters don't function well in the air fryer, but they do in a deep fryer.

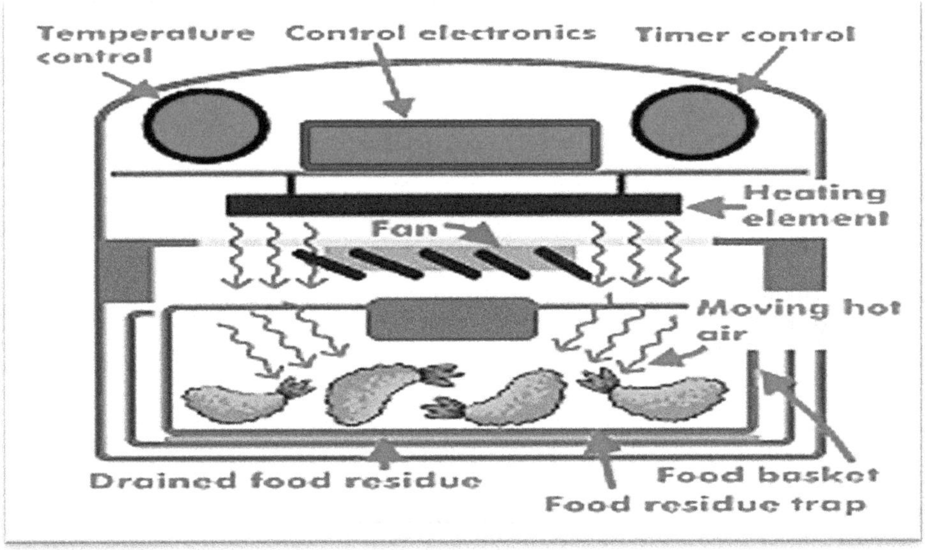

The principle of air frying seems to be a marvel in itself. Is it possible to fry without using fat? Is it really possible? What is an air fryer, and how does it work? It, like all other enigmatic phenomena, has a perfectly logical answer. But first, let me state unequivocally that air frying is not the same as frying. To really fry something, it must be fully submerged in oil. There's no getting around that. On the other hand, an air fryer will have a crispy, crunchy texture that makes Southern fried chicken & French fries delicious. Is that clear?

An air fryer functions similarly to a countertop convection oven. It's a compact electric cooker with a heating element as well as a fan that circulates air in the cooking chamber. In an air fryer, though, the air is swirled quite rapidly in a circular pattern, which allows it to cover all of the food's surfaces to provide a crisp crust. Furthermore, the food is placed in a perforated basket, which raises the amount of time it is in touch with the hot flowing air.

Anything that creates a significant difference? Since there isn't any room between the chamber's walls and the basket, the heat is amplified.

Many families use the air fryer for cooking canned, frozen snacks like tater tots, French fries and chicken nuggets, , yet many parents appreciate that their children can easily prepare a meal in the air fryer when they get home from school. That isn't what it can do, however.

"You can cook something in an air fryer that you can roast — chicken breasts, sandwiches, fish, lamb chops — and they don't have to be breaded. Crawford notes, "The air fryer prepares them to the right temperature — they're juicy and tender."

Cooking vegetables in an air fryer is a brilliant idea. Your vegetables can tan and crisp up with a gentle spritz of olive oil or avocado oil. Crawford claims that most vegetables can be prepared in under 10 minutes. Green beans, broccoli, and mushrooms are among her favorites, and she claims that asparagus & baked potatoes both work well in the air fryer.

To begin with, air fryers do not really fry. Instead, the food is placed in a perforated basket and then cooked through blowing hot air circulated by the device. The air force creates a convection effect, which cooks and browns that foods exterior in the basket. Breaded meats, such as frozen chicken tenders, and unbraided starchy foods, such as tater tots or French fries or, can turn brown if the air temperature rises over 320 F.

Chapter 3: Mistakes to Avoid About Air Fryers

An Air Fryer is a great kitchen gadget, as we all recognize. There's something really rewarding about preparing dinner without ever flipping on the stove in our fast-paced environment!

The use of the air fryer has soared in recent years. There are several air fryer tools available on the internet.

The air fryer is great for saving time, keeping food crispy, and utilizing less oil, but it's essential to use caution while using it. You may be causing several air fryer errors. Here are few examples of how you could be mishandling your air fryer.

3.1 Mistakes When Buying New Air Fryer

1. Buying The Wrong Size of Air Fryer.

There's a reason these appliances come in various sizes! Get a smaller one if you're catering with one or two guests. Get a bigger one if you choose to cook for a larger family.

There's little more aggravating than discovering that your air fryer can't handle the amount of food you're cooking and needing to prepare several batches to get it done.

An air fryer with a capacity of no more than 4 quarts is recommended for 1-3 individuals. Have something of 5 quarts or more for a bigger family. In general, we recommend that you order one size larger than you think you like!

2. Buying An Air Fryer of Low Quality.

You get what you paid for, much about anything else you do. Stick with companies with a history of producing high-quality small appliances and read Amazon reviews to see how the devices do with other buyers.

The Amazon reviews are beneficial. Members of several Facebook groups discuss the excellent, terrible, and fantastic aspects of various air fryer products! You can look up almost every brand to get a recommendation!

3.2 Mistakes While Cooking with Air Fryers

1. Not Using Oil

While you can fry food with less oil versus deep frying, certain foods use a small amount of oil using an air fryer.

Before placing your food in the air fryer, spray or lightly coat it in oil, particularly if it's breaded. Your fries and vegetables would be crispy and tasty!

2. Using Of Right Oil In Air Fryers

Air fryer baskets & trays have a fickle covering. Any air fryer guides advice against using a propellant oil mist.

(Especially Pam) Over time, this form of oil may trigger the basket or attempt to chip.

It's a difficult decision; locating a pump oil jar that reliably fits is difficult.

You should apply the oil to a paper towel and use it to rub the basket. It is one possibility.

Make sure you're working with a high-smoke-point oil. Avocado oil is preferable as it has a better smoke point. If the bottle says 500 degrees Fahrenheit, it might seem a little heavy, but you won't be frying something that hot in the air fryer, so you should be fine!

3. Overfilling The Air Fryer

The air fryer cooks your food by circulating hot air inside it. If you stuff so much food into the basket, some of it will miss out on the hot air, and the food will not cook equally.

Using the best judgment when deciding how much food to bring in your air fryer basket. Make sure the food has enough space to pass about.

The sole exception to this law is that frozen chicken wings may be stacked in the air fryer. When air frying, they cook down but don't stay together.

Essentially, every single image on any single air fryer package depicts the food stacked to the very top. Please don't do that; it won't cook anything! Yes, such images are misleading.

4. Not Checking on Food.

Since you can't see inside most air fryers, it's crucial to keep an eye on things while cooking, particularly if you're frying something you haven't done before.

It's a brilliant idea to open your air fryer halfway through every recipe's cooking period to search, shake, or sometimes flip the food.

5. Not Using A Thermometer During Air Frying

A meat thermometer can offer you the most precise reading of whether or not your food is cooked.

Using a thermometer while frying meat through an air fryer because there are so many different versions (and they all cook differently) or so many other recipes!

6. Cooking The Wrong Things

There are several foods you can never attempt to cook in an air fryer. One is things that have been battered. Air frying battered foods are not the same as deep-frying them. The batter would simply drip all over the place, causing a sloppy mess.

This may be perplexing since a straight liquid batter can typically solidify until it meets the HOT oil in the deep fryer. In the air fryer, that doesn't work quite well.

However, you can cook stuff like air-fried pickles and Oreos in an air fryer. The Oreos are made using a crescent roll as the crust, but the pickles are made by dredging them in a liquid and covering them with a solid such as breadcrumbs to keep everything intact.

Another thing you shouldn't do in the air fryer is cook things that are delicate or lack weight. (Think leafy greens and uncooked grains.) Since the air fryer circulates air, everything that gets caught in it can burn as it hits the heating element.

3.3 Air Fryer Care and Safety Mistakes

1. Do Not Set the Air Fryer on Your Stove

Typically, Air fryers get hot! So, it's essential to make sure the appliance doesn't come into contact with something that might melt or burn.

When handling the air fryer pieces and the food inside, it's also essential to use tongs & potholders.

2. Not Washing the Air Fryer After Use.

You will believe that you should leave your air fryer just on the counter and not clean it until it becomes extremely dirty.

If you leave extra crumbs in the air fryer, it will retain the smells from previous meals, and it will be more likely to burn.

3. Used a Dishwasher to Clean the Air Fryer

It is a mistake that is unique to a particular brand. Check the manual before putting your air fryer baskets, trays, or drip pans in the dishwasher. Not all air fryer buckets can be washed in the dishwasher.

Some air fryers come with dishwasher-safe parts, while others don't. And sure to double-check for your owner's manual!

If your air fryer is emitting white smoke, you can wash the air fryer basket, plate, or pan. A buildup of fatty foods often causes it.

After each use, hand-wash the air fryer pieces in wet, soapy water.

4. Not reheating food in an air fryer

Your air fryer can be used for more than just cooking from scratch; it can even be used to reheat food.

Reheat some leftover pizza in your air fryer. Set it to 350 degrees Fahrenheit for a few minutes, and that will be "restaurant quality" once again!

3.4 Common Air Fryer Mistakes

Here are a few more of the most popular Air Fryer Mistakes to Avoid.

Can you have an air fryer? Make sure you stop these famous air fryer blunders and get the most out of your air fryer!

In recent years, air fryers have been all the rage, and with good cause! They make dinner preparation a breeze and save you effort and time while frying food!

You should know a few items before using your latest air fryer to ensure that you get the best performance possible. Rather than practice these lessons the hard way, and here's a list to assist you!

These were some of the more popular air fryer mistakes which people make.

1. Overcrowding the frying pan

Overcrowding the pot is one of the most significant principles of frying food. This will result in poor cooking outcomes and cooking that is inconsistent. The same can be said with your air fryer! Overcrowding the food can result in it being half-burned, undercooked, and unsatisfactory.

If you're producing many significant quantities, a larger air fryer might be worth considering. If you don't have a pressure cooker, you'll have to cook the food in portions, much as you would if you were cooking it in a pot.

A good rule of thumb is to never fill the air fryer more than halfway. When looking for an air fryer, it's best to concentrate on the basket's perimeter size rather than the entire quart size.

2. You don't buy a good air fryer.

If you think you're doing all right but your food always tastes burned or strange, it's possible that the issue isn't with you.

Purchasing a low-cost, even sub-par air fryer will help you save money and have this hot new gadget on a shoestring budget. If you don't buy a decent one, though, you risk having burned or unevenly cooked food, spoiled counters, or worse.

Take some time to read the feedback and invest in a high-quality air fryer. In the kitchen, the Cosori Air Fryer & Philips XXL Air Fryer are excellent choices. If you're uncertain about an air fryer to buy, read reviews and stay with a reputable company.

3. You're either using too much or not enough oil.

The ability to produce "fried" food without oil is a significant selling reason for the air fryer. Most foods, though, will take some oil to achieve an utterly crispy finish. However, if you use so much oil, you'll wind up on the other end of the scale.

When air frying food, there are a few explanations why you'll need oil.

- Crisp up foods (similar to air fryer French fries)
- Helps in the adhesion of spices and seasonings to the food (like with the air fryer steak)

Here are a few things to bear in mind while using oil on air-fried foods.

1. No additional oil is necessary while frying foods that have fat or skin, such as chicken wings and air fryer bacon. Spray the food with oil near the completion of the cooking process if you like it extra crispy.

2. When using the air fryer for baking, then you won't require any oil since you'll be using it like a convection oven but a fryer. You won't need to use any oil on foods like:

- Air fryer cookies
- Air fryer molten cake
- Air fryer bagel pizza bites
- Air fryer margherita pizza

3. For breaded items like fries, you'll only need about 1 to 2 teaspoons. Your air fryer circulates hot air, but they don't get crispy without the oil. Make sure your food is nicely coated, but not excessively so. Remember that if you want more crispness, you can always add extra near the end of the cooking cycle.

4. It is safer to stay away from canned and pressurized propellant oil sprays to secure your investment. What is the reason for this? These spray oils include propellants and additives, as can be seen in their ingredients. These propellant oils were already known to cause the lining of your air fryer baskets to peel and chip, which is not safe for your skin.

5. If you're going to air fry your food, please ensure to use a high-smoke-point oil. Have you ever heard of the term "smoke point"? The temperature where oil or fat starts to produce smoke is known as the smoke point (or burning point). Each oil or fat does have a different maximum temperature at which it can be safely cooked.

- The smoke point for avocado oil is 375-400°.
- The smoke point of coconut oil, butter, and EVOO is 350°.
- The smoke point of 400° is for Canola oil
- Peanut oil and Vegetable oil has the higher smoke point 45o°

Personally, find avocado oil to be beneficial. It has a more excellent smoke point than EVOO, much healthier than vegetables which canola oil, and does not alter the flavor of the food the way peanut oil does.

Only keep in mind if you're using butter and cook at 400 degrees, the air fryer can smoke a little more and feel a little more unpleasant.

4. You don't shake or rotate the food

Air fryers provide for almost hands-free cooking, though not entirely.

At the halfway stage of cooking, flip or swap the food for a fully cooked dinner, which means that the product is crisped equally on all sides.

When frying air fryer chicken or some other poultry, you can definitely check it with an instant-read optical meat thermometer to make sure it doesn't overcook.

Since the thickness of the meat can differ for each batch, cooking meats with the air fryer can be tricky.

You would want to check on it now and then make sure it's finished to stop overcooking.

5. Checking your food's temperature

If you don't already have one, invest in a digital reading food thermometer to prevent undercooked or overcooked food. This would ensure that the meat is thoroughly cooked before you serve it. This is particularly critical when it comes to meats. It can also assist you in learning and gauging the suitable cooking period for your meals since all air fryers have different cooking times.

6. Putting your air fryer basket on the countertop with a hot fryer

While you won't see steam come from the air fryer, it does get very hot! It's similar to using a small oven inside a small appliance.

To stop damaging your counter, make sure your air fryer is taken off the counter with little feet or has something beneath it. This even applies to the basket! When you're done, place it on some heat-safe surface instead of your counter.

7. Cooking fatty foods not correctly

Oil isn't needed for all foods, particularly those that are already fatty. Add a small amount of water at the bottom of the air fryer to make these items cook correctly. This can also save things like bacon from emitting an unpleasant smoky smell.

8. Cooking wet food

This is particularly true when it comes to proteins and vegetables. If you don't pat them dry, you'll get steamed food on your hands. To get the crispy fried flavor, make sure to pat those foods dry.

9. Helpful tools are not in use

To make the most out of your air fryer, you should purchase air fryer attachments. You don't have to, however! You probably still have several things in the kitchen that can be included! As an alternative,

It would help if you made a foil sling out of foil to make it easier to put fragile foods in & out of the air fryer. It is ideal for delicate meats or sweets (like air fryer salmon). Just make sure the foil isn't pressed to the edges of the air fryer basket, or the air won't flow.

To cover the bottom of the air fryer basket, you can use air fryer friendly parchment paper with holes. This is ideal for foods that get a little messy during the cooking period, such as parmesan chicken or coconut shrimp.

10. Not removing the basket when finished cooking.

When your food is ready, make sure to remove the fat-collecting basket from the bottom before tossing it into your serving bowl. This is to prevent the oil from spilling all over the food.

11. Not using the air fryer's full potential.

Anything that your grill or oven can prepare can be cooked in an air fryer. Your air fryer may also be used to roast! Imagine using your air fryer to make hot dogs, quiche, pizza, cinnamon buns, steak, roasted veggies, and so much more.

Ignoring the importance of fire protection. Air fryers are extremely hot! It's essential to make sure the air fryer doesn't come into contact with something that might melt or fire. To avoid burning yourself, use tongs & potholders while removing the lid from your air fryer. When frying, leave a 5-inch gap around your air fryer to allow it to function correctly. It is highly recommended that you place your air fryer on something to prevent it from burning or melting your countertop.

12. Cooking fresh vegetables.

In the air fryer, vegetables cook quickly. Remember to spray them with a thin layer of olive oil and season them well if you like them to crisp up. Shake it up sometimes, and you'll have a delicious roasted vegetable meal on your table in no time.

The majority of air fryer ovens & baskets operate in a similar manner. Air fryer ovens & air fryer baskets cook at the same temperature and for the same amount of time, plus-minus 1 or 2 minutes. You will use the same ingredients for both. This is a common misunderstanding created by marketing firms that believe one brand is superior to another. Both of them are air fryers. They all cook in a similar manner.

13: Not cooking frozen food.

When using an air fryer, so no need to defrost your stuff. Foods include beef, hamburger patties, lasagna casseroles, and other frozen items that may be cooked.

14: Not read the user manual.

Don't forget to read the user guide. The manual has a wealth of information about how to get the most out of your fresh air fryer.

15. Not baking with it.

Don't let this machine devolve into a pricey French fry generator! It may be used to bake something that will usually be baked in an oven. In your air fryer, you will make cinnamon rolls, pie, cheesecake, dinner rolls, and more.

16. Not having enough patience

It would be best if you spent some time learning how to use your air fryer. Check to see whether it cooks quicker or slower than the recipes on Pinterest & YouTube. And if you obey anyone else's formula strictly, you can find that your air fryer has already burnt the roasted cauliflower, so keep that in mind.

17. Low-quality air fryer.

Air fryers aren't always made equal. Choose a well-known brand while buying an air fryer. Still read the feedback on places like Amazon to see if other users rate the air fryers. Here are three suggestions: Instant Pot Vortex Plus, Omni, and GoWise are three of the company's models.

18. Using an air fryer to prepare liquid batter foods.

Batters that are dense and hold together perform well in air fryers. Tempura and other liquid batters do not do well in an air fryer. If in need, the classic breading process for the air fryer (flour, breadcrumbs coating, egg dip) may be used.

Chapter 4: Air Fryers vs. Deep Fryers

There are the air fryers on one side and the deep fryers on the other in the environment of fried foods, but they are not the same thing! We've compiled what you need to know about the calories, health, cooking time, flavor, and price of air fryers vs. deep fryers. By contrasting these two kinds of fryers beside one another, you will decide whether to go for the better air fryer or the best deep fryer.

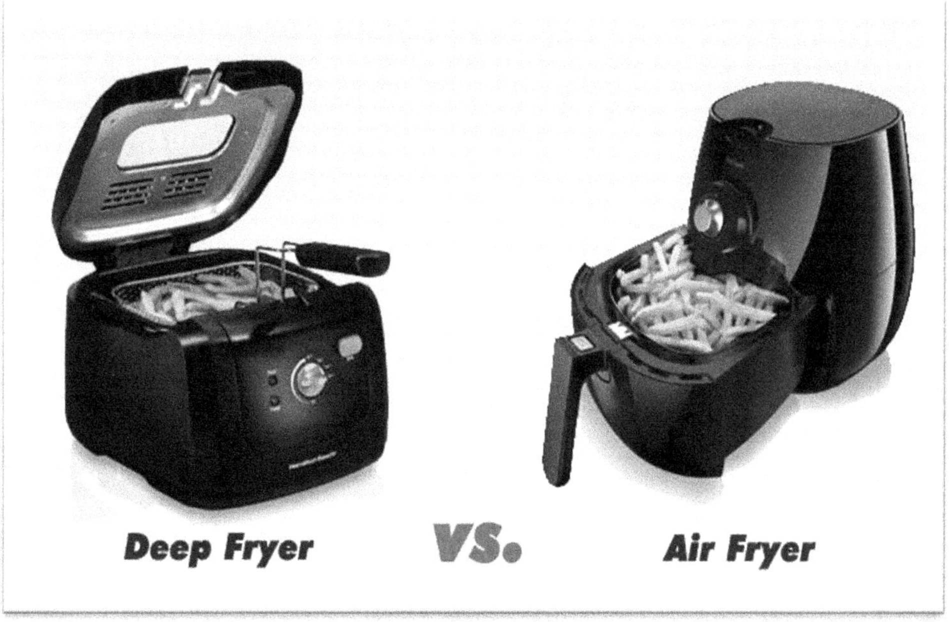

4.1 Is It Worth It to Buy An Air Fryer?

This would be a one-sided competition, with air fryers bringing home the most of the prizes. And if the Air Fryer is still not a significant technological breakthrough that can alter the trajectory of human evolution, it would undoubtedly improve the lives of many housewives and husbands. It also paves the way for a healthier new cooking lifestyle.

If you're in the market for a new fryer, then you're presumably deciding between an air fryer and a deep fryer. Both have advantages and disadvantages, but both provide delicious crunchy stuff. You can get the familiar fried texture without extra oil and calories by using one of our best-rated air fryers or go all-in by purchasing in a deep fryer.

Deep fryers & air fryers seem to be somewhat close at first sight. Both impart a delectable flavor and a crunchy exterior to ordinary foods (such as vegetables or meat). However, a deep fryer's process (dunking food into a massive volume of hot oil) differs significantly from an air fryer's, which covers the food with a small amount of oil before blasting it with hot air.

An air fryer is the most recent technological advancement in the kitchen, revolutionizing how you cook and serve food. An air fryer is just a gadget that claims to fry tasty foods without the use of excessive oil, which may render you overweight or unhealthy. It operates by circulating superheated air through its chamber to cook your food.

A fan inside the air fryer allows circulating the hot air, which generates a reaction known as the Millard Effect. However, how would an air fryer stack up against a deep fryer? In this deep fryer vs. air fryer comparison, you'll learn why they're healthier. Recently, healthy, organic meals have become common. "Individuals are beginning to search for the term sustainable on market packaging, which means no extra preservatives, fewer oil, and "no trans-fat, "or "fresh produce".

What is causing this? Many of us are stressed and worried as a result of our current lifestyle. In a world full of quick and simple yet sometimes unhealthy decisions, you'll need somebody to support you keep your sights on the prize. Air-fryers are small machines that will help you get a good crisp on your favorite foods while avoiding the use of oil and grease.

If you haven't done it yet, you should seriously try it. While technology could be the primary driver of the world's rapid acceleration, it compensates through reintroducing safe and natural alternatives. Being safe is a behavioral decision we make every day, not simply a product of discipline.

4.2 Brief History of Use of Air Fryers

In Europe and Australia, the air fryer was first introduced in 2010. It was developed in Japan and North America, and it is now a standard feature in western kitchens.

The Japanese use it to create fried prawns, while the UK & the Netherlands use it to make chips. It's used to prepare chicken wings in the United States, and it's used to produce samosa in India.

The purpose of an air fryer is to circulate hot air around the food being fried. A mechanical ventilator circulates hot air at high speed around the food.

Which causes the food to get crusted and fried. Other items frizzed include chicken, fries, pastries, and fish. The disadvantage is that cooking food requires little or very little oil.

Many air fryers have time & temperature sensors, which assist in properly cooking food throughout the process. The food is set in the basket above the drip tray.

There are several labels in the market. We expect it to be able to save up to 80% more oil than a traditional oven.

The buckets in most of the fryers are often shaken to ensure even cooking. The majority of versions do not have an agitator that continuously churns the food while it cooks.

People are becoming more interested in it every day because it is an oil-free cooking process. Many people believe that this form of cooking has an effect on the flavor, texture, and appearance of the food.

The traditional oven needs more oil throughout the cooking process. This has a significant impact on the users' well-being.

The deep fryer can be your best choice if you like traditional fried foods. If you're more health-conscious and want to produce comparable outcomes without completely sacrificing the fried flavor and feel, an air fryer may be the best option. You may also question if air fryers are as good as deep fryers. Probably invest in an air fryer if you're able to give up a little taste and even texture in exchange for healthy fried foods.

You've already set a budget for yourself, whether you're looking for an air fryer or a deep fryer. You may have also suggested features like portability or automated temperature regulation. You will narrow down the usable deep fryers & air fryers by comparing specifications, durability over time, overall healthiness, and other considerations to find what's right for you.

4.3 Deep Fryer's Features vs. Air Fryer's Features

The features (or lack thereof) of a fryer may be a determining factor for specific customers. The Secura Electric Triple Basket Deep Fryer is a typical fryer with a lot of features. A reusable oil tank, an optional oil filter, adjustable heat sensors, a see-through window in the frame, and an automatic timer are all included in this fryer.

In general, both types of fryers have several features in common, particularly concerning digital displays, customizable temperatures & user-friendly controls. In this case, deciding between an air fryer and a deep fryer can come down to only one or two essential features. The further functionality a fryer has, the more expensive it is. A well-equipped fryer, for example, comes with an adjustable temperature sensor and a timer with the ready signal & automated shut-off. Some fryers also have pre-programmed cooking times to eliminate the guesswork.

If you value simplicity, an air fryer that has a quick touch function and a compact on/off button is a good choice. A fryer with an automated countdown and buzzer may be a perfect option if you're the one to forget regarding food when it's frying. Easy-to-clean fabrics or fryers that come with a recipe book are other features to consider.

When deep-fried food is frying, it smells delicious, but it could also leave an awful odor behind, particularly if it's been overcooked. If you choose to stop this lousy encounter, search for a deep fryer that has a sound odor management system (particularly ones with charcoal filters). Since cooking with too much oil can be inconvenient, particularly while cleaning up, you might want to suggest a removable container with some oil pouring spout.

Cool-touch or collapsible handles and a wireless timer with a clearly accessible display panel are both useful features. Look for a deep fryer that has an adjustable thermostat if you want to keep track of your food during the cooking period. Some units have built-in viewing windows in their lids, allowing you to look inside without needing to lift the top. Another thing to think about is the unit's total strength. At first sight, a 1,600-watt power fryer and a 1,800-watt dryer seem similar, but the more efficient machine usually heats & cooks food faster.

4.4 Taste Comparison

It's also essential to consider the flavor of food cooked in an air fryer over a deep fryer. Air fryers will provide crunchy, crispy food which your taste buds can come to enjoy. The conventional form of deep-frying, on the other hand, is superior because the foods produced have a crispier deep-fried finish. As a result, if you're looking for a satisfying crisp flavor, a deep fryer is a safer option.

4.5 Size and Efficiency

Since air fryers are usually smaller than deep fryers, deep fryers may cook food in more significant amounts than air fryers.

If you only need a fryer to cook treats or a small meal now and then, an air fryer is the better choice since it will cook food in a shorter amount of time.

On the other hand, a deep fryer is preferred for daily use and preparing large quantities of food since it has a large capacity that can accommodate the whole family.

Reduce the possibility of heart failure and other health conditions as far as possible.

Air Fryer designs have been made easier to maintain to render them more maintenance-friendly.

People have reacted positively to a new kitchen device that has recently been introduced to the market. The Air Fryer is a relatively modern device that has exploded in popularity due to its many benefits. It has made cooking simple, safe, and affordable, making it the best cooking gadget to date. There are many reasons to use this versatile tool in the kitchen. Let's look at a few of the most prominent explanations why you can use it to help you prepare nutritious food in a limited amount of time. In essence, since no oil is used, this assists in the preparation of healthy meals. So, bring this device to better use and eat balanced, tasty stuff.

The Air Fryer has a variety of cooking choices, including roasting, frying, baking, and many more, allowing you to prepare a wide range of foods. With all of the cooking choices in one unit, you don't need to waste money on various devices to cook different food items. So, get this well-known device and cook a variety of foods with ease.

4.6 Cooking Time & Capacity Comparison

The average scale of air & deep fryers is one of the most significant distinctions. Since their products may not need to be dunked into a considerable volume of oil for deep frying, most air fryers are considerably smaller than deep fryers. The AIGEREK Electric Digital 3.2L air fryer is one model with large size. For most home cooks, this should be enough room.

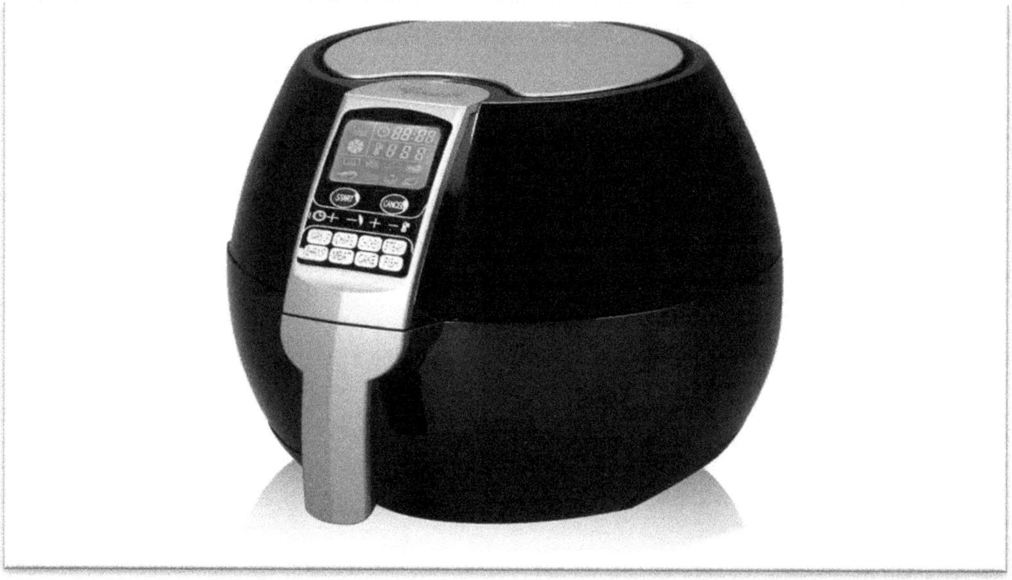

The air fryer is the best option if you're searching for a fryer that would work on your counter. Don't be fooled by the smaller size; most air fryers have had plenty of room for a reasonable amount of food. You will quickly find an air fryer to an altitude of 1.5 to 2 pounds, which is plenty for two to four people to eat. You may get away with a smaller food capacity if you choose to use the air fryer for just a snack or a small meal, but you can look for a bigger model if you want to make meals with it. Unless you want to make a deep-fried side dish every now and again, you'll need a deep fryer that has enough room to hold everything you're preparing. Although the number of deep fryers sits right in the center, the normal range is 2 - 12 cups. Although serving sizes can differ depending on personal preferences, a 6-cup fryer will usually have enough food for two individuals.

If you choose to make a smaller batch, specific fryers come with two big baskets or a combination of large and small baskets. Many deep fryers in the market today are very big, necessitating additional counter or storage room. Deep fryers are commonly used in restaurants, but they're still gaining popularity among home cooks.

To make your food nice and crispy, all types of fryers take some cooking time. Air fryers, including their limited size, take longer to cook since they use hot air instead of oil to cook the meal. The hot oil in a deep fryer heats food quicker, resulting in a shorter cooking period.

4.7 Healthiness Comparison

Fryers, let's face it, aren't the healthiest cooking tool around. Another factor to remember when deciding between an air fryer and a deep fryer is calories. It's impossible to achieve those delectable results (and the perfect amount of crispiness) unless using oil that means more calories. Deep fryers work by pouring a considerable volume of oil from which the food is dipped and then extracted. Air fryers, on the other side, should not submerge food in hot oil vats. Although you can cook your food in an air fryer basket, it will be coated with a bit of amount of oil. The air fryer then cooks the food by blowing hot air over it.

If you're looking for a dry fryer that cooks food without using oil, one using Rapid Air Technology may be worth looking into. This form of technology is relatively new on the market, and it usually uses very little oil. According to some of the best air fryers on the market, air fryers use up to 70% less oil than conventional fryers.

To achieve the perfect amount of crispiness, you'll need oil. On the other hand, air fryers use minimal amounts of oil to produce the same effects, i.e., delicious and crisp goods, whereas deep fryers use a substantial volume of oil to obtain the same amount of crispness.

So, go for an air fryer over a deep fryer since the food processed is less sticky, reducing the risk of obesity, heart disease, and other health issues associated with fatty foods.

The Phillips Air Fryer, which has Rapid Air Technology, is one air fryer we want. If you choose a deep fryer, the Hamilton Beach Professional-Style Deep Fryer may be a good choice because it comes with two baskets with hooks for fast drainage, allowing you to get every single drop of excess oil out from your food's surface.

4.8 Maintenance and Reliability Comparison

If you don't want high-maintenance gadgets, a deep fryer or air fryer will suffice. Both styles of fryers are designed to last a long time with no work on your part. The GoWISE USA Electric GW22621 Air Fryer, which produces a range of crispy foods with little or no oil and won't break the bank, is one alternative that might appeal to you.

Customers of both kinds of fryers worry most about the plastic parts, such as knobs and even bowls, to collect extra oil, breaking off, or wearing down with time. However, within a few years of consistent usage, these issues (if they exist at all) tend to accumulate. The easiest way to keep all forms of fryers in good working order is to test them regularly, disinfect them at frequent intervals, and search for signs of wear & tear. The oil must also be drained or purified in most fryers (both types).

Few air fryers have sections that can be washed in the dishwasher, making them easy to clean. They also come with a stainless steel interior and a nonstick basket, which makes them easier to clean. They still don't emit an odor that might alter the flavor of fresh foods fried in them.

Alternatively, due to the residual oil that could be left behind, you'll need to spend some time cleaning your deep fryer thoroughly. If you hate washing in the first instance, oil drops on the counter might be an eyesore.

4.9 Calories

Regarding calorie comparisons between air fryers and deep fryers, air fryers are the better choice since they use 70 to 80 percent less grease. As a result, air-fried foods are better for you. Serving a size of 99g air-fried French fries yields 226 calories, while the same amount of deep-fried French fries will produce up to 312 calories in a real-life situation.

If you like fried chicken wings, turkey, chips, or French fries, you can consider a healthier choice to deep frying that contains fewer calories. Obesity, heart attack, and elevated cholesterol are also reduced as a result of it.

4.10 Price Comparison

In both kinds of fryers, you usually get a ton of bang for your buck. You'll spend a bit extra upfront for either, but a fryer is a perfect investment because of its general dependability, low costs over time, and reliably delicious performance. Since deep fryers are far more significant than air fryers, they can seem to be more costly. On the other hand, most air fryers are more expensive, particularly if they use cutting-edge technology or advanced frying systems. For the high-quality deep fryer, a reasonable pricing range is between $50 and $100. However, you can eventually identify a well-rounded fryer for even less money, particularly if it is smaller.

The price of an air fryer, on the other side, is generally between $100 – $200. Unlike deep fryers, the air fryer's final price is determined by the equipment it applies rather than its scale. Rapid Air technology is available on more expensive versions for quicker and more effective cooking (not to mention significantly less oil use while cooking). Many customers would appreciate the programmable settings, odor reduction, and softly lit monitor screens with countdown alarms and timers that are included in these devices. If you're on a limited budget, though, this doesn't rule

out the possibility of finding a perfectly decent air fryer for a marginally lower price. The Deep Fryers of VonShef Stainless Steel which costs just $39.99, is one low-cost alternative you may enjoy.

There are inexpensive air fryers and also deep fryers in this price category. You'll almost certainly come into those that are very costly. However, an air fryer is more expensive since a good model will cost over $100 and last a long time. On the other hand, deep fryers may be used for $50 – $250, which is less expensive than an air fryer.

It is worth noting that an air fryer becomes less expensive to use in the long term because it uses less oil. Unlike a deep fryer, you won't have to purchase gallons and gallons of oil.

Chapter 5: Using Air Fryer – The Advantages

Air frying is generally better than frying in oil. It reduces calories by 70% – 80% and has a lot less fat. This cooking method can also reduce any of the other negative consequences of oil frying.

5.1 Key Advantages of Air Fryer

An air fryer can do almost everything. We say any of the following: fry, grill, bake, even roast.

The air fryer is made of durable plastic and metal, and it has a lot of cool features.

Are Easier to Clean

Since air fryers are dishwasher-safe components, an air fryer is simple to clean. These components are the basket, tray, and plate, which are all cleaned in the same manner as most dishes: with hot water and soap. Apart from that, you may need to clean your air fryer with a soft bristle brush on a regular basis. You have the choice of using the best dishwasher anywhere. However, for protection reasons, you must first consult the model's instruction manual. After that, dry each component entirely before reassembling the air fryer.

Furthermore, because air fryers are not using a ton of oil, washing is much easier. In most situations, all that is needed is hot water, cleaning soap, and a little elbow grease. Apart from that, Air fryers are also easier to clean than deep fat fryers, which become very sticky when frying and make the cooking process more difficult since they use a lot of oil.

You'll Cook Healthier Foods That Still Taste Fantastic

An air fryer does not need any oil to create crisp, browned foods such as French fries. If you obey the manufacturer's directions, you'll get consistent results. And if any oil is needed for a high-quality finished product, all you have to do is spray a small amount of healthy oil, such as canola or olive, onto the products before starting the cooking cycle.

Fresh or thawed onion rings, mozzarella sticks, chicken wings, or even sweet potato fries can be made in an instant. Any extra oil drains free. According to the Cleveland Clinic, by utilizing their air fryers, certain people will cut their calorie consumption by up to 80%.

Cooking Becomes More Efficient

Many air fryers require just a few minutes to complete their preheating period when used at home. The majority of the hot air remains inside the appliance, resulting in less energy waste throughout the cooking period. Since there is even less temperature loss in operation, the product can cook

quickly and evenly, resulting in more crispness. Because of the extreme impact that the circulating air produces within the cooker, even frozen products cook quickly.

You won't heat up the house as well as you can with a conventional oven since the hot air is trapped inside. Cooking your food requires less energy, the periods are faster, and it needs less time to finish dinner.

Air fryers are a remarkable gadget in terms of versatility. An air fryer may be used to prepare a wide range of foods. If you like, they will roast, steam, or bake your food. Most versions come with roasting and broiling capabilities. If you enjoy a fast stir fry without a lot of oil, this small kitchen gadget is an excellent option. Rotisseries are also used in some versions. If your device is big enough to accommodate the product, you can barbecue a burger, make hot dogs, and even bake the whole chicken. It does a lot more than just mimic the deep-frying method.

Air fryers are small and take up no room in your kitchen.

The number of air fryers on the market today is around the size of a 12-cup coffee maker. Smaller versions are available that are very portable and can be used in a dorm space, kitchen area, or even an RV. Most of these tiny kitchen appliances can serve in place of an oven if you don't have one, and they're still more convenient than a steamer or toaster oven. You'll find that using this technology to make a short snack or a whole dinner is simple and convenient, giving the kitchen a remarkable degree of versatility.

Air fryers are usually 1 foot cubed, which is a reasonable scale for a kitchen cooking device. They are around the same size as a standard coffee maker but smaller than a toaster to place this in context.

Their compact scale has a number of benefits. For starters, they are tiny enough to be hidden away in a pantry while not in service. Even if left on the counter, they would not take up much room.

A countertop deep fryer differs from a conventional deep fryer in that it has a cooking basket that protrudes from the front. Since this detracts from their cosmetic appeal, most people like to store their deep fryers in the pantry while not serving.

Anyone can use easily an air fryer

The majority of air fryers on the market currently are designed to be simple to use. All you have to do now is set the temperature, time, and food in the container or basket for cooking. To ensure that it cooks at the same temperature, shake your food a number of times as its cooking. This is particularly true for things such as nuggets or wings. Most children can learn to use this tiny kitchen gadget safely so that they might prepare treats after school or assist in the preparation of a meal.

Wonders Works on Vegetables

When you glance through the different lists of advantages and disadvantages of air fryers available online today, you'll see that many people consider meats or fried foods, such as French fries, to be the primary applications for this unit. If you have touchy vegetable eaters at home, this tiny kitchen gadget can be used to prepare your vegetables. They'll crisp up perfectly, and your house won't stink like a deep fat fryer for hours. You won't have to vacuum out the oil & grease off your cabinets anymore.

Are Safer to Use

Air fryers are better than most cooking machines since they are auto kitchen appliances that shield the consumer from the heat source and any oil that might splatter when cooking. Unlike traditional deep fryers, which splatter and burn everything in their immediate proximity, air fryers keep the immediate area clean and prevent others from being burned. This is excellent, particularly considering they use hot oil, which is over 300 degrees Fahrenheit.

Unlike traditional deep fryers, which splatter and burn everything in their immediate proximity, air fryers keep the immediate area clean and prevent others from being burnt. This is a significant thing to remember before purchasing a cooking device since they use hot oil over 300 degrees Fahrenheit. Furthermore, apart from reducing the possibility of personal injuries, air fryers have a low risk of causing explosions, which may cause property loss and even death.

The most extensive explanation for their protection is that they have auto-shutdown safety mechanisms that switch them off when the timer is over. This not only prevents the food from being burned or drying out, but it also means that the air fryer can switch off when the timer beeps. This is a significant advantage over convection ovens and grills, which lack such a protection function.

Are Economical to Use

Cooking oil is a costly product, particularly when you need a gallon or more to prepare for a mate, guests, or even coworkers.

To cook food in a countertop deep fryer, you'll need to buy a gallon or two of frying oil, which may be costly, and that's where an air fryer helps in because it requires very little oil.

Some might claim that cooking oil may be reused, but it can only be used a few times until it becomes rancid. Once this occurs, you would have no choice but to discard it and replace the frying oil in your deep fryer.

In the economic sector, the volume of electricity required is another factor to remember. Deep fryers need a considerable amount of electricity to function. On the other hand, air fryers are cost-effective since they do not need long to heat up, requiring less energy to operate. Overall, air fryers are less costly and more accessible to operate than most frying equipment.

Use Less or Even No Oil For Cooking

Traditional deep fryers, as previously said, will use about a gallon of oil while running at maximum capacity. In contrast, depending on the food you're preparing or the recipe you're using, air fryers may use as little as a tablespoon of oil.

There are several benefits of consuming less oil. First but foremost, it is cost-effective and inexpensive, implying that you would not have to waste a lot of money on cooking oil. Second, it simplifies the task of washing the air fryer. Deep fryers that are clogged with so much oil are more complicated to clean. Third, cooking with less oil requires consuming fewer calories, making air frying much better. When frying with an air fryer, you can use an oil spray bottle or mister to ensure that the food is correctly coated with oil.

Food cooked in an air fryer has fewer calories and fats

When using an air fryer, keep in mind that a tablespoon of widely used frying oil contains just around 20 calories and 10 to 14 grams of fat. This leads to less calories while using an air fryer, depending on the amount of oil you use.

When using an air fryer, just a tablespoon or so of oil is used. When comparing food fried in an air fryer to food cooked in a deep fryer, we can confidently assume that one's calorie consumption would be more minor. It also ensures you'll be able to eat crispy, tasty, textured, and crunchy foods without consuming a lot of calories.

The meal is wholly immersed in frying oil when cooked in a deep fryer, which ensures it can consume a ton of oil, which adds up to around 240 calories or 25 grams of fat. While the added fat makes the food taste better, it comes at a significant expense to your good health.

Can Promote Weight Loss

Fried food use is directly linked to an increased incidence of obesity. This is due to the high fat and calorie content of deep-fried foods.

Weight reduction may be aided by switching from deep-fried to air-fried foods & reducing daily consumption of unhealthy oils.

Are Safer Than Deep Fryers

Deep-frying foods necessitate the use of a large container filled with hot oil. This may be dangerous. Though air fryers do get heated, there is no danger of leaking, splashing, or hitting hot oil by mistake. To ensure protection, people can use frying appliances carefully and obey directions.

Toxic Acrylamide Formation Is Reduced by Using Air Fryer

Frying food in cooking oil can result in the formation of harmful compounds like acrylamide. During high-heat cooking processes, such as deep-frying, this compound occurs in some foods.

According to the International Research Agency on Cancer, acrylamide has been linked to the growth of cancers such as endometrial, vaginal, pancreatic, breast, and esophageal cancer. Additional research while the findings remain unknown, Trusted Source has indicated a correlation between kidney & dietary acrylamide, endometrial, or ovarian cancers. People may reduce the chance of acrylamide contamination in their food by converting to air frying.

Reduced Deep-Fried Food Consumption Lowers Disease Risk

Cooking or baking with oil and eating traditional fried foods on a daily basis has been linked to a variety of health problems. Deep frying may be replaced with other cooking techniques to reduce the chance of these problems.

Chapter 6: Getting Started to Cook with Air Fryer

Want to change up your cooking style without putting in more effort and time in the kitchen? Of course, you can, and this is when the quality air fryers come into the picture.

Air fryers, which are identical to convection ovens except that they use air for cooking up the food, are an alternative method to rustle up dinner. This ensures the hot air is circulated all around until it is thoroughly fried and crispy on the outside.

Cooking times are far shorter than you'd imagine from a conventional gas or electric grill or hob, for example, so the meal is prepared using hot air instead of conducted heat in a container or direct heat from the grill.

Although it is easy to deep-fry food in a couple of minutes or seconds, air fryers benefit from requiring relatively little oil, rendering them a healthier alternative to deep or shallow frying.

If you're thinking about buying an air fryer, you'll probably want to find the best deal with your money, and because these devices take up a lot of counter space, it's worth learning about all the meals you can create with one – there are hundreds.

Many people equate air fryers, like the Tefal ActiFry Genius, with healthy fries or ideally crispy potatoes, but what else do these devices cook?

6.1 What can you prepare in an air fryer?

Air fryers can cook a wide variety of foods, from crispy fries to cakes, and they do so quickly. When it comes to savory recipes, you can prepare frozen fried foods right from the fridge, and thanks to the multi-drawer nature of an air fryer like the Dual Zone Ninja Foodi, you can cook two dishes at once.

Since air fryers cook food using extreme heat and air circulation, please remember that cooking times would be much shorter than you're used to with a conventional oven. For instance, fries can be prepared in as little as 10 min.

Chicken wings, root vegetables, meats, and homemade potato chips are all excellent candidates for air fried, but you may be shocked to hear that gnocchi and ravioli, as well as mini pizzas, may also be prepared this way. Chickpeas crisp up good in an air fryer, and you can cook your own vegetable chips with kale or zucchini/courgettes if you're searching for a better snack.

It's not all side dishes that can be prepared in an air fryer. Fajitas, for example, maybe entirely made in an air fryer, but, as in everything else you're air frying, stop overfilling the frying basket, as this can result in long cooking time and unevenly cooked food.

Chapter 7: Air Fryer Breakfast Recipes

1. Air-Fryer Eggplant Fries

Cook Time: 10 min (per batch)

Servings: 6

Difficulty: Easy

Ingredients

- Large eggs 2
- Toasted wheat germ 1/2 cup
- Grated parmesan cheese 1/2 cup
- Italian seasoning 1 tsp
- Cooking spray
- Eggplant 1 medium (about 1 to 1/4 lbs)
- Garlic salt 3/4 tsp
- Meatless pasta sauce 1 cup, warmed.

Instructions

1. Preheat the fryer to 375 degrees. Whisk the eggs together in a bowl. Mix the cheese, wheat germ & seasonings in another bowl.
2. Trim the eggplant ends; cut the eggplant into 1/2"-thick slices lengthwise. Cut lengthwise to 1/2" slice strips. Dip the eggplant in the eggs, then fill with the mixture of cheese.
3. Arrange the eggplant in batches on an oiled tray in the air-fryer basket in a layer, dust with cooking spray. Now Cook until the brown is crispy, 4-5 mins. Turn; spritz with spray for cooking. Cook until brown 4-5 mins. Serve with pasta sauce immediately.

2. Air-Fryer Turkey Croquettes

Cook Time: 10 min (per batch)

Servings: 6

Difficulty: Easy

Ingredients

- Grated parmesan cheese 1/2 cup
- Mashed potatoes 2 cups (with added milk & butter)
- Shredded Swiss cheese 1/2 cup
- Minced fresh rosemary 2 tsps. or dried rosemary 1/2 tsp, crushed.
- Shallot 1 finely chopped.
- Minced fresh sage 1 tsp/dried sage leaves 1/4 tsp.
- Pepper 1/4 tsp
- Salt 1/2 tsp
- Finely chopped cooked turkey 3 cups

- Large egg 1
- Water 2 tbsps.
- Cooking spray butter-flavored
- Panko bread crumbs 1-1/4 cups
- Optional sour cream

Instructions

1. Preheat the fryer to 350 degrees. Mix the mashed potatoes, cheese, shallot, rosemary, salt, sage, and pepper in a big bowl, whisk in the turkey. Form into 12 1"-thick patties.
2. Whisk the egg and water together in a small dish. In a different bowl, place the bread crumbs. In the egg mixture, dip the croquettes, pat them onto the bread crumbs to adhere to the coating.
3. Place croquettes in batches in a layer in an air-fryer basket on an oiled tray; sprinkle with cooking spray. Cook until brown, 4-5 mins. Turn; spritz with spray for cooking. Cook until brown; 4-5 mins. Serve with sour cream if wanted.

3. Stuffed bagel balls

Cook Time: 25 min

Servings: 4

Difficulty: Easy

Ingredients

- Baking powder 2 tsps.
- Unbleached all-purpose flour 1 cup, whole wheat/gluten-free mix
- Kosher salt 3/4 tsp
- Egg white 1, beaten.
- Less fat cream cheese 4 tbsps., in 8 cubes
- Non-fat Greek yogurt 1 cup
- Optional toppings

Instructions

1. Mix together the flour, salt & baking powder in a med bowl and whisk properly. Add the yogurt & mix with a spatula or fork until it appears like tiny crumbles, well combined.
2. On a work surface, gently brush the flour and from the bowl remove the dough; knead the dough many times until the dough is tacky and not sticky, around 20 turns.
3. Split into 4 balls equal to each other. To shape bagels, roll each ball to 3/4-" thick ropes and link the ends.
4. Cover with egg wash & sprinkle with the seasoning of your choice on all ends.

5. Preheat to 280F degree air fryer. Shift without overcrowding into batches and bake for 15 to 16 mins, or till golden. No reason to take turns. Before cutting, let cool for 15 mins at least.

4. Air-Fryer Green Tomato BLT

Cook Time 10 min (per batch)

Servings: 4

Difficulty: Easy

Ingredients

- Salt 1/2 tsp
- Green tomatoes 2 med. (about 10 ounces)
- Pepper 1/4 tsp
- All-purpose flour 1/4 cup
- Large egg 1, beaten.
- Panko bread crumbs 1 cup

Cooking spray

- Reduced-fat mayonnaise 1/2 cup.
- Green onions 2, finely chopped.
- Snipped fresh dill 1 tsp or dill weed 1/4 tsp.
- Whole wheat bread 8 slices, toasted.
- Center-cut bacon strips cooked 8.
- Bibb/Boston lettuce leaves 4.

Instructions

1. Preheat the fryer to 350 degrees. In 4 slices, split each tomato crosswise. Using salt & pepper to sprinkle. In different shallow containers, position the egg, flour & bread

crumbs. After that, patting to adhere, drop tomato slices in flour, shake off the residue, and eventually dip into the egg and eventually into the bread crumb mixture.

2. Arrange tomato slices in batches on an oiled tray in the air-fryer basket in a single layer; spritz with the cooking spray. Now Cook until brown, 4-6 mins. Turn; spritz with spray. Cook until brown, 4-6 mins more.

3. Meanwhile, mix the mayonnaise, dill, and green onions. Layer each of the 4 bread slices with 2 strips of bacon, 1 leaf of lettuce, and 2 slices of tomato. Spread the mixture of mayonnaise over the remaining bread slices; put it over the top. Immediately serve.

5. Air-Fryer Reuben Calzones

Cook Time: 10 min (per batch)

Servings: 4

Difficulty: Easy

Ingredients

- Swiss cheese 4 slices
- Refrigerated pizza crust 1 tube (13.8 ounces)
- Sauerkraut 1 cup, rinsed & well drained.
- Sliced cooked corned beef 1/2 lb.
- Salad dressing thousand island

Instructions

1. Preheat the fryer to 400 degrees. Unroll the pizza crust dough on a gently floured surface and pat it into a 12" square. Break into four squares. Layer A slice of cheese & a fourth of sauerkraut & corned beef diagonally over each square half to within 1/2 " of the edges. Fold 1 corner to the opposite corner, creating a triangle over the filling; force the edges to close with a fork. In an air-fryer basket, put two calzones in a layer on a greased plate.
2. Flipping halfway during cooking, cook till golden brown for 8-12 mins. Serve with salad.

6. Air Fryer Blueberry Muffins

Cook Time: 15 min

Servings: 12

Difficulty: Easy.

Ingredients

- Old-fashioned oats 3/4 cup (oatmeal)
- All-purpose whole white wheat flour 1 1/2 cups
- Brown sweetener 1/2 cup
- Cinnamon 1/2 tsp
- Baking powder 1 tbsp
- Salt 1/2 tsp
- Milk 1 cup
- Melted unsalted butter 1/4 cup (at room temp)
- Eggs 2 (at room temp)
- Vanilla 2 tsps.
- Blueberries 1 cup

Instructions

1. In a big mixing bowl, mix the flour, salt, cinnamon, rolled oats, brown sweetener, and baking powder together. Mix.
2. In a separate, med-sized bowl, combine the milk, vanilla, eggs, and butter. Using a silicone spoon, blend.

3. In the mixing bowl, wet ingredients are added with the dry ones. Stir.
4. Fold and stir in the blueberries.
5. Divide the batter into 12 muffin cups of silicone and add them to the air fryer. It is optional to coat the liners with oil. Generally, the muffins don't stick.
6. Place the fryer at 350 degrees. Carefully track the muffins for enough cooking time since each model can cook differently. Muffins require 11-15 mins to cook. Into the center of a muffin, insert a toothpick, and the muffins have done baking if it returns clean. At around 13 mins, it will set.

7. Air Fried Tofu Rancheros with Veggies & Little Face Salsa

Cook Time: 30 min

Servings: 4

Difficulty: Easy

Ingredients

Spice Crusted Tofu:

- High Protein Tofu/Super Firm Tofu 1 - 20 0z container into cubes
- Ground cumin powder 1 tsp
- Ground chili powder 1 tsp
- Smoked paprika 1/2 tsp.
- Salt 1/4 tsp
- For the Salsa Beans:
- Organic black beans 1 15.5 ounces can, drained.
- Jalapeno Cilantro Salsa 1/4 cup or your fav mild salsa
- Liquid smoke 1/8 to 1/4 tsp (or use smoked paprika 1/8 tsp)
- Jalapeno powder 1/8 tsp
- Cumin Powder 1/8 tsp
- Salt
- For the Veggie Topping:
- Grated carrot 1/3 cup
- Grated zucchini 1/3 cup

- Grated yellow squash 1/3 cup.
- Salt 1/8 tsp
- Pinch black pepper

For the Base:

- Flour/ gluten-free tortillas 4 large
- Shredded vegan cheese 1 cup.

Instructions

Make Crusted Tofu:

1. Toss the cumin, smoked paprika, chili powder, and salt into the tofu cubes.
2. If your model doesn't need it, preheat the air fryer to 390 °. When it is warmed to the basket of the air fryer, add the coated tofu.
3. Adjust to 5 mins the cooking time and shake/stir the tofu when the time is finished. For an extra 5 mins, repeat.

Salsa Beans Making:

1. In a little bowl, combine all the ingredients together.

Base Preparation:

1. Preheat the oven to 350o, take 2 tortillas & place them on a baking sheet. Sprinkle (or spread) on each tortilla top with vegan cheese (1/4 cup). In the center of the tortilla, put salsa beans (1/4) & bake for 15 mins, which will warm the beans & keep them crunchy with the tortilla.
2. When warm, add the chopped tomatoes, shredded veggie topping, or other vegetables you'd want to pile on avocado/shredded lettuce to the Spiced Crusted Tofu.

3. With a spoonful of Small Face Salsa, top it all off.

8. Air Fryer Bacon

Cook Time: 11 min

Servings: 11

Difficulty: Easy.

Ingredients

- 11 slices bacon

Instructions

1. The bacon is divided in two, then put in the air fryer, the first half.
2. Set the temp to 400 degrees and set the time limit to 10 mins.
3. To see if anything has to be rearranged, search it halfway through.
4. Check for the doneness needed.

9. Air Fryer Breakfast Frittata

Cook Time: 20 mins Servings: 2 Difficulty: Easy

Ingredients

- Breakfast sausage ¼ lb, fully cooked & crumbled.
- Eggs 4, lightly beaten.
- ½ cup shredded cheddar-Monterey jack cheese blend
- Red bell pepper 2 tbsps., diced.
- Green onion 1, chopped.
- Cayenne pepper 1 pinch (optional)
- Cooking spray

Instructions

1. Combine the sausage, eggs, bell pepper, Cheddar cheese, onion, and cayenne in a bowl and blend.
2. The air fryer should be preheated to 360 ° F. Spray with cooking spray on a nonstick 6x2" cake pan.
3. Put the mixture of eggs into the prepared cake pan.
4. Now Cook in an air fryer for 18 to 20 mins before the frittata is set.

10. Easy Sweet Potato Biscuits

Cook Time: 15 min

Servings: 8

Difficulty: Easy.

Ingredients

- All-purpose flour 2 cups
- Baking powder 1/2 tbsp
- Tsp salt 1/2
- Sweetener or sugar 2 tbsps.
- Cinnamon 1 tsp
- Unsalted butter 2 tbsps butter should be cold.
- Plain non-fat Greek yogurt 1/4 cup
- Cooked mashed sweet potato 1/2 cup.
- Egg 1
- Water 1 tbsp
- Optional honey butter
- Butter 4 tsps.
- Honey 1 1/2 tsps.

Instructions

Biscuits

1. In a bowl, mix the flour, cinnamon, baking powder, sweetener, and salt.

2. Add yogurt, butter & mashed sweet potatoes.
3. To combine, use a fork. Do not over-blend. Take the fork all the way into the mix & knead the butter. You will find that the dough is about to get flaky & there will be little flour in the bowl that remains. It's okay. It would result in biscuits that are hard and tough if the dough is overmixed.
4. On a floured board, spread out the dough. To roll the dough out 7 x 7 and 1/2 " in height, use a pin or hands. Roll the dough out such that it is 1″ high if you like thicker biscuits. This is likely to end in fewer biscuits. Don't make the dough overwork.
5. To cut out the biscuits, or cut them the way you wish, use a biscuit cutter. When you are using a biscuit cutter, the dough is reallocated, and use the remaining dough to roll it again for extra biscuits.
6. In a shallow bowl, beat the egg and mix it with the water & stir. Using egg wash to clean each biscuit top.

Instructions

1. Line the basket of the air fryer with parchment paper. Just parchment paper designed for the air-fryer can be used. This helps avoid browning very easily and subsequent burning the bottom of the biscuit. Without it, you may go but consider that.
2. Air-fry at 300 degrees for 4 mins.
3. For 2-5 mins, raise the temp to 400 degrees before the biscuits turn a rich golden brown.

11. Air Fryer Beef Taco Fried Egg Rolls

Cook Time: 25 min

Servings: 8

Difficulty: Easy

Ingredients

- Egg roll wrappers 16
- Ground beef 1 lb
- Chopped onion 1/2 cup.
- Garlic cloves minced 2.
- Can diced tomatoes & chilies 16 oz.
- Refried black beans 8 oz.
- Shredded Mexican cheese 1 cup.
- Cooking oil spray
- Whole kernel corn 1/2 cup

Homemade Taco Seasoning

- Chili powder 1 tbsp
- Cumin 1 tsp
- Smoked paprika 1 tsp.
- Salt & pepper

Instructions

1. On med-high heat, add the ground beef along with the pepper, salt, and taco seasoning to a skillet. While splitting the beef into smaller chunks, cook until browned.
2. Add the sliced onions & garlic as the meat has begun to brown. Cook until onions are fragrant.
3. Add the sliced tomatoes, chilies, beans, Mexican cheese, and maize. To ensure the combination of the mixture, stir.
4. On a hard surface, egg roll wrappers are laid. Dip in water the cooking brush. Glaze each egg roll wrappers along the edges with a wet brush. This would soften the crust & make rolling smoother.
5. Fill each wrapper with 2 tbsp of the mixture. Don't overstuff yourself. You can have to double cover the egg rolls according to the type of egg roll wrappers.
6. Diagonally fold the wrappers to close. For the filling, push tightly on the region and cup it to keep it in place. For triangles, fold on the left & right ends. To close, fold the topmost layer over the top. For wetting the area, use the cooking brush and keep it in place.
7. Spray a basket of air fryers with cooking oil.
8. Load the rolls of the egg into the Air Fryer basket. Using cooking oil to spray each egg roll.
9. Bake at 400 degrees for 8 mins. Flip the rolls. Cook extra 4 mins or until crisp and browned.

12. Air Fryer Bacon & Egg Bite Cups

Cook Time: 15 min

Servings: 8

Difficulty: Easy

Ingredients

- Large eggs 6
- Heavy whipping cream/milk 2 tbsps.
- Salt & pepper
- Green peppers chopped ¼ cup.
- Onions chopped ¼ cup.
- Red peppers chopped ¼ cup.
- Fresh spinach chopped ¼ cup.
- Cheddar cheese shredded ½ cup
- Mozzarella cheese shredded ¼ cup
- Cooked & crumbled bacon 3 slices.

Instructions

1. To a wide mixing bowl, add the eggs.
2. Add the cream, pepper, and salt. Whisk to combine.
3. Sprinkle with the red peppers, green peppers, spinach, onions, bacon, and cheese.
4. Whisk in order to blend.
5. In each silicone mold, pour the mixture of the egg.

6. Sprinkle with all of the vegetables in the remaining portion.
7. Cook the egg cups at 300 degrees for 12-15 min. Through a toothpick, you can examine the middle. The eggs have set when the toothpick falls out clean.

Chapter 8: Air fryer Lunch Recipes

1. Air-Fryer Sweet & Sour Pork

Cook Time: 15 min

Servings: 2

Difficulty: Easy

Ingredients

- Cider vinegar 1/2 cup
- Unsweetened crushed pineapple 1/2 cup, undrained.
- Sugar 1/4 cup
- Packed dark brown sugar 1/4 cup.
- Ketchup 1/4 cup
- Reduced-sodium soy sauce 1 tbsp.
- Dijon mustard 1-1/2 tsps.

- Garlic powder 1/2 tsp
- Pork tenderloin 1 (3/4 lb), halved.
- Salt 1/8 tsp
- Pepper 1/8 tsp
- Optional sliced green onions
- Cooking spray

Instructions

1. Combine the 1st 8 ingredients in a saucepan. Get it to a boil; lower the heat. Simmer it uncovered, till thickened, 6 to 8 mins, occasionally stirring.
2. Preheat the fryer to 350 degrees. Sprinkle salt & pepper on the pork. Place the pork in the air-fryer basket on a greased tray; spritz with the cooking spray. Cook for 7-8 mins before the pork starts to brown around the edges. Pour two tbsps of sauce over the pork. Cook until at least 145 ° is read by a thermometer placed into the pork, 10 to 12 mins longer. Let the pork stand before slicing for 5 mins. Serve with the sauce that remains. Top with the sliced green onions if needed.

2. Air-Fryer Keto Meatballs

Cook Time: 10 min

Servings: 4

Difficulty: Easy

Ingredients

- Shredded mozzarella cheese 1/2 cup
- Grated Parmesan cheese 1/2 cup
- Large egg 1, lightly beaten.
- Garlic clove 1, minced.
- Heavy whipping cream 2 tbsps.
- Lean ground beef 1 lb (90% lean)

Sauce:

- Tomato sauce with garlic, basil, and oregano 1 can (8 ounces)
- Prepared pesto 2 tbsps.

- Heavy whipping cream 1/4 cup

Instructions

1. Preheat the fryer to 350 degrees. Combine the 1st five ingredients in a wide bowl. Add beef; mix thoroughly but lightly. Mold to 1-1/2" Balls. In the air-fryer basket, place in one layer on an oiled tray; cook till lightly browned & cooked through 8 to 10 mins.
2. Meanwhile, stir together the sauce ingredients in a tiny saucepan; heat up. Serve along with meatballs. The option of Freeze: In freezer containers, freeze the cooled meatballs. Partly thaw overnight in the refrigerator for use. Preheat the fryer to 350 degrees. Reheat until heated, 3-5 mins. Make the sauce.

3. Air-Fryer Quinoa Arancini

Cook Time: 8 min

Servings: 3

Difficulty: Easy

Ingredients

- Large eggs 2, lightly beaten.
- Seasoned bread crumbs 1 cup, divided.
- Ready-to-serve quinoa 1 package (9 ounces)/cooked quinoa 1-3/4 cups.
- Shredded Parmesan cheese 1/4 cup
- Olive oil 1 tbsp
- Minced fresh basil 2 tbsps. or dried basil 2 tsps.
- Garlic powder 1/2 tsp
- Salt 1/2 tsp
- Pepper 1/8 tsp
- Mozzarella cheese 6 cubes part-skim (3/4 inch each)
- Cooking spray
- Optional Warmed pasta sauce

Instructions

1. Preheat the fryer to 375 degrees. According to box directions, prepare quinoa. Add 1 egg, bread crumbs (1/2 cup), parmesan cheese, basil, oil & seasonings.

2. Divide it into 6 bits. To cover entirely, shape each part around a cheese cube, creating a ball.
3. In different small bowls, incorporate the remaining egg & 1/2 cup of bread crumbs. Dip the quinoa balls into the egg and roll in the bread crumbs. Put in the air-fryer basket on an oiled tray; spritz with the cooking mist. Cook until brown for 6-8 mins. Serve with pasta sauce if needed.

4. Air Fryer grilled cheese sandwich

Cook Time: 5 min

Servings: 1

Difficulty: Easy

Ingredients

- Butter 1 tsp
- Cheddar cheese 2 slices
- Bread 2 slices
- Turkey 2 slices (optional)

Instructions

1. The air fryer is preheated to 350 degrees.
2. On the side of the loaf, spread the butter. If using, add cheese & turkey & cover with another bread piece, buttered on the other side.
3. Inside the Air Fryer, put the sandwich. Set 5 mins time. Halfway turn.
4. The sandwich should look like a toasty and melting cheese sandwich.

5. Air Fryer Vegan Veggie Balls

Cook Time: 12 min

Servings: 4

Difficulty: Easy

Ingredients

- Sweet Potato 100 g
- Carrot 70 g
- Cauliflower 200 g
- Parsnips 90 g
- Garlic Puree 2 Tsp
- Chives 1 Tsp
- Paprika 1 Tsp
- Mixed Spice 1 Tsp
- Oregano 2 Tsp
- Desiccated Coconut ½ Cup
- Gluten-Free Oats 1 Cup
- Salt and Pepper

Instructions

1. Place a clean tea towel with the cooked vegetables and strain out the excess water.
2. Position them & add the seasoning in a mixing bowl. Blend well and render med-sized balls.

3. Place them for 2 hours in the fridge, so they have the ability to firm up a little.
4. Mix the coconut & gluten-free oats in a mixer and whizz before it resembles hard flour. In a bowl, pour it.
5. In the mixture, roll the veggie balls and then put them in the grill pan in the air fryer.
6. Cook it at 200c/400f for 10 mins. Rollover & cook on the other side for another 2 mins at the same temperature.
7. Serve.

6. Jamaican Jerk Meatballs

Cook Time: 14 min

Serving: 4

Difficulty: Easy

Ingredients

- Chicken mince 1 kg
- Jerk dry rub 1 tbsp.
- Breadcrumbs 100 g

Jamaican Sauce Ingredients:

- Jerk dry rub 1 tsp.
- Honey 4 tbsp
- Soy sauce 1 tbsp

Instructions

1. Along with the breadcrumbs and the jerk seasoning, put the chicken in a mixing bowl and combine well. Using a meatball press or make meatball forms.
2. Put the Meatballs in the air fryer & on 180c/360f cook for 14 mins.
3. Combine the honey, soy sauce, and the remaining jerk dry rub in a bowl. Mix thoroughly.
4. In the sauce, toss them and on sticks serve them when the meatballs are cooked.

7. Crispy Air Fryer Eggplant Parmesan

Cook Time: 25 min

Servings: 4

Difficulty: Easy

Ingredients

- Eggplant 1 large
- Whole wheat bread crumbs 1/2 cup
- Finely grated parmesan cheese 3 tbsp
- Salt
- Italian seasoning mix 1 tsp
- Whole wheat flour 3 tbsp
- Water 1 tbsp + egg 1
- Olive oil spray
- Marinara sauce 1 cup
- Grated mozzarella cheese 1/4 cup
- Fresh parsley/basil to garnish

Instructions

1. Cut the eggplant into slices of roughly 1/2". Rub some of the salt on slices on both sides and hold for 10-15 mins at least.
2. Meanwhile, combine the egg with water & flour in a bowl to make the batter.

3. Combine bread crumbs, Italian seasoning blend, parmesan cheese, and some salt in a shallow med plate. Thoroughly mix.
4. Now add the batter equally to each slice of eggplant. To coat it uniformly on both sides, in the breadcrumb mix, drop the battered slices.
5. On a clean & dry flat plate, put breaded eggplant slices and spray the oil on them.
6. Preheat to 360F Air Fryer. Then place the slices of eggplant on the wire mesh & cook for around 8 min.
7. With roughly 1 tbsp of marinara sauce, top the slices and gently sprinkle fresh mozzarella cheese. Cook the eggplant for a further 1-2 mins or till the cheese melts.
8. On the side of the favorite pasta, serve warm.

8. Air fryer rotisserie chicken

Cook Time: 60 min

Servings: 4

Difficulty: Medium

Ingredients

- Whole chicken 1, about 3–4 lbs
- Ghee 2 tbsps.
- Magic mushroom powder 1 tbsp
- Salt couple pinches

Instructions

1. Remove the chicken inside & with a paper towel pat it dry. Mix the ghee and the mystical mushroom powder together in a shallow bowl. On the chicken (breast side), drawback the skin & use a spoon to scrape up some of the mixtures of ghee between the breast & skin and use the fingertips to force the mixture in. Till the ghee mixture is out, do that on the other breast. Sprinkle salt all over the chicken.
2. Take out the air fryer with the inside wire basket. Drop the side of the chicken breast in the wire basket. Cover the air fryer, set the temp to 365 ° F, and click the start button for up to 30 mins.
3. Use tongs/wooden spoons to flip the chicken over until the 30 mins are done, up is the breast side. Switch the temp back up to 365o F and then click Start for up to 30 mins. When the time is finished, let the chicken rest before slicing for 5-10 mins.

9. Air Fryer Parmesan Truffle Oil Fries

Cook Time: 40 min

Servings: 6

Difficulty: Medium

Ingredients

- Large russet potatoes peeled & cut lengthwise 3.
- White truffle oil 2 tbsp
- Parmesan shredded 2 tbsp.
- Paprika 1 tsp
- Salt & pepper
- Parsley chopped 1 tbsp.

Instructions

1. Put the sliced potatoes with cold water in a wide bowl.
2. Let the potatoes for 30 mins at least ideally an hour, soak in the water.
3. On a flat surface, spread the fries and completely dry them with paper towels. Now coat them with seasonings and 1 tbsp of white truffle oil.
4. To the Air Fryer basket, add half of the fries. Adjust the temp to 380 degrees & cook for 15-20 mins. Set a 10 mins timer, and at the 10-min point, stop & shake the basket (once).
5. If you need the fries to be crisper, give them some time to cook. Remove them if the fries appear crisp prior to 15 mins.
6. Cook the remaining portion as the first half ends.

7. Upon taking them from the Air Fryer, immediately add the leftover truffle oil & parmesan to the fries.
8. Add shredded parsley on top. Serve.

10. Air Fryer Crispy Crunchy Sweet Potato Fries

Cook Time: 25 min

Servings: 6

Difficulty: Easy

Ingredients

- Large, sweet potatoes peeled & cut lengthwise 2.
- Cornstarch 1 1/2 tbsps.
- Paprika 2 tsps.
- Garlic powder 2 tsps.
- Salt & pepper
- Olive oil 1 tbsp

Instructions

1. Put the sliced sweet potatoes with cold water in a wide bowl. Let the sweet potatoes for an hour to soak in the water.
2. Remove them from water & dry them out. Sprinkle it all over with cornstarch.
3. Sprinkle the paprika, salt, garlic powder, and pepper.
4. In the air fryer basket, put the fries and spray them with olive oil. And do not overload the basket. If necessary, cook in batches. Spray with olive oil if white spots of cornstarch are visible on the fries.
5. To 380 degrees, set the temp and cook for 23-25 minutes. Set a 10 mins time, and at the 10-min point, stop & shake the basket (once).
6. Cook them longer if you want crispy fries and check on them.

11. Air Fryer Pepperoni Pizza

Cook Time: 8 min

Servings: 1

Difficulty: Easy

Ingredients

- Whole wheat pita 1
- Pizza sauce/marinara 2 tbsp
- Mozzarella cheese shredded 1/8th cup.
- Cheddar cheese 1/8th cup, shredded.
- Pepperoni 8 slices
- Olive oil spray
- Chopped parsley 1 tbsp, optional.

Instructions

1. On the pita bread top, drizzle the sauce, then load the pepperoni & shredded cheese on top.
2. Using olive oil spray to spray the pizza top.
3. In Air Fryer, Place it at 400 degrees for 8 mins. At the 6-7 min point, check the pizza to make sure it doesn't overcook.
4. From the Air Fryer, remove the pizza. Serve.

12. Sweet Potatoes Au Gratin

Cook Time: 60 min

Servings: 6

Difficulty: Hard

Ingredients

- Sweet potatoes 2 lbs sliced in 1/4-1/2" rounds.
- Butter 1 tbsp
- Garlic cloves 2 minced.
- Cream cheese 4 oz.
- Heavy whipping cream 1/4 cup
- Shredded cheddar cheese 1 cup divided 1/2 cup portions.
- Shredded parmesan Reggiano cheese 1/4 cup
- Onion powder 1 tsp
- Salt & pepper
- Shredded mozzarella cheese 1/2 cup

Instructions

1. Preheat the oven to 350°C.
2. On medium heat, heat a saucepan & add the butter.
3. When it has melted, add garlic & cook for a few mins until it is fragrant.

4. Add the whipped cream, Parmesan Reggiano, cream cheese, and shredded cheddar cheese (1/2 cup). Stir. To taste, add the onion powder, pepper & salt. Repeatedly taste the sauce and change the seasoning to taste as desired.
5. Continually stir till the cheese melts.
6. Remove and set aside from the heat.
7. In a 9/13 baking dish, arrange sliced sweet potatoes in the line. Drizzle cheese sauce.
8. Sprinkle the plate with the remaining shredded cheddar (1/2 cup) and the mozzarella.
9. Using foil to protect & bake for 30 mins.
10. Remove the foil and bake till the sweet potatoes are soft for an additional 25 mins.
11. If you want a crisp top, switch on the broil feature on the oven a few mins before the dish has done baking. Broil for 1-3 mins till crispy at the tip.
12. Serve.

Chapter 9: Air Fryer Dinner Recipes

1. Cilantro Pesto Chicken Legs

Cook Time: 20 min

Servings: 2

Difficulty: Easy

Ingredients

- Chicken drumsticks 4
- Jalapeño Peppers 1/2
- Cilantro 1/2 cup
- Garlic 8 cloves
- Ginger 2 thin slices
- Oil 2 tbsps.
- Lemon Juice 2 tbsps.
- Kosher Salt 1 tsp

Instructions

1. Put drumsticks in the flat tray. Use the sharp knife's tip, cut small slashes in the chicken at steady intervals so the marinade can easily penetrate the chicken.
2. Equally chop pepper, ginger, cilantro, garlic & put it in a bowl.
3. Put oil, salt & lemon juice in the chopped vegetables & combine well.
4. Spread this combination on the chicken.
5. Allow chicken to marinate at least for thirty minutes / up to twenty-four hours in the refrigerator.
6. When completely ready to cook, put chicken legs in the air fryer basket; skin must be side up.
7. Adjust air fryer at 390F for twenty minutes for the meaty legs of chicken. In the center, turn the legs of the chicken over.
8. Use a meat thermometer to confirm that the chicken has touched the internal temp of 1650F. Remove & serve with sufficient napkins.

2. Crispy Pork Belly

Cook Time: 30 min

Servings: 4

Difficulty: Easy

Ingredients

- Water 3 cups
- Pork belly 1 lb
- Kosher Salt 1 tsp
- Ground Black Pepper 1 tsp
- Soy Sauce 2 tbsps.
- Bay Leaves 2
- Garlic 6 cloves

Instructions

1. Cut pork belly in three thick chunks so that it can cook evenly.
2. Put all of the ingredients in the inner liner of the Instant Pot/ pressure cooker. Cook pork belly at maximum pressure for fifteen minutes. Let the pot sit for ten minutes & release the remaining pressure. Use a set of tongs, cautiously remove meat from the pressure cooker. Let meat drain & dry for ten minutes.
3. Cut every three chunks of the pork belly into two long slices.
4. Put pork belly slices in the basket of air fryers. Adjust air fryer at 400°F for fifteen minutes, till fat on pork belly has been crisped & then serve.

3. Air Fryer Scallops

Cook Time: 10 min

Servings: 2

Difficulty: Easy

Ingredients

- Tomato Paste 1 tbsp
- Heavy Whipping Cream 3/4 cup
- Chopped fresh basil 1 tbsp.
- Minced Garlic 1 tsp
- Kosher Salt 1/2 tsp
- Ground Black Pepper 1/2 tsp
- Frozen Spinach 1 12 oz.
- Jumbo sea scallops 8

- Cooking Oil Spray
- Extra salt & pepper to season scallops

Instructions

1. Spray seven inches in a heatproof pan & put the spinach in an equal layer at the bottom.
2. Spray each side of scallops with the vegetable oil, drizzle with little salt & pepper on it & place scallops in pan on the top of spinach.
3. In the bowl, combine tomato paste, garlic, pepper, salt, basil, spinach & scallops.
4. Adjust air fryer at 350F for ten minutes till scallops are thoroughly cooked through an internal temp of 135F & the sauce is hot & bubbling. Serve instantly.

4. Air Fryer Chicken Jalfrezi

Cook Time: 15 min

Servings: 4

Difficulty: Easy

Ingredients

- Onions chopped 1 cup.
- Boneless Chicken Thighs 1 lb & cut it into the large, two-inch pieces.
- Chopped Bell Peppers 2 cups
- Oil 2 tbsps.
- Kosher Salt 1 tsp
- Turmeric 1 tsp
- Garam Masala 1 tsp
- Cayenne Pepper 1/2-1 tsp

For the Sauce

- Tomato sauce 1/4 cup
- Water 1 tbsp
- Garam Masala 1 tsp
- Kosher Salt 1/2 tsp
- Cayenne Pepper 1/2 tsp

Instructions

1. In the bowl, combine onions, pepper, chicken, salt, oil, garam masala, turmeric & cayenne.
2. Put vegetables & chicken in the basket of an air fryer.
3. Adjust the air fryer at 360F for fifteen minutes. Mix & toss midway thru cooking time.
4. In the meantime, make the sauce: In a microwave bowl, mix water, cayenne, garam masala & tomato sauce.
5. Microwave it for one minute. Remove & mix for one minute. Put aside.
6. When chicken is prepared take away & put chicken & vegetables in the bowl. Put prepared sauce on them & toss to cover chicken & vegetables equally with sauce. Enjoy with the naan, side salad/ rice.

5. Air fryer Asian-glazed boneless chicken thighs

Cook time: 30 min

Servings: 4

Difficulty: Easy

Ingredients

- 32 ounces, skinless chicken thighs, eight boneless
- Low sodium soy sauce 1/4 cup
- Balsamic vinegar 2 1/2 tbsps.
- Honey 1 tbsp
- Garlic three cloves, crushed.
- Sriracha hot sauce 1 tsp
- Fresh grated ginger 1 tsp
- Green one scallion only sliced for garnish.

Instructions

1. In the bowl, mix ginger, soy sauce, honey, balsamic, garlic, honey & sriracha & mix it well.
2. Put half of (1/4 cup) marinade into the bowl with chicken, cover all marinate & meat minimum two hours/ overnight.
3. The remaining sauce will be saved for later.
4. Heat air fryer at 400F.
5. Take chicken from marinade & transfer it to the basket of an air fryer.

6. For fourteen minutes, cook in batch, flip halfway till cooked thru in the middle.
7. In the meantime, put the remaining sauce in a pot & cook over med-low heat till it decreases a little & thickens around one to two minutes.
8. For serving, sprinkle sauce on chicken & top with the scallions.

6. Za'atar lamb chops

Cook Time: 10 min

Servings: 4

Difficulty: Easy

Ingredients

- Garlic three cloves, crushed.
- Lamb loin chops 8, trimmed.
- Extra-virgin olive oil 1 tsp
- Fresh lemon 1/2
- Kosher salt 1 1/4 tsp
- Za'atar 1 tbsp
- To taste, fresh ground pepper

Instructions:

1. Lamb chops rub with garlic & oil.
2. Squash lemon on each side & season with zaatar, black pepper & salt.
3. Preheat the air fryer at 400F. Uneven layer & in batches cook to the desired, around four to five minutes on every side.
4. On every bone, chops must have raw meat 2 1/2 oz.

7. Toad in The Hole

Cook Time: 35 min

Servings: 4

Difficulty: Easy

Ingredients

- All-Purpose Flour 1/2 cup
- Eggs 4
- Whole Milk 1 cup
- Kosher Salt 1/2 tsp
- Ground Black Pepper 1/2 tsp
- Dijon mustard 2 tbsps.
- Vegetable oil 2 tbsps., or bacon fat/melted lard.
- Sausages 4, around ounces 4 each

Instructions

1. In the med bowl, add salt, pepper & flour.
2. Make well in the middle & break in eggs & milk. Beater the eggs & milk, then mix gradually into flour. You need batter that is around thick as the batter of a pancake. If it is very dense, put water/ milk. You should cover a batter and allow it to rest until you complete the remaining steps.
3. In a heatproof 6 x 3 pan, put the oil. Sausages should be cut in half & put into oil. Adjust air fryer at 400F for fifteen minutes.
4. Cautiously put in batter on the top of oil & sausages.

5. Adjust air fryer at 360F for twenty minutes/ till batter has been risen & browned on the top.

8. Air Fryer Tacos

Cook Time: 10 min

Servings: 6

Difficulty: Easy

Ingredients

Marinade

- Gochujang 2 tbsps.
- Dark Soy Sauce 1 tbsp
- Minced Garlic 2 tsps.
- Minced Ginger 2 tsps.
- Sugar 2 tsps
- Sesame Oil 2 tbsp.
- Sesame Seeds 2 tbsps
- Kosher Salt 1/2 tsp

Meat and Vegetables

- Sirloin beef 1.5 lbs, thinly sliced.
- Onion 1 cup, sliced.

For Serving

- Tortillas 12 flour, warmed.
- Romaine Lettuce Leaves one head for low carb
- Chopped Green Scallions 1/2 cup, cut into 2-inches pieces.

- Kimchi 1/2 cup, (optional)
- Cilantro 1/4 cup, chopped.

Instructions

1. Put sliced onions, sliced beef & green onions into the zip-top plastic bag. Put soy sauce, gochujang, garlic, ginger, sesame oil, sweetener & sesame seeds. Squish a bag to get meat & sauce to combine well.
2. Let beef marinate at least for thirty minutes/up to twenty-four hours in the refrigerator.
3. Put meat &veggies into a basket of an air fryer. Adjust air fryer at 400°F for twelve minutes, shaking halfway thru.
4. For serving, put little meat in tortillas & top with cilantro, kimchi & green onions.

9. Un-Fried Chicken

Cook Time: 15 min

Servings: 4

Difficulty: Hard

Ingredients

- Buttermilk 1 cup
- Hot sauce 1 tbsp, as Louisiana Hot Sauce
- Boneless 4, chicken breasts skinless
- Kosher salt/black pepper
- Breadcrumbs multi-grain panko 1 1/2 cups
- Grated Parmesan 3 tbsps.
- Lemon 1, quartered, plus lemon zest 1 tbsp.
- Flakes red pepper 1 tsp.

Instructions

1. Mix buttermilk & hot sauce in the bowl. Flavor chicken with the pepper & salt & dip in a mixture of buttermilk.
2. Mix parmesan, breadcrumbs, red pepper flakes & pinch of pepper & salt in the dish. Remove chicken from the mixture of buttermilk, allow the extra drip off & dredge in a mixture of breadcrumb until evenly coated. Put pieces flat on the nonstick baking sheet & chill it uncovered at least for 30 mins.

3. Warm the oven to four hundred degrees F. Bake the chicken till just cooked thru, twenty to twenty-five minutes. Split the chicken into four plates & crush the lemon on the chicken.

10. Air Fryer Hamburger

Cook Time: 10 min

Servings: 1

Difficulty: Easy

Ingredients

- Ground beef 1 lb
- Ground black pepper.
- Salt
- Cheese four slices
- Burger buns 4 (gluten-free)
- Garnishes
- Tomatoes lettuce

Instructions

1. Air fryer Preheated to 350F.
2. Combine the salt, black pepper & beef in the bowl.
3. Shape the mixture of the beef into four burger patties.
4. Spray the basket of your air fryer t, put in your burgers.
5. Cook for about 8 to 12 mins & flip them mid-way thru cooking.
6. Before 1 min they are completed, take a basket of air fryer & top every burger with the cheese, and turn back to air fryer & cook until completed.
7. Make burgers & now serve them.

8. The doneness of hamburger by with splendid meat thermometer.

11. Chicken Stuffed with Fontina and Prosciutto

Cook Time: 10 min

Servings: 2

Difficulty: Easy

Ingredients:

- Fontina cheese 4 ounces cut into two inches sticks, rind removed.
- Prosciutto two-slice
- Boneless chicken 2breast halves
- To taste salt
- To taste, ground black pepper.
- Unsalted butter 4 tbsps.
- Olive oil extra-virgin 2 tbsps.
- Portabella sliced mushrooms 1 cup.
- Dry white wine ½ cup
- Rosemary three sprigs
- Baby arugula one bunch
- Lemon ½, juiced.

Instructions

1. Put halves of chicken breast b/w sheets of the wax paper & using the rolling pin/mallet, lb thin.

2. Cover every fontina cheese stick along with the one slice prosciutto & put in the middle of every half-flattened chicken breast. Roll the chicken around cheese, prosciutto & secure with the butcher's twine /toothpicks. Flavor chicken rolls along with the salt, black pepper & salt.
3. In the heavy skillet, warm two tbsps of butter & one tbsp of olive oil. Speedily rolls of brown chicken on med heat, two to three minutes each side. Put chicken rolls in the air fryer basket. Adjust t temp to 350 degrees & air fry for seven minutes. Remove chicken rolls to the cutting board & allow them rest for 5 minutes. Cut the rolls at an angle into the six slices.
4. Reheat skillet & put remaining butter, wine, mushrooms & rosemary; sprinkle with pepper & salt; & boil for ten minutes.
5. In a bowl, toss leaves of arugula in the remaining lemon juice, olive oil, pepper & salt. To serve, place chicken & mushrooms on the bed of arugula.

12. Cajun Fried Okra with Creamy Chili Sauce

Cook Time: 15 min

Servings: 6 to 8

Difficulty: Easy

Ingredients:

- Okra
- Cornmeal 1 cup
- All-purpose flour 1 cup
- Paula Deen's House Seasoning 2 tsps.
- Cajun seasoning ¼ tsp
- Buttermilk ½ cup
- Fresh okra 2 lbs, ½ inch thick sliced
- For spraying, oil
- Creamy Chili Sauce
- Mayonnaise 1 cup
- Thai sweet chili sauce 3 tbsps.
- 1 tbsp garlic chili sauce
- Ground red pepper 1/3 tsp.

Instructions

1. In the med bowl, mix flour, cornmeal, Cajun seasoning & House Seasoning. Put the buttermilk in a bowl. Put okra in the buttermilk, & dredge in the cornmeal combination.

Put it on the cookie sheet with the parchment paper. Refrigerate the battered okra for thirty minutes.

2. Working in the batch of ten, spray the okra with oil & place it in the air fryer basket. Adjust temp to four hundred degrees, & air fry for 5 minutes. Mix okra nicely, sprays with the oil, & air fry for five minutes. Mix okra nicely sprays with the oil, & air fry for three minutes more. Repeat it with the remaining okra. Enjoy warm with the Creamy Chili Sauce on the side.
3. For creamy chili sauce, add mayonnaise. Garlic chili sauce, Thai sweet chili sauce & red pepper in a bowl & mix well. Cover & chill till ready to serve for 1¼ cup.

Chapter 10: Air Fryer Vegetables and Snacks Recipes

1. Air Fryer Bacon Wrapped Asparagus

Cook Time: 20 min

Servings: 6

Difficulty: Easy

Ingredients

- Bacon 1 lb cut in half.
- Asparagus 1 lb trimmed.
- Salt, pepper, & Creole seasoning/seasoned salt to taste
- Olive oil 1 tbsp

Instructions

1. Slice the bacon in two, and the asparagus ends are trimmed.

2. Drizzle the asparagus with olive oil. Add salt, pepper, & Creole seasoning to season. To coat evenly, toss.
3. Bacon half slice is wrapped around two asparagus spears.
4. Cook for ten minutes in an air fryer, then switch & cook for a further ten mins. You can cook your bacon for less time, depending on how crispy you like it.
5. Serve promptly, or store for up to a week in an airtight jar.

2. Air Fryer Cajun Sweet Potato Fries

Cook Time: 30 min

Servings: 2

Difficulty: Easy

Ingredients

- Sweet Potato Yam 1 med
- Cajun Seasoning 1 tsp
- Cornstarch 2 tbsps.
- Olive oil 3 tbsps.

Cajun mayo

- Hellman's mayonnaise 1 cup
- Dijon Mustard 2 tbsps.
- Lime 1

- Cajun Seasoning 1/2 tsp
- Cayenne pinch

Instructions

1. Chop the yam to 1/4 " fries on a wide cutting board.
2. Place them in a wide bowl and soak them in water.
3. Soak for at least 30 mins, strain, and put in a different bowl.
4. Season it with cornstarch & toss it to coat.
5. Drizzle over the top with olive oil & season.
6. Bake for 30 mins at 400 f.
7. Create the spicy mayo as it's frying, eat alongside & enjoy.

3. Roasted Rainbow Vegetables in the Air Fryer

Cook Time: 20 min

Servings: 4

Difficulty: Easy

Ingredients

- Red bell pepper 1, seeded & cut into 1" pieces.
- Yellow summer squash 1, cut into 1" pieces.
- Zucchini 1 cut into 1" pieces.
- Fresh mushrooms 4 ounces, cleaned & halved.
- Sweet onion ½, cut into 1" wedges.
- Extra-virgin olive oil 1 tbsp
- Salt & pepper

Instructions

1. According to recommendations from the manufacturer, preheat the air fryer.
2. Put in a wide bowl the red bell pepper, zucchini, mushrooms, summer squash, and onion. To combine, add olive oil, black pepper, and salt and shake.
3. Place the vegetables in a layer in the basket of the air fryer. Air-fry vegetables till roasted, stirring halfway through the cooking time, around 20 mins.

4. Air Fryer Roasted Cauliflower

Cook Time: 12 min

Servings: 4

Difficulty: Easy

Ingredients

- Chopped cauliflower 4 cups.
- Olive oil 1 tbsp
- Parsley 1 tsp
- Thyme 1 tsp
- Minced Garlic 1 tsp
- Salt 1 tsp
- Parmesan cheese ¼ cup
- Salt & pepper

Instructions

1. Combine the cauliflower, olive oil, parsley, minced garlic, thyme, and salt in a wide bowl.
2. Toss to mix, and it is well coated with cauliflower.
3. In an air-fryer basket, put the cauliflower. For 20 mins, adjusted to 400 degrees.
4. After 10 minutes, mix the cauliflower and add the parmesan cheese.
5. Season with salt & pepper to taste and serve immediately.

5. Sweet & Spicy Air Fryer Brussels sprouts

Cook Time: 20 min

Servings: 4

Difficulty: Easy

Ingredients

- Brussels sprouts 1 lb cut in half.
- Honey 2 tbsp
- Vegetable oil 1 1/2 tbsp
- Gochujang 1 tbsp
- Salt 1/2 tsp

Instructions

1. In a bowl, mix the honey, gochujang, vegetable oil, and salt and stir. Set around 1 Tbsp of the sauce aside. Add the sprouts to the bowl and mix until all the sprouts are fully coated.
2. In the Air Fryer, put the Brussels sprouts, ensure that they do not overlap, and cook for 15 mins at 360 ° F, shaking the bucket halfway through. Set the bowl aside.
3. Increase the temperature to 390 ° F after 15 mins and cook for five more mins. Place in a bowl when the sprouts are finished and cover with remaining sauce and stir. Enjoy, enjoy.

6. Air Fryer Green Beans

Cook Time: 10 min

Servings: 4

Difficulty: Easy

Ingredients

- Green beans 2 c
- Oil 1/2 tsp

Instructions

1. Wash the green beans & cut the ends off if necessary. With oil, toss the beans.
2. Place the beans in an air fryer. Cook for 10 mins at 390 ° F.
3. Enjoy.

7. Air-Fried Ranch Zucchini Chips Print

Cook Time: 20 min

Servings: 2

Difficulty: Easy

Ingredients

- Whole-wheat panko breadcrumbs 2/3 cup
- Ranch dressing 1 tbsp. /dip seasoning mix
- Zucchini 10 oz. Ends removed.
- Egg whites 1/4 cup or liquid egg substitute fat-free
- Light ranch dressing, ketchup

Instructions:

1. Mix the breadcrumbs in a large bowl with the seasoning.
2. Split zucchini into coins that are a quarter-inch wide. Put in another large bowl. Place an egg on top, & flip to coat.
3. Shake the zucchini coins one at a time to extract the excess egg, then gently cover with the breadcrumb mixture.
4. In one layer, put the zucchini in an air fryer & top with any leftover seasoned crumbs.
5. To 392 degrees, set the air fryer.
6. Cook till golden brown, 8 to 10 mins, working in batches.

8. Air Fryer Garlic Roasted Green Beans

Cook Time: 8 min

Servings: 4

Difficulty: Easy

Ingredients

- Fresh green beans 3/4-1 lb (trimmed)
- Olive oil 1 tbsp
- Garlic powder 1 tsp
- Salt and pepper

Instructions

1. Drizzle the green beans with olive oil. The seasonings are scattered throughout. Toss it to coat it.
2. Put green beans in the basket of an air fryer.
3. Cook green beans at 370 degrees for 7-8 mins. Toss halfway through the overall cooking time for the basket.
4. Get the green beans removed and serve.

9. Quick & Easy Air Fryer Roasted Asparagus

Cook Time: 10 min

Servings: 4

Difficulty: Easy

Ingredients

- Fresh asparagus 1 bunch
- Olive oil 1 tbsp
- Herbes de Provence seasoning 1 1/2 tsps. optional
- Salt & pepper
- Optional fresh lemon wedge

Instructions

1. Wash & trim Asparagus hard ends.
2. Drizzle the olive oil & the seasonings with the asparagus. Cooking oil spray may also be used.
3. In an air fryer, add the asparagus.
4. Cook at 360 degrees for 6-10 mins until crisp. Drizzle over the roasted asparagus with freshly squeezed lemon.
5. Begin to track it closely after asparagus is cooked for 5 mins.

10. Quick & Easy Air Fryer Roasted Broccoli

Cook Time: 10 min

Servings: 4

Difficulty: Easy

Ingredients

- Fresh broccoli florets 3-4 cups (cut)
- Olive oil 1 tbsp
- Salt & pepper
- Optional herbes de Provence seasoning 1 tsp

Instructions

1. Drizzle with olive oil on the broccoli or spray with the cooking oil. The seasonings are sprinkled throughout.
2. Spray a basket of air fryers with cooking oil. Load up the broccoli. Cook at 360 degrees for 5-8 mins.
3. Open the air fryer and check the broccoli once the broccoli is cooked for five mins. Each type of air fryer cooks differently. To make sure the broccoli is not overcooked, use your judgment.

11. Air Fryer Crispy Balsamic Brussels sprouts

Cook Time: 10 min

Servings: 5

Difficulty: Easy

Ingredients

- Fresh Brussels sprouts 1 1/2 -2 cups each sliced in half.
- Sliced red onions 1/2 cup.
- Balsamic vinegar 1 tbsp
- Olive oil 1 tbsp
- Salt & pepper

Instructions

1. In a bowl, add the Brussels sprouts & sliced red onions. Olive oil and balsamic vinegar are drizzled throughout.
2. Sprinkle salt & pepper to taste. To coat uniformly, stir.
3. Spray a basket of air fryers with the cooking oil.
4. Add onions and Brussels sprouts.
5. Cook at 350 degrees for 5 mins.
6. Open the air fryer and use tongs to shake/toss the vegetables.
7. For an extra 3-5 mins, cook. Each type of air fryer is cooked differently. In order to determine the optimum cooking period, use your judgment.
8. Before serving, cool it.

12. Garlic-Herb Fried Patty Pan Squash

Cook Time: 15 min

Servings: 4

Difficulty: Easy

Ingredients

- Halved small pattypan squash 5 cups (about 1-1/4 lbs)
- Olive oil 1 tbsp
- Garlic cloves 2, minced.
- Salt 1/2 tsp
- Dried oregano 1/4 tsp
- Dried thyme 1/4 tsp
- Pepper 1/4 tsp
- Minced fresh parsley 1 tbsp.

Instructions

1. Preheat the fryer to 375 degrees. Put your squash in a wide bowl. Mix together the oil, the garlic, the salt, the oregano, the thyme, and the pepper, drizzle over the squash. Toss it to coat it. Place the squash in an air-fryer basket on a greased plate. Cook until soft, 10-15 mins, occasionally stirring. With parsley, sprinkle.

13. Air-Fryer General Tso's Cauliflower

Cook Time: 20 min

Servings: 4

Difficulty: Easy

Ingredients

- All-purpose flour 1/2 cup
- Cornstarch 1/2 cup
- Salt 1 tsp
- Baking powder 1 tsp
- Club soda 3/4 cup
- Head cauliflower 1 medium, cut into 1" florets (6 cups)

Sauce:

- Orange juice 1/4 cup
- Sugar 3 tbsps.
- Soy sauce 3 tbsps.
- Vegetable broth 3 tbsps.
- Rice vinegar 2 tbsps.
- Sesame oil 2 tsps.
- Cornstarch 2 tsps.
- Canola oil 2 tbsps.
- Dried pasilla 2 to 6

- Green onions 3, green part thinly sliced white part minced.
- Garlic cloves 3, minced.
- Grated fresh ginger root 1 tsp.
- Grated orange zest 1/2 tsp
- Hot cooked rice 4 cups

Instructions

1. Preheat the fryer to 400 degrees. Mix the flour, salt, cornstarch, and baking powder together. Stir in the club soda when combined. (Batter will be thin). Toss the florets in the batter, transfer over a baking sheet to a wire rack. Let it stand for 5 mins. Place cauliflower in batches on a greased tray in the air-fryer basket. Cook till tender & golden brown, 10-12 mins.
2. Meanwhile, whisk the first six ingredients of the sauce together: whisk in the cornstarch till smooth.
3. Heat the canola oil over med to high heat in a wide saucepan. Add chilies; cook & mix for 1-2 mins until fragrant. Add the white onions, ginger, garlic, and orange zest; simmer for around 1 min, until fragrant. Stir in the mixture of orange juice; add to the saucepan. Take to a boil; cook & stir for 2-4 mins till thickened.
4. To the sauce, add cauliflower; toss to coat. Now Serve with rice & sprinkle with green onions, thinly sliced.

14. Air-Fryer Cumin Carrots

Cook Time: 15 min

Servings: 4

Difficulty: Easy

Ingredients

- Coriander seeds 2 tsps.
- Cumin seeds 2 tsps.
- Carrots 1 lb, peeled & cut into 4x1/2" sticks.
- Melted coconut oil/butter 1 tbsp.
- Garlic cloves 2, minced.
- Salt 1/4 tsp
- Pepper 1/8 tsp
- Optional minced fresh cilantro

Instructions

1. Preheat the fryer to 325 degrees. Toast the coriander & cumin seeds in some small dry skillet over med heat for 45-60 sec. until it's aromatic, stirring regularly. Slightly cool. Grind in some spice grinder until finely ground, or by a mortar & pestle.
2. Place the carrots in a wide bowl. Mix melted coconut oil, salt, garlic, crushed spices, and pepper; toss to cover. Place the air-fryer basket on a greased plate.
3. Cook, stirring regularly, until crisp-tender & lightly browned, 12 to 15 mins. Sprinkle it with cilantro if necessary.

15. Air Fryer Blooming Onion

Cook Time: 30 min

Servings: 4

Difficulty: Easy

Ingredients

- For the onion
- Large yellow onion 1
- Large eggs 3
- Breadcrumbs 1 c.
- Paprika 2 tsp.
- Garlic powder 1 tsp.
- Onion powder 1 tsp.
- Kosher salt 1 tsp.
- Extra-virgin olive oil 3 tbsp.

For the sauce

- Kosher salt
- Mayonnaise 2/3 c.
- Ketchup 2 tbsp.
- Horseradish 1 tsp.
- Paprika 1/2 tsp.
- Garlic powder 1/2 tsp.

- Dried oregano 1/4 tsp.

Instructions

1. Slice off the stem of the onion and place the onion on the flat side. Into 12 - 16 sections, cut an inch down from the root, being cautious not to cut across all the way. To separate petals, turn over and softly take sections of onion out.
2. Whisk together 1 tbsp of water and eggs in a small bowl. Whisk the breadcrumbs & spices together in another small bowl. Dip the onion into the egg wash, and dredge it in the breadcrumb mix, then coat it fully with a spoon. Sprinkle the onion with some oil.
3. Put the air fryer in the basket and cook 20 to 25 mins at 375 ° until the onion is tender. Drizzle as needed with more oil.
4. Meanwhile, mix together the mayonnaise, horseradish, paprika, ketchup, garlic powder, & dried oregano in a med bowl. Season it with salt.
5. For dipping, serve the onion with sauce.

Chapter 11: Air Fryer Chicken Recipes

1. Garlic Parmesan Chicken Wings

Cook Time: 30 min

Servings: 3

Difficulty: Easy

Ingredients

- Sea salt 1/2 tsp
- Chicken wings 1.5 lbs
- Black pepper 1/2 tsp
- Garlic powder 1/2 tsp
- Smoked paprika 1/2 tsp.
- Onion Powder 1/2 tsp
- Baking powder 1 tbsp
- Wings sauce garlic parmesan

- Melted & unsalted butter 1/4 cup.
- Grated parmesan 1/2 cup
- Onion powder 1 tsp
- Garlic powder 1 tsp
- Dried parsley 1 tsp
- Black pepper 1/4 tsp

Instructions

1. Take your chicken wing parts from a fridge & pat dry.
2. Mix the black pepper, paprika, sea salt, garlic powder, baking powder & onion powder in the dish/ramekin.
3. Drizzle the mixture of seasoning on the wings & toss to coat.
4. In the air fryer, put wings on the flat layer.
5. Using an air-fryer programmed settings for the chicken, cook for 25 to 30 mins. Set your timer for around 15 mins, turn the wings, then check your wings at 5 mins intervals till the skin becomes crispy. To make the wings crispy very quickly requires turning them around halfway thru.
6. In the bowl, mix all the components for the sauce of the garlic parmesan.
7. Toss your wings in the mixture of garlic parmesan & serve immediately.

2. Crispy Air Fryer Chicken Wings

Cook Time: 35 min

Servings: 4

Difficulty: Easy

Ingredients

- Black pepper 1/4 tsp
- Baking powder gluten-free 2 tsp
- Chicken wings 2 lb
- Sea salt 3/4 tsp

Instructions

1. In the bowl, toss your wings with the sea salt, black pepper & baking powder.
2. Grease the two racks for an air fryer oven.
3. Put the wings onto an oiled rack or put only enough wings into a basket to be in the single layer.
4. Put the racks/basket into an air fryer & cook for fifteen mins at 250 degrees.
5. Turn the wings & switch the trays. Increase temp to 430. Air fry for around 15- 20 mins, till chicken wings are cooked & crispy.

3. Brazilian Chicken

Cook Time: 25 min

Servings: 4

Difficulty: Easy

Ingredients

- Cumin seeds 1 tsp
- Dried oregano 1 tsp
- Dried parsley 1 tsp
- Turmeric 1 tsp
- Kosher salt 1 tsp
- Coriander seeds 1/2 tsp
- Black peppercorns 1/2 tsp
- Cayenne pepper 1/2 tsp
- Lime juice 1/4 cup

- Oil 2 tbsp
- Chicken drumsticks 1.5 lbs

Instructions

1. Grind together the oregano, cumin, parsley, kosher salt, turmeric, coriander seeds, peppercorns & cayenne pepper in the clean coffee grinder.
2. In a med bowl, mix the ground spices with lime juice & oil. Put the chicken drumsticks & flip them, coating well with the marinade. Let the chicken marinate for thirty mins or can be for one day in the refrigerator.
3. Once you are prepared to cook, put the chicken legs into an air fryer basket.
4. Set the air fryer temp to 390 f & timer for 20 to 25 mins for meaty chicken legs. Halfway thru, turn the chicken legs over.
5. Remove & serve with enough napkins.

4. Basic Air Fryer Chicken Breasts

Cook Time: 11 min

Servings: 2

Difficulty: Easy

Ingredients

- Chicken breasts 2
- Salt 1 pinch
- Olive oil 1 tbsp
- Garlic powder 1 tsp
- Paprika 1 tsp

Instructions

1. Rub the olive oil & coat them with a mix of salt, garlic powder, & paprika onto the chicken breasts.
2. Place into your air fryer, making sure there is some space between them.

3. Set the air fryer to 400f and let it cook for 7 mins before flipping the chicken and cooking for another 4 mins.

5. Air fryer chicken nuggets

Cook Time: 14 min

Servings: 4

Difficulty: Easy

Ingredients

- Pickle juice 1 cup
- Chicken breast 2 6 oz.
- Egg 1
- Milk 3 tbs
- All-purpose flour 3/4 cup
- Corn starch 3 tbsp
- Powdered sugar 2 tbsp
- Salt 1 1/2 tsp
- Paprika 3/4 tsp
- Black pepper 1/4 tsp
- Garlic powder 1/4 tsp
- Onion Powder 1/4 tsp
- Oil to spray

Instructions

1. In a plastic bag, put chicken slices & pickle juice. Close & put in the freezer for 20 to 30 mins.

2. Therefore, in the bowl, stir together the egg & milk.
3. In the other bowl, stir together corn starch, flour, salt, powdered sugar, paprika, powder, onion, garlic powder & black pepper. Set aside.
4. Take the chicken pieces from the freezer. Oil your air fryer basket with a little bit of oil. Coat the chicken pieces in the mixture of an egg; after this, coat it in the mixture of flour; shake off the extra flour & put it in a basket. Repeat till the bottom of your air fryer basket is full. Ensure that no pieces are overlapping.
5. Close your air fryer basket & cook at 360 degrees f for twelve mins, turning halfway. Spray the flour spots when turning.
6. After twelve mins, increase the air fryer heat to 400 degrees f & cook for another two mins.
7. Remove & serve with your preferable dipping sauce.

6. Air fryer jalapeno stuffed chicken

Cook Time12 min

Servings: 12

Difficulty: Easy

Ingredients

- Seeded & cut lengthwise jalapenos 6.
- Boneless & skinless chicken thighs 12
- Cream cheese 125g
- Minced garlic three cloves
- Onion Powder 1/2 tsp
- Chili powder 1/2 tsp
- Fresh ground pepper 1/4 tsp
- Salt 1 tsp

Oil mixture

- Avocado oil 4 tbsp
- Chili powder 1/4 tsp
- Onion Powder 1/4 tsp

Instructions

1. In the med bowl, mix the garlic, cream cheese, chili powder, onion powder, salt & pepper. Set aside.
2. Remove a stem of jalapenos, slice them lengthwise, & remove the seeds.

3. Use the butter knife & add the cream cheese to each half of the twelve jalapenos.
4. Roll out the piece of a chicken thigh. Put the jalapeno popper on your chicken & roll it up. To hold it secure. Use the toothpick.
5. Do the above step again till all the ingredients are used.
6. In the bowl, mix all the ingredients for the mixture of oil.
7. Brush the mixture of oil on each side of every piece of the chicken.

7. Buffalo chicken egg rolls

Cook Time: 10 min

Servings: 12

Difficulty: Easy

Ingredients

- Shredded chicken 1 ½
- Egg roll wrappers 12
- Buffalo wing sauce ½ cup
- Blue cheese crumbles ½ cup
- Softened cream cheese 4oz
- Shredded cheddar cheese ½ cup
- Chopped green onions 2.

Instructions

1. In the bowl, mix cream cheese, buffalo wing sauce, blue cheese crumbles & cheddar cheese till well combined. Whisk in chopped green onions & shredded chicken. Combine well.
2. As per the egg roll package instructions, assemble the egg rolls by using around two tbsp of filling for every egg roll.
3. In the air fryer basket, put wrapped egg rolls, leave the space b/w egg rolls. Spray lightly with the non-stick cooking spray.
4. Cook in an air fryer over 370 degrees for ten mins, turning halfway thru cook time.
5. Serve warm with the blue cheese dressing.

8. Air fryer rotisserie chicken

Cook Time: 40 min

Servings: 5

Difficulty: Easy

Ingredients

- Full chicken
- Oxo cube chicken 1
- Paprika 1 tbsp
- Thyme 2 tsp
- Pepper & salt
- Chicken rub
- Olive oil 1 tbsp
- Paprika 1 tbsp
- Celery salt 1 tsp
- Pepper & salt

Instructions

1. Into the freezer bag, put all the brine ingredients. Put the whole chicken & then add cold water till the chicken is fully covered. Put it in your fridge for a night.
2. Once you are ready to cook the air fryer rotisserie chicken the next day, remove your chicken from the bag, remove the brine stock, remove the giblets, & pat dry the full chicken with the towel.

3. In a bowl, make the chicken rub.
4. Place the whole chicken & rub ½ olive oil & ½ of a chicken rub into every visible skin in the air fryer.
5. Cook your chicken for twenty mins on 360f.
6. After twenty mins, turn over with the kitchen tongs; after this, add the remaining oil & your chicken rub onto the other chicken side.
7. Cook for an additional twenty mins.
8. Serve hot.

9. Air fryer chicken tender "hot dogs."

Cook Time: 30 min

Servings: 1

Difficulty: Easy

Ingredients

- Chicken tenderloins 1.25 lb
- Gluten-free breadcrumbs 1½ cup
- Buttermilk 1 cup
- Celery salt 1 tsp
- Garlic powder ½ tsp
- Onion powder ½ tsp
- Cayenne ¼ tsp
- Crushed black pepper ½ tsp.
- Honey 3 tbsp
- Yellow mustard 2 tsp
- Stoneground mustard 2 tsp
- Diced red onion ¼ cup.
- Homemade hot dog buns 8 (gluten-free)

Instructions

1. In the buttermilk, soak your chicken tenders for ten to fifteen mins.

2. In the bowl, mix the breadcrumbs, celery salt, onion powder, garlic powder, cayenne & black pepper. Stir well.
3. Please pick up the one tender of chicken, shake off the extra buttermilk & roll it in your seasoned breadcrumbs. Set aside on a separate plate.
4. Repeat these steps with the leftover tenders.
5. Put some slices in a lightly oiled air fryer basket in a single layer. Spray the prepared tenders lightly.
6. Air fry on 370 f for fifteen mins, turning at the midway mark.
7. Do again with all of the prepared tenders of chicken.
8. Whereas the tenders of chicken are air frying, mix yellow, stoneground mustard & honey then combine it well in the bowl.
9. To serve: cut open the hot dog buns lengthwise.
10. Put the air fried chicken tender in it & finish with the honey mustard (already prepared) & minced red onion. Serve it immediately.

10. Air fryer cheesy chicken tender's

Cook Time: 30 min

Servings: 4

Difficulty: Easy

Ingredients

- Pulverized cheese crackers 2 cups
- Boneless & skinless chicken tenders 2- 2.5 lbs
- Cooking spray olive oil
- Paprika 1/4 tsp
- Onion Powder 1/2 tsp
- Milk 2 cups

Instructions

1. In the bowl, soak the thawed chicken tenders filled with the milk for one hour. It could be soaked for a night or a whole day.
2. Pulverize your crackers in the electric food chopper.
3. Place the chopped cheese crackers into the resealable bag (gallon size).
4. Put the seasonings on your crackers & shake to mix.
5. Drain the tenders of chicken.
6. Put around 2/3 tenders at one time in a bag with the cracker combination & shake to coat.
7. Put the coated tenders into an air fryer basket.

8. Drizzle each one with the cooking spray.
9. Set the temp at 400 degrees & also set the timer for 12 mins & cook.
10. Test the tenders at the end of the first twelve mins, flip over & drizzle this side with the cooking spray.
11. Cook for another 10 to 15 mins.
12. Now enjoy it with your favorite toppings.

11. Air fryer turkey meatballs

Cook Time: 16 min

Servings: 4

Difficulty: Easy

Ingredients

- Cooked vegetables 150 g
- Leftover turkey 30 g
- Greek yogurt 1 tbsp
- Couscous 1/2 cup
- Soft cheese 30 g
- Turkey stock 30 ml
- Cumin 1 tbsp
- Desiccated coconut 20 g
- Moroccan spice 1 tbsp
- Coriander 1 tbsp
- Pepper & salt

Instructions

1. In the blender, put the cooked vegetables, turkey leg meat, Greek yogurt (soft cheese), turkey stock, & seasoning. Blend for some mins or till the mixture resembles thick.
2. Move the blender ingredients into the mixing bowl, put in a couscous & combine well.
3. Form the combination into balls & roll in desiccated coconut.

4. Put in your air fryer for sixteen mins on 360f & then serve.

12. Air-fryer Nashville hot chicken

Cook Time: 10 min

Servings: 6

Difficulty: Easy

Ingredients

- Divided dill pickle juice 2 tbsp
- Divided hot pepper sauce 2 tbsp.
- Divided salt 1 tsp
- Chicken tenderloins 2 lbs
- All-purpose flour 1 cup
- Pepper 1/2 tsp
- Egg 1
- Buttermilk 1/2 cup
- Cooking spray
- Olive oil 1/2 cup
- Cayenne pepper 2 tbsp
- Dark brown sugar 2 tbsp
- Paprika 1 tsp
- Chili powder 1 tsp
- Garlic powder 1/2 tsp
- Dill pickle slices

Instructions

1. In the bowl/shallow dish, mix one tbsp pickle juice, half tsp salt & one tbsp hot sauce. Put the chicken & turn to coat. Cover & refrigerate for one hour. Discard the marinade; drain.
2. Air fryer preheated to 375 degrees. In the bowl, combine flour, half tsp salt & pepper. In the other bowl, stir egg, one tbsp pickle juice, one tbsp hot sauce & buttermilk. Dip your chicken in the flour to coat each side; shake off extra. Dip in the mixture of egg, after which again in the mixture of flour.
3. In batches, assemble the chicken in a single layer on an oiled tray in an air-fryer basket, drizzle with cooking spray. Cook till its color changes to a golden brown, 5 to 6 mins. Flip; drizzle with cooking spray. Cook till its color changes to golden brown, 5 to 6 mins longer.
4. Stir together cayenne pepper, oil, brown sugar & seasonings, place on hot chicken & toss to coat. Enjoy with the pickles.

13. Air fryer Cornish hen

Cook Time: 25 min

Servings: 3

Difficulty: Easy

Ingredients

- Cornish hen 1
- Salt
- Black pepper
- Paprika
- Coconut spray/olive oil spray

Instructions

1. With spices, rub the Cornish hen. Spray your air fryer basket with olive/coconut oil spray.
2. Put the Cornish hen into the air fryer at 390f for around 25 mins. Turning halfway thru
3. Safely remove & serve.

Chapter 12: Air fryer Beef Recipes

1. Air Fryer Asian Beef & Veggies

Cook Time: 8 min

Servings: 4

Difficulty: Easy

Ingredients

- Cornstarch 2 tbsp
- Cut into strips sirloin steak 1 lb.
- Sliced into strips red pepper one med.
- Sliced yellow onion 1/2 med.
- Minced garlic three cloves
- Grated ginger 2 tbsp
- Red chili flakes 1/4 tsp

- Soy sauce 1/2 cup
- Sesame oil 1 tsp
- Water 1/4 cup
- Rice vinegar 1/4 cup
- Brown sugar 1/3 cup
- Chinese 5 spice 1 tsp

Instructions

1. On a gallon-shaped zip bag, put all the ingredients. Make sure that all the ingredients are mixed. For up to four months, mark & freeze.
2. Overnight, thaw the zip bag in the freezer.
3. Remove the vegetables & steak using tongs & move them to the Air Fryer. Take the marinade away.
4. Preheat the air fryer to 400 degrees F & set the timer to 8 mins.
5. Serve with rice, then garnish with scallions & sesame seeds.

2. Air Fryer Steak Tips

Cook Time: 20 min

Servings: 4

Difficulty: Easy

Ingredients

- Steaks 1 lb
- Butter 2 tbsp
- Potatoes 1/2 lb
- Worcestershire sauce 1 tsp
- Salt
- Garlic powder 1/2 tsp
- Minced parsley for garnish
- Black pepper

Instructions

1. Carry a pot of water to a simmer & after this, add the potatoes. Cook for five minutes or till almost soft. Place away & drain
2. Combine the tips for steaks with blanched potatoes. Mix the melted butter, garlic powder, Worcestershire sauce, salt, and pepper.
3. Preheat your Air Fryer for four mins at 400 °F.
4. In the air fryer basket, scatter the steak & potatoes in a layer. Air fry for 10 to 18 minutes at 400 ° F, shaking & flipping & the steak & potatoes two cycles during the cooking process.
5. To see how well cooked it is, see the steak. If you want to do something about the steak, put an additional 2 to 5 minutes of cooking time.
6. Sprinkle with parsley. If needed, drizzle with extra salt and pepper. Serve hot.

3. Air fryer meatloaf

Cook Time: 50 min

Servings: 3-4

Difficulty: Easy

Ingredients

- Ground beef 1/2 lb
- Thick-cut bacon 1/2 lb.
- Ground pork 1/2 lb
- Diced yellow onion 1/2
- Almond flour 1 cup
- Diced red bell pepper 1.
- Spicy brown mustard 1 tbsp
- Ketchup 2 tbsp
- Salt 1 tsp
- White pepper 1/2 tsp
- Garlic powder 1 tsp
- Celery salt 1/2 tsp
- Egg 1
- Cayenne pepper 1/4 tsp

For the sauce:

- Ketchup 1/2 cup

- Maple syrup 2–3 tbsp

Instructions

1. Preheat your air fryer to 350 °.
2. In a bowl, whisk together the meatloaf ingredients till thoroughly mixed. In the other bowl, stir the sauce ingredients together & set aside.
3. Top a 9-to-5 loaf pan with mildly overlapping bacon strips. Put the meatloaf combination on top of the bacon to fully cover the meatloaf, wrap the strips near the meat. After this, tip the pan on to remove your meatloaf.
4. In an air fryer, put the meatloaf. Heat the oven to 350 ° F and set the timer for approximately 50 minutes.
5. When the timer reaches the mark of 30 minutes, click pause & brush around Three tbsp of the sauce over top of a meatloaf by using the basting brush. Slightly cover the piece of tin rolls with the meatloaf.
6. Cook for Sixteen more minutes, now remove a foil, baste your meatloaf once again in around three tablespoons of sauce, and then cook for the next 4 minutes without the foil.
7. When cooked, before slicing & serving, allow the meatloaf rest for ten minutes. Only a head up, it's certainly a little tough to pull the meatloaf out. You'll be able to gently press up and lift the wire rack from the basket till the wire rack has chilled.

4. Air-Fryer Beefy Swiss Bundles

Cook Time: 10 min

Servings: 4

Difficulty: Easy

Ingredients

- Ground beef 1 lb
- Chopped onion 1/2 cup.
- Sliced fresh mushrooms 1-1/2 cups.
- Minced garlic 1-1/2 tsp
- Crushed dried rosemary 3/4 tsp.
- Worcestershire sauce 4 tsp
- Salt 1/2 tsp
- Paprika 3/4 tsp
- Pepper 1/4 tsp

- Refrigerated mashed potatoes 2/3 cup.
- Thawed frozen puff pastry one-sheet.
- Shredded Swiss cheese 1 cup.
- Water 2 tbsp

Instructions

1. Air fryer preheated to 375 degrees. In a big skillet, cook mushrooms, onion & beef, on med heat till meat is no further pink & veggies are softer, 8 to 10 mins. Put garlic; cook one minute further. Drain. Whisk in Worcestershire sauce & seasonings. Take it from the heat; set aside.
2. On a lightly floured surface, roll the puff pastry into a 15 into a 13-inch rectangle. Cut into rectangles. Put around two tbsp potatoes on every rectangle: scatter to within one in of edges. Drizzle each with a 3/4 cup beef combination; season with 1/4 cup cheese.
3. Beat egg & water; brush a few on pastry edges. Carry opposite pastry corners on each bundle; put a pinch of seams to seal. Brush with leftover egg combination. In batches, put pastries in the single layer on a tray in an air-fryer basket; cook till color changes to a golden brown.
4. Freeze option: Freeze your unbaked pastries on the parchment-lined cookie sheet till hard. Move it to an airtight jar, back to the freezer. To use it, cook frozen pastries till their color changes to a golden brown & heated fully.

5. Air Fryer Beef Bulgogi

Cook Time: 12

Servings: 6

Difficulty: Easy

Ingredients

- Minced Green Scallions 3
- Sirloin Steak 1.5 lbs
- Shredded carrots 1 cup
- Brown Sugar 2 tbsp
- Soy Sauce 3 tbsp
- Sesame Oil 2 tbsp
- Minced Garlic 2 tsp
- Sesame Seeds 2 tbsp
- Ground Black Pepper 1/2 tsp

Instructions

1. Put sliced carrots, green onions & beef into the zip-top bag (plastic). Put brown sugar, soy sauce, sesame oil, garlic, ground pepper & sesame seeds. Squish a bag well to get the meat & sauce mixed well.
2. Let the beef marinate for thirty mins or up to one day in the freezer.
3. Put the meat and vegetables into the air fryer basket, leave behind the marinade as you can. Heat the air fryer to 400 degrees F for about 12 mins, shaking halfway thru.
4. Serve with rice cauliflower, steamed rice.

Chapter 13: Air Fryer Dessert Recipes

1. Air-Fryer Bread Pudding

Cook Time: 15 min

Servings: 2

Difficulty: Easy

Ingredients

- Half-&-half cream 1/2 cup
- Chopped semisweet chocolate 2 ounces.
- Sugar 2/3 cup
- Egg 1 large
- Milk 1/2 cup
- (Crusts removed & sliced into cubes) day-old bread four slices.
- Vanilla extract 1 tsp

- Salt 1/4 tsp

Instructions

1. Melt chocolate in the microwave-safe bowl, whisk till smooth. Mix in cream; set aside.
2. In the bowl, stir milk, sugar, egg, salt & vanilla. Mix it in a mixture of chocolate. Put bread cubes & toss to cover. Let it rest for fifteen mins.
3. Air fryer preheated to 325 degrees. Spoon the bread combination into the two greased 8 oz. ramekins. Put on a tray in an air-fryer basket. Cook till a knife inserted in the middle comes out.
4. If you like, then top it with whipped cream & confectioner sugar.

2. Air-Fryer Caribbean Wontons

Cook Time: 10 min

Servings: 2

Difficulty: Easy

Ingredients

- Sweetened shredded coconut 1/4 cup.
- Softened cream cheese 4 ounces
- Mashed ripe banana 1/4 cup.
- Canned chopped pineapple 2 tbsps.
- Chopped walnuts 2 tbsp.
- Marshmallow crème 1 cup
- Wonton wrappers 24
- Cooking spray

Sauce:

- Hulled fresh strawberries 1 lb.
- Sugar 1/4 cup
- Cornstarch 1 tsp
- Ground cinnamon & confectioners' sugar

Instructions

1. Air fryer preheated to 350 degrees. In the bowl, stir cream cheese till smooth. Whisk in banana, coconut, walnuts & pineapple. Fold it in the marshmallow creme.
2. Put the wonton wrapper with one point toward you. Keep the leftover wrappers covered with the damp paper towel till ready to use. Put two tsp filling in the wrapper middle. With the water, moisten edges; fold other side corners together on filling & press to cover. Do that step again with the rest of the wrappers & filling.
3. Arrange the wontons in a single layer on an oiled tray in an air-fryer basket in the batches, drizzle with the cooking spray. Cook till its color changes to golden brown & crisp, ten to12 mins.
4. Therefore, put the strawberries in the food processor, cover & process till pureed. In the saucepan, mix sugar & cornstarch. Whisk in the pureed strawberries. Carry to a simmer; cook & whisk till thickened, two mins. If you like, then strain the mixture, saving sauce & discard seeds. Drizzle wontons with the confectioners' sugar & cinnamon. Serve it with sauce.

3. Air-Fryer Apple Fritters

Cook time: 8 min

Servings: 15

Difficulty: Easy

Ingredients

- All-purpose flour 1-1/2 c
- Cooking spray
- Sugar 1/4 cup
- Salt 1/2 tsp
- Ground cinnamon 1-1/2 tsp
- Milk 2/3 c
- Baking powder 2 tsp
- Eggs 2 large
- Lemon juice 1 tbsp
- Divided vanilla extract 1-1/2 tsp.
- Peeled & chopped Honeycrisp apples two med.
- Butter 1/4 c
- Confectioners' sugar 1 c
- Milk 1 tbsp

Instructions

1. Line the air-fryer basket with the parchment. Drizzle with the cooking spray. Air fryer preheated to 410 degrees.
2. In the bowl, mix sugar, baking powder, flour, cinnamon & salt. Put eggs, milk, lemon juice & vanilla extract (one tsp); whisk just till moistened. Fold them in apples.
3. Drop the dough by one/four cup in batches onto the air-fryer basket. Sprinkle with cooking spray. Cook till its color changes to a golden brown, five to six mins. Turn the fritters; air-fry till its color changes to a golden brown, 1 to 2 mins.
4. Melt your butter in the saucepan on med-high heat. Safely cook till butter begins to brown & foam, five mins. Take it from the heat; cool it slightly. Put 1 tbsp milk, confectioners' sugar & leftover vanilla extract into the browned butter; stir till smooth. Before serving, sprinkle on fritters.

4. Air-Fryer Carrot Coffee Cake

Cook Time: 35 min

Servings: 6

Difficulty: Easy

Ingredients

- Buttermilk 1/2 cup
- Lightly beaten egg one large
- Sugar1/3 cup + sugar 2 tbsp
- Dark brown sugar 2 tbsp
- Canola oil 3 tbsp
- grated orange zest 1 tsp
- Vanilla extract 1 tsp
- All-purpose flour 2/3 cup
- Wheat flour (white whole)1/3 cup

- Baking powder 1 tsp
- Pumpkin pie spice 2 tsp
- Salt 1/4 tsp
- Baking soda 1/4 tsp
- Shredded carrots 1 cup
- Dried cranberries 1/4 cup
- Toasted chopped walnuts 1/3 cup.

Instructions

1. Air fryer preheated to 350 degrees; Grease & flour the 6-in. Round cooking pan. In the bowl, stir egg, 1/3 cup sugar, buttermilk, oil, orange zest, vanilla & brown sugar. In the other bowl, stir flours, 1 tsp pumpkin pie spice, baking soda, baking powder, & salt. Slowly beat into egg combination. Fold in the carrots & dried cranberries. Place into the prepared pan.
2. In the bowl, mix walnuts, remaining one tsp pumpkin spice & remaining two tbsp sugar. Drizzle equally on the batter. Nicely put the pan in the big air fryer basket.
3. Cook till the toothpick inserted in the middle comes out clean, 35 to 40 mins. If the top gets too dark, then seal firmly with foil; before removing it from the pan, cool it in the pan over the wire rack for ten mins. Serve warm.

5. Raspberries With French Toast Cups (Air-Fryer)

Cook Time: 20 min

Servings: 2

Difficulty: Easy

Ingredients

- (Cut into 1/2-inch cubes) Italian bread two slices.
- Fresh/frozen raspberries 1/2 cup
- Cream cheese 2 ounces
- Eggs 2 large
- Milk 1/2 cup
- Maple syrup 1 tbsp

Raspberry syrup

- Cornstarch 2 tsps.
- Water 1/3 cup
- Fresh/frozen raspberries 2 cups

- Lemon juice 1 tbsp
- Maple syrup 1 tbsp
- Grated lemon zest 1/2 tsp

Instructions

1. Split half bread cubes b/w two greased custard cups (8-oz). Sprinkle with cream cheese & raspberries. Top with the leftover bread. In the bowl, stir milk, syrup & eggs, place over bread. Cover & refrigerate for one hour.
2. Air fryer preheated to 325 degrees. Put custard cups on the tray in an air-fryer basket. Cook till its color changes to golden brown & puffed, 12 to15 mins.
3. Therefore, in the saucepan, mix water & cornstarch till smooth. Put 1.5 cup raspberries, syrup, lemon zest & lemon juice carry to a simmer; lower the heat. Cook & whisk till thickened, around two mins. Strain & discard seeds; chill it slightly.
4. Nicely whisk leftover 1/2 cup berries into the syrup. If required, drizzle cinnamon on French toast cups; serve with the syrup.

Chapter 14: Air fryer Side Recipes

1. Air Fryer Tater Tots

Cook Time: 15 min

Servings: 4

Difficulty: Easy

Ingredients

- Russet potatoes 1 1/2 lbs
- All-purpose flour 2 tsps.
- Cooking oil
- Salt n pepper
- Optional spices/seasoning
- Garlic powder 1 tsp
- Thyme 1/4 tsp

- Smoked paprika 1 tsp.

Instructions

1. Bring a saucepan or pot 3/4 of the way full of cold water to a boil with a pinch of salt. Add enough water to cover the potatoes.
2. Add the potatoes and simmer for 6-12 mins. You should be able to pierce the potatoes easily on the outside and tell that the inside of the potatoes is still firm.
3. Remove the potatoes from the water. Dry and allow them to cool. Wait for about 10 mins.
4. Once cooled, use the large area of a cheese grater to grate the potatoes. Squeeze out any excess water from the potatoes.
5. In a bowl, place the grated potatoes with the flour & seasonings. Russet potatoes are bland. Salt according to taste. Then stir.
6. Use your hands to form tots with the mixture. Spray both sides of the tots with cooking oil. Place the tots in the air fryer. Air fry for 10 mins at 400 degrees.
7. Open the air fryer and flip the tots. Cook for an additional 5 mins or until the tots have reached your desired crisp.

2. Greek Baked Feta Psiti

Cook Time: 10 min

Servings: 4

Difficulty: Easy

Ingredients

- Feta cheese 8 ounces, in a block
- Olive oil 2 tbsps.
- Crushed red pepper 1 tbsp.
- Dried Oregano 1 tbsp
- Honey/Choczero Syrup for Keto 2 tbsps.

Instructions

1. Cut the feta block in half and then cut half of each thinner slice to produce four pieces.
2. On a serving bowl (heatproof), arrange these.
3. Using a basting brush (silicone) to disperse the oil uniformly. With olive oil, drizzle the cheese. Then sprinkle with oregano and red pepper flakes.
4. Using a basting brush (silicone), cover with honey and uniformly scatter the honey throughout.
5. Put the dish in the basket of the air fryer.
6. For 10 mins to 400F, set the air fryer.
7. When finished, remove and serve with the basting brush to disperse any honey and oil that has been transferred to the bottom.

3. German Currywurst Recipe

Cook Time: 12 min

Servings: 4

Difficulty: Easy

Ingredients

- Canned tomato sauce 1 cup
- Vinegar 2 tbsps.
- Curry powder 2 tsps.
- Sweet paprika 2 tsps.
- Truvia 1/2 tsp, or sugar 1 tsp
- Cayenne pepper ¼ tsp
- Diced onion ½ cup.
- Bratwurst 1 lb

Instructions

1. Whisk together the tomato sauce, curry powder, paprika, vinegar, sugar, & cayenne pepper in a heatproof container 6 x 3. Stir the onions in.
2. Slice the bratwurst into 1" thick chunks on the diagonal. To the sauce, apply bratwurst and mix well.
3. The pan is placed in the basket of an air fryer.
4. Till the sausage is cooked & the sauce is bubbling to 400F, set the air fryer for 12 mins.

4. Air-Fryer Ravioli

Cook Time: 10 min (per batch)

Servings: 1-1/2 dozen

Difficulty: Easy

Ingredients

- Seasoned bread crumbs 1 cup
- Shredded parmesan cheese 1/4 cup
- Dried basil 2 tsps.
- All-purpose flour 1/2 cup
- Eggs 2 large, lightly beaten.
- Frozen beef ravioli 9 ounces, thawed.
- Optional fresh minced basil
- Cooking spray
- Marinara sauce 1 cup, warmed.

Instructions

1. Preheat the fryer to 350 degrees. Mix the bread crumbs, the parmesan cheese, and the basil in a bowl. In different bowls, position the flour & eggs. To cover all ends, dip the ravioli in flour; shake off the waste. Dip in the eggs, then pat in the crumb mixture to help adhere to the coating.
2. Arrange the ravioli in batches on a greased tray in the air-fryer basket in a single layer, dust with cooking spray. Then Cook until crispy brown, 3 to 4 mins. Flip; spritz with

spray for cooking. Cook until crispy brown, 3 to 4 mins longer. Sprinkle instantly with basil and extra Parmesan cheese if needed. With marinara sauce, serve warm.

5. Air fryer French toast sticks

Cook Time: 8 min

Servings: 12

Difficulty: Easy

Ingredients

- Texas Toast 12 slices
- Milk 1 cup
- Eggs 5 large
- Butter 4 tbsp, melted.
- Vanilla extract 1 tsp.
- Granulated sugar 1/4 cup
- Cinnamon 1 tbsp.
- Optional Maple syrup

Instructions

1. Slice each slice of bread into thirds.
2. Add the milk, butter, eggs, and vanilla to a cup. Whisk until they're mixed.
3. Add the sugar and the cinnamon to a separate bowl.
4. Dip each stick of bread into the mixture of eggs easily.
5. Sprinkle both sides with the sugar mixture.
6. Put in the air-fryer basket & cook for around 8 mins or until only crispy at 350 °F.
7. From the basket, remove and allow to cool. If desired, serve it with maple syrup.

Chapter 15: Air fryer Seafood Recipes

1. Fried Shrimp Po' Boy Sandwich Recipe

Cook Time: 10 min

Servings: 4

Difficulty: Easy

Ingredients

- Deveined shrimp 1 lb
- Creole seasoning 1 tsp
- Buttermilk 1/4 cup
- Louisiana fish fry coating 1/2 cup
- Cooking oil spray
- Canola or vegetable oil
- French bread hoagie rolls 4
- Shredded iceberg lettuce 2 cups

- Tomato slices 8
- Remoulade sauce
- Mayo 1/2 cup
- Minced Garlic 1 tsp
- Lemon juice 1/2
- Worcestershire 1 tsp
- Creole seasoning 1/2 tsp
- Dijon mustard 1 tsp
- Hot sauce 1 tsp
- Green onion chopped 1.

Instructions

Remoulade Sauce

1. In a small bowl, put all ingredients. Before serving, refrigerate, whereas the shrimp cook.
2. Breading and shrimp.
3. In Creole seasoning, marinate shrimp and for 30 mins buttermilk.
4. In the bowl, add fry fish. Take your shrimp from a bag & dip each into a fish fry. In the basket of air fryer, add shrimp.

Air Fryer

1. Spray the air fryer basket with cooking oil. Add the shrimp to the air fryer basket.
2. With cooking oil, spritz the shrimp.

3. Cook shrimp for 5 mins at 400°. Open the basket & flip the shrimp to the other side. Cook for an additional 3-5 mins or until crisp.
4. Assemble the Po Boy
5. Spread the remoulade sauce on the French bread. Add the sliced tomato and lettuce, and then the shrimp.

2. Easy Air Fryer Fifteen Minute Crab Cakes

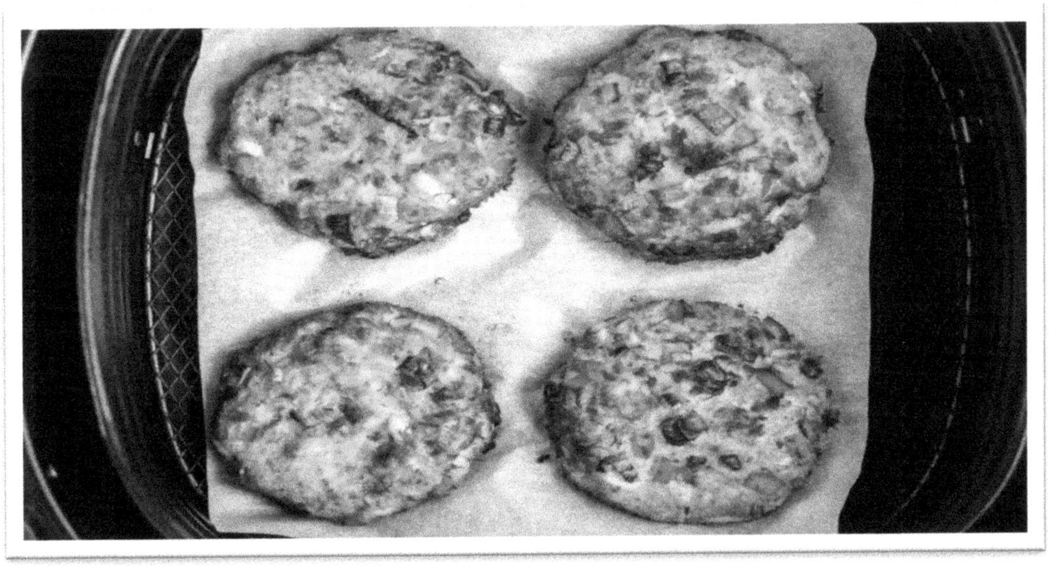

Cook Time: 10 min

Servings: 4

Difficulty: Easy

Ingredients

- Cooking oil
- Jumbo lump crab meat 8 ounces
- Old bay seasoning 1 tbsp.
- Breadcrumbs 1/3 cup
- Cup red peppers diced.
- Green peppers diced ¼ cup.
- Medium egg 1
- Mayo ¼ cup
- Lemon juice ½

- Flour 1 tsp
- **Instructions**

1. With the cooking oil, spray an air fryer basket.
2. Well, mix all the required ingredients except the flour.
3. Shape mixture into the four patties. To each patty, add a dash of flour.
4. Put crab cakes in Air Fryer. With cooking oil, spray crab cakes.
5. At 370 degrees, cook for 10 minutes.
6. Before serving, cool it.

3. Air Fryer Crispy Fish Sandwich

Cook Time: 10 min

Servings: 2

Difficulty: Easy

Ingredients

- All-purpose flour 2 tbsp
- Garlic powder 1/2 tsp
- Pepper 1/4 tsp
- Salt 1/4 tsp
- Egg 1
- Fresh lemon juice 1 tbsp
- Mayo 1/2 tbsp
- Cod fillets sliced 10 oz.

- Panko bread crumbs 1/2 cup
- Cooking oil
- Buns two
- Primal kitchen tartar sauce

Instructions

Breading

1. Build a cooking station. In a large bowl, put garlic powder, flour, pepper, and salt to dredge a fish.
2. Put the egg, lemon juice & mayo in to separate large bowl from dredging a fish. Whisk the egg & mix the ingredients.
3. Put the panko breadcrumbs in another bowl. Have a moist towel closely.
4. In flour, dredge a fish, then a mixture of egg & then breadcrumbs.

Air Fryer Fish

1. With the cooking oil, spray the air fryer basket & put the fish in the basket.
2. Spritz the top area of fish with the cooking oil.
3. For crispy & golden, cook fish for eight to ten minutes at four hundred degrees.
4. Whitefish is tender & delicate. Be alert if you move the fish and whereas handling it when eliminating it from the air fryer.

Oven-Baked Fish

1. Preheat the oven to 425 degrees.
2. Scratch a baking sheet with parchment paper. Place the fish on it.
3. Overheat for 10-12 minutes till crisp & golden.

4. Air Fryer Salmon Patties

Cook Time: 16 min

Servings: 8

Difficulty: Easy

Ingredients

- Canned Salmon wet weight 20 ounces, dry weight 16 ounces
- Mashed potatoes 2 ½ cups
- Milk can substitute ¼ cup with heavy cream.
- Parsley generous 1 tbsp
- Chives generous 1 tsp
- Dill 1 tsp
- White pepper ½ tsp
- Cayenne pepper ¼ tsp
- Creole seasoning ¼ tsp

Breading Ingredients

- Flour ½ cup
- Beaten eggs 4.
- Breadcrumbs 1 cup

Instructions

1. Mix all ingredients except breading ingredients.
2. Shape salmon mixture in patties form. Put in flour, then a mixture of egg, & then in breadcrumbs.
3. On Air Fryer, cook at 400-degrees for eight minutes, & drizzle with olive oil. Again flip & drizzle with the olive oil & cook for further 8 minutes.
4. Serve instantly, refrigerate in a sealed container for one week. It can be enjoyed with creamed peas.

5. Parmesan Crusted Fish Fillets with a Dijon Mustard Sauce

Cook Time: 10 min

Servings: 4

Difficulty: Easy

Ingredients

- Fish Fillets fried
- Fish Fillets thawed 1 lb.
- Coconut Flour 1/4 cup
- Parmesan Cheese 1/4 cup
- Lemon Pepper Seasoning 1/2 tsp
- Dijon Mustard Sauce
- Sour Cream 1/4 cup
- Heavy Whipping Cream 1 Tbsp
- Dijon Mustard 1 Tbsp
- Chives dried 1/2 Tbsp

Instructions

1. Small rectangular bottle put coconut flour, lemon pepper, parmesan cheese, and seasoning. Mixing well to combine.
2. Spray each side of the fish with the cooking spray. Then put to a parmesan mixture & coat each side. Use your fingers to press the parmesan mixture into the fish if required.

3. Put to an air fryer basket & cook at 400 degrees for 10 minutes until the fish flakes effortlessly.
4. Dijon Mustard Sauce
5. On medium heat, in a small saucepan, put heavy whipping cream, sour cream, chives & Dijon. Mix to combine & heat it thoroughly but do not allow it to boil.
6. Pour mustard sauce on cooked fish & serve instantly.

6. Shrimp Scampi

Cook Time: 10 min

Servings: 4

Difficulty: Easy

Ingredients

- Butter 4 tbsp
- Lemon Juice 1 tbsp
- Minced Garlic 1 tbsp
- Red pepper flakes 2 tsp
- Chopped chives 1 tbsp.
- Chopped fresh basil 1 tbsp.
- Chicken Stock 2 tbsp
- Raw Shrimp 1 lb

Instructions

1. Turn air fryer to a 330F. Put 6 x 3 metal pan in it & allow to start heating till you gather all ingredients.
2. Put garlic, butter & red pepper flakes into a hot six inches pan.
3. Let it cook for two minutes, mixing once till butter has been melted. That infuses garlic into butter, which makes it taste good.
4. Open-air fryer put butter, minced garlic, lemon juice, chives, red pepper flakes, basil, shrimp & chicken stock into a pan.

5. Let the shrimp cook for five minutes, mixing once. At that step, butter must be good melted & liquid, dip shrimp in spiced goodness.
6. Stir very well, eliminate 6-inches pan with silicone mitts allow it rest for one min.
7. Mix at the end of the min. Shrimp must be well cooked at this step.
8. Put extra fresh leaves of basil & enjoy it.

Conclusion

Air fryers, including their inaccurate name, are used in the same way as a convection oven. The benefit is that they use considerably less oil to "fry", but the downside is that it would not prepare all food in the same manner, resulting in certain people becoming more efficient in the kitchen than others.

In general, frozen, canned food cooks almost as well in an oven as it does in an air fryer, but more slowly, while unprocessed raw foods like raw vegetables and pounded raw meat does not cook equally in some places underdone and others overcooked on the same piece of food.

Furthermore, air fryers become versatile equipment, with various features ranging from timers to various trays and racks that make cleaning and customization simpler. Ultimately, the decision to buy an air fryer comes down to personal choice. Do you want something with a lot of options and customization, or you want something easy that only gets the job done? Of note, the former would be more expensive, but you will get whatever you pay for.

Finally, if you're hoping for a better alternative to those indulgent frozen meals, keep dreaming. The Air Fryer, on the other hand, could be the gadget for you if you're searching for an easy-to-clean way of roasting regular meals without using oil.

IF YOU LIKED THIS BOOK, RECOMMEND IT AND

WRITE A REVIEW PLEASE.

I'LL BE GRATEFUL.

Patton Trevis

Lightning Source UK Ltd.
Milton Keynes UK
UKHW050815240821
389380UK00002B/71

Garth Haythornth

Christ Church, Oxford

A Portrait of the House

Christ Church, Oxford

A Portrait of the House

EDITED BY
CHRISTOPHER BUTLER

MANAGING EDITOR – FIONA HOLDSWORTH

CO-EDITED BY
JUDITH CURTHOYS, COLLEGE ARCHIVIST
BRIAN YOUNG, TUTOR IN HISTORY

PHOTOGRAPHY
CAMBRIDGE JONES
MATT POWER • BI SCOTT

III
THIRD MILLENNIUM
PUBLISHING, LONDON

First published in 2006 by
Third Millennium Publishing Limited, a subsidiary of Third Millennium Information Limited

2–5 Benjamin Street
London
United Kingdom
EC1M 5QL
www.tmiltd.com

ISBN 10 : 1 903942 46 2
ISBN 13 : 978 1 903942 46 8

British Library Cataloguing in Publication Data

A CIP catalogue record for this book is available from the British Library.

Managing editor – Fiona Holdsworth
Designed by Michael Davies
Production by Bonnie Murray

Printed by 1010 Printing International Ltd
on behalf of Compass Press Ltd

Image Acknowledgements

We would like to thank all those who supplied images for this book:

Cambridge Jones, for new photography
2, 9, 10, 14, 15, 18 (top), 20, 21, 22, 24, 25, 29, 32, 34 (bottom right), 35, 40, 42, 43, 46, 47, 49, 50, 51, 52 (top), 58, 60, 62, 64, 68, 72, 74 (right), 76, 81 (top), 86, 89, 90, 93, 96, 98, 99, 100, 102, 103, 104 (left), 108, 109, 110, 111, 114, 116, 117, 118, 119, 120, 122, 123, 125, 126, 131, 134, 136, 141, 143, 145, 147, 148, 149, 154, 158, 159, 161, 163 (right), 167, 168, 169, 173, 175, 179, 184 (bottom), 187, 189, 190, 193, 194, 197, 200, 202, Back cover.

Matt Power
11, 16 (top left), 18 (centre), 19, 23, 27, 28, 30, 31, 34 (top left), 37, 38, 46 (left), 53, 57 (bottom left), 74 (left), 82, 91, 92, 94, 97 (bottom), 106, 113, 121, 124, 127, 137, 140, 151, 153, 155, 165, 174, 177, 181, 184 (top two), 191, 192

Bi Scott
Front cover, 6, 7, 17, 36, 45, 48, 77, 85, 87, 105, 130, 138, 139, 156, 157, 164, 166 (two on left), 170, 171 172, 180 (top), 199

Julian Gaisford-St Lawrence (1976), 101

William Cheung (1948), 128

Oval House, 132, 133

Dacre Trust, 142

Edward Cazalet (1956), 144

Alan Pulgrave Brown (decd) (1943), 146

Michael Beaumont (1958), 162 (both images)

Barbara Blood, wife of Anthony Blood (decd) (1944), 163

Catherine Story (1987), 166

Eric Prabhaker (1948), 176

Christopher Lowe (1949), 178

David Gillespie (1960), 180

Ian Wyatt (1964), 182

HP Films, 186

Thanks also to Jane Inskipp for the pictures of the paintings in the gallery and Louise Roswell of Verve Digital who helped to reformat a number of the images in the treasures section. We would also like to thank all those who sent in photographs and mementoes that we were not able to include.

High-quality prints of Christ Church images by Cambridge Jones and Bi Scott reproduced in this book can be ordered direct from the photographers via their websites, where many other Christ Church subjects can also be found:

Cambridge Jones: **www.cambridgejones.com**

Bi Scott: **www.biscott.co.uk**

Every effort has been made to trace and credit copyright holders; we will be pleased to correct any unintentional errors or omissions in subsequent editions of this book.

CONTENTS

Editor's Foreword

This is not a full scale history of Christ Church – that still needs to be done. There are no detailed scholarly accounts here of the remoter aspects of college life, such as the true historians of academe tend to write. All the same, what we have here is informed by deep scholarship, as can immediately be seen from Christopher Haigh's masterly account of our foundation. I have tried to get together an entertaining account, of the most important things, along with evocative illustrations, so that such matters as Tom and the Hall steps, Aldrich and Gladstone, the Cathedral and Picture Gallery, Trevor-Roper, Dundas, and three Morrises are all here, somewhere. Since anecdote is often more illuminating than footnote, I have included much that is true, and also some few bits which are perhaps *ben trovato* – but none, I hope, which are entirely misleading. This applies most particularly to the memoirs, where I have left my contributors to speak in their own voices. A great deal of my time was spent in making extracts from the very many which were offered to us. I have printed about a fifth of what I received, and cut much of that fairly drastically – so my apologies, to those who are left to fight another day, and also to those who are in, if I have too much changed their emphases. The generational differences here are all fascinating – in the 20th century in particular, Christ Church has been occupied by undergraduates with widely varying intellectual, political, and social assumptions. I hope that some of this variety is to be seen in what follows. There can be no doubt, of course, of the distinction of our Christ Church authors – and I hope that I have succeeded to some degree in the art of arranging their contributions. Academics, particularly under present circumstances, are often uncomfortably aware of the remark in Ecclesiastes : 'of making many books there is no end'. This one has been written with and for pleasure; and in making it I have been greatly helped, informed and encouraged by my co-editors. My thanks go to Judith Curthoys, whose archival knowledge is immense, sense of humour unfailing, and willingness to tackle food, servants, and estates, to anything else I asked for, was seemingly endless; and to Brian Young,

whose historical conscience has (occasionally) restrained me, has seen his subjects in an engagingly ironical light, and has urged me to allow the humane Tory voice (appropriately enough for much of Christ Church's history) to speak clearly in these pages. Our managing editor, Fiona Holdsworth (1981), has the lively perspective of so many of our old members, and an indefatigable ability to organise and keep the text editors supplied with floods of paper, from text to illustrations to spread sheet analyses of content. She has also managed to correspond with all involved, with a charm and enthusiasm that is beyond all but the most benevolent of persons. A huge amount of administrative, secretarial and generally encouraging support was given by Margaret Molloy to all the editors. It has also been a pleasure to know that this portrait has been illustrated entirely by members of Christ Church photographers – by Cambridge Jones (1985), who was commissioned to do the special photography, and read PPE here, by Bi Scott, who is a former Junior Research Fellow and current member of Common Room, and by Matt Power, the Cathedral Sacristan. These three gave us hundreds of images to chose from.

No portrait can be 'complete', because it is always aspectual, and some portraits do not manage to convey much character. I nevertheless hope that our differing perspectives, and the human interest within a remarkable history, and pictures which convey the great beauty of our buildings and works of art, have combined here to express a great affection for the House as a community, where the life of student and teacher is as vigorous now as it ever has been.

Christopher Butler

The Foundation Period

CHRONOLOGY

1525 *Foundation of Cardinal College in July*
Beginning of the demolition of the abbey church, and construction of Tom Quad
1529 *Completion of kitchen and Hall*
1529 *Fall of Thomas Wolsey in October*
1530 *Closure of Cardinal College*
1532 *Foundation of King Henry VIII College in July*
1542 *Foundation of the diocese of Oxford with its cathedral at Oseney*
1545 *Surrender of King Henry VIII College and Oseney to the king*
1546 *Foundation of Christ Church on 4 November*
Installation of Richard Cox as Dean
Signing of the Charter of Dotation [endowment] on 11 December
1547 *Christ Church begins on 14 January*
1553 *Installation of Richard Marshall as Dean*
1554 *Disinterment of Catherine Martyr*
1555 *Degradation of Archbishop Cranmer in the cathedral in February*
1559 *Installation of George Carew as Dean*
1561 *Creation of the Westminster Studentships*
Installation of Thomas Sampson as Dean
Beginnings of the Library in the old refectory of St Frideswide's Priory
1565 *Installation of Thomas Goodwin as Dean*
1566 *First visit of Elizabeth I to Christ Church*
1567 *Installation of Thomas Cooper as Dean*
1570 *Installation of John Piers as Dean*
1576 *Installation of Tobie Matthew as Dean*
1583 *Visit of Prince Alasco of Poland, and the performance of plays by William Gager*
1584 *Installation of Dean William James*
1592 *Second visit of Elizabeth I*
1596 *Installation of Dean Thomas Ravis*

The Foundation of Christ Church by Wolsey and Henry VIII

I [N] promise and swear that I will faithfully observe and keep to the uttermost of my power all statutes and ordinances of this Church now made and hereafter to be made by our most excellent prince and founder King Henry VIII. And that I will yield due obedience and reverence to the Dean and Subdean and other officers of this Church. And that I will do willingly all things which I shall be lawfully commanded by the Dean or Subdean or their deputies. And that so long as I live I will be faithful and kind unto this Church, ready at all times to profit and honour this Church and in no manner of means to hinder or hurt the same. In doing the contrary I will yield myself obediently to suffer all pains and punishments in the foresaid statutes and ordinances contained against the transgressors thereof. As God liveth, and as I would by him have my life continued. So help me God and the holy gospel of God.

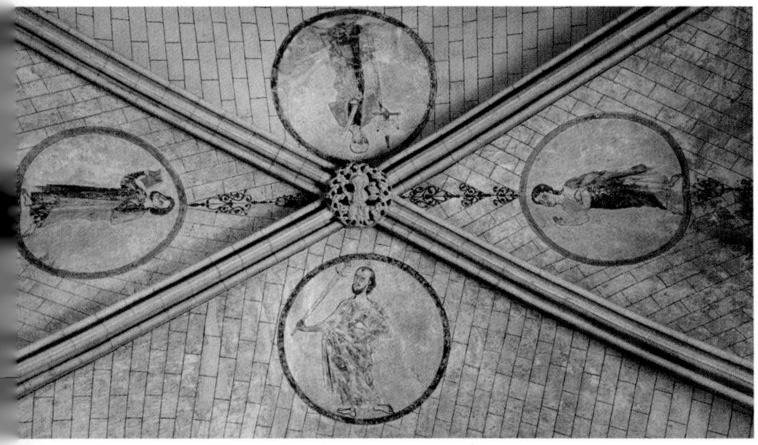

Painted figures on the chapter house vault, showing St Peter, a female figure with a book, a male figure with a book, and another male figure with a sword

On 14 January 1547 the first Canons and Students of Christ Church were formally enrolled as members of the House, and they took the oath of obedience and loyalty. For many, perhaps all, it was a proud day: they were joining the biggest and best foundation in Oxford, deliberately established by King Henry VIII to dominate the University and give it a lead. But for some of them it must have been a day of uncertainty, for the new Christ Church was only the latest in a series of institutions suppressed, established and altered by the fancies of a cardinal and a king. Was 'the cathedral church of Christ in Oxford of the foundation of King Henry VIII' going to last? – or would it go the way of the nunnery and the priory of St Frideswide, the Cardinal College, King Henry VIII's College, and the shadowy 'Frideswide's' of 1545–6?

St Frideswide's had begun as an Anglo-Saxon nunnery, and was refounded in 1122 as an Augustinian priory. Four centuries later it fell victim to the policy and pride of Thomas Wolsey, cardinal archbishop of York and chancellor of England. For all his vanity and venality, Wolsey was a reformer. He wanted to leave a monument to his own greatness, but he meant it to be a training college for theologians and priests, with a modern curriculum and teaching methods. Wolsey obtained licenses from the pope and the king to abolish twenty-two religious houses in England, and use their properties to found a major college on the site of St Frideswide's: building began in July 1525. The college

The arms of Cardinal Wolsey, showing the Tudor rose of the king, the Cornish choughs of Thomas à Becket, the silver cross from the Ufford earls of Suffolk, the four blue leopards from the de la Pole earls and dukes of Suffolk, and the red lion of his patron, Pope Leo X. From *Wolsey's lectionary*, Library MS 101

was to have a dean, six professors, sixty canons, forty Students, thirteen chaplains, twenty-eight choristers and a choirmaster, supported by an endowment more than twice that of the next two richest Oxford colleges combined. Wolsey did not stint on his new project. The king's masons set to work on a grand quadrangle, a great kitchen was built, the heralds granted elaborate arms, and the cardinal commissioned illuminated service books and gold and silver plate for the chapel altar and the tables in Hall. But Wolsey came unstuck. He failed to provide what King Henry most wanted, an annulment of his first marriage so he could marry Anne Boleyn. So Wolsey fell from power, and in October 1529 he was convicted of infringing the royal prerogative. His property – and his college – was forfeited to the Crown.

The Dean and canons were now out of a job, though for the moment they received their stipends. They sent representatives to plead with the king, and they were promised something. But, when it came, it was not very much. On 18 July 1532 Henry founded a new college, his college: it had a dean, twelve canons, a divinity lecturer, eight chaplains and a choir of eighteen. Wolsey's great establishment of 129 was replaced by a mean thing of forty men and boys, with an endowment only one-third of Wolsey's – and everyone else was told to leave. The new foundation was sometimes called King Henry VIII's College, sometimes St Frideswide's College, but it was not a college as we would understand it nor as Wolsey had intended it: it was a house of prayer, with no educational function. Its early days were difficult, and after a few months the canons complained to the king of their poverty and claimed that without help they would go hungry at Christmas. Some of its staff were eminent: the Dean, John Oliver, was an influential civil lawyer, and the canons included two vice-chancellors of the University, the king's Latin secretary, a tutor to the prince of Wales, and the antiquary John Leland – but some of them were absentees, appointed only so they could draw salaries from the endowment. When the Dean and Chapter surrendered the college and its property to the king in May 1545, only five of the canons were there to sign the deed. The Dean and canons were pensioned off – but most of them hardly noticed the difference. The fourth of the foundations that led to Christ Church was no more.

What came next was very odd. It was referred to as 'Frideswide's', but it had no constitution, no property and an uncertain future. It was funded mainly by cash transfers from the royal Court of Augmentations to Dr Richard Cox, called 'dean of Oxford' and William Haynes, called 'subdean'. But there was nothing for them to be dean and subdean of. From June 1545 some of the money was paid out in wages to Cox, Haynes and three others (presumably canons), to eight petty canons, two schoolmasters, twenty schoolboys, two more priests, a choirmaster, twenty-one choristers, a butler, a barber, two cooks, a carter and a porter. There were payments for fabric repairs, cleaning, candles, new windows in the church, equipment for services, and wine and wafers for communion. Soon others were on the payroll: the Vice-Chancellor, and professors of Greek, Hebrew and Divinity. And from September 1545 exhibitions were paid to fifty scholars. Someone had had a big idea, and the big idea was to become Christ Church.

Sampson Strong, *Cardinal Wolsey*. Strong was paid £3 in 1610 for the painting

Frideswide's was a transitional institution, an amalgamation of the new cathedral at Osney and King Henry VIII's College. Cathedral and college had both been surrendered to the king on 20 May 1545, for now there was a new plan. The cathedral was moved to the Frideswide's site. A joiner called Poppingjay took down the choirstalls and high altar at Osney, and then set them up again in the chancel at Frideswide's. Osney was gutted: its timber, slates, lead and stone were carried to Frideswide's and used in rebuilding. The choirboys and schoolboys from Osney were moved into Frideswide's: their beds were taken down and rebuilt in their new home, and six loads of 'the children's stuff' were transferred. Moving Osney's bells was the biggest job of all. John Westbury, chief carpenter, and his men worked for ten days at Osney taking down the bells, and extra help was needed to handle Tom, 'the great bell'. Willoughby of Eynsham carted Tom across to the Frideswide's site on 26 September, and then it took Westbury, three carpenters and four labourers six days to hang the bell in the steeple. But Frideswide's was going to be more than a cathedral, with choirboys and bells: it was going to be Christ Church.

It is not clear when it was decided to have a combined cathedral and college at Frideswide's – but it was probably by the middle of 1545. The Frideswide's site was to be enlarged to make room for something even bigger than Cardinal College had been: the king demanded neighbouring Peckwater Inn from New College and Canterbury College from Canterbury Cathedral. The three Oxford professors and fifty scholars who had, on the king's orders, been funded by eleven English cathedrals, were now transferred to the Frideswide's establishment, and half-yearly stipends were paid to them from September 1545. 'An erection of a cathedral church in Oxford where your Majesty's College of St Frideswide's was' was signed in November 1545, and in January 1546 a formal document for the establishment of the cathedral was ready. But then something went wrong, and the foundation was delayed for nearly a year. Frideswide's trundled on, but its future was shaky. Henry VIII was strapped for cash, with war against France and Scotland.

He planned to make further seizures of ecclesiastical property, Parliament authorised the confiscation of chantry and collegiate endowments –

and commissions were issued for the survey of the properties of colleges in Oxford and Cambridge. Would Frideswide's go the way of the nunnery, the priory and the first two college foundations? No, for the Vice-Chancellor of Cambridge was Dr Matthew Parker, who had influential friends at Court; the dean of Frideswide's was Dr Richard Cox, tutor to the prince of Wales. They got themselves appointed as commissioners to survey the college properties in their own universities, so they could keep grasping courtiers and hard-headed civil servants out of the process, and report to the king directly. The surveys were completed with great speed, and the reports were tailored to demonstrate that the colleges were efficiently run on shoe-string budgets. The king was impressed: 'he thought he had not in his realm so many persons so honestly maintained in living, by so little land and rent'. The colleges usually spent more than their ordinary income, and made ends meet by savings in good years, laying off staff in bad years, and by legacies and donations from old members and friends. Then, as now, colleges depended upon the generosity of their supporters, and there was no excess wealth to be seized. Cox and Parker had seen off the threat to college estates, and Henry sent Cox back to Oxford with a message to the University: the existing colleges were safe, and the king confirmed that he would establish two great new foundations, one at Oxford and another at Cambridge. Frideswide's was safe, and soon it would be Christ Church.

Unattributed, *King Henry VIII*

On 4 November 1546 the charter of Dotation was enrolled in Chancery, formally establishing a cathedral with a dean and eight canons and naming the first incumbents. Dean Cox was an experienced educationalist: he had been headmaster of Eton – 'the best schoolmaster of our time', but also 'the greatest beater'. Four of the first canons came from Osney, one from King Henry's College, and three were new men. Cox was soon busy, choosing the first Students and sorting out the financial arrangements. The letters patent of dotation, granting Christ Church its property, was enrolled in Chancery on 11 December, and Christ Church had an endowment worth £2,200 a year, or as much as All Souls Magdalen, Merton and New College put together. It was to be a splendid establishment, and it had to be kitted out. For the cathedral there were six dozen candles, wax for the tapers, a new sacring bell, communion wine and wafers, and six new surplices for the choir: the old copes, albs and vestments were mended and washed. For Hall there were new tablecloths, four dozen spoons, seven dozen pots, and twenty dozen trenchers. The kitchen stocked up with a mortar and pestle, a colander, a pair of scales, and a huge brass pot weighing 102lbs. The new foundation was celebrated with a service in the cathedral (for which the eight best copes were specially mended for the canons), and 'the erection dinner' – a grand affair, costing more than a canon's annual stipend and commons. The communal life of Christ Church began on 14 January 1547, with the formal admission of the Canons and Students.

The House did not yet have its full complement, and in the first weeks there were just the dean, eight canons, twenty-six Students, thirteen chaplains and choir men, twelve BA Students, twenty logicians and twenty-nine grammarians – but Dean

Cox was already busy recruiting more. But this was not yet the Christ Church we know. The draft Henrician statutes prescribed a college of a dean, eight canons, forty senior Students, three professors, twenty junior Students and forty schoolboys. For a short time, Christ Church was a tripartite foundation, cathedral, college and school: the Students were drawn mainly from the exhibitioners who had been paid by Frideswide's from 1545, and the schoolboys were those who had been moved over from Osney in that year. There were also nine chaplains, nine lay clerks, eight choirboys and twenty-four almsmen. The clergy and choir were recruits from Osney, and the organist was Bartholomew Lant. The staff included an auditor, a manciple, three sacristans, a verger, two porters, three stewards, three cooks, a groom, a carter and a barber. Christ Church had its own 'barber's lodge' and the first barber was Davy Jenkinson. He was set up with a chair, a bucket, two pans, two shaving basins, a brass ewer, towels, a brush, and 'shaving knives' which cost 6d. It was in everyone's interest for the razors to be sharp: in the first year there were payments 'to Davy for grinding his knives, 2s',and 'To Davy for washing his cloths and grinding, as the prebendaries agreed until Mr Dean's pleasure was further known, 6s-8d'.

Apparently Mr Dean was pleased enough with Davy, but less happy about the Henrician constitution of Christ Church. In particular, Cox seems not to have liked the inclusion of a grammar school as part of the foundation. The surviving copy of Henry's draft statutes was heavily amended, the provision for a school was deleted, and instead the number of Students was increased. The revised version became the basis for a new and more detailed set of draft statutes. In May 1549 the Crown had appointed a royal commission to investigate Oxford: Cox was one of its members, and he did most of the work. The new statutes were his, and reflected his vision of Christ Church: although these statutes were never formally enacted, the Chapter Register and the college accounts show that in practice they were implemented. Christ Church now had a hundred Students divided into five grades: twenty Theologians, twenty Philosophers of the first rank, twenty Philosophers of the second rank, twenty Scholars of the first rank and twenty Scholars of the second rank. Up to twenty Commoners were allowed by the statutes, and the first four of them were already in residence. There were to be no schoolboys. This was the constitution that was to operate from 1549 until the Ordinances of 1858.

The statutes regulated the new community strictly. The duties of the Dean, Subdean, Canons, Censors and other officers were described, and the rates of pay and allowances prescribed: the Dean's food allowance was £30 a month, but the others were

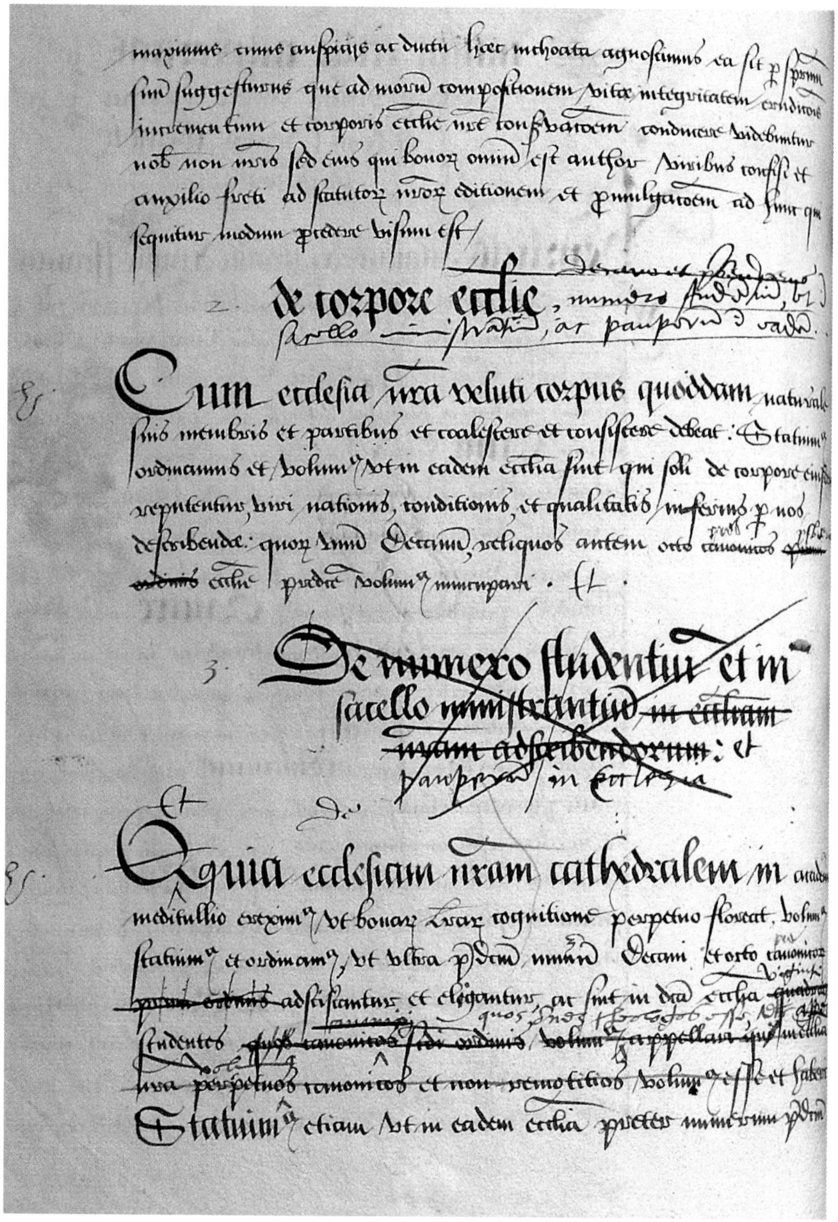

A page from the draft statutes for Christ Church prepared by Edward VI, showing the heavy annotations and alterations by the Dean and Canons. The administration of Christ Church was *de facto* until its first statutes were finally ratified in 1867

allocated less – from 2s 4d a week for Canons, down to 12d a week for Scholars, choirboys and the staff. Promotion from one rank to another was through election by the Dean and Canons, and there were incentives for success – higher stipends, better food, bigger clothes allowances, and bonuses for degrees gained. New arrivals were to bring their own bedding, a surplice and a book of psalms, and learn the 'catechism set forth in the Book of Common Prayer' and 'grace accustomed to be said in Hall'. All members were to dress as was appropriate for clerics and scholars, with no velvet, damask, silk or satin; they were not to wear cloaks in college, or carry arms at any time. The curfew hour was 9.00pm in summer and 8.00pm in winter, when the great bell was to be rung and the gates closed.

This was now a Christ Church we could recognise. Each Scholar was to have a tutor from among the Theologians or first-rank Philosophers, though in practice Canons sometimes acted as tutors. The first list of tutors in 1550 shows that most had one or two pupils, four had four, and the most popular tutors, with six pupils each, were Richard Marshall and Christopher Goodman. In 1550 Goodman was a Censor, together with Edward Cratford: on 5 October they sat with the Subdean (in the Dean's absence) to hold the first recorded Collections. They examined twelve of the Scholars, and the results were not good: three had made no progress, three more only a little, four moderate progress, one had progressed, and only one had made good progress – he was Henry Westfaling, Canon in 1562, vice-chancellor in 1576, and bishop of Hereford from 1585.

The kitchen, painted by Augustus Pugin, and reproduced in Ackerman's *History of Oxford* in 1814

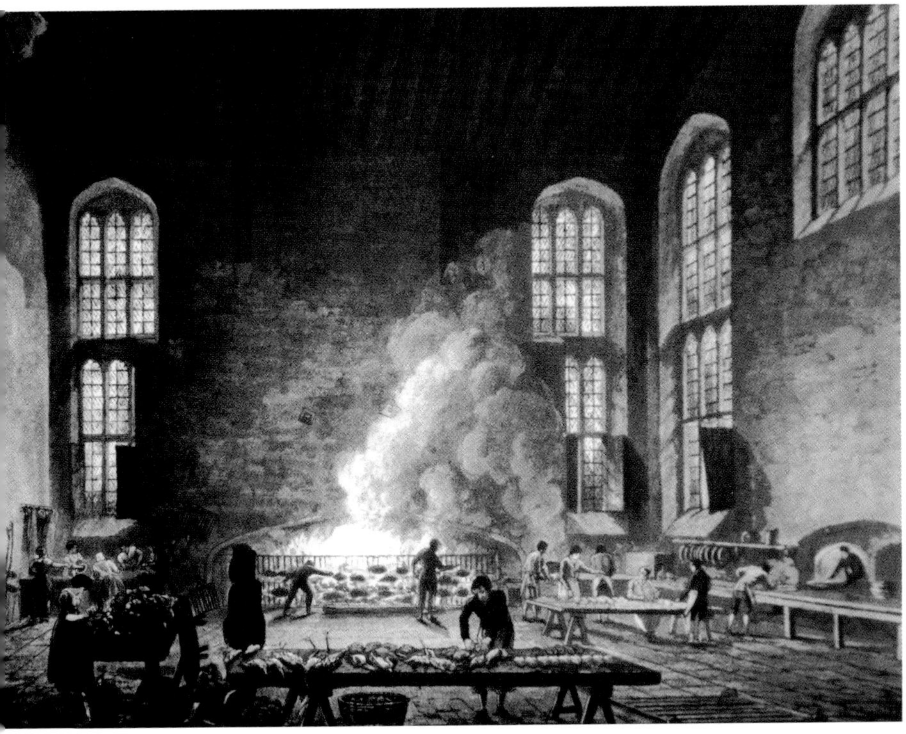

The academic regime for undergraduate Scholars was demanding. There were lectures in dialectic, mathematics and philosophy at 6.00am, beginning with an examination on the preceding day's lectures. There were two-hour disputations in logic and mathematics, in either the morning or the afternoon. Those whose work was unsatisfactory were to be expelled by the Dean and Censors; those who did well might be promoted up the academic hierarchy. For those funded by the foundation, there was no question of letting the young follow their own interests or work at their own pace: those who did not work did not eat. For the Commoners, who paid their own way, the routine was more relaxed and there was only a tutor to satisfy. But one commoner bragged in 1552 that his day began at 6.00am with Aristotle's *Politics*, and proceeded through Roman Law, Peter Martyr's theology lecture, and reading Cicero and Melanchthon: for relaxation, he and his friends strolled around college in the evening debating philosophy questions.

The new Christ Church dwarfed the other colleges, in its scale, its numbers, its endowment, and the eminence of its members. It was stuffed with the men who ran the University. The first dean was appointed Chancellor of Oxford, and the provost of Oriel came in as subdean. Vice-Chancellor Tresham was made a canon, and, when Tresham resigned as Vice-Chancellor, his successor was Richard Marshall, a senior Student of Christ Church. When Dean Cox was removed by Queen Mary in 1553, Vice-Chancellor Marshall replaced him as Dean. When St John's College was founded in 1555, Canon Alexander Belsyre was made President – and he remained a canon of Christ Church. Three of the University's five public professorships were attached to Christ Church by royal order – and the Crown retained the

ECCLESIA CHRISTI.
Prima stat australis domus ampla, Ecclesia Christi,
Primo iam duplici nomine digna loco.
Tum quia te, patremque tuum sit nacta patronum,
Tum quia sit reliquis auctior ista cohors.
Coepta quidem Thomae Wulsaei sumptibus olim,
Sed patris Henrici censibus aucta tui.

WOLSEY'S CARDINAL'S COLLEGE
From the Bereblock MS. in the Bodleian Library

nomination of the Dean, the eight canons and the three professors. The monarch controlled Christ Church, and Christ Church was to control Oxford: that had been Henry VIII's plan. In a period of religious change, it was important for the Crown to regulate higher education, and Trinity College, Cambridge, was founded with the same purpose in mind. Christ Church was not only a royal foundation: it was an instrument of royal policy.

Christ Church's hegemony was to be academic as well as political. Its undergraduate curriculum reflected the fashionable ideas of Renaissance humanism, and its teaching methods the latest educational orthodoxy. The undergraduates tackled dialectic, rhetoric, Greek, Hebrew, mathematics and cosmography, as well as the more usual Latin, philosophy and theology. They were closely supervised by tutors, and examined regularly on their progress. It was a model that the rest of Oxford was soon to follow, as the colleges became the paramount University institutions. Indeed, the foundation of Christ Church ensured the victory of the college system in Oxford, over the looser and laxer ways of private lodgings and unregulated halls. At a census of the University in 1552, there were only 260 men in halls, as against 761 in the colleges – 131 of them in Christ Church. King Henry's wish to impose some sort of order on the anarchy of Oxford led him to found an institution big enough to call the academic tune. It was the intention to make Christ Church dominant that had made Christ Church great.

Christopher Haigh

Left:
John Bereblock's representation of the Great Quadrangle, drawn as one of a series presented to Queen Elizabeth I when she visited Oxford in 1566

Above:
The Old Library. Once the refectory of St Frideswide's Priory, this building housed the Library from 1561 until the middle of the eighteenth century when the New Library, in Peckwater Quad, was completed. It was then converted into rooms for Westminster Students. From Joseph Skelton, *Oxonia Antiqua Restaurata,* 1823

The Medieval Priory of St Frideswide

The cathedral and the college have been inextricably intertwined in a dual foundation since both were established in 1546. They were the heirs to a building, the priory church of St Frideswide, which had been standing for nearly four centuries before they came into existence. They were also heirs to a religious and social ethos, which this essay will attempt briefly to describe in relation to the building. St Frideswide's had long been a house of secular canons, with an Anglo-Saxon church just to the north of the main body of the present Romanesque church, when it was transformed into a house of Augustinian canons around 1120. This transformation was probably achieved with the active support of King Henry I (1100–35), under whom the Augustinians were sweeping through Britain, and of his chief minister, Bishop Roger of Salisbury. The idea of the Augustinian canons, who followed a rule of life established by St Augustine at Hippo, was to combine being pastors with forming celibate communities of a semi-monastic character which prayed and worshipped together. Their ideals were finely articulated by an Augustinian canon in Yorkshire during the mid-twelfth century, Robert of Bridlington, who in the so-called *Bridlington Dialogue* had much to say about prayer, contemplation and the performance of the divine office, before he went on to deal with more practical issues of living.

The first prior of the newly constituted house was one Master Wimund. But it was under his successor, Master Robert of Cricklade, whom John Blair has described as a 'notable scholar who moved in circles interested in artistic patronage', that the present church was planned and begun. He was prior from circa 1139 to some time in the late 1170s. His presence in Oxford for nearly four decades may well have done much to kick-start the higher studies of our university, of which the first serious evidence comes in the 1170s. We might say that the ideals expressed by Robert of Bridlington in writing were here expressed by Robert of Cricklade in architecture. When we look at the chancel, certainly completed in Prior Robert's time, we have to strip away in our mind's eye all the furniture of Gilbert Scott's restoration of the 1870s to make it look like a conventional college chapel, in order to see it as a grand unified space and a stage for the performance

Top: Moustached figure, above the senior members' stalls in the chancel

Centre: St Frideswide, with the priory that would become Christ Church in the background, and the ox for the city. From *Wolsey's lectionary*, Library MS 101 of the communal liturgy. The chancel aisles, present from the start, give this stage breadth and extra solemnity; the 'giant order' elevation, whereby the piers are surmounted by an arcade of great arches which engross the triforium, give it a sense of height. The finely carved scrollwork on the eastern capitals of the piers enrich it as a liturgical setting.

There are some remarkable twelfth-century carved faces at the bottom points from which spring the vaulting shafts which once supported a simpler chancel vault than the flamboyant affair of circa 1500 which now regales us. These faces may at first sight look humorous to the unwary, but they were not in the least intended to be funny. The huge moustache of the north-westernmost face, for example, may strike us as bizarre. The silver pennies of Henry II, however, exactly contemporary with our chancel, represent the king himself with just such a moustache. In fact these faces are images of power and contemplation, and of the power that comes from contemplation as described by Pseudo-Dionysius in the highest orders of angels.

From its early days the priory church had a parish church within it, for which the canons were responsible. Where the parish altar was located, whether in the long nave (Wolsey knocked down the three western bays of it in building Tom Quad) or as some have reasonably argued in the north transept, is a matter of uncertainty. But it is not uncertain that the priory also served a parish. Moving outside the priory precinct, by the mid-twelfth century there were many stone churches already established in Oxford, that is before there was a sizeable number of scholars here. Within a few hundred yards of Carfax there were, to name only some, St Ebbe's, St Aldate's, St Michael at the Northgate, St Peter in the East and St John the Baptist (next to the site which came to be that of Merton chapel). Like many other English towns, Oxford enjoyed growing prosperity during the twelfth century, basically due to navigation on the Thames. Who were the priests who served these churches? This is a difficult question to answer, so spasmodic is the evidence, at least until the thirteenth century. But on the basis of what we know about the Augustinian canons elsewhere, they are likely to have played a large part in this service. They may not have always or usually served as parish priests, but they are likely to have 'served the altars', as the expression is,

Part of one of the fourteenth-century windows in the Latin chapel showing the Madonna and Child. Christ is holding an orb with images from the legend of St Frideswide: a river, a tree and a church

by celebrating mass, preaching and hearing confessions. In the late twelfth century, Guy, Augustinian prior of Southwick (Hampshire), wrote a treatise on confession. The Augustinian canons came into a situation where there was growing pastoral need and as yet an insufficiency of university-educated clergy to meet it.

The finest evidence of the pastoral outlook of the Augustinians in their first century at St Frideswide's is the shrine of St Frideswide itself. The legend of St Frideswide is well known and is delightfully represented in the jewel-like glass of the east window of the Latin Chapel by Edward Burne-Jones (1859). There is little doubt, however, about the historical existence of the saint or that her bones were buried in her Oxford church. Early in 1180, Prior Philip, who had not long succeeded Master Robert of Cricklade, translated the relics to a new shrine, apparently in a chapel just to the east of the north transept. Immediately, this new shrine began to attract considerable crowds and miracles started to occur there. Prior Philip himself acted as 'registrar' of the shrine and recorded some 100 miracles that had taken place at it. Of course there is no denying that crowds of visitors and pilgrims and a reputation for miracle healings brought money to a shrine and its custodians. Prior Philip's narratives show, for the time, extraordinary insight into the whole social context of those suffering from physical or mental illness, an unusual lack of censoriousness, and a strong sense of how, through crowd ritual and therapy, a sufferer might be accepted back into (an often excluding) society.

In Prior Philip's miracles, the case histories of women heavily outnumber those of men. Philip obviously understood the strains arising in these women from sexual fear or rebuff. There was one woman who had had sexual intercourse with her husband and had then gone mad for three years until she came to the shrine. Another had had sexual intercourse with her husband and promptly got a headache which lasted for two years. The concubine of a priest had ceased to be attractive to him and was repudiated by him; she suffered acute internal pains and insomnia. In an age when women had far fewer outlets of activity than men, when women were socially disparaged by purchase of marriage rights, and when stories were legion of girls who fled into vows of virginity to avoid arranged marriages (like that of Frideswide herself), it is no wonder that the teenage years were a time of unbearable anxiety to many girls, and this too shows up in several of the case histories.

Centre:
The reconstructed shrine of St Frideswide in the Latin chapel.
The shrine, which would have housed a jewelled casket, was destroyed at the Reformation and the saint's bones buried anonymously. Although the body was reburied with honour in 1563, with that of Catherine Martyr, the pieces of the shrine itself were not rediscovered until the cathedral was reorganised by George Gilbert Scott

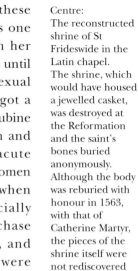

No further miracles were recorded at the shrine after 1180 or thereabouts. That is not to say that people ceased to resort to the shrine for prayer and to receive comfort. Between 1269 and 1289 the canons constructed an expensive new shrine. Pieces of the shrine base were discovered during the Scott restoration of the 1870s, and today, thanks to the expertise of several archaeologists and above all to the discoveries of John Blair, it has been possible to piece together, or in parts accurately reconstruct, this base (now once again located in the Latin Chapel), as we can know in almost every detail that it was constructed in 1289. Thereby the thirteenth-century community has left us one of the masterpieces of Gothic design and ornament in the whole country.

Henry Mayr-Harting

The Cathedral

The glorious church within the walls of Christ Church is unique in being both a college chapel and the cathedral of a diocese. It was founded in the eighth century as the centre of the priory established for St Frideswide, and was re-established as an Augustinian house in 1122. The early Saxon church was probably just a timber building, but there are remnants of tenth and eleventh-century stonework, which suggest that it was growing bigger and more substantial before the Normans began to build the sturdy pillars and rounded arches which are still evident and so characteristic.

During the medieval period, the Lady chapel – with its St Cecilia window by Burne-Jones – and the Latin chapel – with the lovely, subdued saints in the windows on the north side, contrasting almost violently with the vibrant colours of Burne-Jones's uncharacteristic take on the life of St Frideswide – were added. It was in the Latin chapel that the Regius Professor of Divinity gave his lectures well into the nineteenth century. The beautiful ceiling of the chancel is late fifteenth century, contemporary with the cloisters to the south of the church, and may well have been built by the same man who built the Divinity School, William Orchard.

In 1542 Henry VIII divided the diocese of Lincoln, creating, in the south, the new diocese of Oxford. At first, the old Oseney abbey on the west of Oxford was the cathedral, but it only survived as such

A pair of silver candlesticks, given to Christ Church by the Roebling family of New York, standing in front of Brindley's reredos

William Francis, Dean's verger, who served Christ Church for nearly seventy years

until 1545, when Henry devised his new scheme to found an extraordinary joint foundation of college and cathedral on the site of the old priory, in the half-built Cardinal College, the scheme of his former minister, Thomas Wolsey. The new dean and canons took control of both sides of the establishment, and a new era was under way.

Not a great amount happened to the body of the cathedral until the seventeenth century when Dean Brian Duppa reordered the interior. It is not certain quite what Duppa did; he probably removed the early memorials surviving from the medieval priory, and maybe commissioned the painted windows by the van Linge brothers of which only the Jonah window survived the iconoclasts of the Commonwealth. It may well have been Duppa, too, who arranged the tombs of Lady Montacute, Alexander Sutton and the giant Sir Nowers into a line with the watching loft.

It was in the nineteenth century, under the reforming hand of Dean Henry Liddell, that the great changes were made. He began almost immediately he took up residence, in 1855, to repair some of the fabric, and then, twenty years on, commissioned George Gilbert Scott to overhaul the interior entirely, particularly the chancel. The east end was completely rebuilt, its fourteenth century window removed, and the two arched and one rose windows installed, based on Norman evidence that Scott had found in the fabric. The old canons' stalls were removed, and the new stalls were bounded by elaborate wrought ironwork created by the artist F.A. Skidmore. The cathedral verger was evicted from his home in the south transept, which was brought back into the church, and the canon in the south lodgings on the east side had his residence chopped in two to make the new arches and tunnel into the cathedral from Tom Quad. Scott's survey revealed that the steeple was in danger of collapse from the weight of the peal of bells (Tom, of course, had been taken out and hung in the tower over the Great Gate in 1684), and so the bells were moved to the 'meat safe' over the Hall stairs. It was Charles Dodgson who had coined the derogatory title for the wooden structure which was replaced, rather more elegantly, by the Wolsey bell tower in the 1880s.

Changes are still made, although maybe not quite so drastic as those of Scott. The shrine of St Frideswide has recently been moved into the Latin chapel, probably its original location, and a new altar, from oak felled in Windsor Great Park, is dedicated to the memory of George Bell. The cathedral is still, though, an integral part of both college and diocesan life.

Judith Curthoys

King Charles's Hay Store

The magnificent chancel vault in the cathedral was the work of the Oxford master mason William Orchard. Orchard had already built Magdalen College Tower when, in around 1500, he was commissioned to design the vault at Christ Church, a virtuoso piece of Gothic architecture: twelve lantern-shaped pendants hang miraculously in mid-air, whilst intricate ribs of stone form star-shaped patterns along its centre, the stars of heaven high above the floor of the church.

In the nineteenth century, during the height of the Victorian enthusiasm for all things Gothic, a visiting architect to the college took an interest in the construction of the vault. He was sent to see Mr William Francis, the Dean's Verger, who recorded the visit many years later:

> *In Dean Liddell's time, I once had occasion to go up to the space between the vaulting of the choir and the lead roof in order that a London architect might examine how the stone pendants were keyed in. We went armed with tapers as there is only a very feeble light there. On striking a match we found to our dismay that there was a great deal of hay stored there, especially in the pockets of the vault; we had to exercise the greatest caution.*

Puzzled by the existence of the hay, Francis took a sample of it to the Dean who then had it examined by a botanist. It turned out to be of a coarse type that had not been grown in Oxford since the seventeenth century, a fact that explains why the hay found its way into the cathedral in the first place. During the English Civil War, Charles I made Oxford his headquarters, and Christ Church his royal residence. Interestingly, he kept his cattle in Tom Quad, and in order to feed them demanded the right, traditionally reserved for the citizens of Oxford, to take hay from Port Meadow. He needed somewhere high and dry to store this hay, and so the chancel vault loft was used.

Charles left Christ Church in April 1646, all hope of a Royalist victory having long disappeared. He fled the city, leaving everything behind, including the hay, and it was to remain undiscovered in the loft for the next two and a half centuries. When it was finally removed three bags were saved and sent to the British Museum, the Oxford University Museum and the Treasury at Christ Church; the last poignant remnants of Charles's last straw.

CANDLESTICKS

During the summer of 1960 the cathedral sanctuary underwent a complete reordering. Gilbert Scott's Victorian high altar was replaced by a new altar, and his bishop's throne substituted by a modern cathedra designed by Sebastian Comper. The original colour of the reredos was restored and the stone in the sanctuary and chancel cleaned.

The restoration was the work of Dean Cuthbert Simpson, who had been able to call on a number of his North American friends to help fund the project. One such donor was the Roebling family of New York, who gave two sets of candlesticks: one for the new high altar, and a second large free-standing set for the sanctuary. The Roeblings had made their fame and fortune building the Brooklyn Bridge, in its day the longest suspension bridge in the world. It was the work of John Augustus Roebling and his son Washington Augustus, though only the son lived to see the bridge completed; John Augustus had died of a tetanus infection, the result of an accident during the final survey of the bridge. Interestingly, of the two sets of candlesticks given to the cathedral by the Roebling family, only one set survives today.

The east end of the cathedral, showing the rose, or wheel, window installed by George Gilbert Scott, as a more Romanesque replacement of the fourteenth-century traceried window

In 1980, during restoration work on one of the stained-glass windows in the cathedral, thieves broke in through temporary hoardings and made off with both sets of candlesticks. On discovering the theft it was decided to put out a nationwide appeal for their recovery by asking 'Crimewatch' to interview the Dean about what had happened. Whilst TV cables were being laid out in one of the college gardens in preparation for the broadcast, BBC technicians came across two silver candlesticks poking out of a bush! They turned out to be the high altar set, which had, no doubt, proved too cumbersome to be carried more than a short distance. Today they are back on the high altar, though now securely chained down.

Jim Godfrey

Music At Christ Church

A group of choirboys and clerks are singing John Taverner's votive antiphon Christe Jesu in the former priory church of St Frideswide.~ This scene, which encapsulates so many of the features of the musical life of Christ Church, is as familiar now as it was in the 1520s, and it is fundamental to the rich and diverse cultural history of the college. In fact, Christe Jesu exists in several versions, successively extolling the virtues of Cardinal Wolsey, Henry VIII and Elizabeth I, and it is thanks to the investigations of generations of scholars poring over the manuscripts in the magnificent Christ Church Library collection that it can be performed today. This combination of scholarship and performance has proved fertile ground for the nurturing of a wide range of talent since the recruitment of John Taverner as Organist in Wolsey's sumptuous musical foundation. His intention to establish the finest virtuoso choir in the land was no accident. The sixteen choristers, their schoolmaster and twelve clerks (one of whom was to serve as Organist) are all specifically mentioned in the Statutes. What better way for Wolsey to define his status as the most powerful man in England? When the College and Cathedral were re-established in 1546 the choral forces were more modest. Nevertheless Henry VIII's foundation still included nine lay clerks and eight choristers as well as provision for their education. This remains the case to this day, although since the late nineteenth century the cathedral School has occupied its present site in Brewer Street. An impressive list of alumni includes William Walton and~Jan Morris.

Posterity has judged Taverner to be the finest English composer of his generation through his mastery of the polyphonic idiom and the sheer scale of his musical conception. Many of his successors have enjoyed similar reputations, amongst them Henry Aldrich, William Crotch, William Walton and Peter Warlock. Walton's formative years were spent as a chorister in the cathedral choir and then as an undergraduate in the college. It is a great tribute to the enlightenment of Dr Strong (the Dean) and Dr Ley (the Organist) that Walton enjoyed such generous patronage. William wrote to his mother in 1918: 'My fate hangs in the balance. The Dean is writing to Dad to see whether I shall go into Christ Church … .or go into an office. Fortunately for the development of twentieth-century English music, he stayed in Christ Church: the imaginative flair and energy of his musical language undoubtedly had its roots in his experiences here.

William Walton's potential was spotted at an early age, but nothing could compare with the prodigious talent of the eighteenth-century William Crotch, whose first public appearance was at the age of three at the organ in the Holywell Music Room. He became Organist at Christ Church at the age of only fifteen and went on to be Professor of Music at Oxford for fifty years. Renowned nationally as a composer, editor, lecturer, writer, collector and performer, as well as the first Principal of the Royal Academy of Music in London, Crotch elevated the study of music to a new level.

As an infant prodigy, he was probably the college's most formidable performer, although there are plenty of rivals for this accolade, particularly amongst organists. Henry Ley (late nineteenth century) and Simon Preston (late twentieth century) are close contenders, as are other brilliant figures such as Allan Wicks and Christopher Robinson. It is remarkable that many occupants of cathedral organ lofts around the country were organ scholars at Christ Church: Bury St Edmunds, Canterbury, Chester, Edinburgh, Exeter, Lincoln, Llandaff, St Albans, St David's, St George's Windsor, Wells and Worcester to name but a few.

Pre-eminent amongst other performers was the conductor Sir Adrian Boult. When his mother was choosing an appropriate Oxford college for him in 1905, she wrote to his housemaster at Westminster: 'We should like Christ Church ... if it has really ... outlived its evil reputation.' In fact, Boult found Christ Church to be a very civilised place in which he flourished as a musician, enjoying the luxury of rooms in Tom Quad, where he had sufficient space for two pianos! He became one of England's greatest conductors, and a particular champion of contemporary music. As for the many singers who have been part of the cathedral choir, top prize should go to the eighteenth-century counter-tenor Walter Powell, whose obituary described him as having the best voice in England and included these flattering lines:

Is Powell dead? – Then all the earth
Prepared to meet its fate;
To sing the everlasting birth;
The choir of heavn's compleat!

The achievements of performers have been matched in the academic study of music at Christ Church. Several of Crotch's predecessors were also Professors of Music at Oxford (Edward Lowe, Richard Goodson, father and son), and in the twentieth-century, Sir Thomas Armstrong was particularly influential not only as Choragus of the University and the first Organist to be a Student of the College, but also as Principal of the Royal Academy of Music. The extensive Library collection has provided a compelling resource for many academics from all over the world. In addition, undergraduates and graduates who studied musicology here have enlightened the research community with their published work: for example Herbert Oakley (who was Professor of Music at Edinburgh University), Ivor Keys (who became Professor of Music at Birmingham University), or more recently in Oxford, Edward Olleson and John Milsom.

John Taverner's reputation was unparalleled given the limitations of communications in the sixteenth century. The advent of recordings has enabled the music and scholarship of Christ Church to spread throughout the world. In particular, the choir boasts a lasting legacy of ground-breaking recordings which have excited the critics and the listening public over the last thirty years. These range from Simon Preston's Purcell and Handel recordings for Archive and Decca to Stephen Darlington's extensive catalogue of early music recordings for many labels, the choir securing a Grammy Award nomination in 1989. There is also a strong media profile, the choir having appeared on all the major UK television channels. The Christ Church sound (for that is how it is known!) of recent years is open, vigorous and uninhibited. It is also compellingly allied to the transparent acoustic of the building. The choir's tonal quality has been praised and admired throughout the world from Sydney to Rio, from Tokyo to New York, from Helsinki to Paris.

St Cecilia, the patron saint of musicians, by Edward Burne-Jones, in the north choir aisle, holding a regal or hand organ

L' O R F E O
FAVOLA
IN MVSICA
DA CLAVDIO MONTEVERDE
MAESTRO DI CAPELLA
DELLA SERENISS. REPVBLICA.
RAPPRESENTATA IN MANTOVA
L'Anno 1607. Et nouamente Riſtampata.

IN VENETIA MDCX.V.
Appreſſo Ricciardo Amadino.

Far left:
A day-dreaming figure, above the Dean's stall

Left:
The title page of Monteverdi's *Orfeo,* from Library Mus. 795, printed in Venice, 1615

The present generation can look to the past for inspiration on its journey of musical discovery. W.H. Auden's words about music in an international context seem to express the essence of this musical tradition:

For all within the cincture of the sound
Is holy ground,
Where all are Brothers,
None faceless Others.

The unique power of music to beguile and uplift the spirit continues to lie at the very heart of the ethos of Christ Church.

Stephen Darlington

Bibliophilia

I didn't use Christ Church's magnificent high Baroque library much in my first or second years as an undergraduate. In those days (the late 70s), Peckwater Quad had the unmistakable ambience of an expensive boys' public school, and since I had escaped from just such a place to attend my excellent local comprehensive earlier in my teens I found its Hooray swagger evoked unhappy memories. One late summer evening in my first term I chose to write my essay in the Library only to be assailed by an inebriated, pantless toff in a 'toga' (pillowcase) who had strayed from a party in Peck. That pretty much did it for me until Finals year, when, with proper exams looming, I fell in love with the polished tranquillity of the Library and took up residence therein. An added bonus was that the woman to whom I am now married would stroll past every afternoon on her way to her then boyfriend's rooms, not that it did me much good at the time.

I vaguely knew that the college library contained somewhere a dusty collection of manuscripts, sheet music and early music publications but assumed that it was no match for the glories of the Old Bod. I have since discovered my mistake. Twenty years after I'd left the House, whilst researching for a Channel 4 TV series, *Howard Goodall's Big Bangs,* I found myself desperately in need of an original manuscript of Monteverdi's opera *Orfeo,* the piece to which we more or less owe the form. The great composer's old haunts, the Ducal Palace at Mantua and St Mark's Basilica in Venice, where we had been filming, yielded nothing, and neither did the Italian State Archives nor the mighty Bibliothèque nationale in Paris (the French

Etching by J. Sanders, *William Crotch, organist 1790–1807, as a child*, 1778

have been ransacking Italy's written treasures for centuries). My assistant (also a Christ Church graduate, as it happened) gleefully told me, however, that one priceless copy of the authentic 1609 edition – the one Monteverdi himself worked from – was in Christ Church library, of all places. I booked an appointment and the carefully gloved Librarian kindly left me with the amazing manuscript to peruse. It was as if the intervening 400 years simply hadn't existed. I was looking directly – composer to composer – at Monteverdi's own instructions, unfiltered, unedited, unchanged. My questions, for example on his use of the band, on his 'figured' bass lines, on how much ornamentation he offered to, or expected from, his singers were all answered within an hour. No amount of scholarship or expertise by someone else, however brilliant, can substitute for the direct contact with a composer's own score. This extraordinary booklet of yellowing pages, still completely legible after 400 years, is opera's Holy Grail, more significant than all of Wagner's frenzied jottings or even Mozart and Da Ponte's revelatory correspondence, since without *Orfeo* the fledgling form of opera might never have taken flight at all. If this weren't enough, I recently noticed that Christ Church also has an original 1602 printed edition of Vincenzo Galilei's seminal treatise, *Dialogo della musica antica e moderna*, which formed the intellectual 'plan of action' for the invention of the first operas.

The Library's music collection houses substantial amounts of work by virtually every European composer from the early Renaissance to the Treaty of Utrecht, including Henry Purcell's Funeral Music for the Death of Queen Mary, Handel's *Zadok the Priest*, John Dowland's *Flow my teares*, possibly the most famous (and beautiful) song of the entire Elizabethan and Jacobean period, and no less than five operas by Jean-Baptiste Lully, Louis XIV's court composer and friend. Now those two really *did* know how to host a toga party.

Howard Goodall

Memories of a Chorister

Visiting St Peter's in Rome in 1845, Charles Dickens declared himself impressed but unmoved: 'I have been infinitely more affected in many English cathedrals when the organ has been playing, and in many English country churches when the congregation have been singing.' Every time I return to Christ Church and walk around its little cathedral I am reminded of these words. Dickens would surely have loved it here, in a building whose intimacy is as redolent of village church

as of episcopal seat; and – as I discovered aged eight – there can be few experiences as powerful as standing in those choir stalls in the candlelight singing a Byrd mass.

As a chorister one was always aware of the House's rich musical past, both distant and more recent: of great former organists like Henry Ley, William Crotch and Basil Harwood, whose names were also those of the cathedral school dormitories; of Sir Thomas Armstrong, who had known Vaughan Williams and who well into his nineties would struggle into choir practice on two sticks to greet the choristers he had first taken charge of in 1933; but above all of the gigantic shadow of John Taverner, whose extraordinarily beautiful music we sang in continuance of a tradition four and a half centuries old.

The value of such traditions was one of many things we learnt as choristers. Stephen Darlington, newly appointed Organist, provided an object lesson in the importance of high standards and what one has to do to achieve them. Though a kind man, to a small boy this could make him appear an intimidating figure – even if his exacting nature was often leavened by unexpected humour. 'What are you looking at?' he once roared, terrifyingly, at a tiny chorister distracted by a verger lighting a candle. "There are only two people in this building who matter: me, and God! *In that order*!'

One of the biggest thrills was being allowed to act as page-turner for the organist after evensong. We relished this privilege, which was given only to the four senior members of the choir and entailed a hazardous sprint up the narrow metal staircase to the organ loft at the end of the service. Discerning critics, we liked very loud and fast music: Vierne and Messiaen were favourites, but the chorister who had turned the pages of Widor's *Toccata* was envied for a week.

At thirteen my voice broke and it was time to move on; but in a sense the House never stopped being part of my education. My piano teacher at Winchester College, Robert Bottone, was a wonderfully natural musician who turned out to have been Organ Scholar at Christ Church. He regaled me with stories of his tutor, the idiosyncratic Sidney Watson, and painted vivid pictures of a frail and depressed W.H. Auden shuffling around Tom Quad in his slippers.

When I returned to Christ Church as an undergraduate, my experience of the place was radically different. No longer a singer, I was more likely to meet members of the choir in the pub than in the chapter house rehearsal room. The highly organised cathedral school regime was succeeded by a much lazier existence in which I preferred real tennis to lectures and sat up half the night writing last-minute fugues for morning tutorials. Stephen Darlington, now my tutor, had retained his genial charm but showed no interest in shouting at anybody. Though I played endless chamber music, learnt how to write cod Palestrina and unpicked Brahms string quartets, and enjoyed them all, in a way this all seemed to miss the point. For I was no longer expected to go to the cathedral seven times a week; and it's surely in the cathedral that the musical soul of Christ Church is to be found.

Tom Morris

In-House sensuality

I have been a member of the House, in one kind or another, on and off since I was nine years old – as a chorister, as an undergraduate and now, to my infinite pride, as an Honorary Student. I have reluctantly to admit, though, that through all these years its chief influence upon me has not been cerebral, but soppily sensual. It has been a matter of light and shade, of nostalgia, of attitude, occasionally of greed and always of suggestion.

My earliest Christ Church memories, for example, revive in me to this day the hushed and ancient mysteries of the cathedral, contemplated through a child's eye. How infinite the subtleties of the fan-vaulting when one is nine years old! How deep the blues of the rose window! How magically tantalising the glimpse of young Tom Armstrong the organist, reflected in the mirror above his keyboard in the organ loft! And as a lifelong agnostic, even now I have experienced nothing that has taken me nearer to God than the benediction after evensong, delivered in the frail sweet voice of Canon Claude Jenkins, Regius Professor of Ecclesiastical History and an eccentric sort of saint, from far, far away in the sanctuary of the altar.

Nor have I ever tasted more celestial food than the meringues they used to make in the college kitchens, which occasionally reached our hungry maws on occasions of festivity. Do they make them still? They may, but I am fairly sure they don't still carry them in trays on their heads, to distribute them among the quadrangles and give a few to us appreciative choristers. They used to make delectable sandwiches too, and these we would gobble down in our practice rooms in Tom Quad in an atmosphere that remains marvellously pungent in my mind, because it was fragrant with the beer they served to the basses, tenors and altos.

My tutor, when the years had passed, was J.I.M. Stewart, who taught me nothing about English Literature that I couldn't have discovered for myself, but who was never less than fascinating. His high-pitched voice was strangely emollient, he read poetry with visceral emotion, his teaching methods were peculiar, consisting chiefly, as I remember, of consulting huge scrapbooks filled with literary quotations, and I was profoundly impressed by his attitude to books. Books poured into his rooms, new ones arriving constantly during all our tutorials, and his reception of them was salutary, I thought. The minute he opened a package and checked the title, he ripped off the dust-jacket and threw it away with a gesture I thought marvellously insouciant, as

The murder of Thomas à Becket, from the Becket window in the Lucy chapel

if nothing mattered in the least except the content: and fifty years on I still do my best to emulate him – stifling, as I do so,~ any vulgar thoughts about resale values.

I have always particularly loved the top left-hand corner of the choir school playing fields, with a tall clump of trees overlooking Dead Man's Walk. There is nowhere better in the world, to my mind, for lazing in long summer grass, sucking straws and contemplating the towers and silhouettes of Christ Church. When I came to write a book about Oxford, in the 1960s, sometimes I wandered in there just to let the place play upon my sensibility, smelling the grasses, feeling the faint breezes, hearing old Tom sounding from beyond the cathedral and generally soaking myself in sentimental complacency – to belong to such a place, and to feel, however presumptuously, that it belongs to you!

Now that I am old, still my seventy-odd years of acquaintance with the House chiefly leaves with me effects of pure sensuality. I love to walk into Hall on a winter evening, into the dim hubbub of dinner, with all those portraits looking down out of the murk, and a palpable smell of potatoes. I love scholarly lights still burning among the treasures of the Library, laughter from upstairs rooms in Peckwater, young dons in gowns earnestly debating as they emerge from the Common Room, bowler-hatted porters like idols in their cabins – I love the whole aesthetic being of this grand old body, so pompous, so full of haughty memory, so rich in humanity and humour, so generous in its sympathies. And most of all, even now, I am bewitched by the two dark orifices that give such arcane access to the cathedral, seen from the other side of Tom Quad. I know that inside there, beyond the tragic rosters of the war dead in the porch, is a timeless retreat of dignity and kindness. I am an agnostic still, but in my mind Sir Thomas Armstrong (died 1994) is always hunched over his Bach in the organ loft, and old Claude Jenkins (died 1959) perpetually blesses us.

Jan Morris

College Servants

Riley, *A scullion of Christ Church*, circa 1685

Right from the very beginning, when Sylvester Tennant and Peter Dormer, the first porters, took charge of the keys to the gate, when Thomas Long, the first head chef, brandished a knife and a saucepan, when Richard the carpenter first had to repair a broken window, and Thomas Palmer, the first auditor, sat down to his pint of beer andhis ledgers, Christ Church has depended on its servants and staff to keep college and cathedral up and running.

The skills of John Furnivall, the account-keeping manciple, are extolled elsewhere in this volume, but there were many others, from the foundation onwards, whose talents have been crucial or whose characters have made them memorable. Sylvester Tennant was one of the first porters; little is known of his life in the lodge, but we do know that he was considered trustworthy by one of the almsmen, John Wykyns, who was evidently not as poor as his position might suggest, and who asked Tennant to be his executor. The will, which survives in the University archives, tells that Tennant was left a goodly portion of Wykyns's estate. One of the cathedral clerks was left a length of good russet worsted, too.

Late nineteenth- and early twentieth-century head porters kept a log book describing all the incidents that they had to deal with. They flew flags for all sorts of occasions, welcomed important visitors, returned lost pyjamas to Gaudy guests who might have over-indulged, caught undergraduates climbing over walls, recorded the purchase of new fangled gadgets, such as the Hoover bought in 1925; one even had to rescue a zealous decorator who walked backwards into Mercury while admiring his handiwork. Much later, Mr Borrett, Head Porter from 1936 to 1962, left an account of his long service atthe college.

The names of cathedral vergers are scattered throughout the records. The first was Robert Jones, who served Christ Church for twenty years, but few were as much part of the furniture as William Francis. Francis was born in 1840, and started work at Christ Church as Dean Liddell's footman in 1859. In 1866, he became an under-porter whose duties included ringing the '101' every night. Francis became canons' verger and sub-librarian and evidently loved his place of employment, taking photographs which recorded parts of Christ Church which nolonger exist. He remembered Edward VII as an undergraduate, met Queen Victoria and George V when they visited, and served both college and cathedral almost until his death in January 1937. There is a memorial to him in the cloister.

Clockwise from left: George Cripps, the scout, who worked at Christ Church from 1876 to 1918, with James, his boy; Christ Church private fire brigade in 1948 with 'Hooky' Hill; Christ Church and Trinity College Cambridge servants' cricket teams, 1947

In the offices were the Chapter Clerk, responsible for recording all the business of the Dean and Chapter, and the auditor. John Willis, Chapter Clerk after the Restoration, was charged with producing the first real catalogue of estate records, long before we had an archivist. His work is still invaluable today. The role of the auditor was laid down in the statutes of Cardinal College, and it was required that he had somewhere to work, and a good supply of ale to tide him over the tedious business of checking all the accounts. It's still uncertain where the audit house was, but the auditors of today certainly do not get their barrel of beer.

Long before these regulations were made, the Dean and Canons made certain that no man would be tempted by young and beautiful scouts. Rarely were women allowed across the threshold of the main gate, let alone into the rooms of the students; laundresses had to collect and deposit linen at given times at the lodge. But there were bedmakers in the seventeenth century, and it was strictly laid down that none of these could be younger than forty – a goodly age in those days. Scouts, of course, were always men until fairly recently and, until the second World War, acted almost as valets and butlers to undergraduates, bringing water, making breakfast, serving lunch – which was, in the nineteenth century, rushed from staircase to staircase by kitchen porters – running baths, as well as undertaking housekeeping activities on their staircases.

Between the wars, college servants across the University were a community unto themselves; they had their own social club, and there were sports clubs for tennis, rowing and cricket. The role of the scout has changed, but they are still a crucial part of the college community. In modern times, college 'servants' now do a huge variety of jobs; there are office administrators, accountants, librarians, gardeners, all sorts of maintenance staff, messengers, custodians, cooks, hall staff and butlers, some of whom are the modern successors to men who have worked here for centuries, and others whose tasks would have been incomprehensible in the sixteenth century.

Judith Curthoys

Robert Burton

Burton's memorial in the north transept of the cathedral

Robert Burton is one of the most singular and distinguished literary figures to have been associated with Christ Church, his literary character being at once substantial and elusive. He is best known as the author of *The Anatomy of Melancholy*, a work that was first published in 1621 but subsequently appeared in seven further editions in the seventeenth century alone, constituting what Burton's most recent editors call, with some understatement, 'a work in progress'. This is in keeping with the literary character of the *Anatomy*: in many ways it lives up to what its title and division into 'partitions' promise, namely a comprehensive discussion and analysis of all the ramifications and sub-divisions of a vast and provocative subject; but it is also intentionally digressive and even transgressive, a belated product of sixteenth-century rhetorical copiousness, a 'paradoxical encomium', an encyclopedia, a satire, a 'house of learning' and a covert (and sometimes overt) autobiography.

The learning that Burton was able to demonstrate in this voluminous and commercially successful work (White Kennett, bishop of Peterborough in a much later generation, notes that 'the Bookseller ... got an Estate by it') is a direct product of his having spent most of his life at Christ Church. Burton acknowledges this in his guise as 'Democritus Junior', telling his reader that 'I have beene brought up a Student in the most flourishing Colledge of Europe ... for 30 yeeres I have continued ... a Scholler, and would be therefore loth, either by living as a Drone, to be an unprofitable or unworthy Member of so learned and noble a Society, or to write that which should bee any way dishonourable to such a royall and ample Foundation'. Burton's tenure of a studentship from 1599 to 1640 is most obviously commemorated in the monument to him in the cathedral, its self-composed epitaph variously confirming and arousing the suspicions of generations of readers with its enigmatic observation that 'Melancholy gave [him] both life and death'. But Burton's other legacy to Christ Church is a monument to his period as librarian, and to his persona as, in the words of Anthony à Wood, a 'devourer of authors', in the form of his bequests to its library and to the Bodleian. To what à Wood called 'the antients of Ch[rist Ch[urch]', Burton was 'very merry'. White Kennett hints at something more bipolar, stating that nothing provoked more laughter in Burton than 'going down to the Bridge-fast in Oxford, and hearing the Bargemen scold & storm & swear at one another ... Yet in his College and

Chamber [he was] so mute and mopish that he was suspected to be *Felo de se*' (i.e. a suicide: an unsubstantiated rumour). The analysis of Burton's character, as far as this can be deduced from his writing, was consummated in Hugh Trevor-Roper's essay on him in *Renaissance Essays*. In keeping with the purposefully digressive literary techniques of his subject, Trevor-Roper used this occasion to smuggle into his narrative a tangential, potted history of Christ Church in the seventeenth century: '[it] was not', he asserts meaningfully, 'like the other colleges of Oxford'. The essay is a suggestive meeting of Christ Church minds, the historian persuasively assessing Burton's quest for equanimity in both the private body and the body politic and thereby diagnosing in his subject a case of temperamental and intellectual Anglicanism.

Mishtooni Bose

Five Centuries of Travellers and Explorers

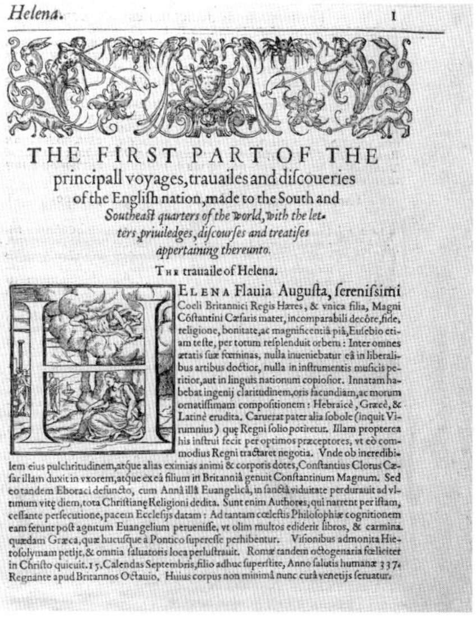
Helena. 1

THE FIRST PART OF THE principall voyages, trauailes and diſcoueries of the Engliſh nation, made to the South and *Southeaſt quarters of the world, with the letters, priuiledges, diſcourſes and treatiſes appertaining thereunto.*

The trauaile of Helena.

HELENA Flauia Auguſta, ſereniſsimi Coeli Britannici Regis Hæres, & vnica filia, Magni Cōſtantini Cæſaris mater, incomparabili decôre, fide, religione, bonitate, ac magnificentiâ piâ, Euſebio etiam teſte, per totum reſplenduit orbem: Inter omnes ætatis ſuæ fœminas, nulla inueniebatur eâ in liberalibus artibus doctior, nulla in inſtrumentis muſicis peritior, aut in linguis nationum copioſior. Innatam habebat ingenij claritudinem, oris facundiam, ac morum ornatiſſimam compoſitionem: Hebraicè, Græcè, & Latinè erudita. Caruerat pater alia ſobole (inquit Virumnius) quę Regni ſolio potiretur. Illam propterea his inſtrui fecit per optimos præceptores, vt eò commodius Regni tractaret negotia. Vnde ob incredibilem eius pulchritudinem, atque alias eximias animi & corporis dotes, Conſtantius Clorus Cæſar illam duxit in vxorem, atque ex eâ filium in Britanniâ genuit Conſtantinum Magnum. Sed eo tandem Eboraci defuncto, cum Annâ illâ Euangelicâ, in ſanctâ viduitate perdurauit ad vltimum vitę diem, tota Chriſtianę Religioni dedita. Sunt enim Authores, qui narrent per iſtam, ceſſante perſecutione, pacem Eccleſijs datam: Ad tantam cœleſtis Philoſophiæ cognitionem eam ferunt poſt agnitum Euangelium perueniſſe, vt olim multos ediderit libros, & carmina quædam Græca, quæ hucuſque à Pontico ſupereſſe perhibentur. Viſionibus admonita Hieroſolymam petijt, & omnia ſaluatoris loca perluſtrauit. Romæ tandem octogenaria fœliciter in Chriſto quieuit. 15. Calendas Septembris, filio adhuc ſuperſtite, Anno ſalutis humanæ 337. Regnante apud Britannos Octauio. Huius corpus non minimâ nunc curâ venetijs ſeruatur.

Opening page of Richard Hakluyt's *Principall navigations, voiages and discoveries of the English nation …*, 1589

The 'Golden Age' of adventuring, with the dashing and romantic heroes of the likes of Drake and Raleigh, has to be the late sixteenth and early seventeenth centuries. Christ Church men were no less determined to make their mark across the globe. Poets, writers, collectors of travellers' tales, adventurers and profiteers, men like Humfrey Coningsby (ChCh 1581) made their way around the globe. Coningsby travelled across Europe, visiting France, Germany, Italy, Sicily, Bohemia, Poland, Hungary, Greece and Turkey, before vanishing into thin air, last seen in Venice, in 1611. Richard Hakluyt (ChCh 1570), most famous for his book, *Principal Navigations, voyages, traffiques and discoveries of the English nation, made by sea or overland, to the remote and farthest distant quarters of the earth*, actually never travelled further than Paris himself, but he was a great encourager of others like Stephen Parmenius and Robert Hues. Both men lodged with Hakluyt at Christ Church, but unlike their friend, they both travelled; Parmenius, a poet who wanted to be the English Camões and eulogise the exploits of English explorers, went to Newfoundland, which he hated, and died there when his ship ran aground. Hues was a scientist, interested in navigation. He circumnavigated the globe with Thomas Cavendish between 1586 and 1588, with the main aim of 'taking the true latitude of places', and travelled later to the Azores to make astronomical observations and to demonstrate the use of astronomy for navigational purposes. However, the underlying purpose of all this romantic wandering was for commercial gain. William Herbert (ChCh 1600), whose father is described in the *Oxford Dictionary National Biography* as a 'writer, pirate, merchant, and public official', seemed determined to follow in his parent's footsteps, at least in all but the last. He wrote poems on early English history, but evidently had a severe case of wanderlust. In 1616 Herbert sold his house to fund Walter Raleigh's expedition to Guiana in search of gold mines. They set off together in 1617, but Herbert nearly lost his life in an armed attempt to take control of a mine. On their return, Raleigh was imprisoned, betrayed by Herbert. Raleigh still insisted, rather honourably, that Herbert be paid his dues from the voyage but, unsurprisingly, after Sir Walter was executed, his widow was rather reluctant to hand over anything! Nothing daunted, though, Herbert reinvested, this time in a scheme to export Welsh butter. He died, almost inevitably, in a debtors' prison. During the later seventeenth century, politics and diplomacy, rather than profiteering, were the reasons for travel. William Penn, of course, having

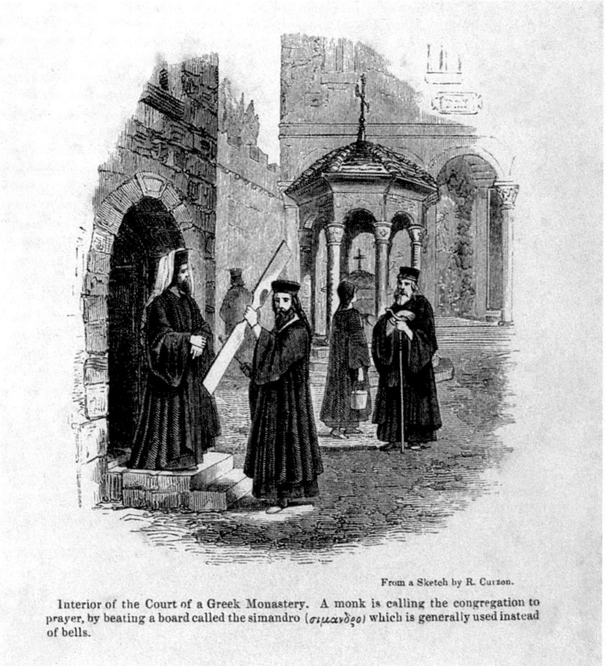
From a Sketch by R. Curzon.
Interior of the Court of a Greek Monastery. A monk is calling the congregation to prayer, by beating a board called the simandro which is generally used instead of bells.

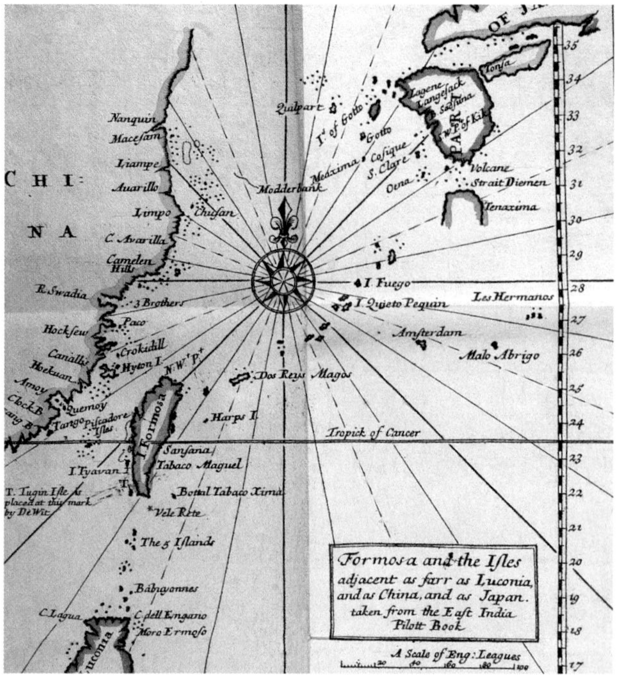

Left: Title-page illustration from Robert Curzon's *Visits to monasteries in the Levant,* 1850; right: a map, showing Formosa and the Chinese coastline from *An enquiry into the objections against George Psalmanaazaar of Formosa*

honed his political and business skills in Ireland, used his talents to promote the cause of non-conformity, and to promote his own interests. His manoeuvring, among the king's men in court, eventually led to his land grant in America, and the creation of Pennsylvania. Less well known, perhaps, is Francis Vernon (ChCh 1654), who was a diplomat and ambassador. Based initially in Paris, Vernon took great delight in the advances promoted by the new Academy of Sciences, especially in astronomy, and it wasn't long before the politicians back home in England decided that Vernon was not going to be a terrific asset to England, at least on the diplomatic front. He travelled, like so many contemporaries, through Europe and Asia Minor, but came to a sticky end in Persia having foolishly picked a quarrel with some Arabs in Esfahan.

In the eighteenth century, the country seems to have been divided by industry and diligence on the one hand, and dilettantism on the other. Henry Skrine (ChCh 1774) was a wealthy gentleman whose travels may only have been within the British Isles, and his travel writings more for the general reader, but they covered everything the informed gentleman of the time would need to know. His particular interest was in the living standards of the various communities through which he passed. The flip side of the coin was George Psalmanazar, a Frenchman who, having received an education from first Franciscan and then Dominican monks, forged a certificate claiming Irish origins, and set off on a 'pilgrimage' to Rome. Needing funds, he changed his origins from Irish to the more exotic Japanese. He created an alphabet and bits of a language that he thought would give the impression of a far-eastern tongue but, still destitute, he had to join the military, now claiming that he came from Formosa. Having been baptised in Holland by a diligent English chaplain, Psalmanazar was invited by the bishop of London to come to Oxford to teach Formosan to potential missionaries. His books about the Formosans were spectacular, both in their claims, many of which were completely fictitious, and in their popularity. He continued to write, and to flourish, if not financially, in spite of an increasingly incredulous public, until his death. Although his links with the House are rather tenuous – he stayed here for only three months – he was probably our first 'tabloid' journalist.

The gentleman scholar epitomised the nineteenth century. Philip Webb had been a pupil of Buckland's at Christ Church, and had developed a fascination for geology and the natural world. A man of means, he made his way across southern Europe, Turkey, Tangiers, ending up in the Canary Islands where he and some friends set about producing the definitive work on the islands' natural history. Botany was his first love, and Webb possessed an herbarium almost second to none. Webb also worked on the flora of the Cape Verde islands, of Ireland, and of Italy where his collections are now housed. Francis Oates was another natural historian, this time in the Americas and on the Zambezi. Robert Curzon collected, too, but manuscripts from the monasteries of Mount Athos and Sinai, a practice which has been the subject of much disapproval in more recent times. Even less politically correct was James Harrison, who travelled to Bermuda, Canada, India and finally to Africa, where he collected six pygmies from the Congo. Harrison 'displayed' them first at a garden party at Buckingham Palace, then for an extended period at the Hippodrome in London, and 'on tour' around the holiday hot-spots of England. Even at the time, there were complaints about the exploitation – which included postcards, posters, gramophone recordings, as well the exhibition itself – but one million people had paid to see the pygmies before they finally left for home.

More of a professional scholar, Halford Mackinder may not have travelled particularly far himself, except for making the first recorded ascent of Mount Kenya in 1899 – no mean feat, of course – but he was the one who, more than any other, put geography as an academic subject firmly on the syllabus both in schools and at Oxford, where he was the first director of the School of Geography. How far Mackinder's work influenced Christ Church's explorers of the twentieth century is probably incalculable. If the sixteenth- and seventeenth-century adventurers are best known for pushing back the bounds of navigation and commerce, eighteenth-century travellers for both improvement and pleasure, and explorers in the nineteenth century for scholarship, then those of the twentieth century can be seen as embracing all these activities at the same time. Apsley Cherry-Garrard managed to inveigle his way onto Scott's ill-fated expedition to the South Pole, purely by being a shooting acquaintance of Edward Wilson rather than expert in anything useful at the Pole. As 'assistant zoologist', Cherry-Garrard found himself picked for a hazardous trip to acquire eggs from an emperor penguin rookery. His experiences led Cherry-Garrard to entitle his book about the expedition, *The Worst Journey in the World.* No doubt much of what Scott and his companions went through would have been recognised by Andrew Croft (ChCh 1925), who participated in the longest self-supporting dog-sled drive on record, in Arctic expeditions working on radar development and ethnography, and serving in the intelligence services during the war. Croft became one of the world's experts on cold weather warfare. Christopher Sykes, too, was a member of both the SAS and the SOE, this time operating in the rather warmer climes of Iran and Egypt before he joined the BBC after the war. Many Christ Church men wrote about their adventures, but none captured the public imagination quite as much as the stories of Peter Fleming. Fleming, hating being dragged into the family financial business, took himself off to a Guatemalan volcano on a thinly veiled work trip. On his return, Fleming joined *The Spectator*, and later *The Times*, recording his travels in Brazil, China, and India in a series of books and articles which were unprecedented in their light-heartedness and humour, and turned the travel-writing genre on its head.

Judith Curthoys

The Deans

The conversation turned to cannibalism. My entomologist cousin was dining with his wife in the 1930s near a tropical village which had a reputation. 'How long', they asked each other, 'would it take for the tragedy of our being cooked and eaten to become a joke – indeed the only thing remembered about us?' Not long. Most of us will suffer the fate of being remembered for few things and those not of our own choosing; deans of Christ Church are no exception. There are towering figures whose activities are minutely recorded, because they moved mountains or were brazen. Then there are those for whom the record is less impressive, perhaps because of the nature of the age in which they lived: when a biography of Thomas Strong (Dean 1901-20) came out, the *Annual Report* of the House said that the book had been written in spite of the fact that 'nothing particular ever happened to him'. Perhaps the very fact of being attached to an institution results in a kind of memorial, for even fairly trivial stories (especially if amusing) stick to the House as if glued to it.

George Morley, engraved by George Vertue from a painting by Sir Peter Lely, circa 1740. Morley was Dean of Christ Church for six months in 1660

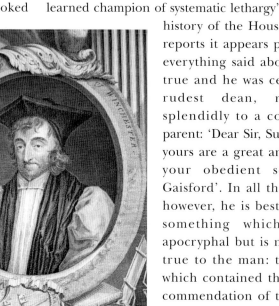

The verdict on some deans is uncertain. John Ruskin saw Thomas Gaisford (Dean 1831–55) as a 'rotundly progressive terror' or indeed as 'a semi-maniac', yet Hugh Trevor-Roper describes him as 'the learned champion of systematic lethargy' in his short history of the House. From the reports it appears possible that everything said about him was true and he was certainly the rudest dean, responding splendidly to a complaining parent: 'Dear Sir, Such letters as yours are a great annoyance to your obedient servant, T. Gaisford'. In all the accounts, however, he is best known for something which may be apocryphal but is nevertheless true to the man: the sermon which contained the immortal commendation of the study of Greek as 'serving to elevate above the vulgar herd, and not infrequently leading to positions of considerable emolument'. Those were the days!

The chapter on Christ Church in the nineteenth-century volume of the University's history is dominated not by Gaisford, but rather by his reforming and building successor, Henry Liddell (Dean 1855–92), appointed by the Whigs. Although known more for his daughter Alice than for himself, there is no doubt that under his aegis the House developed into something near to what it is today. It was he who presided, with some diplomacy, over the transition from Chapter government to a Governing Body similar to that of other colleges. He quelled discussion in the new body with an authoritative cough and built the hybrid Victorian block which overlooks the Meadow.

Godfrey Kneller, *Francis Atterbury, Dean of Christ Church 1711–13*, circa 1711

On the wall of my study is the best-known reminder of Liddell's successor, Francis Paget. It is two cartoons which describe the Blenheim Palace row of 1 December 1893. The Dean and Censors had refused permission for some undergraduates to attend a ball at Blenheim, so they danced in Tom Quad and painted the outside of the deanery and other places red, including their considered, if somewhat repetitive, opinions: 'Damn Sampson' (the senior Censor); 'Damn the Dean'; 'Damn the dons'. The bell-rope for Tom was cut, so the curfew did not ring that night. Paget is shown, with his distinctive centre parting, in night shirt and cap. The cartoons are a suitable reminder of the shortcomings of authority figures. Whether they are fair to Paget is hard to gauge; he was an anxious and competent administrator who probably did takc himself too seriously. In 1891 he wrote a book on 'Accidie' which was promptly dubbed 'the Dean's new sin'.

Liddell and Paget were what might be called 'career deans'. Looking back over the forty four occupants of the post, one of whom was dean twice (at both ends of the Commonwealth: Edward Reynolds, 1648–51 and 1660), that cannot be said of many. For about a hundred years from the foundation, tenures were short for either of two reasons: deprivation or promotion. The first dean, Richard Cox (Dean 1546–53) was banished by Queen Mary. He was a staunch protestant who, when headmaster of Westminster, was described as 'the best schoolmaster of our time' and 'the greatest beater'. Cox was succeeded by Richard Marshall (Dean 1553–59), known for his extremism in the other direction as demonstrated by his removal of the mortal remains of Peter Martyr's wife from her grave in the cathedral and its burial in the deanery dunghill. He was, of course, deprived in his turn. During Elizabeth's reign and beyond, there was a string of Calvinist deans, many of whom held other appointments at the same time and became bishops. Their activities were political and religious, as in the case of William James (Dean 1584–96) who was described as a 'stout oppugner of papists', and they do not seem to have done much for the House, except perhaps to build up its library. Thomas Ravis (Dean 1596–1605) achieved notoriety by replacing the Students' food allowance with mean cash payments.

For distinction in deans, the prize must go to Stuart times. Here was Samuel Fell (Dean 1638–48), responsible for the building of the fan-vaulted stairs to the Hall. He it was who gave over the deanery to the king during the Civil War and whose family was evicted on 12 April 1648, carried out of the House by Parliamentarian soldiers. He passed on his interest in printing to his son, John Fell (Dean 1660–86), the father of the Oxford University Press, the University's earliest and most successful spin-out company. He became dean at the age of thirty five and worked on the development of the House and of the University: a stickler for discipline, a proponent of elitist admissions, a great fund-raiser and builder, not only of parts of Tom Quad but also of the Sheldonian as a place for academic ceremonial, and as the

University's first printing house. The piece of doggerel ('I do not love thee Dr Fell...') by which he is most remembered may have truth, for he was described as 'an awesome figure, fanatical in diligence, celibacy and learning', and it was he who expelled John Locke in 1684.

James II then appointed John Massey (Dean 1686–89) who thus became the Catholic dean of a Church of England cathedral, with his private chapel in Canterbury Quad. His tenure is most notable for its end, for at the time of the 'Glorious Revolution', he made his escape out of the deanery drawing room window before dawn on 30 November 1688. He went to London and then, disguised as a trooper, made his way to the exiled court in St Germain.

The prize for deans must go to Henry Aldrich (Dean 1689–1710): entertaining polymath, architect, engraver, classicist, philosopher, poet, musician, collector, humorist, bon viveur. There are nine portraits and three marble busts of him in Christ Church, but a fuller monument is his design of Peckwater Quad (built 1706–13). He was involved in the affairs of the church: in its Convocation which met to counter the Protestant tendencies of the new reign. As Vice-Chancellor he was keen to restore discipline and to promote music and toryism. Yet it is as someone who was good company and an enthusiast for community that he is best remembered, in part (as his biographer remarks) on account of 'the endearing evidence of the battel book'. He wrote drinking catches, set to music by Henry Purcell, and smoked a pipe although not while a sermon was being preached in the cathedral. Aldrich was succeeded by the most volatile of all the deans, Francis Atterbury (Dean 1711–13). Like many others, he had a long association with the House, but unlike them he showed impatience with its ways and always yearned for a larger stage on which to display his 'incendiary talent'. For fifteen years he was at the centre of ecclesiastical politics, giving his immense energy to the High Church movement. His appointment to Christ Church was a move by Queen Anne to keep the Tories on board, but his time at the House was tempestuous. The University was not responsive to his Tory scheming and the Canons sabotaged his more domestic plans. In a sense Christ Church saw him off, but then he was glad to go. His haughty portrait looks down on the deliberations of all our committee meetings, challenging us to an awareness of a wider world. He went on to be dean of Westminster and Bishop of Rochester, where he became a Jacobite conspirator; his Westminster portrait bears a plaque which says 'Banished 1723'.

Francis Paget (Dean 1892–1901), in nightcap and gown, looking over the riot in Tom Quad on the night of the Blenheim Row

To be fair to deans, there should be some reference to more recent and less turbulent times. Legends are sometimes true, and it is the case that John Lowe (Dean 1939–59) was seen off on his helicopter ride to Torquay in 1950 by a strange band which included a sheeted bard in classical semi-nudity whose ode has happily not survived. *The Oxford Magazine* did, however, contain a Latin epigram:

Stupet Peck quadrangulum: Christi super Aedem
Rapit Helicopterus novum Ganymedem.
Magno mos miraculo vertitur mundanus:
Caelo in-Torquay-bitur 'Humilis' Decanus!

On his return, the Dean was greeted with the singing of 'Lowe, he comes with clouds descending'; some wrote demanding severe penalties for this blasphemy, but were disregarded. John's son Christopher remembers the occasion, a couple of years earlier, when Lowe became Vice-Chancellor and marked the elevation by buying his secretary a new typewriter to cope with the increased volume of correspondence. This was the birth of university administration.

Left and right: 'Lowe he comes with clouds descending', May 1950; centre: Princess Margaret, with Dean Lowe, arriving for a wedding in the cathedral

As for deans after John Lowe, there are wells full of reminiscences on which to draw. They are too recent properly to be the subject of history.

The role has changed and yet remained the same. Neither the process of appointment nor the task is as overtly political as it once was, and the religious aspect of it is less adversarial. Nowadays deans are not deprived, nor, alas, do they flee. Their lives are more pedestrian, pastoral and representative. Having said that, the relations with old and present members have been fairly constant over 500 years. Deans have always been concerned about the buildings and had to raise funds. They worry about admissions and standards. They have been the court of appeal and the trouble-shooter, although some like Francis Atterbury and Charles Hall (Dean 1824–31) caused more trouble than they shot. Atterbury found college life frustrating: 'I'm perfectly weary of this nauseous circle of small affairs', but most have reckoned it to be exciting, indeed one of the most strange and quirky jobs to be found, presiding over a unique institution. It was Dean Strong who said that 'the public mind is somewhat particularly attracted to this place'. So is the private mind.

Christopher Lewis

The Seventeenth and Eighteenth Centuries

CHRONOLOGY

1605 *Installation of Dean John King*
1611 *Installation of Dean William Goodwin*
1620 *Installation of Dean Richard Corbet*
1629 *Installation of Dean Brian Duppa*
1630s *Alterations to the cathedral, including the installation of the van Linge windows*
1638 *Installation of Dean Samuel Fell*
1640s *Planting of Pocock's fig and plane trees*
Building of the fan-vaulting above the Hall stairs
1640 *Bequest of the books of Robert Burton*
1642 *Arrival of Charles I and his court at Christ Church*
1646 *Fall of Oxford to Parliament*
Parliamentary visitation
Installation of Dean Edward Reynolds
1648 *Forcible removal of Mrs Fell from the Deanery*
1651 *Removal and destruction of the 'idolatrous' windows from the cathedral*
1660 *Installation of Dean George Morley*
Installation of Dean John Fell
1663 *The visit of Charles II, Queen Catherine and Lady Castlemaine*
1665 *Completion of Tom Quad*
Second visit of Charles II
1667 *Creation of the Senior Common Room*
1669 *Fell's Building and Killcanon erected after the destruction by fire of Richard Gardiner's lodgings and part of Chaplain's Quad*
1670 *The digging of Mercury*
1681 *Third visit of Charles II, with Parliament Gift of Richard Allestree's books for the Regius Professor of Divinity*
1682 *Completion of Tom Tower by Christotopher Wren*
1684 *Tom rung for the first time from Tom Tower*
Expulsion of John Locke
1686 *Installation of Dean John Massey*
1689 *Installation of Dean Henry Aldrich*
1705 *Rebuilding of Peckwater Quad*
1711 *Installation of Dean Francis Atterbury*
1713 *Installation of Dean George Smalridge*
1716 *Building of the New Library*
1719 *Installation of Dean Hugh Boulter*
1720 *Fire destroyed the roof of the Hall*
1724 *Installation of Dean William Bradshaw*
1733 *Installation of Dean John Conybeare*
Gift of books and scientific instruments by Boyle, earl of Orrery
1737 *Gift of books, coins and manuscripts by Archbishop Wake*
1756 *Installation of Dean David Gregory*
1760–3 *Bequest of pictures by General John Guise*
1763 *George Grenville (ChCh 1730) became the first of Christ Church's thirteen prime ministers*
1765 *Anatomy School built*
1767 *Installation of Dean William Markham*
1772 *Part of the cloister converted to make a muniment room*
1773–83 *Canterbury Quad and Gate constructed*
1775 *Conversion of Old Library into student rooms*
1777 *Installation of Dean Lewis Bagot*
1783 *Installation of Dean Cyril Jackson*
William Petty (ChCh 1755), earl of Shelburne and first marquess of Lansdowne, elected Prime Minister
William Henry Cavendish Cavendish-Bentinck (ChCh 1755), third duke of Portland, became Christ Church's third Prime Minister, serving again from 1807 to 1809
1785 *Visit of George III*

Tom Tower

A Tale of Three Christophers

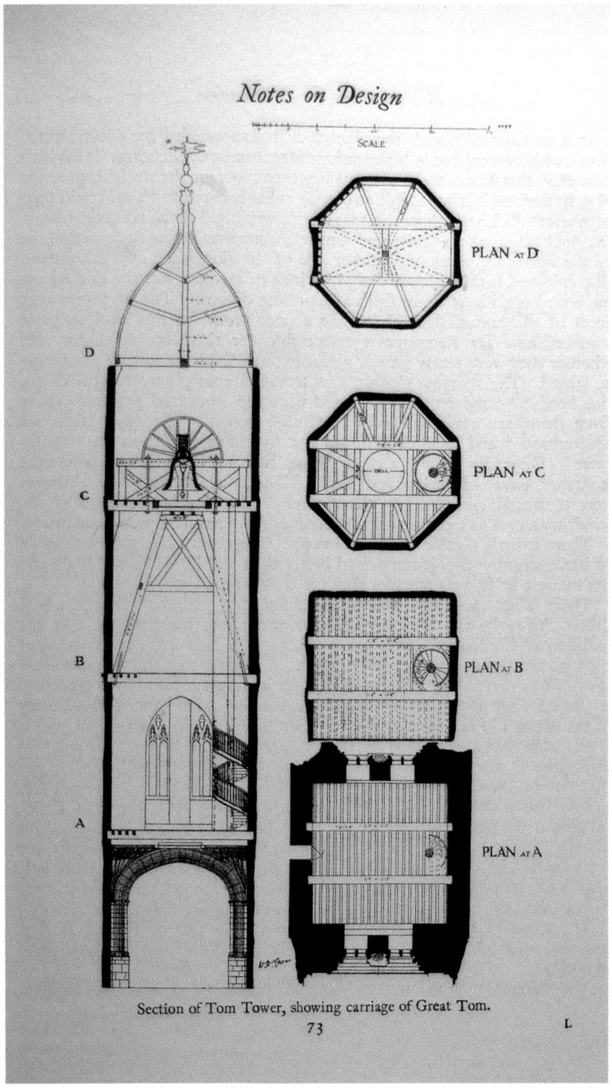

Far left: Sections through Tom Tower, showing the carriage of Great Tom. *From* W.D. Caröe, *'Tom Tower': Christ Church, Oxford, 1923*

In 1529, when Thomas Wolsey fell from Henry VIII's grace, the gatehouse on the St Aldate's front of Cardinal College stood just at the same height as the rest of the quadrangle. What it was that Wolsey had intended for the tower above the gate is uncertain; but it seems likely that there would have been something along the lines of other contemporary colleges, like Corpus Christi or Brasenose, with a two-storey tower perhaps providing part of the residence for the Dean or maybe the college archive. But fate dictated otherwise, and the gatehouse was not completed for many years.

It was not until the Restoration, when John Fell was made Dean, that the building work that had ceased in 1529, apart from a short-lived effort by Fell's father, Samuel, was recommenced. Almost immediately, Fell began to build the north side of

Far right: Queen Anne, presented by Robert Harley, the earl of Oxford, on the quadrangle side of Tom Tower. Unattributed, circa 1712

Tom Quad. Originally intended to be a college chapel to rival that of King's College in Cambridge, Fell decided to complete the square in the same style. The quad was squared in 1665.

Christ Church's bells, including Great Tom, were originally hung in the cathedral spire. Tom was temporarily rechristened Mary in 1546, and had the first of several recastings in 1612. Something was evidently not quite right so, in 1654, Darby, of Southwark, who had worked on the bells at both Merton and New Colleges, was given responsibility for the second recasting. However, according to Anthony Wood, Darby's work was less than satisfactory, and first the Merton bells were recast yet again, and then Great Tom, in 1680, by the first Christopher in the Tom tale, Christopher Hodson.

It was probably at this time that John Fell first conceived the idea of a bell tower, and possibly an observatory, over the main gate to Oxford's largest college. The following winter, Fell and the second Christopher, this time the famous architect and scientist, Wren, met in London. Wren submitted his design for the new tower in late spring 1681. There was considerable correspondence between the two men, discussing all the details of the construction. Fell's notion of including an observatory was successfully taken up by Wren, and only eighteen months later, Tom Tower, constructed by Christopher Kempster from Burford, was completed. The masons and labourers had received a shilling a day.

The niche on the St Aldates side of the tower was probably to have been filled by a statue of Charles II, who had contributed £1,000 to the cost of the building, but this did not happen, and the niche remained empty until 1872, when the image of Cardinal Wolsey was moved from the archway over the hall stairs to fill the space. On the other side, facing into Tom Quad, Robert Harley donated the rather imposing figure of Queen Anne.

It seems unlikely that Great Tom had been rehung in the cathedral after its 1680 recasting. It was installed, with some difficulty, in Tom Tower and was ready, by May of 1684, to be rung to celebrate the fourth anniversary of the Restoration. Ever after, the bell has rung the 101 as well as the hour. Before 1841, the clock on the tower had only one hand originally, and so showed only the hours. It had to be wound and set daily, and an accuracy of within three to four minutes was considered fine, until the 1840s when the railway arrived in Oxford. That Christ Church runs five minutes behind the rest of the country has been legend ever since.

Tom was always hard on its leather; replacing the baldrick appears regularly in the disbursement books. The bell inspired rhymes such as 'Great Tom is cast', published in 1667, before the bell's installation in Tom Tower. The bell has been rehung three more times since 1684; in 1692, when it kept the bell-founder and two carpenters busy for ten days, again in 1847, and then once more in 1953. The bell is now fixed.

Tales are legion about Tom. One porter, charged with the rather long and heavy task of tolling the 101, evidently took a considerable quantity of Dutch courage beforehand. His mind on other things, or perhaps not there at all, the porter lost count half-way through, and had to start all over again. The curfew must have been rather late that evening! And Mr Borrett, long-serving Head Porter, recalled in his memoirs attempts to run around Tom Quad while midnight was being struck – a feat he never saw achieved – and the Beat the Clock relay race which involved three teams of two men on bicycles racing twice around the driveway, stopping at Tom Gate to change over. Apparently, the handover was so chaotic that the undergraduates gave up in a heap of handle-bars and wheels, and with many bruises. At times, though, Tom has been quiet; the bell is muffled for the funerals of deans and, so the porter's log records, was also deadened to mark the occasion of Churchill's funeral in 1965. During the war, Tom was silenced completely; on 1 September 1939, Tom and the cathedral bells were rung for the last time until VE Day in 1945.

Tom Tower and its great bell are to Christ Church and to Oxford what Big Ben and the Westminster Clock tower are to London. The place wouldn't be the same without them.

Judith Curthoys

Smith and the Hall Staircase

Thomas Rowlandson's cartoon of the Christ Church canons at dinner, from his *Tours of Dr Syntax, 1812*

Some time in the 1950s I and a couple of others gave dinner to Lord Hinchingbrooke – familiarly and widely known as 'Hinch' – at the guest table in Hall. His father Lord Sandwich was still alive – it was not till his death in 1962 that his son successfully fought a battle to become the first, I think, hereditary peer to divest himself of his title, and became Victor Montagu, MP. I can't remember why we were entertaining him – it may have been because he had come to speak at the Chatham Club. Anyway, we wined and dined him very well, and he then put on his hat and coat and came out with us into the staircase hall. It was dimly lit, and a group of undergraduates were practising part-songs at the bottom of the stairs. Hinch – a little muzzy and mystified – clearly felt that he must have strayed into a church; he stopped, took off his hat, and reverently bowed his head.

I can't say I blame him; the combination of fan – vaulting and echoing chant was a good deal more evocative of a church than a staircase. And indeed the Christ Church stair hall – infiltrated into the space where Cardinal Wolsey meant to build a stair but didn't – is unlike any other in the world, both a masterpiece and, in so far as it seems two hundred years after its time, a curiosity. It is the most remarkable example of a half century of deliberate revival of Gothic in Oxford. But as it was built when there is a hole in the college accounts, between 1632 and 1640, little is known about it beyond two sentences in Anthony Wood's manuscripts, made in the 1680s or thereabouts, but only published in the eighteenth century: first that the staircase 'most curiously vaulted and supported by one pillar was built about the year 1630', secondly that Samuel Fell 'made [it] as it is now by the help of one -- Smith, an artificer of London'. These statements are not helped all that much by Thomas Baskerville, writing in 1683: 'the college has of latter years been much beautified by Brian Duppa and Samuel Fell, Deans, who also built the fine porch and staircase to the hall around 1630'.

Duppa was Dean from 1629 to 1638, Fell from 1638 to 1648. So was the staircase built by Dean Duppa in about 1630, or by Dean Fell in about 1640? Accounts

have havered between the two. A third possibility is offered by a passage in the diary of Christopher Potter, Provost of Queen's. He was writing in 1634, that is, unlike Wood and Baskerville, in the same period as the stairs were built. Potter commends Fell for his 'skill in contrivance of building' and adds that 'The Deane of Christ Church', that is, Duppa, 'knew not how to have proceeded but for him'. Could the stairs have been masterminded by Fell, but during Duppa's Deanship?

I've always been intrigued by '- - Smith, an artificer of London'. It's about as unhelpful a description as one could hope for. Two attempts have been made to fill the '- -'. In the 1940s John Harvey suggested John Smith of London, who carved not very accomplished statues and enrichments for the great gate of Trinity College, Cambridge, in 1615. In 1988 Mavis Batey and C. Cole suggested William Smith, who was Master of the Masons' Company in London in 1640. Neither is impossible, but neither has any known connection either with Oxford or fan-vaulting.

I can add to the confusion by producing a third name. A year or two ago, in browsing through a comparatively recently published index of 'probate papers' (that is, not wills, but papers to do with the administration of estates after death), I noticed an entry that intrigued me: 'Robert Smith mason/privileged person, Oxford, St Aldates, 1635'. He sounded like someone who was in the right place at the right time. Howard Colvin kindly looked up the original in the Bodleian, and made an abstract for me. Robert Smith died intestate. On 4 August 1635 his wife Mary produced a list of his assets (£70 6s 11d) and debts (£20 1s.) He had clearly died unexpectedly and when still working. He was renting something at Abingdon, owed for stone bought in London, for marble, to a boatman for 'carriage of stone to Abbington', and just for carriage of stone. This suggests that stone, and possibly marble, had been brought for him by barge up the Thames from London, deposited in his yard or quay at Abingdon, and then carried overland to Oxford. The same route was taken by the Purbeck stone that was used for paving Canterbury Quadrangle, St John's College, in or around 1634.

A little more – all too little – is known about Robert Smith. Early in 1632 he, Richard Maude, and Hugh Davies, all freemasons, signed a contract (which does not survive) to build the south, west and east sides of the Canterbury Quadrangle at St John's. Something went wrong, and in August 1633 they abandoned the contract, unfinished. The reasons are not clear; Howard Colvin surmised that the elaborate classical detail finally decided on for the colonnades on the east and west sides was beyond them.

Also in the 1630s, Robert Smith on his own supplied and laid black and white marble paving for the chapel at Queen's College. This could be the 'marble' in his probate account. Finally, the fact that he was 'a privileged person' meant that he was an outsider, who did not belong to the Oxford guild of masons. The University broke the guild monopoly by putting outsiders on their books as college servants, much to the frustration of the Oxford artificers. Smith's being 'privileged' does not necessarily mean that he came from London, but it is not unlikely, not least because his partner Hugh Davies probably did. Or at least, a mason of that name is recorded working in London in 1622–4 and 1625.

Between 1625 and 1634 Davies made one wooden and four pasteboard models of a great staircase that was to go up to the first floor of the Bodleian Library. He had gone to London to show them to Archbishop Laud, Chancellor of the University, and others. Bodley in his will had left money for 'the raysing of a fayre staircase to make the assent more easie and grateful to the first greate librarye'. The number of models, and the care involved, suggest something elaborate, and probably vaulted like the 'Proscholium' under the Arts End of the Bodleian, and all the entrances to the Schools Quadrangle. The project ultimately collapsed, and Davies's bill for the work he had done was finally paid in June 1634.

Buttery

The old Front Quadrangle at St John's was joined to the new Canterbury Quadrangle by a passage or vestibule covered with fan-vaulting. It is likely enough that Maude, Smith and Davies built this before abandoning the contract. A possible pattern begins to emerge. Archbishop Laud paid for the Canterbury Quadrangle (hence its name), but the administration of work was carried out under the President, William Juxon, and it is he who is likely to have appointed Maude, Smith and Davies. Samuel Fell was much involved with the Bodleian at all stages, and was clearly interested in architecture. Juxon doubled up as President of St John's and Dean of Worcester, and Fell, according to Christopher Potter, had 'assisted' him at Worcester. Did the failed 'fayre staircase' at the Bodleian lead on to the realised staircase at Christ Church? Could both Robert Smith and Davies have been involved in building it, between about 1633 and 1635? Did Smith fall off the scaffolding in the last stages of building? And a final thought: in January 1633 Juxon resigned from the Presidency of St John's and a few months later was appointed bishop of Hereford. He was never inaugurated, because in October he was consecrated bishop of London – I don't know if he ever got to Hereford, but it is possible that he at least sent a mason there to report, say, on the condition of the Bishop's Palace. And at Hereford, until unforgivably demolished in 1769, there was the miraculous beauty of an octagonal chapter house, roofed from a soaring central column, like other chapter houses, but the only known example in which the column supported an aureole of fan vaulting. Did a try-out in miniature at St John's, the abandoned staircase at the Bodleian, and inspiration from Hereford all merge together under the beneficent wand of Samuel Fell, and thanks to the skill of a Smith, perhaps not quite so '- -' to delight the generations of dons, undergraduates and visitors who have walked up under that lovely vault to the magnificence and hospitality of the Hall at Christ Church?

Mark Girouard (1951)

Civil War and Commonwealth Christ Church

In July 1642 King Charles I moved into the Deanery; not quite the Deanery we know today, as the northern end of the Great Quadrangle had not yet been completed, but at least a good portion of the east side. He brought with him his courtiers and his military advisers, as well as his complete entourage of servants and household staff. Henrietta Maria, Charles's wife, lodged at Merton College, and new gates were knocked through the boundary walls between Christ Church and Corpus Christi College, and between Corpus Christi and Merton College, to allow the king easy, and private, access to his wife's quarters. The gate between the House and Corpus Christi still survives in the cathedral garden.

In spite of the huge impact that the residence of king and court must have had on Christ Church, surprisingly their presence is barely recorded in the archive. No accounts, no minutes, and very little correspondence. Only the cathedral register, and those few pieces of correspondence, give any clues at all that court, college and cathedral were trying to live and work together. Courtiers, soldiers and canons were marrying, having families and dying. Students, when not occupied in digging the military defences around the city, or drilling in the quads, were still working for degrees but, much to their dismay, they were having to study and to labour for the Crown, on reduced rations. They had complained vehemently that it was not fair that they should only receive one meal a day under these difficult circumstances. Even though Christ Church had opened its doors to Charles, the college and cathedral silver was still lost to the royal coffers, and the college was expected to contribute substantial 'loans' to the war effort. The Dean and Canons did try to appeal to the Commissioners for Fortifications, seeking a more lenient assessment of their contributions to the defences of Oxford in view of the cost of providing for the king. Whether or not they were successful goes unrecorded.

After four long years the king departed, already aware that he had lost the war, but determinedly battling on. The arriving Parliamentarians soon began to clear out all those who had shown loyalty to the Crown. Even the Christ Church almsmen, resident in the house across St Aldates, who had fought for the king were ousted from their places and their rooms reoccupied by soldiers and sailors of the Parliamentary forces. Some Students were sent overseas on special missions for Cromwell, and

two letters survive in the archive, signed 'Oliver P', giving leave from studies and ensuring that their stipends were paid in their absence. One, George Annesley, had been given his studentship in 1647, at the same time as the Parliamentary visitation. He was a major in the Army, and his behaviour evidently affronted the Dean and Canons when he was found, evidently the worse for wear, in a 'tippling house' in the city. Annesley served overseas in Flanders from 1658 and drowned in the Thames, whether by his own hand or not will never be known, 40 days before the Restoration.

The Chapter minutes tell of all the replacements, including the installation of the new Dean. Samuel Fell had been imprisoned by Parliament, and died the day after the execution of Charles I, apparently of a broken heart. Mrs Fell, though, refused to vacate her home, and was evicted from the Deanery in the most undignified manner when two of the more Puritan canons carried the indomitable lady out into the quadrangle in her armchair. Fell's immediate replacement was Edward Reynolds, a Fellow of Merton, but Reynolds was evidently insufficiently radical, and he was soon replaced.

Previous page:
Top:
The seventeenth-century 'Jonah' window by Van Linge, donated to the cathedral in memory of Charles Sonnibancke, a canon of Windsor and a Censor of Christ Church. The window glass is painted, except for the figure of Jonah himself, which is stained glass
Bottom:
Peter Lely, *John Fell, John Dolben and Richard Allestree*, 1670s

Apart from a change in personnel, the obvious changes were in the cathedral; the organ and the 'idolatrous' windows portraying Bible stories were removed and destroyed. These beautiful windows, painted by the Dutch van Linge brothers paid for by individual Students and Canons, had only been installed over the past thirty years. Only the 'Jonah' window survived showing the prophet contemplating Nineveh. Perhaps the subject matter, a sinner rethinking his ways, was considered appropriate.

Student numbers began to increase, and business continued as normal, thanks to the second of the Commonwealth deans, John Owen. A flamboyant man, in appearance much more Cavalier than Roundhead, Owen saw the value of a softly, softly approach. John Fell, the son of the unfortunate Samuel, Richard Allestree (Regius Professor of Divinity, who left us his library for his successors), and John Dolben, once a major in the Royalist army, continued to hold Anglican services just down the road in Merton Street, right under the nose of the Dean, evidently with his tacit agreement. The deanship of John Owen ensured that Christ Church did not suffer too much from the exigencies of the Commonwealth.

At the Restoration, Christ Church returned to its pre-Rebellion days almost overnight. In fact, so little really needed to be done that the first priority was to reinstate the canons' table in the hall. John Fell was installed as Dean in 1660; ejected members, including the almsmen, were given back their places; records began to be kept exactly as they had been before 1642; and governance and education continued almost as if nothing had happened. Even Wolsey's building plan, abandoned in 1529, was picked up where it left off. Unfortunately, the cathedral windows were gone for good – or were they? Bits of glass were found back in the nineteenth century and were placed, almost for safe-keeping, in the upper windows of the north transept clerestory, and then more were found very recently. Enough, perhaps, to put together a whole picture, if only we could find an appropriate space.

Judith Curthoys

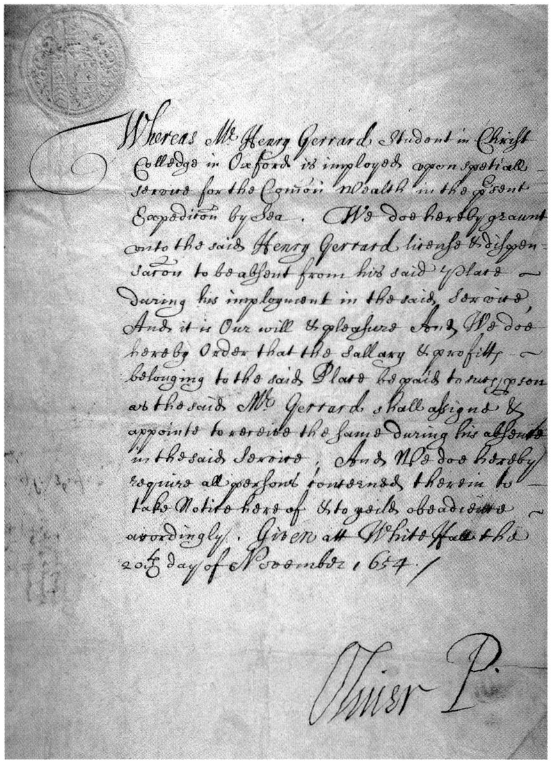
Whereas Mr Henry Gerrard Student in Christ Colledge in Oxford is imployed upon speciall service for the Common wealth in the present Expedition by Sea. Wee doe hereby graunt unto the said Henry Gerrard license & dispensation to be absent from his said place during his imployment in the said Service, And it is Our will & pleasure And Wee doe hereby Order that the Sallary & profitts belonging to the said Place be paid to such person as the said Mr Gerrard shall assigne & appointe to receive the same during his absence in the said Service, And Wee doe hereby require all persons concerned therein to take Notice hereof & to yeild obedience accordingly. Given att Whitehall the 20th day of November 1654.

Oliver P.

Right:
Letter of authority from Oliver Cromwell, Lord Protector, permitting Henry Gerrard to travel overseas in the service of the Commonwealth

Treasures

A medieval Oxford college had two principal sorts of assets, its lands and its plate. Both were treated in some degree as liquid. They were sold off in lean times and accumulated when conditions were more favourable. But among the latter a special place was accorded to the 'founder's plate', those objects in gold and silver which were given at the time of the college's foundation and which took on – in the eyes of its members – something of the quality of religious relics. This special status was surprisingly resilient, even through troubled times like the Reformation and the Civil War, and explains the extraordinarily large number of medieval and Renaissance treasures surviving in Oxford to this day.

At Christ Church things were different. Wolsey's college, had its founder lived to see his grand project through to completion, would doubtless have been more richly endowed with plate than any other college. Plate in the sixteenth century was universally seen as a measure of the status of its owner; Wolsey's holdings were second only to those of the king and he would certainly have wanted his college to reflect his own magnificence.

The only record of what this might have been is a list of some of his plate, preserved in the Upper Library. Compiled by his goldsmith, Robert Amadas, it details his purchases over several years around 1520 and totalling the astonishing sum of £5,002. It includes plate made for his own use, as New Year's

gifts to the king and foreign ambassadors, but also a number of pieces specificially for 'St Frideswide's College in Oxford'. Among these are splendid altar plate, a large salt, a seal, a 'great nut with a cover gilt and upon the cover an image of St Fridewide' and a 'great drinking horn garnished with silver and gilt standing upon three feet of an eagle'.

Whether any of this survived for long is not known. Probably it was forfeited to the Crown along with all of Wolsey's other assets, and when Henry VIII refounded the college it was certainly less well-

Previous page: alms dish from the Fell communion set, 1660–61

Left to right: chalice and paten, candlestick, and a flagon, all from the same 1660–61 service carrying marks for the maker PB and for the London assay office

endowed. But founders were not the only donors of plate, and we know from college records that a certain quantity had been accumulated by the end of the sixteenth century. Exactly what this amounted to is impossible to judge, but various fragmentary documents throw shafts of light onto the presence of plate in the college and the role it played in its business as well as its social life. From silversmiths' bills we see a steady stream of repairs to plate; from memoranda about a visit from the Prince Palatine in 1583 we learn of the 'xi pieces of plate wont to be used in festival dayes', but what these were and how long the college had owned them we cannot tell. Five years later we see plate being drafted into its other traditional role as business fixer when the college presented Secretary of State Burghley and Archbishop Whitgift with a silver cup each in thanks for their finding in the college's favour over some legal dispute.

From that time and indeed from the first half of the following century almost nothing survives. Entries in the college accounts continue to show regular acquisitions of plate, mostly small two-handled drinking vessels called 'college cups' but occasionally larger pieces such as a 111oz ewer and basin acquired in 1630. But the Civil War accounted in one way or another for the almost complete disappearance of these holdings. Charles I's enforced loan in 1642 resulted in Christ Church handing over 172lbs of plate, nor was this the only visitation. Before the king's arrival in Oxford Lord Saye had occupied the city with a Roundhead force and had himself threatened a cull of college plate. According to the diarist Anthony Wood, Christ Church was less than candid about its holdings and was punished accordingly: 'That night they founde out Christchurch plate hid in walles behinde wainescote & in the seller. It was carried awaye in the night time in a great cowle betwixt 2 men to my lord's lodginge at the Starre'. Whereas most colleges had their plate returned in exchange for certain undertakings, that was the last Christ Church saw of it, because it had 'byn hidden at the first'.

Subterfuge may have backfired in that case, but it is also the reason for the survival of what is now the only significant pre-Civil War silver at Christ Church, the luxuriously mounted covers to the cathedral's bible and prayer book, which were given in 1638 and saved from plunder by the spirited action of Dr Richard Gardiner, Canon of Christ Church, who removed them and kept them hidden away until the restoration of the monarchy in 1660.

It is with the Restoration that the history of Christ Church's existing plate really begins, and it is indeed a measure of the euphoria of the moment that the newly appointed Dean Fell decided to celebrate the return of the king and the re-establishment of the episcopal church with the commission of a magnificent service of altar plate for the cathedral. Other than the great service commissioned for the Chapel Royal and a similar

Top:
Silver rosewater dish, London, maker's mark TC, 1678

Bottom:
Bible (1632) and Book of Common Prayer (1636), with silver gilt mounts and clasps. Printed in London, and given to Christ Church by Canon Henry King (1592–1669), later bishop of Chichester

ensemble made for Bishop Cosin of Durham, it is the most spectacular service of its period.

The cathedral commission was an exceptional event, but the acquisition of plate for the college was a continuous process and one which nearly all originated through gift. Fell himself bequeathed one of the oddest pieces in the collection, a silver filigree box containing two mandrake roots, to the Library in 1686. Such a bequest was very much of its time. The poisonous mandrake was thought, even by the sophisticated Oxford mind, it seems, to possess magical powers. Such an attitude lay behind the formation of many sixteenth- and seventeenth-century 'cabinets of curioities', one of the most famous of which was given to the University by Elias Ashmole just three years earlier and became the foundation collection of the Ashmolean Museum.

More typical of college plate and its sources are two of the earliest and grandest secular pieces in the collection, both of which were gifts from aristocratic members: a large basin of 1678, given by the future marquess of Worcester, and an equally outsize tankard given in the following year by Sir Nicholas L'Estrange. Aristocratic gifts, fulsomely inscribed and often intended to serve the interests of the donor as much as the college, were always a breed apart in the college plate cupboard. Most gifts were much more modest and accumulated through a system known as 'plate money', in which undergraduates were expected to make a gift of a piece of plate or of money in lieu. These gifts were meticulously recorded during the late seventeenth and early eighteenth centuries and show an average income of around £10 a year from plate money. By 1683 there is once again much evidence of plate in college life. Silver was regularly lent out to the Dean and canons, and from that year there is also a note that twenty-five tankards and various other pieces had been lent out 'for the use of the Noble and Gentlemen Commoners'.

College plate came in for heavy use and doubtless abuse as well. As fashions changed or old pieces were deemed too worn for use, they were recycled or exchanged with the goldsmith for other things. But in the manner of American museums today, when pictures are de-accessioned and the original donor's name applied to the new purchase that replaces it, the original inscription from the melted piece was transcribed onto the new one, thus preserving the memory of the original gift. As a result, many pieces from one century bear inscriptions from another, such as a pair of 1770 salvers, inscribed as the gift of Sir John Sherard in 1681, or four entrée dishes of 1824, supposedly presented by the duke of Ormond in 1680 and the duke of Buccleuch in 1747.

Not all such benefactions were so piously remembered, nor was the Civil War the only time when the college silver was treated as a financial resource. The college plate repeatedly came to the aid of building and maintenance projects. In 1660 the

Dean and Chapter ordered that gentlemen commoners' plate be sold to fund the building of the north side of Tom Quad and in 1680 when the cost of the new Library was exceeding estimates, the shortfall was partly met by the disposal of 500 ounces of college plate. In 1760 it was the turn of the Hall roof to call in the silver, and a similar amount was sacrificed for the purpose. In all, some 4,500 ounces of silver were voluntarily melted down by the college in the eighteenth century, nearly twice the amount lost in the Civil War.

Plate money has long ceased to add to the burden of a student loan, and replenishment of this resource does not continue today as it did in the eighteenth century. It is true that new acquisitions have occasionally been added to the college's holdings over the last century. A rare sugar box of 1670, for example, was given in 1917 and Albert Carter, law tutor at the House from 1895 to 1927, singled out two items from his famous collection (most of which was left to the Ashmolean Museum) for Christ Church in 1945. Sadly, this aspect of the college's traditions seems to have reached an end, or at least an extended pause. In recent years Christ Church has not followed the example of other Oxford colleges in commissioning new works from some of today's talented silversmiths. But the college outlives us all and certainly outlives changes in fashion: perhaps this is an area in which attitudes will change.

Timothy Schroder (1972)

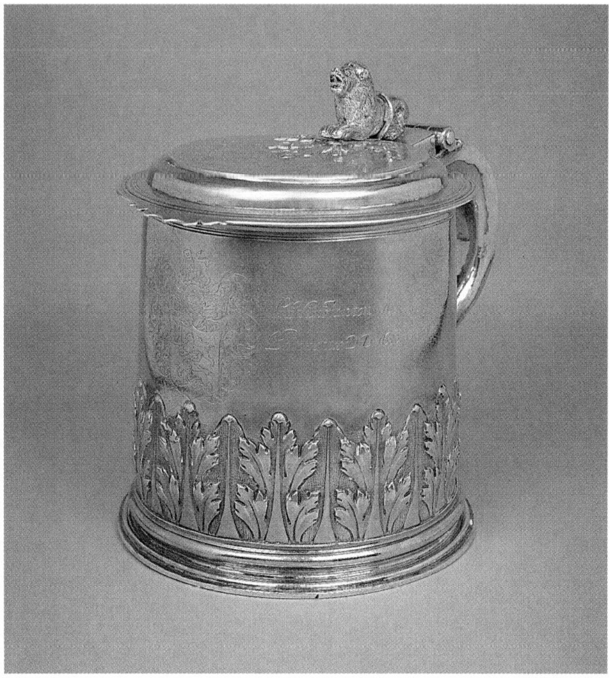

Top right: Silver tankard, London, maker's mark TC, 1679–80, given by Sir Nicholas l'Estrange

Bottom right: Francesco de Rossi, called Salviati, *Design for a sacred vessel*

Below: Silver filigree box, given to Christ Church by John Fell, and originally containing three mandrake roots

HENRY ALDRICH

'Architecture is the art of building well.'

Centre: Albrecht Dürer, *St Jerome in his study*, from the Aldrich collection

So begins *The Elements of Civil Architecture*, the work of Henry Aldrich (1648–1710), the dean whose epitaph could easily replicate that of his older contemporary, Christopher Wren: 'If you seek his monument, look around you' (Si monumentum requiris, circumspice). Aldrich, an amateur architect, designed Peckwater Quad, begun in 1705, and completed in 1711, one year after his death. Peckwater magnificently embodies the claims Aldrich immediately went on to make in his architectural treatise: 'The three chief properties of a good building are these, utility, strength, and beauty ... Beauty arises from parts handsome and necessary, correspondent to each other, and to the whole'. His architectural heroes, Vitruvius and Palladio, were also writers on architecture, whose principles he described in terms that reinforce his achievement in Peckwater: 'Buildings should be uniform; i.e. as they should be strong, so they should show their firmness. Those that are elegant should be conspicuously so.' What better summation of the incomparable qualities of Peckwater as a building!

Buildings are also monuments to social history, and Peckwater has something in it of the Palladian English country house transmuted into the similarly domestic requirements of a college building; it demonstrates in stone the role that Aldrich saw to it that the college played throughout the eighteenth century: it was the supremely elegant finishing school for the nobility, in which not only the intellect – and Aldrich was also the author of the standard *Logic* used in the University well into the nineteenth century – but also the tastes of the governing classes would be greatly improved. Aldrich's selection of illustrations of villas by Palladio had been undertaken according to their appropriateness in transplanting the great master's style to England, as Aldrich concluded that, 'Different tastes will of course approve different models: by an Englishman it has been deemed most proper to select those, which he apprehended would best suit the English manners.' Peckwater thus reflected Aldrich's notion of English taste, as well as helping to shape it for generations to come. Christ Church has subsequently fed the visual taste of many generations in a way of which Aldrich would have greatly approved: Peel, who had rooms in Peckwater, collected Dutch seventeenth-century paintings with great discrimination, and Ruskin, the greatest English commentator on art, lived in Tom Quad: might he have been more tolerant of classicism had he had his rooms in Peckwater? It was not only through building, however, that Aldrich educated his undergraduates (and his colleagues) in the arts: he also built up an extensive collection of prints and drawings, forming the nucleus of the collection that would ultimately constitute the Picture Gallery. Music, fittingly for a dean of Christ Church, was another of his abiding loves, and he was both an accomplished performer and also an accomplished practitioner, writing a good deal of liturgical music, as well as other, lighter pieces, such as one entitled 'O the bonny Christ Church bells'. His considerable, and lasting, achievements in transplanting into Christ Church the arts he relished during journeys to Italy were nicely commemorated in the somewhat pompous language of the late eighteenth century: 'The warm sun of Italy, the domesticity with congenial spirits he contracted there, exalted his inbred taste, and rendered it excursive through the whole field of arts. There he became impassioned for Architecture and Music, from such specimens of both as no other country can afford. That the impression was not merely local and momentary, his executed designs in the one, and his yet daily recited compositions in the other, would enable his historian to prove.' Tribute was paid to him as a person by many in the eighteenth century, who commented on his great humour as well as his considerable abilities; he was also a consummate politician. Becoming Dean in 1689 in the wake of the Glorious Revolution, he promoted the Tory interests of Church and State in all that he did, both in the college and in the University, sometimes in unpropitious circumstances in the first great age of party politics. Rather less extreme in his conservatism than his successor as Dean, the Jacobite Francis Atterbury, Aldrich became a model Queen Anne Tory in the final decade of his life, greatly benefiting the college and its role in national life in the process.

Brian Young

Peckwater Quad, completed in 1711

LOCKE

Godfrey Kneller, *John Locke*

As Anthony Quinton observes elsewhere in this volume, John Locke (1632–1704) is the greatest philosopher ever to have graced Christ Church; and since he is, arguably, the greatest philosopher England has ever produced, this is not a matter for purely local celebration. Locke was, like so many Christ Church men before and after him, a product of Westminster School, where he had been taught by Richard Busby, whose daunting bust sits atop the mantelpiece in the SCR, staring reprovingly across at a portrait of a scraggily sagacious Locke: is it quite fair, one wonders, posthumously to have a famous pupil eternally subject to the penetrating gaze of his former, and notoriously severe, headmaster? Locke originally prospered in the Christ Church where he had held a Studentship since 1652, and which witnessed the happy restoration of both the monarchy, in 1660, and the Church of England, in 1662. Only gradually, in the 1670s, would his politics become altogether more radical, and hence his position in a conservative society rather less secure. This process began when he grew close to Anthony Ashley Cooper, into whose London household he moved in 1667, and where he occasionally acted as his medical man (Locke, who had acquired medical degrees at Oxford, would take up a medical studentship at Christ Church in 1675; he had previously served as Senior Censor in 1664, a position commemorated in a window in Hall).

Locke's political radicalism has become increasingly apparent to historians in recent years. As is well known, the second of his *Two Treatises of Government* expounds the claim that a people has the right to rebel against a tyrannical governor, and, for a long time, this was understood as providing justification for the actions of the English people in rebelling, in 1688, against James II. Subsequent scholarship has demonstrated, however, that far from being the complacent *post facto* justification of the Glorious Revolution that it was long held to be, Locke's argument had in fact first been made during the Exclusion Crisis (1679 to 1681), when Protestant leaders, including Lord Shaftesbury (as Cooper had become), attempted, without success, to exclude the Catholic James, Duke of York, from the succession to the throne. This was as about as dangerous a proposition to promote as could be imaginable at the time; it was altogether less so when the treatises were finally published in 1689, after Locke had returned from a judiciously self-imposed exile in Holland, where he had gone in the wake of the 'Tory reaction' of 1681–85, the final four years of Charles II's reign. In 1684 Locke had been notoriously and very ignominiously expelled from his Studentship at Christ Church, a grave, if historically comprehensible, blot on Christ Church's learned escutcheon.

Locke quietly flourished following the Glorious Revolution, when he published the works that have subsequently made his name. Alongside the anonymous – and never acknowledged during his lifetime – publication of the political treatises, there appeared, in 1690, his greatest claim to fame, *An Essay Concerning Human Understanding*. This work begins with a famously modest appeal to the reader, in which the anonymous author sets himself up, not as a philosophical system-builder, but as a mere 'under-Labourer', engaged in the task of 'removing some of the Rubbish that lies in the way to Knowledge'. This under-labourer found rather a lot of rubbish. Most importantly, he attacked the notion of innate ideas, claiming that far from being born with ideas, human beings were originally born with a mental blank slate, a *tabula rasa*, on which experience gradually inscribed itself. He also speculated in the *Essay*, rather dangerously, on the possibility of thinking matter, a hypothesis briefly bypassing the conventional notion of an immaterial soul (central to the thought of Descartes and others), and this led in turn to much discussion of materialist explanations of the nature of the human mind throughout the eighteenth century – and beyond: would it be too much to adduce such later Christ Church philosophers as Gilbert Ryle – especially as expounded in his great work, *The Concept of Mind* (1949), one of the most gracefully written of philosophical treatises – and also A.J. Ayer and Anthony Quinton, as the eloquent exponents of a Christ Church materialist school? It is certainly pleasing to think that, in clerical Christ Church, such a radical understanding of the mind has been regularly promoted by its philosophers since the time of Locke.

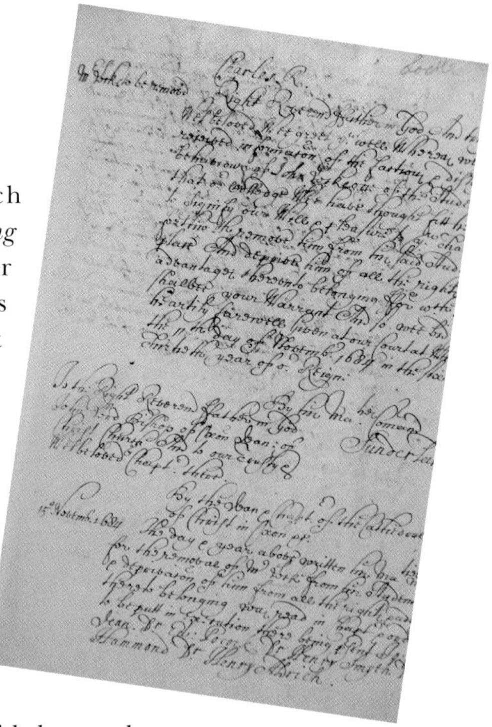

Copy of a letter from Charles II to the Dean and Chapter, recorded in the Chapter Book, requiring the expulsion of Locke, dated 11 November 1684

There is also much humour in *An Essay Concerning Human Understanding*, whether intentional or otherwise. Is there a finer index entry – at least before that supremely Christ Church scholar Hugh Trevor-Roper began a very particular promotion of this potentially mischievous industry in his own writings – than this: 'Parrot, holds a rational discourse'? The *Essay* is also both a new world, and a reflection of the New World: he was keen on examples from the writings of explorers, and the Americas, in particular, afforded many instances for his arguments. He had enjoyed his own engagement with America, when he had had a hand in writing the fundamental constitution for the Carolinas in the early 1670s. Appeal was later to be made to his political thought in the era of the American Revolution, though historians are divided as to how significant, typical, or frequent, such appeals actually were.

Locke was, in his own way, a pious Christian, and there is much space for God in the argument of the *Essay*. He was an early advocate of religious toleration; he advocated a doctrinally minimal version of Christianity in a tract entitled *The Reasonableness of Christianity*, which provoked much controversy in the 1690s. Locke seems to have entertained anti-Trinitarian ideas, in common with his occasional friend, Isaac Newton. He also wrote influentially on education, and on the burgeoning science of political economy.

Locke's contemporary reputation was decidedly complicated, but he quickly became a paragon of philosophical moderation in eighteenth-century England, and even conservative Christ Church was sufficiently reconciled to him to commission a languorously elongated statue of him by Rysbrack, which adorns the stairs of the Library.

Brian Young

Three Scientists

Unattributed, *Charles Boyle, earl of Orrery*

Hooke

Robert Hooke (1635–1703) came to Christ Church in Commonwealth times (1653) and, along with his contemporaries John Locke and Christopher Wren, was engaged in scientific studies, initially with Thomas Willis. Already this group was showing much originality and then it joined a more senior 'invisible college' around John Wilkins at Wadham, to which Robert Boyle also came.

Hooke became Boyle's assistant, and out of their investigations came Boyle's Law, which would play a fundamental role in the industrial age in the following century.

The founding of the Royal Society at the Restoration drew all three into its membership and Hooke, as its Curator of Experiments, was probably the first salaried scientific investigator. His inventiveness was boundless, as he made outstanding contributions to mechanics, astronomy and other fields, but pre-eminently to miscroscopy, in his magnum opus *Micrographia* published in 1665.

Robert Hooke was the most ingenious person ever to come to the House, and many of his inventions are still in use today.

Paul Kent

Orrery

Charles Boyle (1674–1731) came up to Christ Church in June 1690 and took his BA in 1694. Charles was the grand nephew of Robert Boyle, who discovered the Pressure Law, and is memorialised on a plaque on the wall of University College on the High Street. On the death of his father in 1703 he became the fourth earl of Orrery. As well as being a military man and Jacobite politician he was a gentleman scientist. He collected scientific instruments including armillary spheres, microscopes and telescopes, and supported instrument makers through commissioning new instruments. He became a Fellow of the Royal Society in 1706.

Mechanical devices to illustrate the relative motions of the earth, moon and planets around the sun were already known at the time John Rowley built the tellurium for the fourth earl of Orrery in 1712–13 that is now in the Science Museum. It, and all subsequent instruments, were given the name orrery after its owner.

The orrery pictured was designed to illustrate the motions of the earth, moon, mercury and venus. It was commissioned by the fourth earl shortly before his death in 1731 from Rowley's apprentice, Thomas Wright. Orrery bequeathed this instrument to Dr Robert Friend, headmaster of Westminster School who later became a canon of Christ Church. It is now housed in the Museum of the History of Science on Broad Street, along with the extensive collection of Orrery's scientific instruments which are elegantly displayed in the south-east corner of the entrance gallery. These collections, on loan from Christ Church, along with the 10,000 volume collection of books housed in the upper gallery of the Old Library, were bequeathed by Orrery to Christ Church after relations with his legitimate son John had broken down. The fourth earl apparently claimed that John lacked the 'inclination either for entertainment or knowledge which study and learning afford'. The concept of the orrery was extended as new planets were discovered, and they can still be purchased as teaching aids. Their modern equivalents are the widely available computer programmes that generate maps of the sky with precise positions of the sun, moon, planets and stars for any given date and time.

Roger Davies

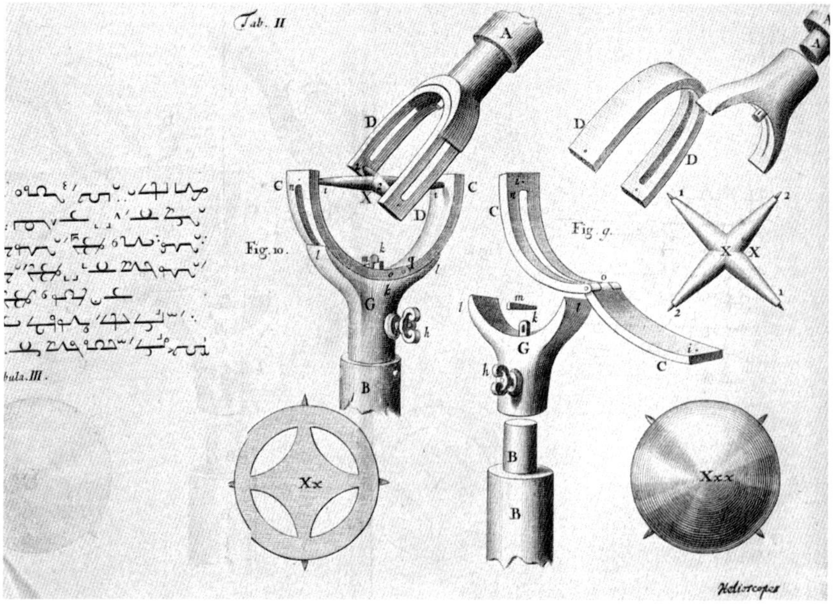

Above:
Robert Hooke's universal joint, from *A description of helioscopes*, 1676

Left:
Francis Chantrey (after William Owen), *Cyril Jackson*, 1824

Above:
A model of the near solar system, commissioned by the earl of Orrery in 1731, and named after him, which was designed by Thomas Wright, and bequeathed to Christ Church in the same year

Right:
An air pump, from Robert Hooke, *New experiments in physico-mechanicall*, 1660

Jackson

Cyril Jackson, FRS (1746–1819) was one of Christ Church's remarkable deans in remarkable times. He was a gifted mathematician, a well-informed botanist and an influential leader who did much to advance the academic and social standing of the House.

Jackson had wide interests outside Oxford: he attended meetings of the Lunar Society in Birmingham, was friends with Edinburgh scientists such as Joseph Black, and did much to support Boulton and Watt in their engineering advances.

As a figure well placed with respect to the royal circle, he was able to use his influence in the interest of good causes. It is said that he was offered numerous bishoprics, even the Primacy of Ireland, all of which he declined, preferring to remain in the deanery. At the end he was offered the bishopric of Oxford which he also declined saying 'Try Will [his brother]; he'll take it'. He did, and William Jackson was bishop of Oxford from 1812 until 1815.

Paul Kent

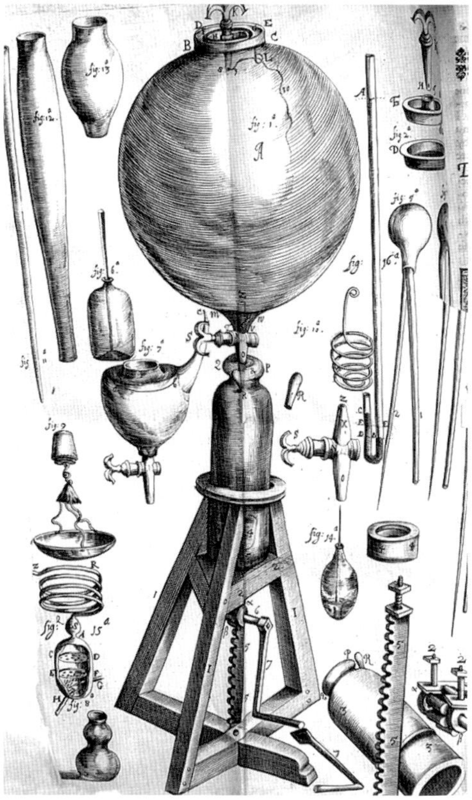

WESLEY

If Christ Church was refounded by the unintentional founder of the Church of England, one of its most distinguished religious figures was likewise to become the reluctant founder of a new denomination, one that broke off from the Church of England in the very late eighteenth century. John Wesley (1703–1791), the founder of Methodism, whose deeply sympathetic portrait hangs in Hall – making it a focus of Wesleyan pilgrimage – was as unlikely a promoter of dissent as had been the young William Penn, later a leading Quaker and the founder of Pennsylvania, who had studied at Christ Church between 1660 and 1662 (the young John Locke, it seems likely, had taught him Greek). Wesley, then a High Church High Tory of the type usual in eighteenth-century Christ Church, took up a fellowship at Lincoln College in 1726, two years after graduating BA, and three years before his younger brother, Charles, the holder of a Westminster scholarship, was elected a Student of Christ Church in 1727. (Charles was to become one of the most prolific and inspired of English hymn-writers, many of whose justly celebrated hymns are still sung in the cathedral today. 'Love Divine, All Joys Excelling' and 'Hark! The herald angels sing' can memorably suffice for illustrative purposes). Just as Penn would take his religious principles with him when establishing his American colony, so the young Wesley began to think most seriously about religion when at work in the newly founded state of Georgia in the 1730s. On his return, and after a personal conversion to vital religion, Wesley began his ministry amongst the poor, all too often neglected by the Church in an age of proto-industrialisation: the subsequent intensity and powerful authority of his ministry was quite without parallel. A deeply charismatic figure, Wesley preached in the open air throughout England and Ireland, gaining a great following amongst those desirous of discovering the many consolations of religion in an increasingly secular culture. Although himself indebted to the Enlightenment (his thinking had its Lockean strain, and he wrote an influential medical textbook: where Locke was a physician-philosopher, Wesley was a physician-priest), Wesley primarily spoke to the heart, and the enormously authentic emotional conviction of his preaching was the key to the immediacy of its success. Such was the eventual growth of his movement that Wesley had perforce to become a great administrator as well as preacher, and his one-man publishing industry at The Foundry in London led to a phenomenal production of books, both original and edited. Wesley was undoubtedly the greatest religious figure in eighteenth-century Britain, and acts as a bridge between the age of Enlightenment and that of religious revival. Although naturally dedicated to serious ends and purposes, Wesley was also happily known to his friends and his intimates for his humour and cheerfulness. In common with another Christ Church preacher to the working people of England, John Ruskin, who yet

George Romney,
John Wesley, 1788/9

described himself as 'a violent Tory of the old school', Wesley's particularly religious variety of Toryism led him to empathise with the plight of the poor in a Whig England dedicated overmuch to prosperity and self-satisfaction (fashionably registered as 'politeness'), and his political theology would ultimately leave a fairly radical inheritance to Methodism. As was famously said by a later leader of the British labour movement, British socialism owed more to Methodism than to Marx (and, incidentally, not a little to Ruskin). Wesley's legacy is, then, a considerable one, both nationally and internationally.

Brian Young

The Picture Gallery

The collection in the Picture Gallery was built up from successive acts of outstanding generosity. It was formed over the last three hundred years from gifts of works of art acquired by a remarkable series of collectors. Although the drawings and paintings for which the gallery is now famous are housed in a modern building, the origins of the collection are quite different.

Christ Church can count a number of collectors and artists among its past undergraduates, ranging from Sir Dudley Carlton (1573–1632), an important ambassador and agent for the connoisseurs of the Stuart court (his full-length portrait is in Hall) to John Ruskin, the art critic and draughtsman, who had a profound influence on nineteenth-century cultural life. But it is not from such obvious sources that the college's collections derive. The commemorative collections – such as the memorials in the cathedral, the portraits in the Hall, and the marble busts in the Library – record the appearance and celebrate the achievements of the many churchmen, statesmen and scholars who have studied and taught in the college. The Hall portraits are not just a gallery of *huomini illustri*, but feature works by painters of the calibre of Gainsborough, Reynolds, Millais and Watts.

The collection that is now displayed and cared for in the Picture Gallery consists chiefly of a series of collections of Old Master paintings, drawings and prints that were bequeathed or given to Christ Church. The earliest and perhaps least known of these collections consists of the 2500 prints bequeathed to the college by Henry Aldrich (1648–1710). As well as being one of the most memorable deans of Christ Church (1689–1710) Aldrich was also an architect, classical scholar, and collector of books, and musical manuscripts. His collection of prints includes examples of works by Mantegna, Marcantonio Raimondi and Dürer, as well as English mezzotints and French portraits. The immense scholarly interest of the collection lies in the fact that it largely survives in its original albums, and so provides an invaluable insight into the arrangements and presentation of a late seventeenth-century print collection.

Above:
Corrado Giaquinto,
St Joachim

Right:
Andrea del Verrocchio,
Head of a young woman

The second collection that came to Christ Church was that of General John Guise (1682/3–1765). Guise was an undergraduate during the time when Aldrich was Dean, and his interest in art may well have derived from studying Aldrich's print collection. The combination of a military career with a passion for collecting was unusual, but Guise established himself as a discerning connoisseur, and formed part of a circle of the most important collectors of his day. Horace Walpole described him as 'a very brave officer, but apt to romance, and a great connoisseur of pictures'. His bequest to Christ Church which consists of almost 2000 drawings and more than 200 paintings, mainly from the Italian schools of the fifteenth to the eighteenth century, makes him one of the greatest artistic benefactors of the eighteenth century. The collection includes works by Leonardo, Michelangelo, Raphael, Bellini, Tintoretto, and paintings by Veronese, Tintoretto and Carracci. The bequest was the earliest donation of a major art collection to a college.

In 1828 and 1834 the Hon. William Thomas Horner Fox-Strangways (1795–1865) gave to his former college a group of thirty-seven 'primitive Italian' paintings. Fox-Strangways (uncle of the pioneer photographer William Henry Fox-Talbot) had joined the diplomatic service and travelled extensively in Europe, but above all it was during his time in Florence (1825–28) and Naples (1828–32) that he thoroughly indulged his love of 'picture hunting'. Interestingly, he concentrated his hunt on Italian paintings from before 1490, works which many then regarded as historical curiosities, rather than as works of art. Perhaps one of the finest works that came to Christ Church with his collection is Filippino Lippi's *Wounded Centaur*.

A further twenty-six early Italian paintings were given to Christ Church in 1897, by the great-nieces of the writer and poet Walter Savage Landor (1775–1864). His collection, which seems to have been brought together more through an altruistic instinct to rescue the works rather than an art historical interest, complements the Fox-Strangways gift, and includes a splendid predella panel by Giovanni di Paolo (active 1420–82).

The last significant bequest of paintings came to Christ Church just before the opening of the

Clockwise from top left: Annibale Carracci, *The butcher's shop*; Giovanni di Paolo, *Calvary*; Frans Hals, *Portrait of a woman*

dedicated gallery building in 1966. Sir Richard Lysle Nosworthy, KCMG (1885–1966) left Christ Church eleven pictures, including works by Salvator Rosa (1615–1673) and Gaspar Dughet (1615–1675).

When these individual collections arrived at Christ Church, they found their place in the Lower Library, which was divided into six compartments in which the paintings could be displayed. By the late 1960s the college became aware of the need to catalogue and to house properly what by then had grown into one of the most distinguished Old Master collections in the country. The acuteness of the case can be illustrated by the fact that some of the most important works were housed in locations appropriate to their themes but far from ideal in terms of conservation – Annibale Carracci's *Butcher's Shop*, for example, hung in the college's Tudor kitchens!

Funding for the gallery building was generously provided by Charles (now Lord) Forte, and the then Dean agreed to part with a third of his garden in order to allow space for the gallery. This is an uncompromising modern structure by the architects Powell and Moya, and it was finally opened by the Queen in 1968. Now a prize-winning and listed building, it was by no means uncontroversial at the time of its building.

Once the gallery was opened, its collection was enriched with further gifts, including an important group of eighteenth-century English glass (the Harding Bequest, 1968) and eighteenth- and nineteenth-century Russian icons (the Patterson Gift, 1980). Most recently, the gallery made its first acquisition, and purchased a preparatory drawing relating to a painting of the *Birth of the Virgin* by the Neapolitan artist Corrado Giaquinto, which is already in the collection. This acquisition was made with the help of several generous donations.

The art historian James Byam Shaw undertook the task of cataloguing the main collection (1967 and 1976), and his catalogues are still the essential

Right:
Filippino Lippi,
The wounded centaur;

Far right:
Salvator Rosa,
A rocky landscape with soldiers studying a plan

guides to the collection of Old Master drawings and paintings in the Picture Gallery, although by now in some need of revision in the light of recent scholarship.

The Gallery meets modern expectations about what a public museum should be and do; and its essential character – as a remarkable series of private bequests and gifts – has been retained. As so many important early collections have been dispersed, their survival intact within Christ Church has made the collection more significant than ever.

Christopher Baker and Jacqueline Thalmann

Memories of James Byam Shaw

To some undergraduates of my time, 1966–9, James Byam Shaw may have seemed a remote figure, his elegance that of an earlier generation whose standards he so consistently maintained. From rooms in Tom and subsequently in the deanery, he worked first on his catalogue of the Christ Church pictures and then on its more monumental successor, that of the drawings.

These projects constituted a coda to Jim's distinguished career as director of Colnaghi's and doyen of the Old Master drawings world: they coincided too with the happy years of his successful third marriage to Christina Gibson. A contemporary of mine was astonished to see the two walking hand in hand past the Library: he might have been equally surprised to learn that so generous a scholar judged men by the polish of their shoes.

Jim became a friend in 1962, when he was fifty-nine and I a boy of thirteen at Westminster. Not long after my arrival as an undergraduate, he asked if I would like to help with some of the more routine work on the picture catalogue, for in those days he had no official assistant. Work on Powell and Moya's Picture Gallery was in progress and the bulk of the collection was stored in Dr Lee's Building. Looking at pictures – or drawings – with Jim was always rewarding. His measured judgement was perfectly expressed in his inimitable terms. He had no taste for experts whose attitude to attributions was competitive. If he observed 'I rather think it is by the *man*', you were left in no doubt of his conviction.

When I arrived many lesser pictures still had to be accessed, and much measuring to be done.

Jim's methods were straightforward. Every picture was represented by an upright card, on which the available information was set out in his clear writing. All references and the views of scholars who visited Oxford were punctiliously recorded. But as the final entries demonstrated, there was nothing second-hand about Jim's sense of quality or connoisseurship.

The college was fortunate that Jim's work on the picture catalogue coincided with the completion of the Picture Gallery. Jim was in close sympathy with the work of the architects, with its emphasis on natural light for pictures, although not of course for the drawings. With his assistance, the building was perfectly calculated for the collection, with the early Italian pictures being placed in the first narrow room, and the great Renaissance and Baroque pictures in the main gallery and in the L-shaped space round the area reserved for the drawings. Jim was not shy of double hanging and understood that small panels are not served by being placed in quarantine against expanses of white walls. He gave the collection a rhythm and a coherence, which in my opinion has been diminished by most subsequent alterations to its arrangement. But Jim certainly welcomed one of these changes, the arrival of the restrained Hals portrait, which had to be excluded from his catalogue as it was deemed to belong to the Senior Common Room.

Francis Russell (1966)

T.M. Rowlandson,
James Byam Shaw,
1929

Food and Drink

Annibale Carracci,
A boy drinking

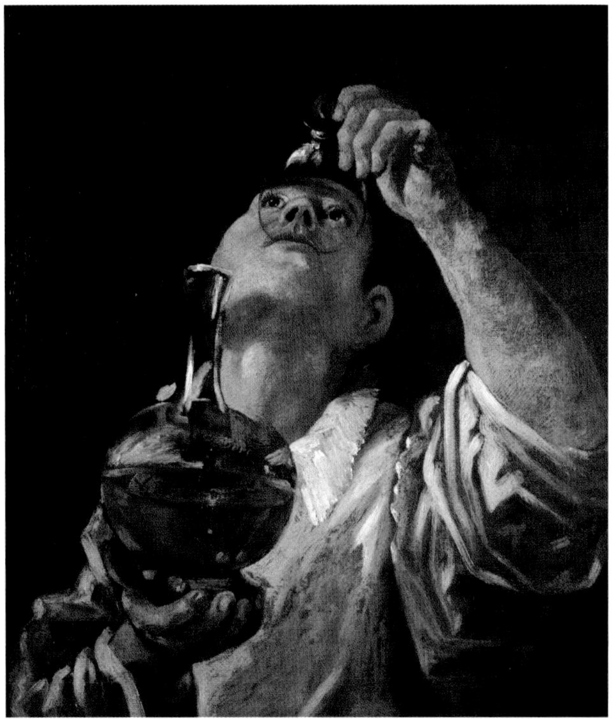

Food and drink have always been important at Christ Church. An army, said Napoleon, marches on its stomach, and the same can surely be said of an academic institution. Without good nourishment, no real research can be undertaken, no essays written, and no accounts properly kept. Right from the beginning, lists of victuals bought and consumed at the House occupy the pages of the college's records, from the daily bread and beer to the expensive and rich items brought in for great banquets and special occasions.

Much to the critical amusement of his enemies, Cardinal Wolsey ensured that the kitchen and the dining hall were the first buildings completed when he first began to build, in 1525, on the site of the old priory. The size of both reflected the grandness of his design. Although Wolsey's statutes stated that meals were not to be lingered over, the Hall was expected to be a place were men gathered around the open fire on cold evenings for useful conversation and entertainment.

Soon after Christ Church was founded, the college was blessed, during the 1560s and 1570s, with a manciple with a passion for record-keeping. John Furnivall kept a detailed account of his purchases for the kitchen day in and day out. Supplies arrived every day of the week, including Sundays and feast days. He purchased eggs, butter, cream by the gallon, mutton in every conceivable joint, whole veal and pigs, chickens, geese, game birds, fruit and wine. There were two fish days during the week – Fridays, and Wednesdays too – with an equal variety on both: ling was the commonest but there was also salmon, skate, cod (both fresh and salt), haddock, eels, whiting, pickerells, oysters and crayfish.

In the last three months of 1583, the kitchen took delivery of £87 worth of bread, 308 kilders of beer at 22d per kilder, £11 worth of butter, and for the Hall sixty-two dozen candles and eighteen

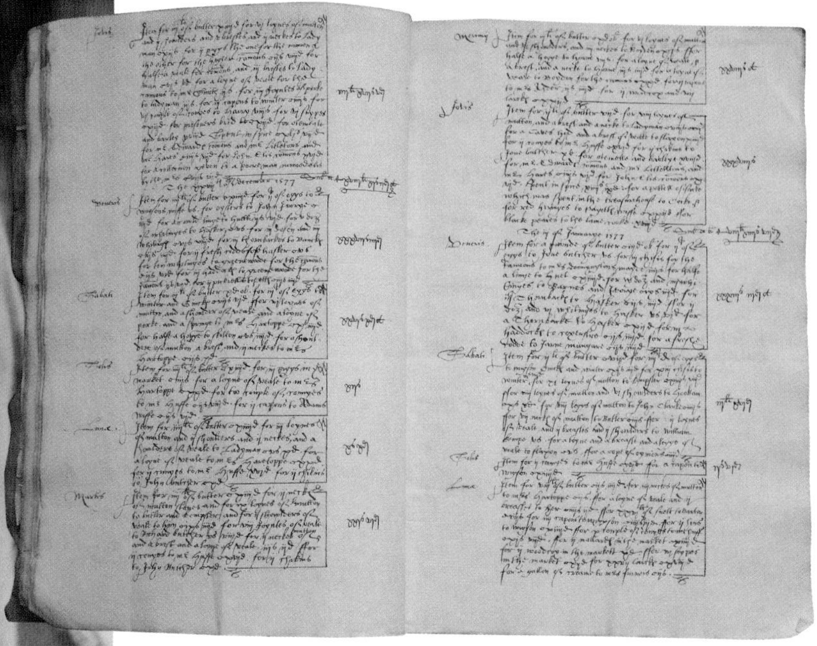

Left:
C.H. Green,
head chef from
1888 to 1916;
Right:
Pages from the
manciple's daily
purchasing lists in
the 1560s

napkins. One hundred old lings were purchased for £9, and the carriage of those fish cost another 24 shillings. But it was sheep that formed the backbone of the Christ Church diet in the sixteenth century; on 17 September 1583 the manciple bought sixty sheep at 6s 4d each from a Mr Elles and a further sixteen at the bargain price of 5s 4d each from Richard Howell of Wootton. Four days later another fourteen arrived. In October, 222 more were added to the stocks. Just to ring the changes, six bullocks were purchased in September. Then, Christ Church had its own slaughterhouse, so meat was bought on the hoof from markets in nearby towns such as Woodstock and Abingdon. The kitchen was regularly supplied with pots and knives; the Hall with drinking vessels, trenchers, tablecloths and napkins; and the buttery ensured that members would never go thirsty. The sixteenth and seventeenth centuries were the great era for royal and embassy visits to Christ Church. We know that banquets were provided for Elizabeth I in 1566 and again in 1592, the latter visit costing the college £127 10s 9d. Two hundred eggs were bought for the day of the banquet alone, but we have little evidence about the dishes offered to the queen. And all we can say from the visit of James at the end of August 1605 is that the wine cost 57s. It is possible that both had swan; during the sixteenth century, Christ Church had the right of swans on the Thames, and the gentleman to whom the rights were leased was obliged, with appropriate notice and the payment of 5s, to provide a swan for table. During the eighteenth century, some college chefs often supplied food for undergraduates to take back to their own rooms for parties – a much grander version of today's delivered pizza. Some even advertised in the local newspaper, and one New College cook ran a sausage-making business from the Wheatsheaf Inn.

But this was also the time of the grandest of dinners and, in 1793, Christ Church hosted some of the celebrations for the installation of the duke of Portland as Chancellor. The Chancellor lodged at Wadham College, and the duchess at Christ Church for a full week. On the afternoon of 4 July, a huge banquet was held in Hall. Turtle soup was one of the most popular dishes at Christ Church from the eighteenth century right into the twentieth, and legend has it that the turtle, which was brought live from London at a cost of 10s 6d just for the carriage, was put into Mercury until the time came for its slaughter, and the smaller of the canons' children were allowed to ride on the turtle's back. All sorts of provisions were brought in including green baize cloth for the tables, extra glassware, crockery and flatware, and additional mahogany tables and chairs. Orders were placed for melons and pineapples, for pies, jellies and other fruits. Agency staff, then as now, were required to serve the meal, which varied depending on the guests' importance. The noblemen, for example, had turbot in lobster sauce, followed by roast beef, lamb, duck, goose, chicken and veal pie, with a fool to finish. The chaplains, at the far end of the Hall, 'made do' with salmon, lamb, and peas. This enormous meal took place in the middle of the afternoon of 4 July, before a concert in the new Chancellor's honour at the Sheldonian Theatre.

Meals at Christ Church have always been appreciated but, as is usually the case in catering establishments, complaints have been made throughout the centuries. In 1596 the Students complained that their 9oz daily allowance of bread was insufficient. They were reprimanded for being greedy at this 'time of dearth' by no lesser men than the archbishop of Canterbury and the Lord Keeper of the Privy Seal. In 1643, with the Civil War in full swing, and with the king and court in residence at Christ Church, the Students once more berated the Dean and Chapter for reducing their commons to one meal a day 'farre below what they conceive as their due', especially as 'the greatest part of them [were] in Armes'.

At the beginning of the First World War, the senior members of Christ Church decided to follow the king's example and to give up alcohol for the duration. Meals were reduced when rationing was introduced in 1918 – meat was only served on Tuesdays and Thursdays, and guests were only permitted on 'meatless' days. The exigencies of war, however, did not stop the complaints: J.G.C. Anderson wrote in July to the Steward's secretary:

> *Turnip soup ... had better be avoided in the future. It is food for cows and there is absolutely no need to serve such stuff. Haddock is a fish that needs far more skilful handling than the Christ Church staff is capable of, to be palatable at all. The spaghetti was solid food but very uninteresting... I think the Ch. Ch. staff would do well to use a cookery book, as they appear not to have the slightest idea of what to serve.*

However, abstemious though the senior members were, the officers of the Royal Flying Corps, who were billeted at Christ Church, managed to make substantial inroads into the Common Room cellars.

There was one complaint, though, which had a more dramatic effect on Christ Church than its signatories imagined. In 1865 a petition against the cost and quality of food prompted the celebrated 'Bread and Butter row'. From about 1600, the food and drink that undergraduates consumed was purchased wholesale by the butler, the manciple and the cook, who then charged the students whatever price they felt they could get away with. The butler was making a sixty per cent profit on the market price of bread and butter. Cost was not the only issue; according to the 108 undergraduates who signed the petition of 4 March 1865, the quality of dinners and the beer was well below par. The matter reached the

Jim Godfrey, *Roland Dépit, head chef since 1980*

press; correspondence appeared in *The Times* and other London papers – largely because one of the prime instigators of the petition was the eldest son of the proprietor of *The Times* – and, like so many small things that go public, the row took on bigger proportions than was originally intended. The debate became entangled with the wider issue of the constitution of the college. But, in its original intent, the petition of 4 March was successful; in December 1865 the office of Steward was created, whose responsibility would be for all the domestic arrangements within Christ Church. Catering staff would be remunerated by fixed salaries, and dinner costs would be fixed.

There have been a dozen stewards since the first. Today's oversees a broader department, one that includes custodians, to look after the tourists, and porters (male and female) to staff the two lodges and keep the place secure. The last twenty years have seen the accommodation grow too: as the House expands across the road to St Aldate's Quad, and beyond the Plain to the Liddell Building. There are now forty eight staircases, and a scout for each.

The Hall, kitchen and buttery are populated by the diligent descendants of the past catering staff, and the Steward's office by a manciple, who still superintends the purchase of food and drink, even if her own meticulous records are on a computer disk and not in a ledger.

The kitchen and Hall continue to provide food to members of the House, just as both have done for almost five centuries. This is more than a truism, and not something to be taken for granted. Today's undergraduate has plenty of eating choice, and Hall dining is not likely to be everyone's choice every night. This sharpens the caterer's appetite for a good turnout at two sittings of dinner, and the preservation of a long tradition. In some places Hall dining is becoming a minority interest. But not at the House, where the gavel bangs and grace is said daily 'at 7.15 p.m. by the Cathedral Clock', as the by-law has it.

Kitchen apprenticeships are still offered at Christ Church, bringing essential new talent – male and female – into the brigade each year. Head chef Roland Dépit, twenty five years in the House's service, supervises the whole thing with benign calm and fatherly control And he needs a talented brigade to cope with the vacations. Today there are no closed periods or quieter times. Business functions, weddings and banquets crowd the vacation and overlap into term. It is in meeting their culinary and dietary expectations, that the House's caterers extend their range and develop their skills. So the process of feeding members and guests has evolved and been modernised. The ingredients have changed too: no longer the high-protein meat diet of medieval times, when, presumably, even ovo-lacto-vegetarians were thin on the ground. No swans, no pickerells, ling or whole sheep, and no turtles in Mercury, though that early story may be substantiated by the presence to this day of two large turtle shells beside Wolsey's arms on the kitchen wall.

Judith Curthoys and John Harris

Left:
One of the fireplaces in the kitchen with the Christ Church arms, and two turtle shells

THE LIBRARY

The first library at Christ Church was set up in around 1562 in the former refectory of St Frideswide's Priory, a late fifteenth-century hall on the south side of the cloisters. Like other college libraries of the period, it was fitted with wooden lecterns to which the books were chained. These were mostly large Latin folios on theology and patristics; about 140 volumes are still in the library collections.

In 1610–11 the Old Library was refitted with bookcases, placed across the main axis of the room, each incorporating its own desk and bench as in Duke Humfrey's Library, and an elaborate painted ceiling was installed. The refurbishment was financed by Otho Nicolson, a wealthy Chancery lawyer, who is better known as the donor of the great water conduit which once stood at Carfax, Oxford's central crossroads. In addition to £800 for the restoration of the Old Library, Nicolson also gave £100 'to buy books'; in recognition of his generosity, his coat of arms is emblazoned on the cover of the new library Donors' Book, started in 1614, and his name appears prominently on the first page. The library was still chained at this date, and was divided into four sections: Theology, Arts, Law and Medicine. The earliest surviving catalogue, written in 1665, shows that Theology was the largest category, but that there were large numbers of books in all subjects. The library was reserved for the use of senior members of the foundation; there was no library provision for undergraduates until Christ Church opened a special reading room for them in 1884. This was in no way unusual: contemporaries plainly took it for granted that undergraduates would learn primarily from their tutors, and had neither the wish nor the need to have access to college or University libraries. Although the library did occasionally buy books, spending over £25 in 1676, the year of the great Bodleian duplicate sales, it was generally reliant on gifts, some of which were very large. These included 780 books from Robert Burton (appointed Librarian in 1624), author of *The Anatomy of Melancholy*. The collection expanded rapidly, and by the end of the seventeenth century the Old Library building was completely full. It was clear that a new building was required.

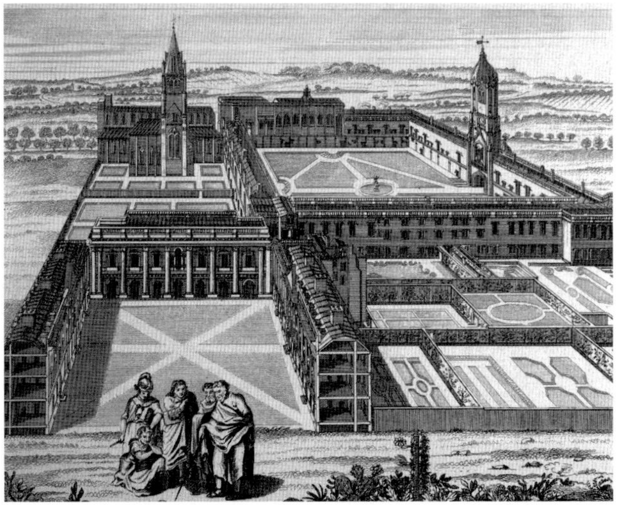

The New Library viewed from Peckwater Quad, 1724, in Joseph Skelton, *Oxonia Antiqua Restaurata*, 1823

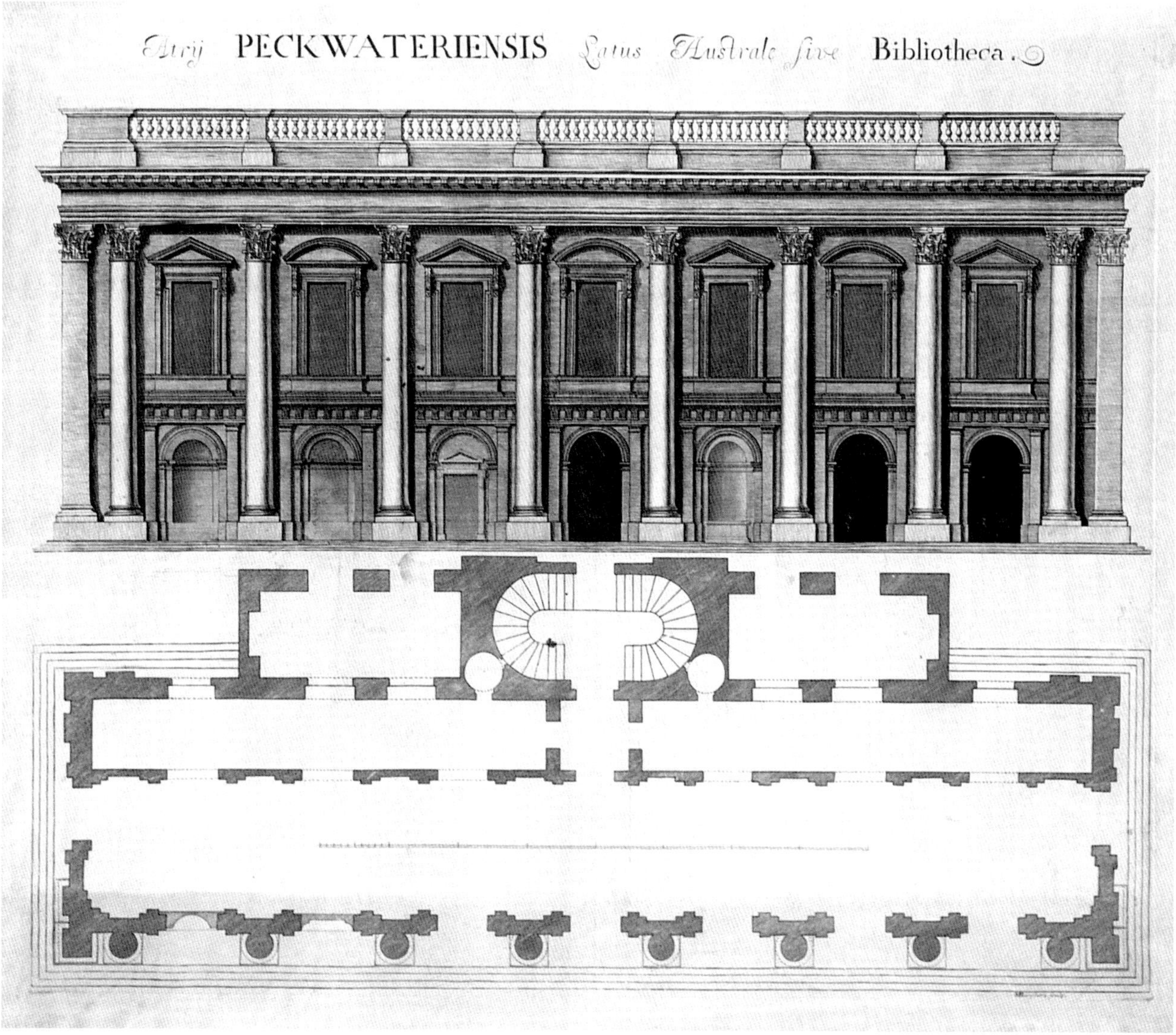

The New Library, designed by Dr George Clarke, from the portfolio of architectural drawings in the Library

Henry Aldrich, Dean of Christ Church from 1689 to his death in 1710, put forward a plan in 1705 for a building, derived from the Palace of Versailles, to complete Peckwater Quadrangle. The ground plan makes it clear that Aldrich envisaged a residential block, but he died before building work could begin. Aldrich bequeathed to the House a substantial collection of printed and manuscript music, twenty albums of fine prints, and a large collection of books on architecture. This gift seems to have precipitated the decision to build a new library, and on 20 September 1716 Canon Stratford wrote to Edward Harley that 'in our new building we shall observe Dr. Aldrich's model as to the case, but we design to turn the inside into a library and to make it the finest library that belongs to any society in Europe'. Aldrich's design was adapted by Dr George Clarke of All Souls, with master mason William Townsend (1668–1739), and early in 1717 the clearing away of the old buildings to make way for the New Library was begun. The new library cost a total of £15,517, the bulk of which (£13,312) was obtained from the 306 members of the House who gave an average of £43 each. The money came in over a long period of time, so that the Library Building Account was finally closed in 1779, sixty-three years after the beginning of construction.

The original plan was for a first-floor library, to avoid damp and flooding, with an open loggia on the ground floor, and the shell of the building was complete by the death of William Townsend in 1739. In the early 1750s, a gallery was inserted in the Upper Library to house the collection of Charles Boyle, fourth earl of Orrery, which had arrived in 1733, and at about the same period four windows in the north wall, two at each end, were concealed by bookcases to accommodate further bequests. In 1752 the execution of the plasterwork in the Upper Library was entrusted to Thomas Roberts, an excellent craftsman who had decorated many important buildings in Oxford and the surrounding district. He was paid £92 12s for the ceiling of the stairwell, and a further £663 11s 3d for the magnificent ceiling of the Upper Library. There were later payments for stucco work, which included the festoons depicting musical and scientific instruments on the north wall.

In the early 1760s, there was another major change of plan from the original design, caused by another benefaction, this time of paintings. General John Guise, a gentleman commoner and then a nobleman of Christ Church at the beginning of the century, drew up his will on 26 April 1760, leaving to the college a large collection of pictures and drawings. After his death in 1765, over 900 drawings arrived, followed in March 1767 by 258 pictures. The ground floor of the Library was still an open piazza with a stairwell leading to the great first-floor room, but under the supervision of the architect Henry Keene the arches were altered into windows, and the ground floor was converted into two large rooms, with a vestibule between them, in order to accommodate the paintings.

The Old Library continued to function during the eighteenth century, while the New Library was undergoing construction, but finally in 1763 books began to go onto the shelving in the new building. Christ Church had received several very large bequests during the early part of the eighteenth century. Lewis Atterbury the younger, brother of the Dean, gave 3,500 pamphlets; Canon William Stratford bequeathed almost 5,000 volumes; Charles Boyle, fourth earl of Orrery, gave a very large collection of books and scientific instruments; and the largest single collection of all was received from William Wake, archbishop of Canterbury from 1716 until his death in 1737. Wake left to the college his printed books, his papers (personal

Upper Library

and official), a large collection of Greek manuscripts, and his collection of coins. Wake's books fill the wall beneath the Orrery gallery, facing on the opposite wall the collections of Nicolson, Aldrich, Stratford and John Morris, Regius Professor of Hebrew, who died in 1648 and who set up a trust fund providing £5 annually to buy books for the study of Hebrew. The addition of these gifts to the existing volumes in the Old Library meant that nearly all the shelves of the New Library were filled as soon as they were installed by the carpenters; only a few gaps remained in the Orrery gallery. The small south rooms were filled with Wake's manuscripts and his coins (the latter now on deposit at the Ashmolean Museum), the music of Aldrich, Orrery's scientific instruments (now on deposit in the Museum of the History of Science, in Broad Street), travel books and pamphlets. The remaining books from the Old Library were unchained, and the Old Library was finally empty by 1770. Five years later it was converted into residential accommodation.

For over a century after its completion, the New Library was used as its builders had intended: the senior members referred to its books, signing out those which

Mrs SHOWWELL.
The Woman who shews General Guise collection of Pictures at Oxford
After an etching by T. NEWTON

Above:
Mrs Showell, who took guided tours of the Guise collection of pictures in the early nineteenth century

they needed in borrowers' registers; occasionally privileged undergraduates were 'indulged' with permission to use the volumes; and visitors were allowed in to view the works of art on the ground floor. At the beginning of the nineteenth century, tours of the paintings were conducted by the Library's janitor and charwoman, Mrs Showell. The Library continued to receive gifts, inevitably including many duplicate copies. Persistent calls for more shelving space led to the first of several duplicate sales in 1793. Annual expenditure on books steadily increased during the nineteenth century, reflecting a sustained effort to build up the various collections: in the last years of the Old Library, about £30 was spent annually, but this rose to £70 in the 1760s, £144 in 1802, and by the 1820s it averaged £250. The modern books were shelved at the east end of the ground floor, with limited space for expansion on account of the paintings. In 1869 certain pictures in a bad state were 'condemned, rolled up, and stored away', according to a Governing Body minute. This allowed the introduction of a Venetian Gothic gallery in oak, designed by Thomas Newenham Deane, the architect of Meadow Buildings, thereby providing much needed shelving. In 1898 the Library received a very appropriate gift through the generosity of a few members of the House, led by Rev. A.W. Oxford: Cardinal Wolsey's hat. It has a provenance from 1710, when it was found in the Great Wardrobe by Bishop Burnet, who was then Clerk of the Closet; it subsequently belonged to Horace Walpole, and was purchased after Walpole's death for £21 by Charles Kean, the actor, who is supposed to have worn it more than once when playing the part of Wolsey in Shakespeare's *Henry VIII.* After Keane's death, it was bought by Rev. Oxford and his friends for £63, and was presented to the Library, where it still resides in a splendid Gothic case, reflecting the style of Walpole's Strawberry Hill.

As in the Old Library, graduates, noblemen and gentlemen commoners were admitted to the New Library, but no other undergraduates, except 'on the common footing of strangers'. In 1884 the needs of undergraduates reading for the Honour Schools were finally met by the setting up of a Reading Room in Tom 4.2. Certain books were transferred from the Library to form the nucleus of a collection, and an annual sum of £35 was expended on new books after an initial payment of £100. In the late 1920s, this rather unsatisfactory arrangement came to an end, when the books were reabsorbed into the main Library collections, and the Reading Room became a Law library. In the 1960s, the new Picture Gallery was built in Canterbury Quadrangle, and the remaining works of art were removed thither, allowing the western half of the ground floor to be shelved for undergraduate use. The Library still retains a number of paintings, chiefly portraits, on the walls above the bookcases, but the chief function of the lower rooms is now to house the modern books used by current undergraduates and postgraduates. Between 1960 and 1962, the north, east and west faces of the New Library building were refaced in Portland Shelly Whitbed and Bath stones, replacing the original Headington stone which had weathered very badly. The stairwell and vestibule were redecorated in 1957 in an intriguing apricot colour, and in 1964–66 it was the turn of the Upper Library: after much debate, a scheme by John Fowler was chosen, in 'Neapolitan pink', with extensive gilding of Thomas Roberts's plasterwork. The result is generally agreed by all visitors to be a very happy choice, for a magnificent building.

Janet McMullin

Estates

In 1726 Canon Thomas Tanner travelled to East Walton in Norfolk to resolve disputes over Christ Church's land ownership in the parish. Things had become rather confused; the Dean and Chapter had their idea of what they owned, land agents and lawyers had theirs, and the tenants and sub-tenants, who worked the fields daily, had yet other thoughts. Tanner struggled to sort things out; the principal tenants and their stewards were reluctant to part with relevant documents, so our worthy canon was obliged, not only to turn to a survey which was 250 years old, but also to loosen the tongues of the men who laboured on the estate, with beer and strong ale.

Tanner was only partially successful. He did manage to collect some documents to bring back to Oxford, only to lose them over the side of his boat into the Thames – where they stayed for a full day before they could be recovered, and still today showing the signs of their submersion – but there was still a muddle over boundaries and lost acres for many years to come.

The worthy canon's experiences were not uncommon; Christ Church's management of its estates was always fraught with difficulties. In 1546 Henry VIII endowed college and cathedral with property in over 180 separate parishes across England and Wales, from north Yorkshire to Devon, and Montgomeryshire to Norfolk, reaping an astonishing income for the time of over £2,000 per annum. Some was real estate, but other property came in the form of tithes, manorial

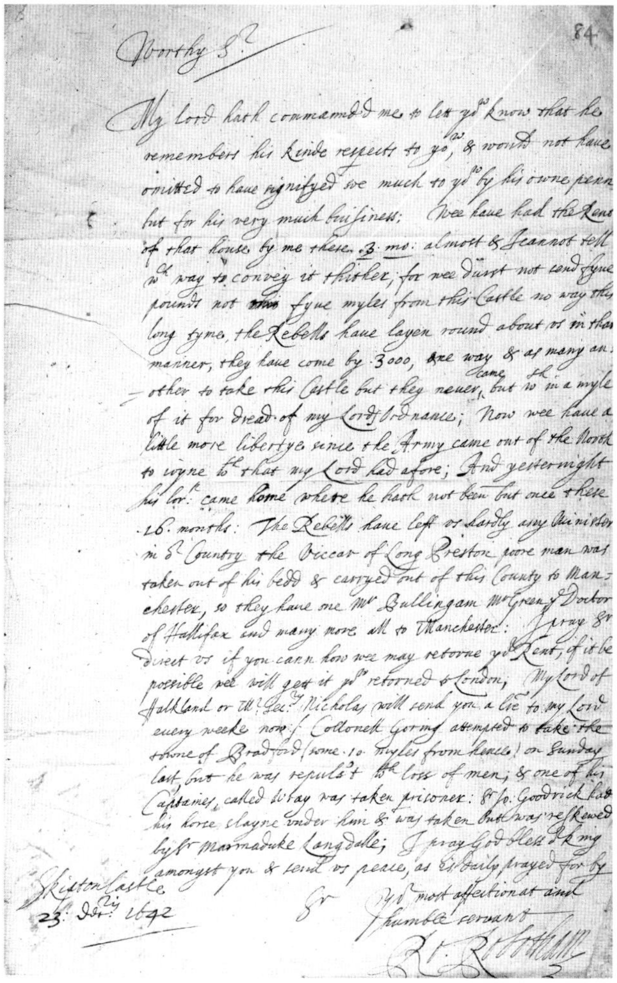

84

Worthy Sr

My lord hath commanded me to lett yow know that he remembers his kinde respects to yow, & would not have omitted to have signifyed soe much to yow by his owne penn but for his very much business; Wee have had the Rent of that house by me these 3 mo: almost & I cannot tell wch way to convey it thither, for wee durst not send fyve pounds not fyve myles from this Castle no way this long tyme, the Rebells have layen round about us in that manner, they have come by 3000, one way & as many another to take this Castle but they never came so nigh as in a myle of it for dread of my Lords Ordnance; Now wee have a little more libertye since the Army came out of the North to joyne wth that my Lord had afore; And yesternight his Lorp came home where he hath not been but once these 16 months: The Rebells have left us hardly any Minister in ye Country the Viccar of Long Preston poore man was taken out of his bedd & carryed out of this County to Manchester, so they have one Mr Bullingam Mr Green ye Doctor of Hallifax and many more all to Manchester: I pray Sr direct us if you cann how wee may retorne yor Rent, if it be possible wee will gett it yor retorned to London, My Lord of Falkland or Mr Secry Nicholas will send you a lre to my Lord every weeke now: Collonell Gorings attempted to take the towne of Bradford (some 10 myles from hence) on Sunday last but he was repulsed wth the loss of men, & one of his Captaines called Wray was taken prisoner: Sr Jo. Goodrick had his horse slayne under him & was taken but was reskewed by Sr Marmaduke Langdalle; I pray God blesse ye King amongst you & send us peace, as is daily prayed for by

Skipton Castle
23 Xbris 1642

Sr Yor most affectionate and humble servant
Rt Robottom

Letter from Robert Robottom, Christ Church's tenant at Long Preston in Yorkshire, apologising that he had not been able to get the rent due to the Dean and Chapter as 'the rebells have layen about us'. Dated 23 December 1642

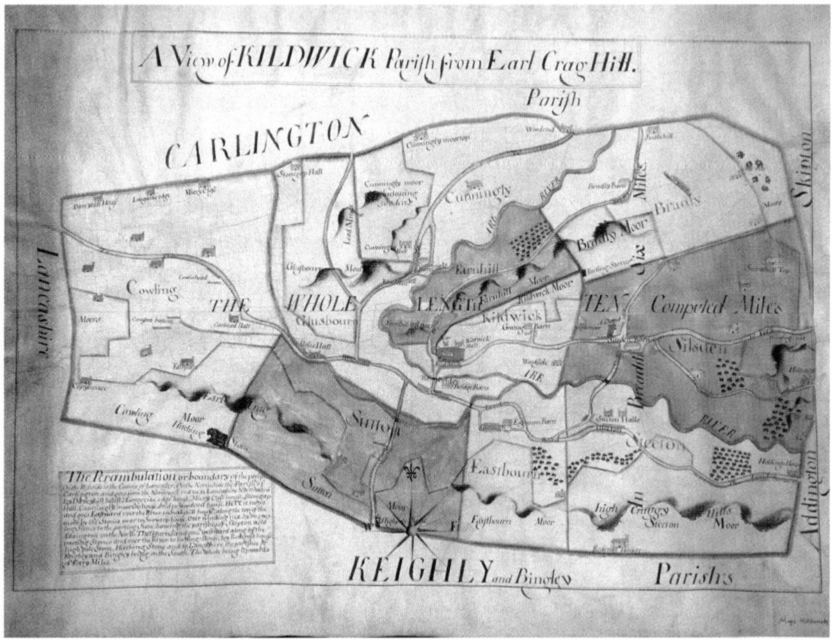

A map of Christ Church's estate in Kildwick, Yorkshire, 1768

profits, mineral rights, market dues and rectories. The vast majority was leased out, on long beneficial leases, which ensured a constant, but definitely not inflation-proof, income. Bailiffs were appointed to collect rents and other income, and an auditor was almost permanently on the books, being paid in both cash and beer for his labours on behalf of the House. Every year, at least once, the Dean and some of the canons were expected to undertake a 'progress' to all the estates to ensure they were being managed correctly. Visiting so many and such wide spread properties must have been impossible, especially as the Dean and the eight canons of the Chapter were, for the first 300 years of Christ Church's existence, the entire Governing Body. How could they be expected to tour all the estates, and manage the education of the students, and run the diocesan cathedral, simultaneously? No wonder individual canons, like Tanner, who had an interest in particular areas, were despatched alone to deal with college business.

Even so, changes in farming and land management techniques, the exigencies of the Civil War, the opportunism of entrepreneurial tenants, depressions, and time, all led to constant difficulties and arguments with tenant farmers, many of whom were aristocratic and significant landowners in their own right.

After the Civil War, the Dean and Chapter decided it was time to formalise arrangements. The Chapter Clerk was asked to compile a survey of Christ Church's title to all its property. The result of his labour was the Book of Evidences which, after the foundation and dotation charters, is probably the most important document in the archives. Completed in 1667, the book recorded details of all the property belonging to the House and all its lessees to that date. Occasionally, the medieval history of a property was included, too. The seventeenth century also ushered in the use of estate maps, and slowly but surely, over the next 200 years, all of Christ Church's land was surveyed more systematically than ever before. New estates were given by benefactors, often for specific purposes, like the huge bequest from Richard South of land in Caversham, Kentish Town and Chatteris to provide better incomes for incumbents and senior members, or Richard Gardiner's 1670 gift of a farm in Bourton-on-the-Water in Gloucestershire to pay for the education of two poor servitors.

Over the centuries, Christ Church's acreage increased as tithes and other dues were commuted to actual land as Parliamentary enclosure spread first across the Midlands, and then across the whole country.

Officially, although rules had always been bent, no college was permitted to sell land until the 1858 Universities and Colleges Estates Act. Once the act was passed, though, properties which were less profitable were sold to buy better farmland (in Lincolnshire, for example). After the First World War, in common with all large landowners, huge quantities of land were bought and sold. Although the total acreage owned by Christ Church is much reduced from its mid-nineteenth-century high, a substantial part of the endowment is still held in property, both urban and rural. College and cathedral staff still live in houses built on Christ Church land, and the income from its estates, which include market gardens, dairy and beef farms, even a carrot farm, still contributes significantly to the annual revenue of the college.

Judith Curthoys

The Nineteenth Century

Chronology

1806 *William Grenville (ChCh 1776) became Prime Minister*
1808 *Robert Peel received the first 'double first'*
1809 *Installation of Dean Charles Henry Hall Fire destroyed the western end of the south side of Tom Quad*
1812 *Robert Jenkinson (ChCh 1787), Lord Liverpool, is elected Prime Minister*
1814 *Visit of European leaders after the signing of the Peace of Paris*
1817 *The beginning of rowing at Christ Church (approximately)*
1824 *Installation of Dean Samuel Smith*
1827 *The first Oxbridge cricket match, instigated by a House man George Canning (ChCh 1787), became Prime Minister*
1828 *Gift of the Fox-Strangways collection of paintings*
1829 *'No Peel'*
1831 *Dean Thomas Gaisford*
1834 *Robert Peel (ChCh 1805) is elected Prime Minister, serving again from 1841–46*
1842 *Restoration of the steps in Tom Quad*
1852 *Edward Stanley (ChCh 1817), earl of Derby, becomes Prime Minister, serving again from 1858–59 and 1866–68*
1855 *Installation of Dean Henry Liddell*
1856 *Alterations to the cathedral began*
1856 *W. Fellows made the biggest hit ever recorded in a first class cricket match*
1858 *Christ Church Ordinances passed*
1859 *Matriculation of the Prince of Wales*
1862 *Beginnings of the Iffley Road sports ground*
1863 *Meadows Building constructed on the site of the old Fell's Building*
1865 *Removal of the natural history collections to the new University Museum*
1867 *Christ Church, Oxford, Act, changing the constitution and giving our first statutes*
1868 *William Gladstone (ChCh 1828), became Prime Minister, serving three further terms*
1870 *Restoration of the cathedral by George Gilbert Scott*
1884 *The Undergraduate Reading Room is set up in Tom 4:2*
1885 *Robert Arthur Talbot Gascoyne-Cecil (ChCh 1847), marquis of Salisbury, became Prime Minister for the first of three terms*
1888 *The almshouse sold to Pembroke College*
1892 *Installation of Dean Francis Paget*
1894 *Archibald Primrose (ChCh 1866), earl of Rosebery, is elected Prime Minister*
1896 *A House man (J.P. Boland) won the first gold medal in the new Olympics*
1898 *The Cardinal's Hat is given to Christ Church*

No Peel

There are two objects in Oxford as a whole that I find especially moving. The first, the Alfred Jewel in the Ashmolean, is an exquisite encapsulation of the rich culture of the Anglo-Saxon era, complete with its haunting inscription, which translates as 'Alfred had me made'. The second, rather different object (one might wish, more trendily, to call it an 'installation'), is the phrase 'No Peel', studded in nails on the door facing the bottom of the Hall Stairs in Christ Church.

Peel was the first of the more educationally accomplished of our national leaders, being the first of two men to take a double first at Oxford: the other was John Keble, whose High Churchmanship was not to Peel's dry Evangelical taste (one can't ask everything of one's heroes!). He managed to turn the Tory Party into a party of ideals and ideas, popularising the neologism 'popularise' when urging his party to seek success at the polls. He was effectively the inventor of the modern Conservative Party; the son of a Lancashire industrialist, he had always been a sound economist, ensuring in the 1820s the creation of a strong metallic currency, and preferring the honest use of income tax to the frequently sneaky ways of indirect taxation. Above all, he dared to change his mind, not least over Ireland, losing in the process his Protestant nickname, 'Orange' Peel (he was also redheaded); and he daringly and controversially supported state support for the Irish Catholic seminary at Maynooth in the 'Hungry 40s'. He not only had the singular political merit of being able to change his mind, but also to have possessed the common decency to let the world know – eventually – when he had done so. It is this all too rare ability that has its moving, if initially critical, memorial in 'No Peel'. In 1829, Peel, then the forty-one-year-old member for Oxford University, had moved over to support the cause of Catholic emancipation, a proposal which, as a consistent

Thomas Lawrence, *Sir Robert Peel*

Protestant, he had previously opposed so strongly as to resign from the cabinet of George Canning, another Christ Church-educated prime minister, and a supporter of emancipation.

Convinced, eventually, that opposition to emancipation would be politically disastrous, and aware of a public mood which increasingly supported it, Peel agonised, and ultimately changed his mind, sagely moving to become the MP for Westbury. Peel himself introduced the act under the premiership of the Iron Duke, masterminding a controversial piece of legislation which freed Catholics from their then total exclusion from the political life of the nation. In Anglican Oxford, and especially in Christ Church, replete with a cathedral and several quadrangles of clergy, such a decision was widely viewed as treachery of the first kind, interpreted by these self-interested parties as the beginning of the undoing of the old order in which the University and the Church had hitherto flourished. A party of offended Christ Church men made their protest known by hammering in, in one of the most public spaces in the college, passed several times a day by most of its members, those two telling monosyllables: 'No Peel'.

This artistic 'happening' had the unfortunate effect of ending Peel's direct association with the college. This was an astonishing failure of political imagination on the part of Christ Church, and it was an error indulged by many of its members. The college's egg cook informed a young Gladstone, then a Student of the House, that it was a great shame that Mr Peel had so let the country down, as he had been such a kind gentleman when an undergraduate. How much less kind, how much less gentlemanly were those who nailed up 'No Peel', and yet what a vivid legacy to the political passions of those divided days they have left us.

Brian Young

The 'No Peel' door, at the foot of the Hall stairs

GLADSTONE

Gladstone's splendid portrait by Millais – he became Sir John Millais, Bt as a result of the commission – hangs in the Hall, the best of the many portraits of Gladstone, and one of the most combative pictures in the Christ Church collection. It was in fact the House's third attempt at a portrait of Gladstone. The first, by G.F. Watts, was mutilated in despair by the artist when the Governing Body sent it back for improvement; and the second, by William Blake Richmond, was rejected when it was shown at a Gaudy – not perhaps the most propitious moment for the exercise of corporate artistic judgement.

John Everett Millais, *William Ewart Gladstone*, 1885

Gladstone was sent by his father to Christ Church from Eton in 1828. The aim was clear: membership of Christ Church, recently reformed by Dean Cyril Jackson, represented the integration of the Scottish, Presbyterian Gladstones into the Anglican elite which ran the nation and the Empire. Success at the House set young William on a clear and determined path. That elite was a remarkable mixture of Whigs and Tories. Christ Church was, of course, known for its liberal Tories: Liverpool, Canning, Peel were all from Jackson's Christ Church, though only Canning got a portrait. But there were many Whigs at the House also. Christ Church played a central part in nurturing a political elite uniquely successful in nineteenth-century European politics – the only elite still in power and recognisably the same in 1920 as in 1820. Of this elite, Gladstone was to be a chief member, stretching and forming its conventions in a life-long drama of radical conservatism.

Gladstone entered Christ Church on Friday, 10 October 1828 and was given rooms in Chaplains' Quadrangle (where Meadow Building now stands). He noted in his diary: 'Very dirty indeed, but I suppose very fair first rooms'. For his later years he was in Canterbury 2 – the height of fashion and at that time a controversial modern building. Gladstone certainly used Oxford as his father intended: he acquired a circle of friends and acquaintances, including many with whom he worked politically until they dropped (for he outlived them all, except his

Mercury. Originally, the reservoir in the centre of Tom Quad, which had been given to Christ Church by Canon Richard Gardiner, was enhanced by a globe. In 1695 the globe was replaced with a statue of Mercury until it was downed by the future Prime Minister, Edward Stanley, in 1819. It was not until 1928 that the statue was replaced by a copy of Giovanni da Bologna's *Mercury*, the gift of Mr H.B. Bompas. The pedestal is one of only two structures in Oxford by Edwin Lutyens

engaging if dissolute aesthetic contemporary John Temple Leader, whom scandal forced to Florence: he hosted Gladstone's last visit to Italy, years after they both came up). Gladstone was elected a Student of the House in 1829 on the nomination of Dean Smith, a mark of the college's expectations. He was Secretary and President of the Union, helping to establish its political prominence by moving its important vote of no confidence in the duke of Wellington's government in 1830 (a nineteenth-century equivalent to the 'king and country' debate).

But Gladstone was in Oxford for more than this. He was a fanatical worker, and recorded in his diary, as well as hours spent in study, hours not spent in study which could have been. Gladstone was tutored by Robert Biscoe and Thomas Short, and was coached by Charles Wordsworth. When he took his double first in 1831 – the first since Sir Robert Peel twenty-three years earlier – he complained that the questions were too easy, for eight of the set books were not required to be written on: he noted sententiously, 'I fear that unless they alter this, no one will get up his books'. When he was viva'ed before a large crowd of well-wishers by Renn Dickson Hampden and others, and the examiner remarked, 'We now leave that part of the subject', Gladstone declared 'No sir; if you please we will not leave it yet', and continued apace.

He also founded a discussion club – known as the WEG – to match the Apostles in Cambridge, which his Eton friend Arthur Hallam had joined. It had lively discussions on politics, history and theology. H.G. Liddell was its Secretary after Gladstone left Oxford, but it did not outlast the 1830s.

Chapel was then compulsory, and Gladstone, a keen Evangelical in his House days, became a Bible clerk and prick bill, that is the person responsible for recording chapel attendance. This he did zealously, probably over-zealously, for he was critical of the conduct of the cathedral and poor attendance at it. This enthusiasm did not endear him to a number of his contemporaries, and it was probably the cause of an incident on 24 March 1830, when the future Prime Minister was beaten up in his rooms 'by a party of men'. He observed piously in his diary: 'if this hostile and unkind conduct be a sample of their ways, I pray that the grace of God may reveal to them that the end

thereof is death'. This was truer than he knew, for the next year Lord Conyers Osborne, son of the duke of Leeds, was killed in a drunken scuffle. Incidentally, Gladstone's only other similar experience was in 1852 in the Carlton Club, when a group of rowdy tories, including Charles Lempriere, the law fellow of St John's and the Tory agent for Oxford, threatened to throw him out of the window when his speech attacking Disraeli's budget brought down Lord Derby's government.

Gladstone left Oxford in 1832 feeling its religious and intellectual tone could be improved. He left a Tory evangelical: he returned in 1847 a tractarian liberal, being elected as one of the two burgesses or MPs from the University by an uneasy coalition of reformers, Tractarians and the Christ Church vote.

Colin Matthew

CHRIST CHURCH AND REFORM

Unsigned, *Edward George Geoffrey Smith Stanley, fourteenth earl of Derby*

Christ Church Dons are proverbially the slowest body in all the university. It is next to impossible to get them to move in any matter of improvement.

However self-evident this assertion may have seemed to the *Morning Post*'s leader-writer in 1865, it was far from being the case at the turn of the nineteenth century. In 1800, when new examinations for University degrees were introduced, Christ Church was still calling the academic tune at Oxford, as its founders had intended. As the prime mover in bringing about the reform of University examinations, Dean Jackson sought to apply Christ Church's rigorous standards across the board. The prospect of honorary distinction was held out to those who excelled, coupled with the terror of failure for others who had neglected their studies. During the early years of the class lists, Christ Church put up a strong showing: it claimed nine of the thirteen firsts awarded in 1808. Well might the heads of some weaker colleges surmise that university honours were merely a device to reinforce the dominance of the House.

A far-sighted observer, however, recognised that Jackson's action had been a public-spirited one. Rival colleges were bound to respond to the challenge, eroding Christ Church's leading position. Some began to hold competitive examinations for their scholarships, attracting the most talented schoolboys; others introduced demanding competitions for

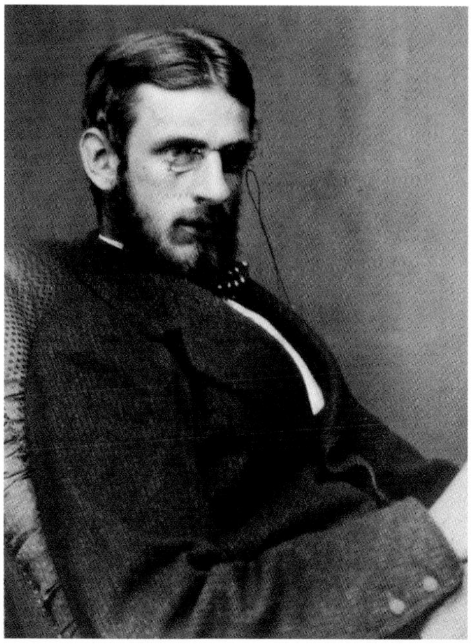

Possibly C.L. Dodgson, *Richard Shute, Student of Christ Church 1872–86*

fellowships, recruiting the pick of each year's finalists. Christ Church's 101 Students, meanwhile, continued to be selected either by nomination of the Dean and canons, or by election from Westminster School. Such methods had served well enough in the past. But Westminster, from which the House had traditionally drawn its tutors, experienced a period of decline (as parents avoided schools located in unhealthy city centres). Patronage by the cathedral chapter meanwhile led to charges of nepotism – in 1853 Canon Faussett nominated his fifth and tenth sons to Studentships – and seemed indefensible in a meritocratic age. Servitors, a category of less-wealthy undergraduates who were remitted fees in return for carrying out various duties within the Hall and cathedral, were denied the opportunity of promotion to Studentships, however able and industrious they were. Although an examination was introduced for commoners seeking admission to the House, noblemen and gentlemen commoners (both of whom wore elaborate gowns and enjoyed certain privileges, in return for paying higher fees) faced less scrutiny as to their credentials. The only test to which the future tenth earl of Wemyss recalled being subjected, when he came up in 1837, was to answer Dean Gaisford's enquiry, 'How is your father?'

Gaisford discouraged Christ Church men from reading for university honours. A few undoubtedly talented individuals – Henry Acland, Robert Cecil and John Ruskin – thrived in conditions that allowed for broader, independent study. Many, however, found themselves under-occupied, and left Christ Church with little to show for their University careers except considerable debts. Temptations to extravagance abounded and were scarcely curbed by the sumptuary regulations periodically issuing from the deanery. Despite attempts to forbid men from wearing red coats in the House, riding to hounds found many adherents, as did other equestrian pursuits. The censors, who struggled to stamp out gambling, feared that the coming of the railway would bring the Ascot races too easily within reach of undergraduates. Another unwelcome attraction was the Bullingdon Cricket Club where – according to reports which reached the Senior Censor W.E. Jelf – 'the scenes which take place, and the songs which are sung at its dinners ... are a curse and a disgrace to a place of Christian education'.

In 1850 the Whig government of Lord John Russell appointed a royal commission to enquire into 'the state, discipline, studies, and revenues' of the university and colleges of Oxford'. 'From the Dean of Christ Church, alone of the Heads of Colleges', the commissioners reported in 1852, 'no answer was received to any of the communications of the Commission'. Gaisford's lack of co-operation did not prevent the commissioners from discovering that he and the eight canons divided among themselves Christ Church's annual surplus revenues of nearly £12,500, leaving them each with some £1,500 in addition to various other payments, while they restricted the most junior Students to an annual dividend of £25 a year, and the seniors to about £45.

H.G. Liddell, who succeeded Gaisford as Dean in 1855, recognised that rather than isolating itself, Christ Church needed to be equipped to compete with the other colleges. The first steps in enabling it to do so were made by executive commissioners, who were empowered to draw up new ordinances for the colleges. Five of the seven commissioners were old members of the House distinguished in public life. Their new ordinances, which received the royal assent on 5 June 1858, reduced the number of Studentships to twenty-eight Seniors (that is, graduates), from whom the teaching staff was to be drawn, and fifty-two Juniors (undergraduates) of whom twenty-one were to be elected from Westminster. All save the latter were to be elected after an open examination; and the stipends of all were to be made comparable to those of other colleges.

The Senior Students were still left with a grievance, for their position remained inferior to that of Fellows in other colleges as regards powers of government. The Cathedral Chapter remained Christ

42. Horses at Canterbury Gate, 1842
From a lithographed drawing by R. W. Buss

After R.W. Buss, *Horses at Canterbury Gate*, 1842

Church's Governing Body, a position which became intolerable to the tutors for two reasons. First, the cathedral canonries were increasingly assigned to holders of University chairs, so that the tutors found themselves exposed to the great bugbear of rule by professors. Second, to compound matters, the canons were now likely to be drawn from outside Christ Church. An agitation to change the constitution of the House was begun in December 1864 by T.J. Prout, a recent tutor and censor, who wrote anonymously to The Times describing the anomalous position of Christ Church's Students. Eighteen of them attended a meeting in Prout's rooms in February 1865, when they agreed to press for the same rights and privileges as Fellows in other colleges. The Chapter's response was unfavourable, causing the Students to circulate a statement of their case, in the hope that influential outsiders might offer their support.

In the meantime, the Canons' position was weakened by the celebrated 'Bread and Butter row'. To prove their residence, undergraduates were obliged to purchase daily from the Butler a fixed quantity (a 'commons') of bread and butter. Like the other principal victuallers, the cook and the manciple, the butler was appointed by the Dean and canons but received only a nominal salary. Instead, he was free to extract profits as a monopoly purveyor to Christ Church's residents, charging a 160 per cent mark-up on the wholesale price of the bread which he supplied his captive customers. An undergraduate petition to the Dean and Chapter in March 1865 protesting about catering charges and quality met with no immediate domestic reform, and in November the undergraduates went public with their complaints. A correspondence erupted in the newspapers as parents and old members added their voices against the extortionate charges levied by the House's domestic contractors. Such practices were by no means peculiar to Christ Church, but they proved a convenient stick with which to beat the Chapter, and an opportunity to assert that a Governing Body which included the Students would put an end to such scandals.

The canons offered the Students arbitration, and after much tussling over the terms of reference, five referees were named. They comprised C.T. Longley, archbishop of Canterbury and a former censor of the House, and four distinguished lawyers. Their award, agreed unanimously and issued in December 1866, represented 'a complete acceptance' of the Students' case. The referees proposed to establish a joint government of the Dean, canons, the Senior Students, and those surviving Students elected before 1858 who were still in residence. New statutes on this basis were drawn up and received royal assent on 12 August 1867, the first meeting of the newly constituted governing body being held on 16 October a settlement had been harmoniously achieved, and a rupture between college and cathedral had been averted.

A third phase of statute-making proved more contentious. Commissioners were appointed in 1877 to draw up new statutes to amend, among other things, the conditions on which fellowships (and Studentships) were held. E.B. Pusey's disciple H.P. Liddon set great store by the requirement that two-thirds of Senior Students should be in holy orders, ensuring that Anglican clergyman remained a majority on the governing body. Since the commission was set up by Lord Salisbury, under a Conservative government, it was expected that Christ Church's clerical interests would be dealt with tenderly. That assumption was undermined when the general election of 1880 returned a Liberal majority to the House of Commons, and with it a political climate unfavourable to denominational privilege. Under the statutes made for Christ Church, and approved on 3 May 1882, only three Students were henceforth required to be clergy. For the future, even allowing for the canons, a majority of Christ Church's Governing Body might be of any

Flooring of Mercury: or Burning the Oaks, a Scene in Tom Quadrangle.

E. Cruickshank, *The flooring of Mercury*, 1824

religion, or none. The suddenness of this change brought a clerical backlash and a period of recrimination.

Such controversies should not overshadow the educational transformation that took place in the House between the mid-1850s and the mid-1880s. Letters written to his family by a Blackheath schoolboy, Edward Kaye Jupp, describe the process of election to Junior Studentships (renamed scholarships in 1882) in History in 1868. Along with the other fifteen candidates for four places, he was summoned by Liddell ('a white-haired giant') to undergo a 'tiring' examination in Greek translation, followed by some 'very dreadful' history papers, whose questions ranged from the siege of Syracuse to the campaigns of Belisarius, the character of the nonjurors, and the comparative constitutional histories of Spain and England. Jupp's success was announced a few days later in *The Times*, to the delight of his relatives. Their grief at his sudden death in 1870 led to the publication of his correspondence, an enduring record of a conscientious undergraduate career spent in the newly reformed foundation. At least two of Jupp's tutors resigned during his period of residence to take up teaching positions at other colleges, where Fellows were beginning to be permitted to marry. Both men had been notable for restoring Christ Church's position in the class lists, and their departure reflected the loss which the House suffered as a result of the continuing requirement that Senior Students must be unmarried, a restriction which was not lifted until 1882. The first Christ Church tutor to be re-elected upon marriage was Richard Shute, a layman and a philosopher whose work was in the field of Aristotelian studies. Like Jupp, he died young (in 1886) a result, it was said, of over work. His colleague in teaching the House's Greats men and also a married tutor, John Alexander Stewart, described what might otherwise have gone unrecorded. Much of Shute's teaching was done through 'private conversations between teacher and single pupil' – that is, the individual tutorials which became the norm in Oxford by the turn of the twentieth century but which in 1880 were still a recent innovation. Lavishing time on his pupils, Shute tried to get them to think. 'He riddled through one's seeming knowledge', one of them recalled, challenging misconceptions in what could be an unsettling process. Many, though, were infected with his enthusiasm for the pursuit of truth, and his commitment to the belief 'that it is a solemn duty which man owes to himself, as a rational being, to try to be clear-headed'.

The commissioners who scrutinised Christ Church in 1852 acknowledged that it was impossible ever again to carry out 'the great designs of Cardinal Wolsey'. No single foundation could dominate the modern University in the way that Wolsey and King Henry had planned Christ Church to do. But to restore Christ Church's standing as a leading place of education was a reasonable expectation, which the brief lives of Jupp and Shute suggest was amply fulfilled.

Mark Curthoys

CHARLES LUTWIDGE DODGSON *(LEWIS CARROLL)*

Charles Lutwidge Dodgson was born on 27 January 1832, in the parsonage of Daresbury, Cheshire, the eldest son of the Reverend Charles Dodgson, perpetual curate of the parish. In 1843 the family moved to Croft-on-Tees, south of Darlington, where the young Charles wrote poems and stories to amuse his sisters and brothers. He was educated at Richmond School and Rugby before following his father to Christ Church, Oxford, where he took up residence in January 1851. He worked hard, obtaining first-class Honours in the Final Mathematical School in 1854. He had already been appointed to a Studentship (the equivalent of a fellowship in other colleges) in 1852, and in January 1855 began his teaching career at Christ Church. The position of Student entitled Dodgson to lodgings and a secure (if limited) income for life, but it also imposed restrictions. He had to proceed to holy orders and never marry. (In fact, although he was ordained deacon in December 1861, he never became a priest.) In February 1855 he was appointed Sub-Librarian at Christ Church, and later in the same year he was made Mathematical Lecturer. In his diary for December 31st 1855, he wrote

> *I am sitting alone in my bedroom this last night of the old year, waiting for midnight. It has been the most eventful year of my life: I began it a poor bachelor student, with no definite plans or expectations; I end it a master and tutor in Ch. Ch., with an income of more than £300 a year, and the course of mathematical tuition marked out by God's providence for at least some years to come.*

He did not know that in the following year an encounter with a small four-year-old girl would change his life and have a profound effect on the subsequent course of children's literature.

John Tenniel's drawing of the White Knight for the first printed edition of *Alice in Wonderland* in 1865

In June 1855 Henry George Liddell was appointed Dean of Christ Church, following the death of Dean Gaisford. The new dean undertook extensive alterations to the deanery, and so it was not until February 1856 that his wife, Lorina, and children could move in to join him. At this time Dean Liddell had four children: Harry, Lorina, Alice (then four years old) and Edith. A second son, Arthur, had died of scarlet fever in 1853. The Liddells were to have five further children: Albert (who died aged eight weeks in 1863), Rhoda, Violet, Frederick and Lionel.

On 22 January 1856 Dodgson records that he wrote to his Uncle Skeffington 'to get me a photographic apparatus, as I want some other occupation here, than mere reading and writing', and in March he went to London with his friend Reginald Southey, to order a camera with lens for about £15. On

25th April 1856, Dodgson went over to the deanery to help Southey to take a photograph of the cathedral from the deanery garden. The three little girls, Lorina, Alice and Edith, were in the garden most of the time, and Dodgson and Southey tried to group them in the foreground of the picture, but they were not patient sitters. Six days later Dodgson's own new camera arrived at Christ Church, and on 3 June 1856 he used it to take the first of many photographs of Alice and the other children. Over the years that followed,Dodgson continued and improved his friendship with the Liddell children,and boating expeditions were quite a frequent occurrence during the summer months.

Hubert von Herkomer, *Charles Lutwidge Dodgson*, 1899

On 4 July 1862 Dodgson and his friend Robinson Duckworth took Lorina, Alice and Edith on an expedition up the river to Godstow. On this occasion Dodgson first related the story of 'Alice's adventures under ground'. The 'interminable fairy-tale', as Dodgson referred to it in his diary, lasted through many later boating trips. Alice asked for the story to be written out for her, and Dodgson records in his diary that he wrote out the headings the very next day (5 July 1862) on his way to London. He began writing the manuscript copy on 13 November 1862, and had finished the text by February 1863. The illustrations caused him much more trouble. On 10 March 1863, he called at the deanery to borrow a natural history book to assist him in the drawings, but even so the pictures were not completed until 13 September 1864. The manuscript was presented to Alice as an early Christmas present on 26 November 1864, by which time the story was already well on its way to publication. Dodgson had shown the story to his friend, George Macdonald, who encouraged him to publish it. He took this advice seriously, and records in his diary on 2 July 1863 that he had 'received from Mr. Combe a second trial page, larger for "Alice's adventures"'. He added more chapters, incidents and characters to the original tale, and found a publisher, Macmillan. Dodgson himself paid for all the costs of producing the book. Although he had initially hoped to provide the illustrations himself, he quickly realised that his artistic skills were not sufficient, and so he engaged John Tenniel, the *Punch* cartoonist.

Many of the details of the Alice stories are based on incidents and characters connected with Christ Church. There is a small door, usually locked, in the wall which separates the deanery garden from the cathedral garden: Dodgson wrote this into his story as the little door, opened by a tiny golden key, which leads into 'the loveliest garden you ever saw', where Alice eventually plays croquet with the Queen of Hearts. The brass fire dogs in the Hall have very long necks, remarkably similar to the illustrations of both Dodgson and Tenniel for the passage in which Alice, after eating the small cake labelled 'EAT ME', finds that she is 'opening out like the largest telescope that ever was'. After she has fallen into the pool of her own tears, Alice finds herself swimming to the bank with a Duck (Rev. Duckworth), a Dodo (Dodgson), a Lory (Lorina) and an Eaglet (Edith). In *Through the Looking-Glass*, Tenniel used Gladstone (a Christ Church alumnus) and Disraeli as models for his illustration of the Lion and Unicorn. Dodgson clearly based the character of the White Knight, an inventor of bizarre contraptions, on himself. Tenniel was given explicit instructions not to

Far left:
The fire-irons in the Hall, which are said to have given Dodgson the inspiration for Alice's growing neck after she had eaten the cake labelled 'Eat me'

Left:
The 'Alice' window in Hall, conceived by Dr John Mason and designed by Patrick Reyntiens in 1983, which shows many characters from *Alice in Wonderland* and *Through the Looking Glass*

make him look old: the resulting picture has the features of the illustrator. In June 1863 Christ Church gave a banquet for the visit of the prince and princess of Wales, 'gorgeously done, with a large collection of grandees' as Dodgson records in his diary. This was probably the inspiration for the feast at the end of *Through the Looking-Glass*, at which Alice, now a queen, is the guest of honour.

In the summer of 1863 came an unexplained breach in his relationship with the Liddells, which has given rise to intense speculation and many different theories, some more plausible than others. Whatever the cause of the alienation, the Liddells feature less and less frequently in his diaries, and when he met Alice and Miss Prickett, the governess, in the quadrangle on 11 May 1865, he recorded 'Alice seems changed a good deal, and hardly for the better – probably going through the usual awkward stage of transition'.

Although Dodgson stopped photographing the Liddell children, he found many other sitters among his colleagues and friends, and his diaries are full of details of this absorbing interest. Dodgson's portraits fall into three clearly defined categories: family, distinguished people, and children. He seems to have been more at ease with children than with adults, and he found little girls particularly attractive sitters. Through photography he formed friendships with them, and often presented them with copies of his books and puzzles. After moving to new rooms in 1868, he persuaded the college to allow him to erect a glass photographic studio on the roof above his rooms, thus enabling him to take photographs even in inclement weather. Often he would dress his sitters in costume. However, in July 1880 he gave up photography, and devoted more time to his writing.
Dodgson was undoubtedly a great photographer, but

Above: Sketches by Charles and Wilfrid Dodgson for the *Alice* stories

Bottom right: Gladstone and Disraeli caricatured by John Tenniel as the Lion and the Unicorn in *Through the Looking Glass*

he is no doubt best remembered as the author of *Alice's Adventures in Wonderland*, published under the pseudonym of Lewis Carroll, a name based on a latinised reversal of his first two names, Charles Lutwidge. The corrected impression of 1865 received admiring reviews, and sales increased steadily. The first German and French translations were published in 1869. A sequel, *Through the Looking-Glass and What Alice Found There*, appeared as a Christmas book for 1871, although bearing the publication date of 1872 on the title-page. Neither 'Alice' book has ever gone out of print, and they have been translated into over seventy languages. Dodgson's other works for children (*Phantasmagoria and Other Poems*, 1869, *The Hunting of the Snark*, 1876, *Sylvie and Bruno*, 1889, *Sylvie and Bruno Concluded*, 1893) never achieved quite the same popularity.

Dodgson had a very inventive mind, and devised games and puzzles for the amusement of his child friends, including word games, games of logic and a game based on croquet, which he played with the Liddell children in the deanery garden. He wrote an incredible number of letters, and his obsession with record-keeping led him for the last thirty-seven years of his life to maintain a register of letters received and sent and other correspondence. According to his nephew, S.D. Collingwood, the last entry in the register numbered 98,721.

As a mathematician, Dodgson also published mathematical works under his own name, having a particular interest in logic, algebra and geometry. He was very concerned to keep his two identities separate, and would return unopened letters which arrived at Christ Church addressed to Lewis Carroll. He became increasingly concerned to complete his numerous writing projects, and this may be one of the reasons behind his abandonment of photography in 1880 and his resignation of the mathematical lectureship in 1881. Yet in 1882 he took on an additional responsibility, in becoming Curator of Common Room at Christ Church, a position which he held for the next nine years.

Dodgson's letters and diaries of the 1890s indicate an awareness of ageing. Minor illnesses plagued him, and he complained of a failing memory. He died on 14 January 1898, thirteen days before his sixty-sixth birthday, at his sisters' home in Guildford, followed to the grave four days later by Henry George Liddell, the father of the little girl 'whose namesake one happy summer day inspired his story'.

Janet McMullin

THREE SCIENTISTS

Samuel Cousins, after a painting by Thomas Phillips, *William Buckland*, 1833

HARCOURT

A.G.V. Harcourt, FRS (1834–1919) came to Christ Church in 1859 having been elected as the first Dr Lee's Reader in Chemistry on the basis, quite unusually, of a competitive examination. Previously he had been at Balliol, where he was taught first by Henry Smith, an outstanding mathematician, and then by Sir William Brodie (Professor of Chemistry).

With Harcourt's election, the Anatomy Museum was refurbished as the college's Chemistry Laboratory. Then began his long career of teaching and research, for which he gained international repute. Harcourt and his colleague Esson embarked on studies of the rates of chemical reactions, studies which marked the beginning of physical chemistry as an exact science. With his pupil H.B. Dixon, the research was extended to the causes of explosions, a necessary subject when town gas was the all-prevailing common illuminant.

Later Harcourt made a valuable contribution to the administration of chloroform as an anaesthetic.

Paul Kent

BUCKLAND

William Buckland (1784–1856) was one of the most colourful people ever to reside in Christ Church, having been appointed a canon in 1825. He had been a Professor of Geology since 1819, and a Fellow of Corpus (1809). His interest in geology probably started when he attended the lectures on mineralogy of Dr John Kidd (Lee's Reader in Anatomy at the House), in his younger days. Buckland rapidly became an established figure through his investigations and the lectures for which he became celebrated. At this time strong interest had been aroused in the history and origin of life on which

Buckland built his ideas of 'catastrophes' – sudden dramatic events which changed both life and geological structures on the earth.

Buckland's ideas and those of his pupils such as Sir Charles Lyell did much to move opinion to revisit the literal interpretation of the 'Noahaic' Great Flood, and prepare the way for Darwin.

Buckland was a great family man who lived in lodgings in the north-west corner of Tom Quad (currently occupied by the Archdeacon). He and the family had a passion for finding animals to share their home including not only a few cats, dogs, rats and the like, but at least one crocodile and a pony, which would enter the dining room should the door be left open (much to the delight of the children and the dismay of Mrs Buckland).

The Anatomy School, now the Lee Building, in Schools Quad, 1827

Buckland's gastronomic eccentricities were well known, believing as he did that all the animal kingdom was edible. He proceeded to munch his way through the various species: mole, bluebottle and panther chops were no impediment!

This cheerful, bustling, energetic man made considerable contributions to Christ Church, not least in the management of the coal mines which the college then owned in Somerset. In this he had the advice of George Sopwith, like William Buckland a member of the Institute of Civil Engineers. He left Christ Church in 1845 to become dean of Westminster, where he oversaw the installation of gas lighting in the abbey and, as an ex-officio governor, greatly improved the lot of boys at Westminster School.

Paul Kent

Acland

Henry Wentworth Acland (1815–1900) came to Christ Church in 1834 from Harrow, and though destined for medicine, was advised in his undergraduate years to go to no lectures related to that subject but rather to broaden his mind. It was only after graduation that he undertook medical studies at St George's Hospital in London, but then because of poor health he went on a remedial voyage on a naval vessel. After this he was advised to avoid any sort of strenuous occupation and was elected to a fellowship at All Souls. There he sought leave to teach the college's handful of undergraduates (Bible clerks) and was allowed to do so provided that he lectured at 6 am.

Further medical studies followed at Edinburgh, and in 1845 he returned to Christ Church as Dr Lee's Reader in Anatomy. When he showed Pusey some of his microscopical preparations, Pusey commented that what he concluded from them could be true, but if it was, he did not believe that God wanted us to know it.

Acland, now Regius Professor, played a notable part in the building of the University Museum and its associated laboratories in Parks Road. These opened in 1860 and gave Oxford a new centre for experimental sciences.

Paul Kent

RUSKIN AT CHRIST CHURCH

John Ruskin, *Christ Church from the south*, 1842

I am going to ... see the drawings of a very wonderful gentleman-commoner here who draws wonderfully. He is a very strange fellow, always dressing in a greatcoat with a brown velvet collar, and a large neckcloth tied over his mouth, and living quite in his own way among the odd set of hunting and sporting men that gentleman-commoners usually are ... they like their own way of living and he likes his, and so they go on, and I am glad to say that they do not bully him, as I should have been afraid they would.

Thus, with visual and psychological acuity, Henry Liddell, then a Tutor of Christ Church, described the young John Ruskin in a letter of 1837. Wonderful in himself, Ruskin drew wonderfully too. Liddell saw to it that Dean Gaisford saw and admired his drawings. The view of the east side of Tom Quad with the cathedral spire which he drew from his room in Tom 3, a delicate and precise exercise in the style of Turner, is in the Senior Common Room now. Then there was Ruskin's dress, shielding him from the damp and cold of an Oxford winter – just as his mother, who took rooms in the High Street to watch over his health, desired. And finally there was his relation to his peers in the 'live and let live' spirit of Christ Church at its usual best. Ruskin was to live his whole life 'in his own way' and, at the same time, socially 'among' his fellow men and women, as a friend of many and as a great Victorian public man.

When he came up in 1837 he was already a much published poet and contributor to Loudon's *Magazine of Natural History* ('On the causes of the colour of the Rhine' and other pieces); very well read in the Bible and the classics; familiar with contemporary literature such as Wordsworth, Scott and Byron; and introduced to Gower and Chaucer at King's College London. He had travelled over much of England and Wales and gone on two long, culturally serious European tours into northern Italy, the second including Venice, with his parents. He was

Unknown artist, *John Ruskin*

to be supplied with good sherry by his father, partner with Domecq. And he had fallen in love with that partner's daughter. He was ready for Christ Church.

He learned quickly that academic excellence was not the thing for a gentleman commoner. A few weeks after coming up, his essay was chosen as the best of the week, to be honoured by his reading it out in Hall. The disapprobation of his peers for this vulgar breach of good form was made abundantly clear to him. He did not trespass again but kept his set work in the slightly-above-average range, even when it was on Plato, Homer, Thucydides or Euclid, all of whom he loved. He liked to be liked. Outside the curriculum, however, he was busy. He drew diagrams for Dr Buckland's lectures along with fine watercolours to please himself. He wrote a series of essays in Johnsonian style on 'The Poetry of Architecture' for the *Architectural Magazine* – unlikely to be noticed by the other gentleman-commoners. He won the Newdigate Poetry Prize and received it at the hands of none other than Wordsworth himself. Clearly, Christ Church kept him in good intellectual spirits.

This happy state of affairs was certainly because, then as now, Christ Church was such a nursery of friendships. He was on close terms with the Tutor and Censor Osborne Gordon, a liberal Christian and, as Ruskin wrote in his great autobiography *Praeterita* (a model for Proust), 'a man of curious intellectual power and simple virtue'. Gordon went for long walks with him and stayed with his family in the vacations. Liddell, as we saw, encouraged him as an artist – and also as an art critic – but Ruskin rather took against him when he published the great *Lexicon* and became Dean, because 'the prosaic and practical element in him prevailed over the sensitive one'. But that was retrospective. In his undergraduate years Liddell was clearly supportive and friendly. But so vertical a man (Ruskin imagined him as the counterpart to Tom Tower) could not be so enchanting a friend as Henry Acland: 'a noble young English life', Ruskin wrote of him 'in its purity, sagacity, honour, reckless daring and happy piety'. This fountain of charity and intellectual courage took a lead in promoting science in Oxford, was an assiduously dedicated doctor, and Ruskin's most devoted friend. For eccentricity, there was Canon William Buckland. His hospitable lodgings in the north-west corner of Tom Quad abounded with animals, often eaten at his table. He used Ruskin as an illustrator and introduced him to Herschel and Darwin, whose momentous discoveries Ruskin was later to treat with uneasily evasive humour. He loved the cathedral and its College Prayers but had no time for that internal alien to the spirit of Christ Church, Doctor Pusey: 'a sickly and rather ill put together English clergyman, who never looked one in the face, or appeared aware of the state of the weather.'

As for his easy-going fellow gentlemen commoners, Ruskin's genial sympathy with them can be caught from his account of Francis Charteris:

> *He could do what he liked with anyone, – at least with anyone of good humour and sympathy; and when one day, the old sub-dean coming out of Canterbury gate at the instant Charteris was dismounting at it in forbidden pink, as Charteris turned serenely to him as he took his foot out of the stirrup, to inform him that 'he had been out with the Dean's hounds,' the old man and the boy were both alike pleased.*

Left:
John Ruskin,
Tom Quad, 1839

Below:
John Ruskin and Henry Acland, photographed in 1893 by Sarah Acland (from Tim Hilton, *John Ruskin: the later years*, 2000)

That cameo can stand for the companionable temper of the Christ Church in which Ruskin thrived. When he turned most unjustly on his father, twenty-five years later, blaming that devoted and nurturing parent for – of all things – a bad upbringing, he accused him of putting him among 'men who had their drawers filled with pictures of naked bawds – who walked openly with their harlots in the sweet country lanes – men who swore, who diced, who drank, who knew nothing'.

He may have been recalling some moments of priggish shock, but he had forgotten what he recalled in old age in *Praeterita*: that they treated him kindly and that he got on with them pretty well. Encouraged in his multifarious interests, surrounded by friends and with his mother at hand to visit in the evenings, the years at Christ Church were benignly formative and creative for him – rather more so than Tim Hilton makes out in the generally splendid first volume of his biography. The only fly in the ointment was not Christ Church's fault: the obduracy of Adele Domecq. Her betrothal to a French baron in his third year brought on a breakdown which removed him from Oxford for eighteen months. He returned only to complete his residence and take the degree which he proudly advertised three years later on the title-page of the first volume of his masterpiece *Modern Painters*, where he concealed his name and ascribed authorship to 'A Graduate of Oxford'.

John Drury

The Study of Ancient Tongues
Gaisford and Liddell

They make a remarkable pair, gremial members of Christ Church who came to dominate sixty years of Christ Church history: Thomas Gaisford, Dean 1831–55; Henry George Liddell, Dean 1855–1892. Gaisford, the Wiltshire boy, stayed a man of few words and blunt manners, variously described as 'the old bear' and 'the Athenian blacksmith'; 'You will never be a gentleman, but you may succeed as a scholar', said (or so it was rumoured) his mentor, Cyril Jackson (Dean 1783–1809). He adhered to the old ways; the college's tone and buildings and constitution altered little in his time. Liddell, on the other hand, nephew to a baron, aristocratic in bearing, installed after a reign as headmaster of Westminster School, took up the mission for change: his buildings (Meadows among them) remain a conspicuous part of the fabric, and his reforms remain the basis of the constitution under which (since the act of 1867) we still live – both projects carried through with firm diplomacy against the opposition of (among others) the cantankerous author of two novels centred on the Dean's daughter Alice, C.L. Dodgson. The portraits in Hall make the contrast: Gaisford's straight stare, Liddell's reflective profile.

Yet the two deans shared one passion: ancient Greek. The subject, indeed, had been built into the House since 1546. When Henry VIII, Renaissance monarch if not Renaissance man, appropriated and refounded Cardinal College as Christ Church, he endowed it with professorships in the going subjects of the day – Medicine and Divinity and the languages of scripture, Hebrew and Greek. The Regius professorship of Greek enjoyed a chequered history. One Elizabethan professor was executed for treason; many of his successors avoided conspicuous intellect as well as conspicuous indiscretion. It was to this chair that Gaisford was appointed (by the Prime Minister) in 1812, and he held it until his death, for more than twenty years in tandem with the deanery. Both offices had duties; but those of the professorship did not include lecturing, or indeed any form of what would now be called 'outreach'. Gaisford made good use of this now unimaginable freedom. As Curator of Bodley he encouraged the acquisition of Greek manuscripts; as Delegate of the Press he arranged the publication of notable works of scholarship; as a scholar, learned

Left:
Henry George Liddell, Dean of Christ Church 1855–92
Above:
Thomas Gaisford, Dean of Christ Church 1831–55

Aphrodite and Eros, found at Pella by Alexander Mackenzie in 1805, and bequeathed to Christ Church

and indefatigable, he studied manuscripts and published texts by a whole series of Greek authors pagan and Christian. The *Etymologicum Magnum* (1848) represents the grandest of these achievements: a dictionary of ancient Greek words which preserves an extraordinary richness of learned detail culled from ancient scholars' comments on their own texts. Two modern attempts have been made to produce a new edition, but the task has proved too much; Gaisford's massive folio remains the standard reference.

Gaisford's death marks a new era. Liddell too was offered the Greek chair at the same time as the Deanery; but he declined the double load. The new professor, Benjamin Jowett, lectured eloquently to undergraduates, and his translations, especially of Plato, reached out to a wider public. The new Dean, however, did not put Greek aside. Throughout his time in office, Liddell pushed ahead with a project begun in 1834, in conjunction with Robert Scott (afterwards Master of Balliol), the Greek–English lexicon still known as 'Liddell and Scott'. Gaisford encouraged the enterprise, which they founded on the Greek–German lexicon of Passow (another sign of the times). The first edition appeared in 1843; in 1882 Liddell, now without Scott, produced a seventh edition, in which form the lexicon enjoyed worldwide acclaim for some sixty years. He made time by working on it before breakfast, leaving the day for college business. At least one old member, otherwise eminent in politics, took pains to advise him: pasted into Liddell's own copy (now in the Library) is a letter which discusses the meaning of a word in Homer, a letter written by that enthusiastic Hellenist, W.E. Gladstone. The lexicon remains Liddell's monument; and a staircase in the deanery, built from the royalties, reminds us of those early morning labours. Gaisford's had been scholarship for scholars. Liddell, much less learned, much more forward-looking, offered a new and fundamental resource for classical researchers and classical students. There was the great lexicon; there were also the shorter and longer abridgements of it, which circulated widely in schools. It took until 1940 to produce a major revision, which, with supplements compiled in 1968 and 1996, is still available in hard copy and in electronic form. That revision required a team in addition to its two individual editors; and the further revision now needed, as new texts accumulate and new ideas accrue, seems unimaginably beyond the reach of one scholar in his spare time.

Gaisford had recommended, in one of his sermons (and it is the sentence that secures his place in anecdote) 'the Study of the Ancient Tongues, which not only refines the intellect and elevates above the common herd, but also leads not infrequently to positions of considerable emolument'. The classical scholars of today will believe the first part of this, and feel wry amazement at the second. From an age of group research and online resources, they look back to Gaisford and to Liddell as to the great achievements of Victorian engineering, an extraordinary reminder of what could (and perhaps still can) be achieved for scholarship and for education by the single-minded commitment of individual vision and individual intellect.

Peter Parsons

St Matthew, from Library MS 32, who wrote his gospel in Greek

The Senior Common Room

The Common Room owes its origins to a benefaction by Dr Busby, the famous headmaster of Westminster School from 1638 to 1695 and for many years a regular supplier of young men to the House.

In an agreement between Busby and the Chapter of 9 June 1667 entitled 'Appointment of Common room for Dr. Busby's Lectures', the terms agreed upon (with 'Rabbinical' in what follows meaning 'Oriental') were:

> *That the new low room beneath the Hall, be for ever set apart and applied to the Mathematick and Rabbinical lectures founded by the Reverend Dr. Busby: as also to the use of the Masters for their Publick fires.That the benefaction in the foundation of the said lectures; & the charge in fitting the said Room be entered into the book of Benefactors.*
>
> *That both the Lecturers read yearly twenty five lectures, viz.: in Michaelmas term 8, in Lent term 8, in Easter term 5, in Act term 4.*
>
> *That the Mathematick reader read on Mondays at nine in the Morning: or if any Accident as Holidays or the like divert at that time, then on Thursdays at the same hour.*
>
> *That the Rabbinical reader read on Thursdays at one of the Clock in the afternoon, & if the said accidents divert at that time, then on Mondays at the same hour.*
>
> *That all undergraduates be obliged to be auditors of the said lectures.*

Whilst there is no record that the lectures indicated were regularly given, this room, now known as the Old Common Room, has ever since remained a place where senior members might meet and keep warm.

A bust of Dr Busby has adorned the Old Common Room since 1875. In its present location above the fireplace it appropriately faces a portrait of John Locke, who was a Censor in the mid-1660s. (It was long accompanied on the mantelpiece by a miniature model of the Eiffel Tower.)

The Common Room as conceived by Busby would not have been a comfortable place, though it certainly became so after it was considerably altered and improved in the 1870s, under the direction of the then Treasurer, Rev. R. Godfrey Faussett. The pillars and vaulting were removed and iron girders were introduced into the ceiling, cased in oak, to support the floor of the Hall above – and even a carpet was provided! At the same time the original western entrance was replaced by the present eastern one from the (newly created) passage into Schools Quad, thus providing access to the Lee Building. Meanwhile the old passage was turned into the butler's pantry and a garden was created to the south of the Common Room. The room's subsequent appearance, with an extraordinary clutter of miscellaneous objects, which can be seen in a photograph of about 1910, remained essentially unchanged down to the 1960s and even later.

J.M. Rysbrack, *Richard Busby*

The Revd. C. M. Blagdon recalled in 1953

the dim religious light of the Common Room, with its panelled walls and its choice of paintings by Cuyp and Franz Hals and Gainsborough, and its many engravings of Chancellors of the University and Governors-General and Viceroys of India, where Telling, the Common Room man who – with his white side-whiskers and choker, looked as if he had come straight out of a Dickens' portrait gallery, who never seemed to sit down or take a holiday, and who, if he were not waiting on us, would be acting as college postman – would be seeing that the polished mahogany was in order, and asking whether any gentleman wished to drink claret.

Blagdon also noted that the pleasant informality which characterised Common Room life in Christ Church then (as now) was not to be found in other colleges:

In the Common Room ... we sat where we liked, not at little tables as in so many other colleges, but round one single table, all of us together; conversation was general if there were not too many of us there, and there was little risk of having the evening spoilt by a taciturn or grumpy neighbour. ... In Hall most of us drank water, and several took little or no wine in Common Room. The cost of dessert and wine was divided amongst those present, and the weekly accounts were light, which is hardly surprising when ... '75 port figured on the wine list at 4s 6d. a bottle, and whisky at 4s. Coffee was served at 8.30 or 8.45, and by 9, before Great Tom began to ring out one hundred and one times, we had scattered and all was quiet again.

Blagdon's account indicates that, when he arrived in 1896, the present spiral staircase from the Common Room up to the Hall, though already in existence, was not in use. Communication between the Common Room and the Hall continued in practice to be by way of the Great Quadrangle and the grand staircase constructed at the start of the nineteenth century beneath the seventeenth-century fan-vaulting.

When the new and enlarged Governing Body came into existence as a result of the Christ Church, Oxford, Act of 1867 bestowing the legal rights and responsibilities of College Fellows upon the Students, its meetings were held in the Old Common Room and continued there until 1971 when the minutes of the meeting of 27 January announced that this was the first meeting to be held in the Lee Building. Indeed there then followed a debate as to what that building should be called.

Even in the mid-1950s the Governing Body was still quite small (thirty-one Students, five Canons and the Dean), but by the late 1960s Governing Body meetings had become crowded and cramped occasions, where close physical proximity perhaps added to the force of rhetoric and certainly added to the depth of perplexity when Sir Roy Harrod, alluding to this canon or that, maintained the Old Ways and insisted on referring to 'Mr Fourth Stall', or whichever it might be. Except on Governing Body days, it was also in the Common Room that lunch was served.

In 1886 a desire was expressed for a separate smoking room, not perhaps a surprise since the then Curator, C.L. Dodgson, was very strongly opposed to

The Lee Anatomy School, later to become part of the Senior Common Room

smoking in the Common Room itself. A committee was appointed to deal with this contentious issue. As a result it was decided to establish such a room in the former set of the ritualist priest Thomas Chamberlain; but this committee was far from expeditious; it took three years to report, and the Smoking Room (now the Bayne Room) did not become available until the early 1890s. At first this was called the 'Drawing Room' until Dodgson ruled (in 1892) that it be the only place where smoking was permitted.

In 1862 the Common Room had considered seeking leave from the Dean and Chapter to take over the Anatomy School (now the Lee Building), the contents of which had recently been moved to the new University Museum in Parks Road. This proposal came to nothing but in 1970, under the devoted supervision of Mr Oscar Wood (then Deputy Curator), and with the advice and assistance of the architect Mr E. Payne, a luncheon room, a drawing room and a dining room were created, these being named respectively after Dr John Freind (physician to Queen Caroline, who gave a course in Chemistry in 1704 and is thought to be the person who first suggested the creation of a college laboratory), Henry Keene (the architect and builder of the Lee Building in 1766–7), and Dr John Kidd (Dr Lee's Reader in Anatomy, 1816–44). Today these rooms are used regularly for lunches, dinners and other social functions, and meetings of the Governing Body.

In the 1950s and 60s the New Common Room was also used for a Tutors' Meeting that took place after dinner on the Saturday at the start of each term. At this brief meeting Tutors would report the names of pupils who had failed to return into residence by the appointed day. The interest and pleasure of such occasions was not infrequently heightened by the fact that it thereby provided the Senior Tutor in English, J.I.M. Stewart, with the opportunity to report in vivid terms and ringing tones on the absence of his own pupils, as when he informed the meeting at the start of one Michaelmas Term that 'there is a heartening report that Mr X. is a prisoner of the Bedouins' [pronounced 'Bedoueen' with relish], and at the start of one Hilary Term, that 'the Honourable ... [who lived in a castle] sends his apologies and regrets that he has been unable to return because heavy snow has made it impossible for him to reach his front gate'.

One of the first mentions of activities within the Common Room dates from Dean Aldrich's time (1689–1710). A group of musicians known as 'The Musick' would play every night to the scholars at dinner in Hall (which seems to have begun at 5 pm) and then 'retreat to the Common Fyre Room where they play to the Masters of Arts till they depart'. Pleasure in musical events continues to this day.

A snapshot of members' day-to-day interests and concerns is provided by the Common Room's betting books. In the first of these, dating from the end of the nineteenth century, we find bets relating to pupils' performances in Schools, the likely outcome of elections to heads of houses, estimates of the weight and height of colleagues, and (in 1899) a claim that the queen (Victoria) would outlive the then Pope (Leo XIII). In both 1902 and 1906 it was predicted that Britain and Germany would very shortly be at war. There were also frequent references to the outcomes of parliamentary elections including, in 1908, a bet in which it was suggested that Winston Churchill would be returned as MP for Dundee.

The more recent betting book contains a greater variety of entries ranging from concerns about military events in the 1930s to publication of authenticated evidence for the existence of the Loch Ness monster and predictions of the outcome of test matches. College matters remained a concern; for example, in 1934, 'Page bets Percival 2/6 that the depth of the water in Mercury is not less than 5 feet 9 inches (under normal weather conditions) near the centre "generally speaking"'. The book then reports that:

> *Measurements of the depth of the water in Mercury were taken at 9.18 am on the 15th September, the basin being full of water. The measuring rod had a sharp point at the end which was pressed firmly into the mud at the bottom of Mercury (basin). The measurements were taken by Mr A.C. Bradbury and testified to the Manciple. The greatest depth was near the centre and was 4 (four) feet, other depths recorded were 3 feet ten inches & 3 feet six inches."*

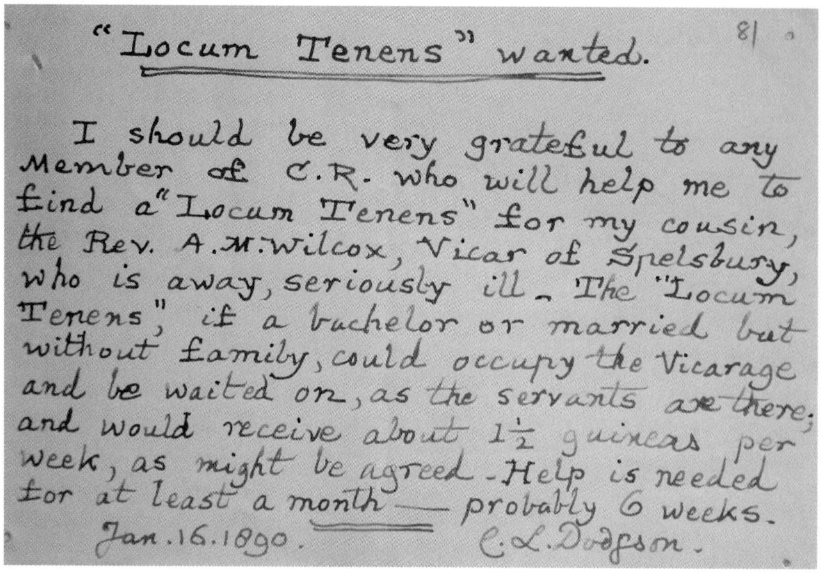
"Locum Tenens" wanted. 81

I should be very grateful to any Member of C.R. who will help me to find a "Locum Tenens" for my cousin, the Rev. A. M. Wilcox, Vicar of Spelsbury, who is away, seriously ill. The "Locum Tenens", if a bachelor or married but without family, could occupy the Vicarage and be waited on, as the servants are there; and would receive about 1½ guineas per week, as might be agreed. Help is needed for at least a month — probably 6 weeks.

Jan. 16. 1890. C. L. Dodgson.

One of Charles Dodgson's many notices issued during his time as Curator of Common Room

In the nineteenth century the Common Room was the agency of the college which mobilised non-resident members to vote on occasions such as parliamentary elections (i.e. for the University's representatives in the House of Commons), the election of the Chancellor and of the Professor of Poetry. The two MPs of the University (one of whom was usually a member of Christ Church) used ceremonially to visit the Common Room as part of the courtesies which they normally extended to resident members of the University. Early in that century the Common Room was the scene of a very different sort of occasion when its Curator, William Corne, was laid in state there after his death. Students sat around the walls in order of seniority, with the coffin in their midst, before they moved off to the cathedral for the funeral service. Corne is commemorated by a tablet in the cathedral's north transept.

After the Second World War, Common Room life returned to pre-war normality. In the 1950s formal dessert flourished and was well attended, Christ Church being one of the few colleges that performed the ceremony of 'Common Room' (i.e. formal dessert) every night of the week. During this period Wystan Auden was Professor of Poetry (1956–60) and contributed both to its social geniality and its amenities. Having discovered to his astonishment that the pantry did not have a refrigerator, he presented the Butler (Cyril Little) with a blank cheque to buy a large and expensive one – prompted in part, one suspects, by his liking for a properly chilled dry martini.

The curators of the Common Room have brought and continue to bring their own individual styles and interests to that role. This was vividly exemplified in the mid-1960s by Sir Roy Harrod, whose characteristically forceful convictions seemed especially strong in matters where aesthetics and social judgement came together. He declared himself to be both perplexed and disappointed when a brass chandelier which he had caused to be put up in the Common Room met with vocal and even vehement dislike on the part of his colleagues. In self-defence he was moved to observe in writing that he did recognise that the privileged milieu in which he had grown up had perhaps given him a sense of fitness in these matters that was not universally shared. He therefore craved the indulgence of the Common Room and asked that the chandelier be allowed to stay. It did so, until such time as its removal would not cause pain to him.

Martin Grossel, John Mason and Ron Truman

The Twentieth Century & Now

Chronology

1901 *Installation of Dean Thomas Banks Strong*
1920 *Installation of Dean Henry White*
1925 *Visit of George V and Queen Mary, recorded on film*
1925–6 *Creation of the Masters' Garden*
1926 *Opening of the Memorial Garden*
1934 *Installation of Dean A.T.P. Williams*
1935 *Building of the Christ Church boathouse*
1939 *Installation of Dean John Lowe*
1939–45 *Brasenose College shares Christ Church for the duration of the war*
1946 *Visit of King George VI and Queen Elizabeth to Christ Church for the quarter-centenary celebrations*
1948 *Visit of Princess Elizabeth*
1950 *Law Library opened*
1954 *Feast of the baron of beef given to mark the end of meat rationing*
1955 *Anthony Eden (ChCh 1919), earl of Avon, elected Prime Minister*
1959 *Installation of Dean Cuthbert Simpson*
1962 *Restoration of the Library stonework, and redecoration of the Upper Library*
Visit of Queen Elizabeth II
1963 *Alec Douglas-Home (ChCh), earl of Home, elected Prime Minister*
1968 *Blue Boar Quad opened by the Queen*
1968 *Picture Gallery opened*
1969 *Installation of Dean Henry Chadwick*
1979 *Installation of Dean Eric Heaton*
1980 *Admission of the first female undergraduates*
1986 *St Aldate's Quad opened*
1991 *Installation of Dean John Drury*
1991 *Opening of the Liddell Building on Iffley Road*
1992 *Visit of Queen Elizabeth II*
1996 *450th anniversary celebration*
2003 *Installation of Dean Christopher Lewis*
2006 *Visit of Queen Elizabeth II*

THIS IS THE ORIGINAL SKETCH
MADE BY
POWELL AND MOYA
(THE ARCHITECTS)
ON THE BASIS OF WHICH THEIR DESIGN FOR
BLUE BOAR QUAD
WAS ACCEPTED BY
THE GOVERNING BODY OF
CHRIST CHURCH,
OXFORD.

GIVEN TO W.R.IX, HON. ORGANISER, BLUE BOAR FUND,
1965.

Christ Church in 1900

Christ Church in 1900 was still the largest college in Oxford, albeit marginally so. Most of the 210 or so men in residence were reading for Honours, though a substantial minority were content to aim for 'pass' degrees, while some – though perhaps fewer than later impressions suggested – left without taking any degree at all. A handful were preparing dissertations for the newly created (1895) research degrees of B.Litt and B.Sc. About forty undergraduates lived out of college in lodgings, mainly in King Edward Street, but also further afield in Iffley Road and Walton Street. Those with rooms in the House were shortly to enjoy the amenity of electric lighting, which was installed in 1901 after nearly a decade of discussion by the Governing Body.

Telephone had yet to arrive, though a speaking tube kept the Dean and Censors in close communication. That triumvirate was regaining the upper hand in disciplinary matters following the upheavals of the Blenheim 'row' in December 1893, and the Bullingdon riot in the following summer. Porters' reports to the censors for the years 1901–3, preserved in the Bodleian Library, provide a daily inventory of broken window panes and shattered soda water siphons, explosions of fireworks, hornblowing, and other disturbances. But the perpetrators were a few habitual offenders, who confined their offences to a limited area (the inhabitants of Meadows were mainly left in peace).

Left: *Thomas Banks Strong*, Dean of Christ Church, 1901–20, and Right: *Marino Vagliano* (mt. 1901), from the album given to Christ Church in 1947 by William Robinow (mt. 1901)

So large a foundation was bound to be divided into many groups or 'sets', 'to the impoverishment of its unity and common sentiment', as a former Student H.L. Thompson wrote in his history of Christ Church, published in 1900. A Junior Common Room had been founded in 1886 'to bring men together', but in its early years it never really flourished. Instead, there was a host of independent clubs and societies: in addition to the well-established Loder's and the Pythic, there were the Anonym, Cardinals, and Twenty debating clubs, as well as the Mermaid play reading society. This dispersion, which Thompson regretted, proved to be one of the House's strengths, for it enabled individuals to find their own niche, especially during Thomas Strong's years in the deanery. Although dunkings in Mercury were not unheard of, dissidents in Christ Church were less likely to face the sort of unpleasant persecutions enforced in places where 'college spirit' was pervasive. The future earl of Halifax, who came up in 1899, considered that it was 'refreshing to find Christ Church large enough to allow an almost indefinite measure of diversity'.

Halifax was able to fall in with a group of serious reading men, who encouraged one another in their studies. For him, like others, the House was an escape from the regimentation and conformity of late Victorian boarding schools.

Although narrow by later standards, the intake of the House was among the more diverse of Oxford's colleges. Former pupils of local grammar schools, along with graduates of Scottish universities, and Welsh and English university colleges, appear in the lists of admissions. With the ending of denominational exclusiveness, there were now Roman Catholic, Protestant non-conformist and Jewish undergraduates. The arrival of overseas students from the late 1860s broadened the range even further. An initial trickle, which included Prince Hassan of Egypt (1869), On Wah Wei from Hong Kong (1887) and Manmohan Ghose from Bihar (1887), became a steady stream by 1900 when the Crown Prince of Siam was among the admissions. Alumni from Harvard and Yale preceded the first Rhodes Scholars, all from the USA, who entered in 1904. On the eve of the First World War there was a remarkable concentration of students from the ruling dynasties of central and eastern Europe, including Prince Paul of Serbia (1913) and Sergius Obolensky (1912) from Russia.

This cosmopolitanism was also reflected in the Senior Common Room. The restoration to Christ Church of the Regius chairs of Greek and Medicine had brought, in 1893, Ingram Bywater, a classicist of European reputation, and in 1905 William Osler, a Canadian clinician revered throughout the English-speaking medical world. Among the tutors, the ancient historians F.J. Haverfield and J.L. Myres embodied the combination of teaching and research inspired by German academic traditions. Yet here, again, there was variety. The philosophy tutor Herbert Blunt was a non-publishing polymath who concentrated his energies upon undergraduate teaching, as did Albert Carter, who established law tuition at the House in the thirty years following his election in 1895. Arthur Hassall, who taught history for forty years, wrote numerous books, mainly for use in schools, but was 'quite out of sympathy' with 'the modern school of intensive research'. The Lee's Readers, A.G.V. Harcourt, Barclay Thompson, and R.E. Baynes meanwhile ensured that Christ Church was Oxford's leading producer of finalists in Natural Sciences.

Harcourt had been the first lecturer in the university to admit women students to his classes after the foundation of women's colleges. Chaperones were present to prevent fraternisation with the male undergraduates present; other than occasions such as Commemoration balls, contact between the genders was discouraged. In February 1900 the Dean and censors heavily fined and 'gated' a third-year historian who had purchased an expensive outfit for a waitress at a café on the High Street, taken her on day trips, and talked vaguely of matrimony – an imprudent act in an age where breach of promise of marriage could give rise to legal action. Changing relations between the genders much exercised Christ Church's debating societies, which regularly discussed the merits (or otherwise) of women's higher education, suffragism and feminism alongside such other concerns as the rise of German power and the growing 'menace' of trade unions. For the present, the world of public life which most House men were destined to enter remained an overwhelmingly male one. And there was reassurance in the result of the general election of October 1900 when, in addition to the Prime Minister Lord Salisbury, Christ Church could claim to have educated more MPs (thirty-five) than any other college.

Mark Curthoys

Punting in 1904, from the Robinow album

Christ Church Gardens

The Memorial Garden, opened in the 1920s, looking towards Auden Cottage and Hall

Gardens are an important part of the space in which Christ Church now stands, but it was not always so. To the north and the west the urban streetscape ran right up to the walls. To the south and east was a great water-meadow. Inside, the original austere quadrangles were so full of formal authority and symbolic meaning that flowers would have been an impertinence, and thus it has remained. Around the immediate edges there was no space for gardens: the needs of domestic offices, food, fuel and sewerage to service this great accumulation of speculative humanity took precedence. With the exception of the private gardens of the deanery and the canonries, then, gardens as public spaces were unknown until relatively recently.

The 'Iris' Garden, created as part of the Memorial Garden
Far right: The Pococke Garden, with its famous plane tree, possibly the first plane tree in the United Kingdom, planted by Edward Pococke, Professor of Arabic, in the mid-seventeenth century

Things began to change with the passing of decanal absolutism in the 1860s. A more open style of governance set in, and the impact of the long slow rise of Victorian middle-class prosperity made itself felt. Eventually even the self-confident dons of Christ Church began to see that lesser colleges had the splendid gardens they were lacking. The appeal was no doubt all the greater in that the natural site for expansion lay to the south of the college, where gardens would provide a better link with those eighteenth- and nineteenth-century recreational creations the Broad Walk and the Long Walk. To reach the Meadow from St Aldate's was to run the gamut of assorted sheds and stores. It punctured the image of grandeur glimpsed in passing Tom Gate. Even Students could hardly be unaware of the mess to their right and the scruffy orchard to the left as they slipped out of the Meadow Building into the Meadow.

Thus began the long slow emergence of the gardens that today reach from St Aldate's, through the Memorial Garden, around the east end of the Meadow Building, to the Masters' Garden, to snake back through what is today Pococke's Garden with its great oriental plane, around behind the chapter house, and out into the Cathedral Garden and up to the very heart of the college.

Almost all these gardens are of twentieth-century origin. The first was the Masters' Garden, the creation in 1926 of the then Treasurer, Captain Hutchinson, who married well, twice, and was able, as a stone tablet in the garden recalls, not only to design the college's first corporate garden, but also to help finance it. It has the masculine orderliness of many of the college's early efforts at garden design. By today's standards it is deeply unadventurous. Unchanged in layout throughout its eighty years, it remains a great grass rectangle, surrounded by heavy grey walls – the north end being the old city rampart. There are four generous mixed borders, the east of which is still punctuated by Hutchinson's yews, wired to conical form but today frequently bursting their bounds to create a disorderly form. But no-one passing through the understated door at the end of the Meadow Building would be churlish enough to remark on the conservatism of the design. What they encounter is one of the best views in Oxford: a garden on a vast scale, and beyond it the backs of Corpus Christi and Merton, and in the distance Magdalen Tower. It is an extraordinary combination of peerless architecture, water-meadow, playing field, and carefully worked gardens. That the Masters' Garden is formal to the point of tedium matters little, and today its huge lawn has adapted to the needs of sunbathers, readers, conferences and weddings.

Almost simultaneously, the then Steward, Major Slessor, constructed the Memorial Garden, honouring college members who died in war. It also transformed the view of the college from the south. Old commercial property was swept away, gates were installed, and a broad York-stone path was laid to link the Broad Walk with St Aldate's. To the left, as the visitor entered the Meadow, was a banked garden that in its delicacy provided a fine contrast to the towering view of the Hall and the south range of Tom. To the right, further on, was an elegant circular walled garden. Its centrepiece holds the tiny serpent fountain which preceded Mercury in Tom Quad. The shambles of domestic offices thus gave way to a fitting entrance to the Meadow. Almost – for as with all things in Christ Church, the past sits in sometimes uncomfortable juxtaposition with the new. Visitors who pass sedately along the broad path of the Memorial Garden to this day pick their way through a small car park and past the buildings and barns of the clerk of works staff, before finally reaching the promised land of the Meadow itself.

Forty years after the Masters' and the Memorial Gardens, another public garden came into corporate hands. The canonry, occupied most recently by Claude Jenkins, was yielded to the college (it subsequently housed the Treasury and the Steward's Office) and behind it the canonry garden became the Cathedral Garden. It was not a perfect garden. It was another example of male rectilinearity. It was overshadowed by the cathedral. It was inaccessible. At the far end, the noisy air-conditioning of the Picture Gallery disturbed the peace and still does. But it did at least have a fine south-facing border protected by a high wall, and here a number of delicate shrubs have prospered in the sheltered micro-climate. It only remained to join all this together, and thirty years later, in the 1990s, came the opportunity. Another large canonry garden – this time behind the Priory House – was divided up, and a new garden created from a generous benefaction from a former college secretary, Miss Page. It links the Masters' garden with the Cathedral garden, but it is much more than a corridor. In many respects it is the best garden in the college. Pococke was the creation of another Treasurer, Richard Benthall, but there the similarity with the Masters' garden ends. It is not flat. It is not a rectangle of grass surrounded by

Bottom:
The gates of the Masters' Garden looking out over the Meadow

borders. It has softly curving paths, and secret places where woodland plants grow under the spreading shade of the 350-year-old plane, and where, under the buttress of the city wall, more tender shrubs flourish in another micro-climate.

Pococke's Garden in the 1990s completed the public spaces that surround the south and east of the college, though they are, for the most part, not fully public. All visitors can enjoy the Memorial Garden, and they can see enough of the Masters' Garden through gates to appreciate it, without normally being allowed in. The Masters' Garden is the collective college garden, and used by all its members. Pococke's and the Cathedral have been reserved for staff and senior members, though special tours and charitable events open all these gardens up to a wider public. What has been achieved in these one hundred years of development is remarkable. It has been executed to a high standard. It has transformed the Christ Church site, and softened its austerity and formality. It adds hugely to the experience of visiting the college and living and working in it. What is lacking is avant-garde garden design and here the jury is out on how we shall see these spaces in the future. The formalism of seventeenth- and eighteenth-century design eventually gave way almost everywhere in England to the artificial naturalism that culminated in the Edwardian mixed border. Through the twentieth century this stuck, and particularly in Christ Church. We shall have difficulty thinking of these gardens in different terms. All to the good the traditionalists will say, but future generations may think differently, and perhaps they should. Taste and message have become immortalised in the distinctive austerity of Tom, Peck and Canterbury. It would be a brave Governing Body that tampered with that. But around the southern garden edge there may be room for experiment. Gardens, unlike buildings, are not permanent fixtures, after all. They can be made and unmade, and made again, as long as records are kept.

David Hine

Bottom:
The Masters' Garden. There is no truth in the rumour that the garden was won from Corpus Christi College in a card game!

Christ Church in the First World War

In 1914 Oxford was directly affected by war to an extent unequalled since 1642. As in 1642, when it was said that the University and college buildings became 'half-arsenals and half-hotels', town and gown united in a common effort.

Just before the outbreak of war in 1914, Christ Church was in its cosmopolitan prime. Under Dean Strong the college attracted the sons of the European nobility, including Prince Paul of Serbia. But, on the outbreak of hostilities, the college was emptied of undergraduates. Before Michaelmas Term 1914 began, huge numbers of students and fellows had volunteered for military service, many processed through the special committee set up by the Vice-Chancellor and the Dean of Christ Church. Only fifteen men came up in the autumn of 1915. The University consisted, in the words of E.R. Dodds, later Regius Professor of Greek, 'chiefly of young boys putting in time while they awaited their call-up, plus a few crocks, a few overseas students, and a number of women'.

Dean Strong, in spite of his early and active participation in officer recruitment, believed in 'business as usual'. In the early days of war, the records show little change in the ordered life of the college and cathedral. Hopes that the conflict would be over by Christmas encouraged the Governing Body to reject a proposal to insure the fabric, books and pictures against bomb damage. Soon, however, in spite of the continuation of the daily business of education, the war and its ramifications came to dominate decisions as undergraduates and the younger Fellows disappeared from the darkened quadrangles. In place of students came the military and refugees from Belgium and Serbia. The Oxfordshire and Buckinghamshire Light Infantry were, in part, billeted in Christ Church – the officers making use of the Common Room smoking room as their mess – until their more permanent barracks in Cowley were ready; and Christ Church, with Brasenose College, became home to the Royal Flying Corps from 1915. One of the canons, Henry Scott Holland, described the scene at the beginning of October 1916: 'Oxford begins next week, and we shall be more entirely a Camp than ever. Our 200 flying-men keep Ch.Ch. alive: and now and again

Oxford University Officer Training Corps, Christ Church Troop, 1912. From the album given to Christ Church in 1976 by G.M. Hamer (mt. 1910)

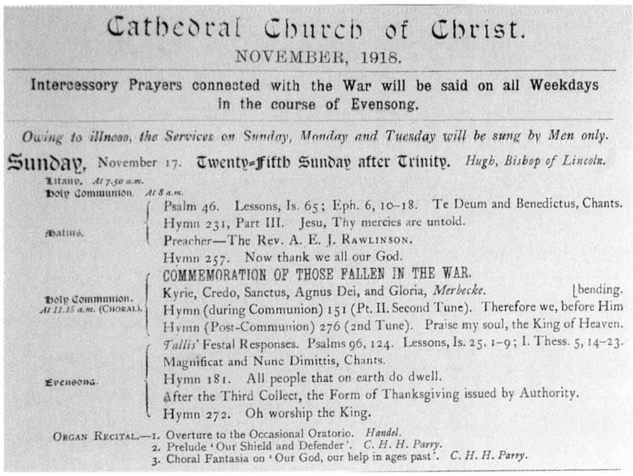
Cathedral Church of Christ.
NOVEMBER, 1918.

Intercessory Prayers connected with the War will be said on all Weekdays in the course of Evensong.

Owing to illness, the Services on Sunday, Monday and Tuesday will be sung by Men only.

Sunday, November 17. Twenty-Fifth Sunday after Trinity. *Hugh, Bishop of Lincoln.*

Litany. *At 7.50 a.m.*
Holy Communion. *At 8 a.m.*

Matins.
Psalm 46. Lessons, Is. 65; Eph. 6, 10–18. Te Deum and Benedictus, Chants.
Hymn 231, Part III. Jesu, Thy mercies are untold.
Preacher—The Rev. A. E. J. Rawlinson.
Hymn 257. Now thank we all our God.

Holy Communion. *At 11.15 a.m.* (Choral).
COMMEMORATION OF THOSE FALLEN IN THE WAR.
Kyrie, Credo, Sanctus, Agnus Dei, and Gloria, *Merbecke.*
Hymn (during Communion) 151 (Pt. II. Second Tune). Therefore we, before Him bending.
Hymn (Post-Communion) 276 (2nd Tune). Praise my soul, the King of Heaven.

Evensong.
Tallis' Festal Responses. Psalms 96, 124. Lessons, Is. 25, 1–9; I. Thess. 5, 14–23.
Magnificat and Nunc Dimittis, Chants.
Hymn 181. All people that on earth do dwell.
After the Third Collect, the Form of Thanksgiving issued by Authority.
Hymn 272. Oh worship the King.

Organ Recital.—1. Overture to the Occasional Oratorio. *Handel.*
2. Prelude 'Our Shield and Defender'. *C. H. H. Parry.*
3. Choral Fantasia on 'Our God, our help in ages past'. *C. H. H. Parry.*

Service sheet for the cathedral for the week commencing 17 November 1918, when a service of commemoration was held. The Armistice service was delayed because of the influenza outbreak; no choristers were available to sing

Peck wakes to quite its historic noises'. The death of Holland in March 1918 showed the changed environment: the cross placed in his hands was a gift from the Serbian students, a squadron of airmen stood to attention as the coffin was processed into the cathedral, and an aeroplane passed low over the cathedral in salute.

The resident officers ensured that the stocks of wine were steadily depleted – to the Common Room's profit – and, when rationing was introduced in 1918, High Table meals were similarly reduced; meat was only served on Tuesdays and Thursdays during 1918, and guests were only permitted on 'meatless' days. Part of the Meadow was temporarily taken from the yeomanry, who had traditionally drilled there, and handed over to the Allotment Association.

But the real toll of the war was brought home in the weekly lists of dead in the *Oxford Magazine* and in the obituary columns of the college's *Annual Report*. Sixteen per cent of the Christ Church men, past and present, who served were killed. Across the University, nearly twenty-nine per cent of those who had matriculated in 1913 died. Among Christ Church's losses were Andrea Angel, blown up developing explosives at Woolwich, and Charles Fisher, the Senior Censor, who died at Jutland.

Throughout the war, the cathedral was the focus for cultural activity, though with the war as a backdrop; the yeomanry's colours were hung above the subdean chair in August 1914 for the duration of hostilities. Organ recitals were given on Saturday afternoons and Sunday evenings in the summer months to raise funds for the Red Cross. On the third Sunday of every month, commemorative communion services for the fallen were held; there were special services at Easter and Christmas for the troops in residence, and regular parades. The military men occupied at first only the north side of the cathedral, but soon khaki began to appear among the choir as the lay clerks joined up. The Precentor had already left as chaplain to the 2nd South Midland Mounted Brigade, and chaplains and singers were roped in from other colleges to join our own choristers in the stalls.

Armistice day celebrations at Christ Church were cancelled as the organist and choristers were all laid low by the influenza epidemic. Instead, a commemoration service was held in the cathedral on 17 November 1918. It was on All Saints' day 1919, close to the first anniversary of the Armistice, and once the grim numbers of dead were finally gathered in, the main service of remembrance was held. The cathedral was full of undergraduates; many were students returning to finish their interrupted degrees, others were servicemen given for the first time the opportunity to study at university, still more were fresh-faced eighteen-year-olds for whom the war had been second-hand. The service and the memories it would have prompted were stark against the determined effort to return the college to normality. J.C. Masterman remembered the 'speed and determination with which Oxford resumed its peacetime life' as well as the 'wide and healthy tolerance of the returning warriors which enabled them to continue and coalesce easily and amicably with the younger men'. These young men would have witnessed the preparations for the tablets of remembrance in the cathedral passage, and the demolition of the houses south of Christ Church to make way for the Memorial Garden.

Never before had the college been so mixed, so democratic, or so full. From January 1919, the floodgates opened, and during that year 245 new faces appeared at Tom Gate to add to those who had arrived at the end of 1918 and all those who returned to complete their interrupted studies.

Judith Curthoys

Sport

Unattributed, *Archibald Primrose,* earl of Rosebery and later Prime Minister, who was sent down from Christ Church after refusing to part with his race-horses

Christ Church have more style than any other crew on the river, but their style is not exactly suited to hard boat pushing.

Thus the *Daily Telegraph* on the House first Eight in the Torpids of 1976. The comment was perhaps discourteous to the participants at the time, but, failing all else, serves as a good starting point for a review of the sporting House in the twentieth century. In truth, although throughout the century there is no doubt that the House – apart from the odd regrettable lapse – had plenty of style, and could reasonably boast many stars in the Oxford sporting firmament, only from time to time was there convincing evidence of 'hard boat pushing'.

In the far off-days of the Edwardian twilight, the intake of undergraduates was from a small and privileged catchment. Everybody, as it were, knew one another, or at least knew one another's sister or cousin. In that social climate, in sporting terms the House Boat Club was a matter of dignified and solemn respect. It was an honour to be selected, and it was an honour that was much prized, not least by Etonians coming from a school with a long rowing tradition. There were, of course, other gentlemanly sports: cricket, for instance, and rugby football. But it was the Boat Club which took undoubted pride of place.

In the early years of the century, those who were chosen for the first VIII in the summer Eights

Top left: hockey XI, 1906–7; Right: beagling at the beginning of the twentieth century

found in their places a set of silver oars about 8in. long, each in a case, one for each place in the boat. There was a special silver rudder for the cox. The rule was that the holder of the trophy was to keep his memento for a year, put his name on the case and hand it on to his successor the following year. But the devil, as so often happens, had his day. The system seemed to work well until 1907, but when the House VIII of that year arrived to claim their due, it was noted that all the silver oars and their cases were missing. There was an immediate request for the culprits to own up, but it was only in 1952 that the cox's silver rudder turned up, without attribution, identified presumably by a guilty descendant of the culprit cox of the day.

It was not only the Boat Club which marked the success of the 1920s. The House recorded Blues in cricket – one in 1923 and 1924, three in 1925 and 1926, two in 1927 and 1928, one in 1929; Blues in rugby in 1923, 1924 and 1925; many half-Blues in boxing (notably Lord Graham in the heavyweight encounter with his Cambridge opponent in 1929), fencing, golf, Eton fives, hockey, lawn tennis, rackets, squash, polo and – improbably – billiards. All in all, the 1920s marked a peak in House sporting achievement, not to be climbed again until after the Second World War.

There was something of a mini-revival in the middle of the 1930s. In 1936 the House won the inter-collegiate Golf Cup, and provided the President of the Oxford Boat as well as no fewer than three cricket Blues. In 1937 the House teams reached the finals of what by then had become known as 'Cuppers' in rugby, soccer and squash – and again fielded three Blues against Cambridge. But by 1938, apart from the cricket Blues and victories in inter-collegiate squash and rackets, Christ Church seems to have entered the sporting equivalent of the doldrums.

The end of the war brought a reflux of undergraduates who had left in the dark days for military service. The Beagles were formed anew and won two prizes at the Peterborough Show; the House provided the Captain of University cricket; and – a sign, perhaps, of the times ahead – a freshman Rhodes Scholar from New Zealand announced his arrival in the Michaelmas Term of 1945 by becoming the father of a son on his first evening and going on to win a rugby Blue; and there was joy in the land when the House first boat went up six places and earned the first Bump Supper since 1927. (Such was the enthusiasm that some who had returned from the war discovered service revolvers which had been kept as mementoes and, loaded with blanks, ran along the towpath firing them off to encourage their comrades.)

The sporting revival continued into 1946 and 1947. Two cricket Blues, a rugby Blue, a soccer Blue and a scattering of half-Blues provided the stars, but there was also a revival of the informal sports – the 'Nondescripts', 'Warrigals' and 'Runcibles' challenging other, equally informal, teams from other colleges and even from villages in the Oxfordshire countyside. In 1946 and 1947 the House won soccer 'Cuppers' and in 1948 went Head of the River in Torpids, and did well in that year in Oxford athletics as well as in golf, Eton fives and fencing. But by 1950 the lament was that 'we have done most things except win'. Style, of course, was still in evidence. 'On the last night (the Eights of 1950) the elegant bijou cox of the first Eight took the sensible and novel precaution of changing into a pair of becoming pants before being ritually hurled into the river'.

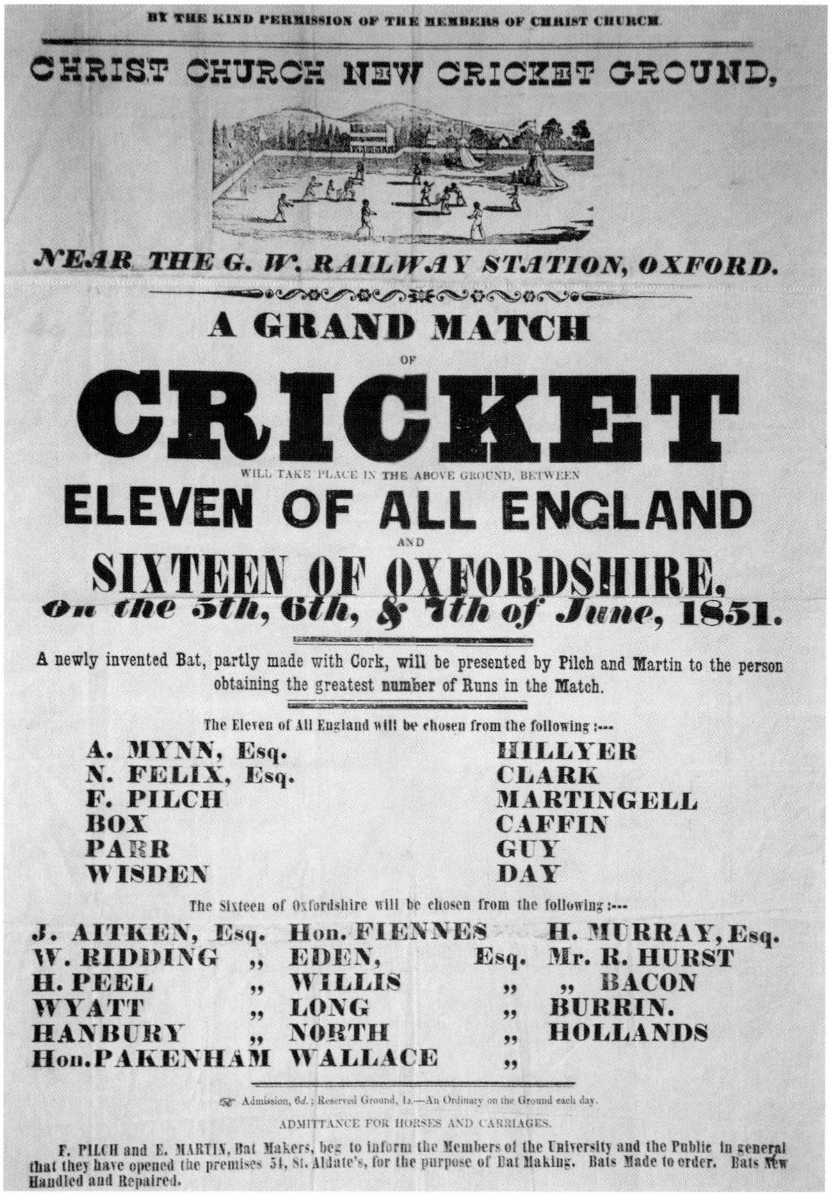
BY THE KIND PERMISSION OF THE MEMBERS OF CHRIST CHURCH.
CHRIST CHURCH NEW CRICKET GROUND,
NEAR THE G. W. RAILWAY STATION, OXFORD.
A GRAND MATCH
OF
CRICKET
WILL TAKE PLACE IN THE ABOVE GROUND, BETWEEN
ELEVEN OF ALL ENGLAND
AND
SIXTEEN OF OXFORDSHIRE,
On the 5th, 6th, & 7th of June, 1851.
A newly invented Bat, partly made with Cork, will be presented by Pilch and Martin to the person obtaining the greatest number of Runs in the Match.
The Eleven of All England will be chosen from the following:---
A. MYNN, Esq.
N. FELIX, Esq.
F. PILCH
BOX
PARR
WISDEN
HILLYER
CLARK
MARTINGELL
CAFFIN
GUY
DAY
The Sixteen of Oxfordshire will be chosen from the following:---
J. AITKEN, Esq.
W. RIDDING ,,
H. PEEL ,,
WYATT ,,
HANBURY ,,
Hon. PAKENHAM
Hon. FIENNES
EDEN, Esq.
WILLIS ,,
LONG ,,
NORTH ,,
WALLACE ,,
H. MURRAY, Esq.
Mr. R. HURST
,, BACON
BURRIN.
HOLLANDS
Admission, 6d.; Reserved Ground, 1s.—An Ordinary on the Ground each day.
ADMITTANCE FOR HORSES AND CARRIAGES.
F. PILCH and E. MARTIN, Bat Makers, beg to inform the Members of the University and the Public in general that they have opened the premises 51, St. Aldate's, for the purpose of Bat Making. Bats Made to order. Bats New Handled and Repaired.

Poster advertising a cricket fixture between and All England XI and an Oxfordshire XVI, to be held at Christ Church's ground near the railway station. The longest hit recorded in any cricket match, of 175 yards according to Wisden, was achieved on the Christ Church pitch

In the 1950s Christ Church fell into something of a trough. The gritty heroes of the war had left. There was an attempt to recreate a supposed pre-war heaven and with it came a renewed Bullingdon. In other words, the 'flanelled fools' and the 'muddied oafs' became again figures of not always innocent fun. There was, of course, the odd star: a rugby Blue and Blues or half-Blues in fencing, athletics, boxing and – oddly enough – lacrosse in 1951; Blues or half-Blues in fencing, boxing, squash and – again – lacrosse in 1952; a Blue in cricket and Blues or half-Blues in boxing and fencing in 1953; another Blue in cricket and two boxing Blues in 1954; and a further cricket Blue in 1955. Yet in all those years the House recorded no win in any of the inter-collegiate sports.

In the 1960s there was not much to celebrate. Cricket went well – other than that, the news was, at best, patchy. In 1962, thanks to a new design for its boat, the House went Head of the River, but this led to another unfortunate lapse in 'style'. There was an outbreak of hooliganism resulting in damage which was 'extensive, wilful and much of it anonymous'. In 1963, the House provided the stroke of the Oxford Boat – a freshman from Yale, as it happened – and another cricket Blue, but there was little success in inter-collegiate sports.

The 1970s promised better. In 1973 a welcome import from Harvard stroked the Oxford Boat, the House provided 'bow' as well, and, to much rejoicing, went Head of the River in the summer Eights. There were successes, too, in Eton fives, boxing and – another surprising first – darts. The headship of the river was followed by a cricket success. Thanks to a sporting decision by the Pembroke captain – reversing a clearly mistaken umpiring decision in the last over of the second round in 'Cuppers' – the House won the final with ease. In fact, such was the ease that the cup itself could not be retrieved from Worcester College, the previous holders, in time for the presentation. The compensation, if any, came from the report of the match in the Oxford *Mail*. 'Cool Christ Church', it proclaimed in its customary breathless prose, 'cruised to a comfortable and convincing "Cuppers" final win.'

Association Football XI, 1958/9

The sequence of sporting success continued for a year or two: Head of the River 'with ease' in 1975, with two Blues in the Oxford Boat; victory in Rugby 'Cuppers', narrow defeat in the semi-final of cricket 'Cuppers' to Keble (who, treacherously, included in their team a Pakistan Test player); a near success in Hockey Cuppers and a triumph in squash. The record by 1977 was 'generally mediocre', and the dreary tale continued into the mid-1980s. But by then it seemed that sport at Oxford was surrendering to the demands of meritocratic examination and sporting professionalism. In the outside world people of any consequence no longer looked to Oxbridge to provide Britain's sporting heroes. In cricket, for example, there were no stars to take the places of the Cowdreys and the Mays of yesteryear. Even the Boat Race was fast becoming a stage for foreign postgraduate students who inhabited colleges which hitherto had been reserved for women. Professionalism seemed to be putting an end to the amateur spirit, and 'style', which had been such a feature of House – and, indeed, University – sport earlier in the century.

So it went on into the last decade of the century. True, the House won soccer Cuppers in 1991 for the first time for fifty-three years, and went Head of the River in Torpids. But beyond that the successes were all achieved by Christ Church women – Blues and half-Blues abounded.

In sum, the history of the sporting House in the twentieth century is one of 'style', but never one of consistent 'hard boat pushing'. None of this is in itself regrettable – *tempora mutantur nos et mutamur in illis.* Yet there were moments in the century when the House did manage to scale not, perhaps, an Olympus, but at least a sporting Parnassus, and they, at the very least, will be treasured by those who took part.

Charles Williams (1951)

Rowing at the House
The First 200 Years

1947 Bump supper, showing the black-out curtains still up on the north side of Hall

The Christ Church Boat Club has a long and glorious history; it can claim to be the oldest of all House athletics clubs. In 1815 racing on the Isis between college crews started with races between Brasenose and Jesus. (In the early days the number of participating colleges was very small.) There were no races in 1816. In 1817 a Christ Church crew entered (the exact origins of the founding of the Boat Club are unknown) and immediately went Head of the River that year and the next, and again three more times before 1830. The House was Head of the River no fewer than sixteen times between 1817 and 1849.

In 1828 Christ Church became the first Oxford college to row away from the Isis, taking on Leander in a race from Westminster to Putney for a stake of £200 a side. Leander won. 1828 was also the year in which Cambridge issued its first challenge to Oxford resulting in the first Boat Race in 1829. The invitation was sent to Thomas Staniforth, captain (and stroke) of the Christ Church Head of the River crew. Staniforth stroked the Oxford crew, aided by three other House men and a House cox, in the race, held at Henley, which Oxford won easily, the House dark blue colour being adopted as the Oxford colour, which it has remained ever since.

An inaugural meeting of college strokes in 1839 led to the formation of the OUBC, with S.E. Maberly of Christ Church a member of the very first Committee, he becoming the second President of the OUBC in October that year. Between 1829 and 1875 there were only five years in which the Oxford boat did not include at least one Christ Church man. C.R.W. Tottenham created a record by coxing the winning boat for five successive years in the 1860s, he following F.E. Hopwood, who had coxed winning crews the two preceding years.

The OUBC sculls were inaugurated in 1841 with a pair of silver sculls 'presented to the Oxford University Boat Club by Members of Christ Church', and won by House men every year from 1842 to 1848. The start of the OUBC coxed pairs had been marked, in 1839, by a pair of Silver Challenge oars presented by Maberly and C. Berwicke of Univ. The pairs (coxless from 1847 on) were won by the House in 1843, 1844, 1846 and 1847.

Given the House's pre-eminence in Oxford rowing, it is not surprising that the Boat Club was quickly attracted to Henley Regatta (the 'Royal' prefix came in 1851) when it was established in 1839. The only event was the Grand Challenge, for which three crews (all from Oxford) competed, the winners being the Oxford Etonian Club stroked by the same Maberly, supported by three other House men and a House cox. In 1845 the House won the Stewards' Cup and the Visitors' Cup, and, in 1848, these two events plus the Silver Wherries and the Ladies' Plate. Including the Grand Challenge Cup, won by an Oxford University crew containing five House oarsmen, Christ Church was involved in winning five of six Henley events.

Because of the college authorities' distaste for undergraduates entering for Henley Regatta when it was held in term time, subterfuge was resorted to in 1851 in an attempt to conceal the true identity of competing crews. Thus Brasenose entered as 'Childe of Hale B.C.', Balliol as 'Oxford B.C.', and Christ Church as 'Westminster & Eton Club, Oxford', since it was known that Dean Gaisford would not give the men leave to attend the regatta. Unfortunately, a newspaper listed the crew as 'Christ Church' and the men were duly punished by the Dean and 'lost a term'.

The most amazing example of sheer rowing ability being recognised in the elevated social atmosphere of the House is found in the case of W.G. (later Canon) Edwards. In the days when the social status of noblemen, and the fine distinction between 'armigeri' and 'generosi' among gentlemen-commoners, were duly noted in the books, Edwards was a mere 'servitor', one of a group of students whose menial duties, in days not so long gone, had included waiting at table upon their undergraduate betters, in return for their education. Having an interest in rowing, Edwards sought out the Etonian President of the Boat Club, Senhouse, and was permitted to join the Boat Club in 1864. He quickly made his mark, stroking the Torpid, and the Eight, in 1866, rowing in ten crews in all, and competing in the

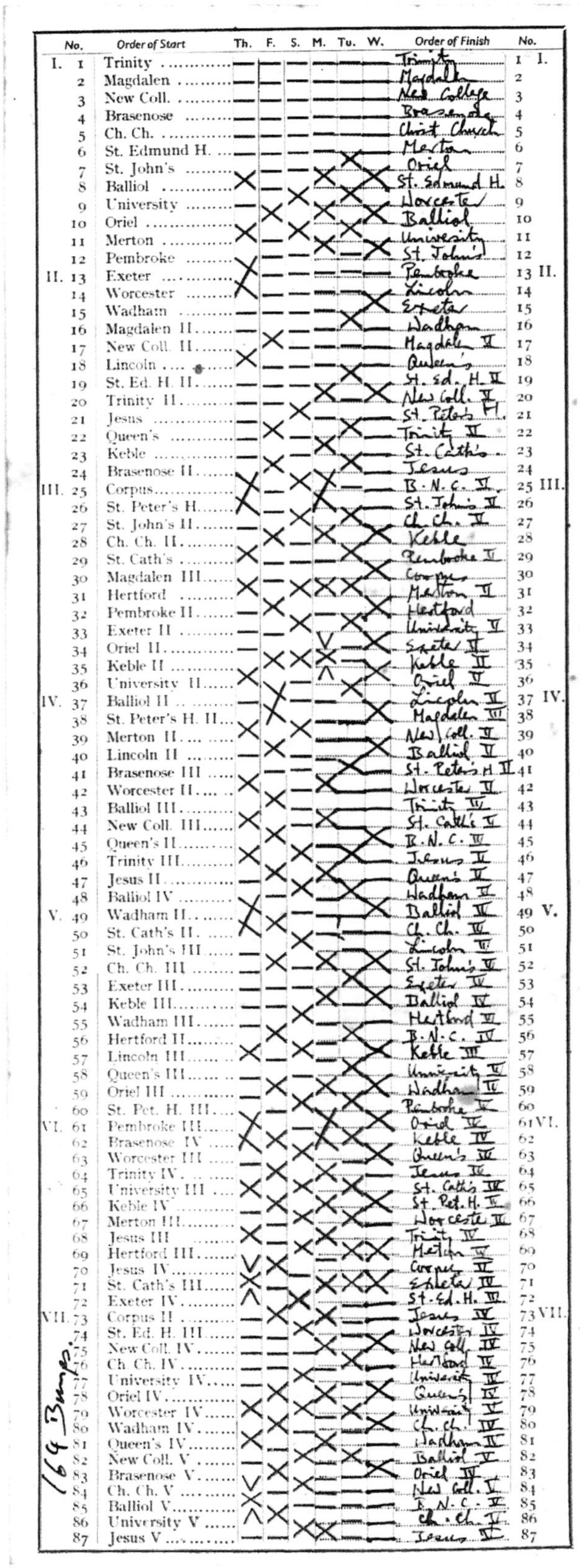

No.		Order of Start	Order of Finish	No.	
I.	1	Trinity	Trinity	1	I.
	2	Magdalen	Magdalen	2	
	3	New Coll.	New College	3	
	4	Brasenose	Brasenose	4	
	5	Ch. Ch.	Christ Church	5	
	6	St. Edmund H.	Merton	6	
	7	St. John's	Oriel	7	
	8	Balliol	St. Edmund H.	8	
	9	University	Worcester	9	
	10	Oriel	Balliol	10	
	11	Merton	University	11	
	12	Pembroke	St. John's	12	
II.	13	Exeter	Pembroke	13	II.
	14	Worcester	Lincoln	14	
	15	Wadham	Exeter	15	
	16	Magdalen II	Wadham	16	
	17	New Coll. II	Magdalen II	17	
	18	Lincoln	Queen's	18	
	19	St. Ed. H. II	St. Ed. H. II	19	
	20	Trinity II	New Coll. II	20	
	21	Jesus	St. Peter's H.	21	
	22	Queen's	Trinity II	22	
	23	Keble	St. Cath's	23	
	24	Brasenose II	Jesus	24	
III.	25	Corpus	B.N.C. II	25	III.
	26	St. Peter's H.	St. John's II	26	
	27	St. John's II	Ch. Ch. II	27	
	28	Ch. Ch. II	Keble	28	
	29	St. Cath's	Pembroke II	29	
	30	Magdalen III	Corpus	30	
	31	Hertford	Merton II	31	
	32	Pembroke II	Hertford	32	
	33	Exeter II	University II	33	
	34	Oriel II	Exeter II	34	
	35	Keble II	Keble II	35	
	36	University II	Oriel II	36	
IV.	37	Balliol II	Lincoln II	37	IV.
	38	St. Peter's H. II	Magdalen III	38	
	39	Merton II	New Coll. II	39	
	40	Lincoln II	Balliol II	40	
	41	Brasenose III	St. Peter's H II	41	
	42	Worcester II	Worcester II	42	
	43	Balliol III	Trinity III	43	
	44	New Coll. III	St. Cath's II	44	
	45	Queen's II	B.N.C. III	45	
	46	Trinity III	Jesus II	46	
	47	Jesus II	Queen's II	47	
	48	Balliol IV	Wadham II	48	
V.	49	Wadham II	Balliol III	49	V.
	50	St. Cath's II	Ch. Ch. III	50	
	51	St. John's III	Lincoln III	51	
	52	Ch. Ch. III	St. John's III	52	
	53	Exeter III	Exeter III	53	
	54	Keble III	Balliol IV	54	
	55	Wadham III	Hertford II	55	
	56	Hertford II	B.N.C. IV	56	
	57	Lincoln III	Keble III	57	
	58	Queen's III	University III	58	
	59	Oriel III	Wadham III	59	
	60	St. Pet. H. III	Pembroke III	60	
VI.	61	Pembroke III	Oriel III	61	VI.
	62	Brasenose IV	Keble IV	62	
	63	Worcester III	Queen's III	63	
	64	Trinity IV	Jesus III	64	
	65	University III	St. Cath's III	65	
	66	Keble IV	St. Pet. H. III	66	
	67	Merton III	Worcester III	67	
	68	Jesus III	Trinity IV	68	
	69	Hertford III	Merton III	69	
	70	Jesus IV	Corpus II	70	
	71	St. Cath's III	Exeter IV	71	
	72	Exeter IV	St. Ed. H. III	72	
VII.	73	Corpus II	Jesus IV	73	VII.
	74	St. Ed. H. III	Worcester IV	74	
	75	New Coll. IV	New Coll. IV	75	
	76	Ch. Ch. IV	Hertford III	76	
	77	University IV	University IV	77	
	78	Oriel IV	Queen's IV	78	
	79	Worcester IV	University	79	
	80	Wadham IV	Ch. Ch. IV	80	
	81	Queen's IV	Wadham IV	81	
	82	New Coll. V	Balliol V	82	
	83	Brasenose V	Oriel IV	83	
	84	Ch. Ch. V	New Coll. V	84	
	85	Balliol V	B.N.C. V	85	
	86	University V	Ch. Ch. V	86	
	87	Jesus V	Jesus V	87	

169 Bumps.

Summer Eights daily results sheet, recording bumps and final positions

Diamond Sculls at Henley (as well as winning a Blue for athletics).

In the second half of the nineteenth century, the Christ Church Boat Club was not, for the most part, especially distinguished. After 1849 the House was not again Head of the River for the rest of the century.

Nevertheless, W.A.L. Fletcher, a massive man for his time at 13 stone (whose nickname "Flea" is the title of a celebrated Vanity Fair 'Spy' cartoon of 1895) was beyond doubt the greatest House oarsman of the nineteenth century. He came up in 1888, having been a member of the Eton Eight that year. He quickly made his mark as a member of the crew which won the Ladies' and the Thames at Henley in his freshman year. For the Boat Race in 1890 he was placed at stroke. Oxford won, as it did the three following years, each time with William Fletcher in the crew. So he won the Boat Race four years in a row, one of a select band of oarsmen from both universities whose record was not exceeded until the run of Boris Rankov's successes in 1978–83.

The House was Head of the River in 1907, and again in 1908 and 1909. These great victories were, to a significant extent, achieved through the work of Fletcher, for he developed a style of rowing known at the time as the 'Christ Church Style' involving, in the simplest terms, a slightly shorter oar and broader blade than was then customary, so as to achieve a more powerful start to the stroke, and sustained power throughout it, slightly at the expense of the long body swing of then 'orthodox' rowing.

Christ Church third Eight bumping Trinity in the 1910 Torpids. From the album given to Christ Church by Eric Parker (mt. 1909)

If W.A.L. Fletcher was the greatest House oarsman of the nineteenth century, the palm for the twentieth century must surely go to H.R.A. Edwards. 'Jumbo', as he was known throughout the rowing world, participated without success in two Boat Races in 1926 and 1930, but won the Grand and the Stewards' for London Rowing Club in the latter year. In 1931 he repeated the feat, adding to it the Goblets with Lewis Clive for a Christ Church win, and achieving the never-since-matched distinction of winning three Henley finals on the same day. In 1932 Edwards and Clive, having won the Goblets for a second time, were chosen to represent Great Britain, in the pairs, in the 1932 Olympics in Los Angeles. 'Jumbo' was also co-opted at short notice into the Four, and won both events. He went on to be a revered coach of the Oxford Blue Boat for no fewer than nineteen years between 1949 and 1972.

In 1957 the House lost two finals at Henley, but the next year went Head of the River in Eights (for the first time for fifty-one years), a feat repeated in 1962, and in 1971, 1973 and 1975. The reward for going Head was of course a Bump Supper, accompanied by assorted hi-jinks on the part of House members at large. Nothing occurred as dramatic as in 1914, when the Torpid had gone Head, and over eighty pianos were dragged to the Meadows from various undergraduate rooms to form the basis for a celebratory bonfire.

No reference to the post-World War II era would be complete without a mention of George Harris, the Christ Church boatman for many years after the end of World War II. As well as being a master of the art of building boats (he was responsible, *interalia*, for the amazing sixteen-oar OUBC training boat, the 'Leviathan', launched in 1951) and much loved by all who came into contact with him, George was an expert coach and trusted advisor to successive presidents. He coached first of all the 1947 Torpids and the Henley Eight before

going on to coach many other crews including the 1962 Head of the River crew, and had the distinction of being the first professional boatman to coach an Oxford Blue Boat, starting in 1964.

The year 1980 marked a watershed in the history of House rowing, for in that year women were admitted to Christ Church for the first time. A women's Eight was formed the next year. In 1982 the Boat Club's constitution was redrawn; a Ladies' Captain (the title was soon changed to Women's Captain) was elected, and provision was made for a woman to hold the office of President of the Boat Club. In that year men's and women's crews entered for both Torpids and Eights. In five short years the women's Eight rose from Division IV to Division II.

The men's Eight, not to be put in the shade, went Head of the River in 1985, and two years later was graced with a woman cox for the first time. Other developments followed in short order. In 1991 Anna Bannon stroked the OUWBC Eight, and Clare Nicholls became President of the OULWRC (for lightweights), while in 1992 and 1994 Elizabeth Chick coxed the (men's) Blue Boat, a male member of the House having coxed the OUWBC against Cambridge in 1985. In 1990 the Women's Eight entered Division I for the first time, achieving ninth place the following year the same year that the men's Torpid went Head of the River. In 1991, also, the House entered no fewer than sixteen men's and women's crews in Torpids and Eights, a number which increased to nineteen in 1999 (thus exceeding that of any other college). In Michaelmas 1985 Sonia Hartwell became the first woman President of the Christ Church Boat Club.

The rising importance of women's rowing also created a demand for an annual race against Cambridge. In consequence, in addition to the traditional Isis/Goldie event over the Boat Race course, other women's, and women's and men's lightweight, races take place at Henley on Boat Race Day for the Francombe Cup, awarded based on results in five events.

The Christ Church Regatta (originally started in 1869 as an in-college event and revived in 1958) attracted, in November 1999, no fewer than 1,400 participants in 132 separate University-wide novice crews. The start of the twenty-first century found House rowing as vibrant and competitive in spirit as ever. In 2004, the women's crews for both Torpids and Eights ended up higher on the river than the men's crews.

One recent stimulus for this ever-flowing interest and support for rowing has been the record and leadership of Robin Bourne-Taylor. He came up in 2000, already a junior World Championship silver medallist, and quickly earned his Blue as a freshman, rowing for Oxford four times and winning three of his races. He also stroked the House first Eight which won its blades and finished fifth on the river in 2001. He represented Britain in world championships for the next two years, winning a bronze medal on the second occasion. At Athens in 2004 he rowed in the Great Britain Olympic Eight. He was President of the OUBC for 2004–5. Indeed Christ Church men earned regular selection for the Olympic Games throughout the twentieth century. First Gladstone and Baker in 1908, then 'Jumbo' Edwards and Clive in 1932. In 1960 D.C.R. Edwards, the son of 'Jumbo', President of the Christ Church Boat Club and twice a Blue, rowed in the Rome Olympics. Next, Jonny Searle, already a World Junior gold medallist when he came up, and three times a Blue, won a gold medal in the coxed pairs at Barcelona in 1992 and a bronze medal at Athens in 1996.

The House has had an interesting history of father/son rowing relationships. For example, in the early 1900s, the brothers A.C. and C.A. Gladstone were both Head of the River crew members, and winners of the Grand for the House, the former also being President of the Boat Club, a four-time Blue and, as noted, a winning Olympic oarsman. C.A. had three sons, William, Peter and Francis. All three came to the House and were in turn presidents of the Christ Church Boat Club, Peter winning a Blue twice. In 1926 three Christ Church Blues were 'Nono' Rathbone, Peter Murray-Threipland and 'Jumbo' Edwards. In 1956 the House won both divisions of the OUBC Fours. These three came to watch their sons, Bill, Mark and Jumbo's two sons, J.H.M. and D.C.R., participate in this success.

The House has been Head of the River more times, won more events at Henley, and produced more Blues, than any other Oxford college. Who knows what may lie ahead?

Gerald Parkhouse (1950)

Oval House

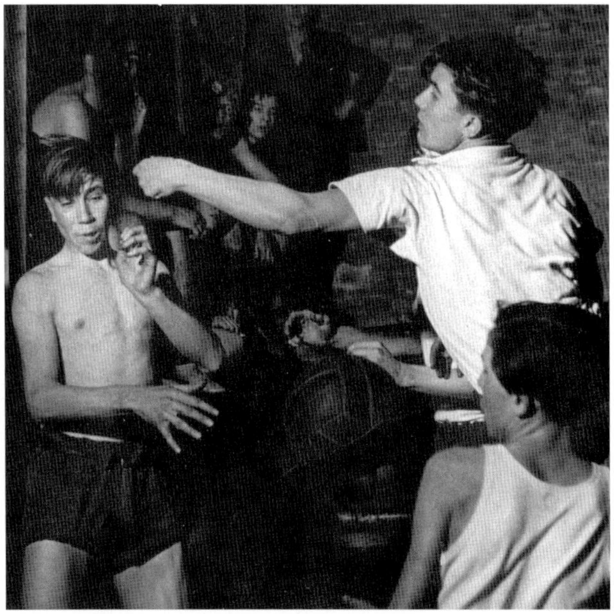

In 1882 the Christ Church (Oxford) Mission was formed by House men to help boys from very poor families in Poplar in east London. Later, the club moved to premises in Walworth near the Elephant and Castle but, by the 1920s, its activities were much reduced. Against that background, John Arkell (1928–31) was asked, on going down from Christ Church, if he would take over responsibility for the Mission and endeavour to breathe new life into it. He started by searching London to see where the need was greatest and chose Kennington in south London. Later in 1931, Arkell refounded the organisation near the Oval cricket ground at 17 and 19 Harleyford Road, provided rent-free by the Duchy of Cornwall through the good offices of the Prince of Wales, whom he had met through another charity.

It was a typical boys' club of the period with much physical activity such as running and boxing, but it also provided debates. What was not so typical was John Arkell's determination to be rid of the somewhat patronising attitude of the earlier organisation. As part of this, he renamed the organisation the 'Christ Church (Oxford) United Clubs' (or 'The House United' for short), thereby regenerating interest from graduates and undergraduates who had been put off by the original name.

House men living in London came to help as volunteers. Financial support came from subscriptions and donations. Additionally, in 1933 or 1934, John started the Red Hat Ball as an annual event raising substantial sums with my mother, Peggie Rathbone, as Chairman of the Ball Committee and my father, William Rathbone (1924–27), as Treasurer.

The Prince of Wales visited the club on several occasions and also came down to the annual camp at Sutton Courtenay. Most importantly, he arranged for the Duchy of Cornwall to give the clubs the empty site next to the two houses in Harleyford Street. A one-storey building was built to provide a boys' club and a gymnasium, whilst other activities continued in the Harleyford Street buildings. The new building, completed in 1936, was officially opened by Lord Halifax in 1937 and visited by H.M. King George VI later in the year.

In 1939, a girls' club was started, closed after a short period and then reopened permanently in September 1942.

Called up in September 1939, John was absent from the activities of the club throughout the war; but thereafter, he involved himself once again in the leadership of the club and remained so for the rest of his life, first as Chairman of the Management Committee and latterly as joint President with the Dean of Christ Church.

In 1955 the two houses in Harleyford Street were required for a major redevelopment and ceased to be available. Happily, St Mark's Vicarage, situated immediately on the other side of the clubhouse, came up for sale and an appeal was launched for £15,000 to purchase the building, to extend the existing clubhouse and to undertake essential repairs.

Interest from the royal family continued. Princess Margaret visited the club in 1950. Then, in July 1955, the clubs were honoured by a visit from H.M. the Queen who later became Patron; not only was she shown the Boys' and Girls' Clubs but also the Grandfathers' Club for pensioners, the Over Fifties' Club for older women, the Mothers' Club and the House United Club for former members of the Boys' Club returning from National Service.

In about 1967, activities at Oval House (as it was now called) moved into the creative activities field under the leadership of Peter Oliver who had recently been appointed as Warden. It also played a significant part in the development of "fringe" theatre in this country.

In the 1970s, Oval House decided to try to bring more local young people into its membership. It therefore recruited a community arts worker and an arts-in-education team to work with local schools. It ran holiday projects and music, dance and drama classes for local members; it also provided rehearsal spaces, a print workshop and a coffee bar.

This emphasis on music, dance and drama has remained at the core of the work of Oval House ever since. Deborah Bestwick, the present Director, supported by a strong management committee, has made Oval House a leader in this field. Over the past five years, its activities have included theatre productions; dance events; organising a London-wide festival featuring work by disabled artists; leading young people in writing words and music for songs which they then perform and record; providing a four-week summer school; and forming a theatre group for profoundly deaf young people. It has provided training for young school leavers on how to fill in a job application form, respond at a job interview and how to behave when you have obtained a job. It has conceived and run 'Back on Track' courses for young people excluded from school or in rehabilitation after anti-social or criminal activity in order to get them back into full-time education or training – and achieved a success rate of over eighty-five per cent. And, of course, it continues to run regular weekly courses in drama, dance and music for the young people who live in the area.

All this is not easy within the vagaries of local authority funding where priorities change each year. Nor is it easy to keep up with new legislation as it applies to buildings; currently over £300,000 is being spent in order to meet the Licensing Act and the Disability Discrimination Act. Nevertheless, Oval House seems to have the knack of surviving in this difficult world and in 2005 was negotiating a move in about six years' time to new premises in Brixton which will be purpose-built for current and future activities. It is a place of excitement and opportunity for young people from very deprived backgrounds and is worthy of the support of all members of the House.

William Rathbone (1956)

Henry Roy Forbes Harrod
1900–78

Marcelle Quinton,
Roy Harrod, 1972

'Roy Harrod is one of the great original economists' – these were the opening words of a tribute spoken by Professor James Meade, himself a subsequent Nobel Laureate, at the celebratory dinner of the Oxford Economics sub-faculty for Sir Roy's retirement in 1967. It was an astonishing forty-five years since he had been appointed to Christ Church as its first Tutor in economics, to initiate the then new Honours School of PPE, 'Modern Greats' in the parlance of its creators.

Roy Harrod's appointment at the age of twenty-two had followed a stellar undergraduate career at New College: a first in proper Greats (Lit. Hum.) in 1921, and another in Modern History twelve months later. The only economics he had then studied was in the context of a special subject in the History School. "We didn't get any instruction in it', he recalled at that retirement dinner, 'but we were given a very long list of original sources: hardly any books that I can remember at all, apart from Bagehot's Lombard Street. We were given the White Papers, reports of Royal Commissions, speeches in Parliament, and so forth, and we had to go through these ourselves ...'

With this memory still vivid, it is no surprise that near the end of his career Harrod should have challenged complacency about the tutorial system, the 'private hour' as he quaintly called it.

> *The original idea was that the hour with a distinguished scholar should be taken up mainly with correcting points of style, presentation, logic,*

modes of criticising the authorities studied, etc. It was not regarded as an occasion when the pupil should be fed with information likely to be needed for the Schools. It has now become a system for spoon feeding. Once the private hour is regarded as an occasion where one gains necessary information, the tutor inevitably has to go over the same ground, parrot-wise, with successive pupils, over and over again. This is not a fitting task for anyone who has real promise in his own line of study. It is a waste of time.

Harrod's own tutorial debts in economics – as he eloquently acknowledged – were acquired not before but after his appointment. He spent two terms (Michaelmas 1922 and Hilary – or rather Lent – 1923) in Cambridge, writing essays for J.M. Keynes and others. On his return to Oxford he had similar encounters with F.Y. Edgeworth, Drummond Professor of Political Economy and an important figure in the history of welfare economics.

Roy Harrod is known principally for having initiated, with a paper of 1939, the modern theoretical analysis of economic growth. But this did not come out of the blue. His creativity as a thinker had earlier shown itself in a variety of domains. He made notable contributions to the geometric apparatus of micro-economics, and was one of the pioneers of imperfect competition theory (models of markets where individual agents can influence the price of what they buy or sell). In the development of macro-economics he was a collaborator far more than a disciple of Keynes, pioneering the concept of the multiplier in an open (i.e. foreign-trading) economy, and also the Keynesian theory of the business cycle in which the multiplier interacts with the response of firms' investment outlays to changes in aggregate spending. In a number of these areas Harrod's proper claim to priority was initially forfeited by delays or obscurities in publication. His contributions have been the subject of considerable recent debate by historians of economic thought – much of it instigated by a young Swiss scholar, Daniele Besomi, but participants have included among others the redoutable Paul Samuelson, now in his nineties.

Harrod's mental energies were not limited to economics. He wrote the official *Life* of J.M. Keynes (1951), an astonishing work to have been published only five years after its subject's death; and also *The Prof* (1959), a more personal memoir of Harrod's somewhat anomalous and controversial Christ Church colleague, F.A. Lindemann, Viscount Cherwell. In Philosophy Harrod produced in 1936 a highly influential article on utilitarianism, and twenty years later a book-length treatment of the foundations of inductive logic.

Along with all this Roy Harrod played the fullest part in the life of the college. In his late years his commitment as Curator of the Senior Common Room, whether entertaining guests at dessert or contemplating new decor for the premises, put his colleagues to shame and occasionally to exasperation. In younger days, notably as Junior Censor in 1927–29 and Senior Censor in 1930–31 – by the latter years he was, incidentally, also a member of the University's Hebdomadal Council – he had not shrunk from crossing swords with veteran colleagues over controversial items of college business. Robert Blake in his memoir of him quotes a letter in which Harrod recalls one of the nine ex-censors of his day reproaching him for having 'raised the college to a pitch of strife such as he could not recall during his long period of service'.

Of course the strife was fleeting. And for Harrod new functions brought new opportunities. As Blake also recounts, it was then, as now, 'the custom for dons living in college to act in turn as caterer for a term with responsibility for the High Table. These were the days of the Great Slump. Harrod in accordance with Keynes' heterodox views held that the right thing to do was to inject as much purchasing power as possible into the economy. He therefore, to the surprise but not one assumes wholly to the displeasure of his colleagues, ordered particularly lavish meals during his term. He was succeeded by the Law tutor, a rigid Conservative. The doctrines of the May Committee replaced those of Keynes, and the gourmets, as they looked glumly at the dismal dishes which appeared at the High Table, reflected with nostalgia upon the reign of Harrod'.

Peter M. Oppenheimer

Einstein and the Jewish Refugees at Christ Church

The popular image of Christ Church in the inter-war years is of Sebastian Flyte holding court in Evelyn Waugh's *Brideshead Revisited*, or of the Bollinger Club dinner at the start of *Decline and Fall*. But there was more to the House in the 1930s than effete and dim-witted aristocrats, for it was also keen to add to its scholarly lustre by taking on German-Jewish professors who had been removed from their posts by the Nazis.

The first German-Jewish academic to take up a post at Christ Church, already before 1933, was Albert Einstein – a remarkably little known connection. Einstein first came to Oxford in 1931, through the initiative of Frederick Lindemann, Professor of Physics at Oxford, later Lord Cherwell, Churchill's wartime scientific adviser. Einstein stayed in Oxford for three short periods between May 1931 and June 1933. He was accommodated at Christ Church, 'the calm cloisters of which he relished as much as Oxford relished him', according to a historian of science at Oxford.

E. Rizzi, *Albert Einstein*, 1933

The correspondence in Einstein's file at Christ Church shows that relations between the scientist and the House were cordially warm. In June 1931 the Dean wrote to Einstein, offering him a research studentship at an annual salary of £400, 'for something like a month during term time in the course of the year'. Einstein replied in July, expressing his unconcealed delight at the prospect of spending time in unfamiliar but highly congenial surroundings. On 23 October the Dean was able to inform Einstein that the Governing Body had elected him to a studentship and to express 'our earnest hope that we may often have the pleasure and honour of seeing you in our Society'.

However, on the 24 October the Dean received a letter from Professor J.G.C. Anderson, protesting vehemently against Einstein's appointment; those who had framed the relevant statutes never intended emoluments to go to people of non-British nationality, Anderson argued, adding that it was wrong to 'send money out of the country' in the dire economic situation of the Depression, especially as the University was receiving a large grant from public funds. The Dean retorted that the academic benefit to the House far outweighed narrow nationalism: 'I think that in electing Einstein

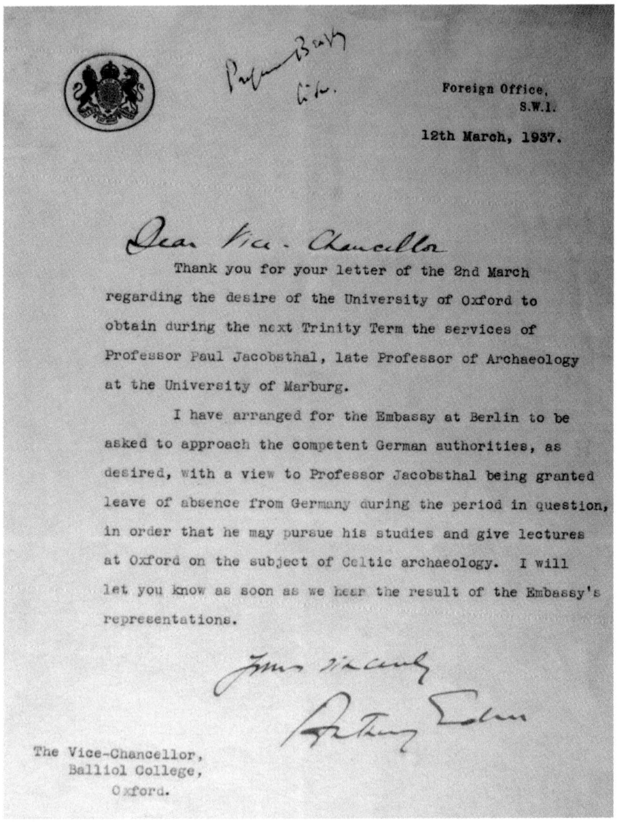

Foreign Office,
S.W.1.

12th March, 1937.

Dear Vice-Chancellor

Thank you for your letter of the 2nd March regarding the desire of the University of Oxford to obtain during the next Trinity Term the services of Professor Paul Jacobsthal, late Professor of Archaeology at the University of Marburg.

I have arranged for the Embassy at Berlin to be asked to approach the competent German authorities, as desired, with a view to Professor Jacobsthal being granted leave of absence from Germany during the period in question, in order that he may pursue his studies and give lectures at Oxford on the subject of Celtic archaeology. I will let you know as soon as we hear the result of the Embassy's representations.

Yours sincerely
Anthony Eden

The Vice-Chancellor,
Balliol College,
Oxford.

Letter from Anthony Eden (mt. 1919) at the Foreign Office arranging for Paul Jacobstahl to stay at Christ Church. Dated 12 March 1937

we are securing for our Society perhaps the greatest authority in the world on physical science; his attainments and reputation are so high that they transcend national boundaries, and any university in the world ought to be proud of having him.'

Einstein, unaware that he had incurred the wrath of Little Englanders reluctant to burden the British taxpayer with foreign scientists, accepted the appointment on 29 October. But on 2 November Anderson fired off a further letter, covering over three tightly packed sides. The Dean circulated this missive to his colleagues, asking for comments. Only one response appears on file, evidently from the one 'outsider', a lecturer in chemistry, mentioned by Professor Anderson as having been appointed to a Studentship. This simply reads 'Is the Professor quite accurate in describing me as an English-speaking member?', signed 'A.S.R'. Alexander Stuart Russell had been appointed Dr Lee's Reader in Chemistry in 1919 and a Student of Christ Church in 1920. He had studied at Glasgow, and presumably spoke with a Scots accent to match. This ended the objections to Einstein; indeed, after such a withering put-down, it is hard to imagine what further xenophobic tirades from Anderson could have achieved.

After 1933 Einstein could not return to Christ Church, so he proposed that his stipend be used to fund posts for Jewish academics dismissed from German universities by the Nazis. In May 1934 Dean Williams was able to inform him that the House proposed to give a sorely needed £200 to the distinguished classical philologist Eduard Fraenkel, formerly of Freiburg University and now in Oxford.

Two distinguished German-Jewish professors found refuge at Christ Church. Felix Jacoby, a specialist in Greek historiography and poetry, had been Professor of Classical Philology at Kiel University from 1907 until his dismissal in 1935. He emigrated to Britain in 1939, where he continued to work on his *Fragmente der griechischen Historiker*, publishing fifteen volumes of texts and commentary over the thirty-five years during which he pursued this magnum opus. One can imagine what it meant to Jacoby, stripped of his position and at the mercy of the Nazis, to receive a letter from Dean Williams in December 1938 inviting him in the warmest terms 'to continue your important work on the fragments of the Greek historians as soon as possible here at Oxford'.

Paul Jacobsthal, who had been Professor of Archeology at Marburg University from 1912 until his dismissal in 1935, was appointed to a post at Christ Church in 1937. An expert on Greek vase painting, his studies of the influence of Mediterranean civilisations on early North Alpine cultures led to his also becoming University Reader in Celtic Archeology. On Jacobsthal's death in 1957, Christopher Hawkes, Professor of European Archeology, wrote to Dean Lowe: 'Everyone at all connected with these studies must always owe a very great debt of gratitude to the House … All that great generosity has of course not only assured [Jacobsthal's] residing and working here, but in so doing has also guaranteed that the prime opportunity for holding the central position in these studies shall lie with Oxford.' A fitting tribute.

Anthony Grenville (1962)

Left:
Richard Busby (by Michael Rysbrack), *William Markham* (by John Bacon), and *Robert Freind* (by Michael Rysbrack) in the Library

A POEM BY EINSTEIN

Einstein occupied the rooms (now the Graduate Common Room) in Tom Quad usually occupied by R.H. Dundas, who was away on extended study leave. On his departure in May 1931, he wrote a poem in Dundas's visitors' book (now in the Bodleian Library). The following is a translation by J.B. Leishman.

Dundas lets his rooms decay
While he lingers far away,
Drinking wisdom at the source
Where the sun begins its course.

That his walls may not grow cold
He's installed a hermit old,
One that undeterredly preaches
What the art of Numbers teaches.

Shelves of towering folios
Meditate in solemn rows;
Find it strange that one can dwell
Here without their aid so well.

Grumble: Why's this creature staying
With his pipe and piano playing?
Why should this barbarian roam?
Could he not have stopped at home?

Often, though, his thoughts will stray
To the owner far away,
Hoping one day face to face
To behold him in this place

With hearty thanks and greetings
Albert Einstein, May 1931
(The 'barbarian' and his host did meet when the latter came home to Christ Church.)

Paul Kent

George Bell

George Bell was, by common consent, one of the most remarkable Anglican clergymen of the twentieth century. He won a Westminster scholarship to Christ Church in 1901, took a first in Mods and a second in Greats and won the Newdigate Prize for a poem entitled 'Delphi' – 'Only I hear the lank eagles crying up the sky'. He was ordained in 1908 and returned to the House, at the invitation of Dean Strong, in 1910 as a Clerical Student with responsibilities akin to those of a chaplain as well as a tutor. Strong expressed the hope that he would be 'when his time came, Censor, and take a full part in the management of the whole place'. It was not to be. In August 1914 he became chaplain to the archbishop of Canterbury, Randall Davidson, and subsequently dean of Canterbury (1924–29) and bishop of Chichester (1929–58). His achievements were many: among others as a leading figure in the ecumenical movement, as the inspiration of religious drama in the Church – at his encouragement Eliot wrote *Murder in the Cathedral* – and as the author of a much-admired biography of Davidson. It is above all, however, for his interest in the German church in the 1930s and his stand in the House of Lords against the area bombing of German towns in 1944 that he is most remembered. In the first capacity he became the friend and confidant of Dietrich Bonhoeffer, and drawing on that friendship he consistently reminded the British public and government that not all Germans were Nazis, at a time when that sentiment was understandably far from popular. During the war he tried in vain to persuade the Government to send a message of encouragement to the German opposition, and in the House of Lords and elsewhere he opposed the indiscriminate bombing of whole towns which had as its objective to break the morale of industrial labour.

His speech to the House of Lords on 9 February 1944 was a fine example of both his courage and conviction and also of his sensitivity to the arguments on the other side. Opposing his views (though not all in the Lords debate) were, as it happens, a number of Christ Church figures. The area bombing of Germany was supported by Charles Portal, the Chief of the Air Staff, who had known Bell when he was an undergraduate and Bell a Clerical Student. It was also supported by Lord Cherwell (Frederick Lindemann), Churchill's scientific adviser, who held the chair of Dr Lee's Professor of Experimental Philosophy (i.e. physics) at Wadham but was elected in

G.K.A. Bell in 1904. From the Robinow album

1921 to a 'studentship not on the governing body' at Christ Church which, as Robert Blake noted, 'entitled him to rooms more spacious than Wadham could provide' where he lived until his death in 1957. Replying to Bell in the House of Lords on behalf of the Government was another Christ Church man, Viscount Cranborne (Lord Cecil, subsequently the fifth marquess of Salisbury).

The crux of Bell's argument was that there was a distinction between military and non-military objectives and that this distinction, which was also a fundamental principle of international law, had previously been accepted by the Government. He acknowledged that the Nazis had begun the bombing of towns and that the legitimate bombing of centres of war industry and transport would inevitably involve civilian casualties. But, he asserted, 'there must be a fair balance between the means employed and the purpose achieved. To obliterate a whole town because certain portions contain military and industrial establishments is to reject the balance'. He gave examples of the casualties and the destruction of libraries and museums which had already occurred in Hamburg, Berlin and elsewhere. He quoted statements from the press and official sources to show that British bombing had become both comprehensive 'and what would ordinarily be called indiscriminate'. He mentioned other towns, including Dresden, as probable targets for future raids. He faced squarely the argument that the policy was designed to shorten the war: 'to justify methods inhumane in themselves by arguments of expedience smacks of the Nazi philosophy that Might is Right. In any case the idea that it will reduce the sacrifice is speculation'. That last argument he developed with remarkable insight (benefitting from the advice of the military historian, Basil Liddell Hart): German military production had not been destroyed and there was evidence from neutral countries that, if anything, German willingness to resist had been strengthened by the bombing. The policy, he alleged, also undermined the efforts of anti-Nazis to encourage resistance, since the Allies offered nothing but annihilation. What they did in war, he warned would affect the whole character of the peace. The Allies stood 'for something greater than power', namely 'Law'. Area bombing was of 'immense importance' because it raised the issue 'of power unlimited and exclusive'.

Bell's opposition did not change government policy, either on bombing or encouragement of the German opposition. Another distinguished Christ Church man, Anthony Eden – then Foreign Secretary – referred to him in a minute as 'this pestilent priest'. But his arguments outlived this failure. On the practical issue of whether the bombing would shorten the war, his case still commands respect. And by raising the moral issue, at a time when it would have been so easy to remain silent, he established a reputation which gave him unique influence with the post-war German church and kept alive respect for the principles for which Britain fought.

Bell was elected to an Honorary Studentship in 1952, joining Eden and Portal (both elected in 1941) and Lord Salisbury (elected in 1949). He is commemorated by a window in Hall and, in 2000, a new altar of scorched oak in the cathedral was dedicated in his memory with the sermon preached by his friend and admirer, Peter Walker (canon of Christ Church, 1972–77).

Jonathan Wright

Christ Church and the Intelligence Agencies in World War II

The first link between Christ Church and the Intelligence Services (or the Security Services, as they are now called) was established by Dick (later Sir Dick) White (1925) who, shortly before the war, was persuaded to abandon a career as a schoolmaster and join MI5. A man of great charm as well as sagacity, the huge expansion of the service on the outbreak of war won him rapid promotion to second-in-command of 'B' Division, concerned with counter-espionage within the United Kingdom. His subsequent career would bring him to the head, not only of MI5 but of its sister service, MI6; and it was largely his pressure that led to the writing and publication of the *Official History of Intelligence during the Second World War* and the opening up of the Security Services to public scrutiny. He deserves to be remembered as one of Christ Church's most distinguished alumni.

It cannot have been entirely a coincidence that White's former tutor at the House, J.C. (later Sir John) Masterman (1914) should have been co-opted by MI5 as Secretary of the 'Twenty Committee', the body responsible for running German 'double agents' within the United Kingdom. He thus played a leading role in managing the 'Double Cross System' – the gigantic spoof that ultimately convinced the German High Command that the Allied landings in Normandy in June 1944 were a feint to distract attention from the main attack that would be launched against the Pas-de-Calais by a purely notional US First Army Group. But that enterprise would not have been possible without the code-breaking that was taking place at Bletchley Park; and in that a major role was played by yet another Christ Church alumnus, H.R. Trevor-Roper (1932).

Major Hugh Trevor-Roper, later Lord Dacre

Trevor-Roper (later Lord Dacre) had joined the Radio Security Service on the outbreak of war, where his work involved the interception and interpretation of German radio traffic. In the winter of 1939–40 his section stumbled on the radio communications between German agents in Western Europe and their controller in Hamburg. Once Bletchley Park had broken their cypher it became possible to foresee and intercept the infiltration of German agents into the United Kingdom, and dictate the information they relayed to their controllers. Trevor-Roper became a leading expert on the operations of the German intelligence services – work in which he was joined by his Christ Church colleagues Denys Page (1926) and Charles Stuart (1938).

Other House men at Bletchley Park were to include John Croft (1941) and Sir Edward Boyle (1945), but there were no doubt many others, both there and elsewhere in the Security Services, whom I regret that I have been unable to trace.

To conclude on a personal note. When I returned to Oxford from military service in October 1945 my own tutors were Masterman and Trevor-Roper. Stimulating though I found them, it was evident that they were not exactly obsessed with the subject-matter of our tutorials, English political life in the seventeenth century. As I was later to discover, both were still hard at work on studies of a very different kind commissioned by their wartime employers; Masterman on *The Double Cross System* and Trevor-Roper on *The Last Days of Hitler*. It would not be too much to say that it is by these books that they are now chiefly remembered.

Michael Howard (1941)

In addition to the gremial senior members discussed by Sir Michael Howard, several other senior members also served in intelligence during the Second World War. The senior figure in this group was Gilbert Ryle, commissioned in the Welsh Guards in 1940, and Student and tutor in Philosophy at Christ Church between 1925 and 1945, whence he moved to his notably distinguished tenure of the Waynflete Chair in Metaphysical Philosophy at Magdalen College. A future Treasurer, Keith Batey, worked at Bletchley alongside his wife, Mavis, who worked on Italian codes, and a future canon, the young Maurice Wiles, Regius Professor of Divinity between 1970 and 1991, deciphered Japanese codes.

Brian Young

Some Memories of Christ Church 1911 to 1944

Wednesday Nov 1st 1911
It so happens that just at present I hardly ever go into the Junior Common Room with the result that I do not see the papers at all so you can imagine what a shock it was yesterday when I saw that Churchill had gone to try his worst on the navy. I wonder whether I have missed anything else exciting.

...

There is an Adam's here who seems very friendly, he comes from Marlborough and is keen on Rugger and Music, but not clever. He took me to hear Kneisler last night which was a great treat. After playing a lot of difficult well known classics he played a few times from early 17th and 18th century people which were charming. It did point the moral that for beauty it is quite unnecessary to be complicated and difficult.

...

Cazenove too is here. Do you remember him at Mrs Egerton's and the good time I had with him. He is a second year man – a polo blue – and one of the rich set so I have not dared to address him yet though I think it must be the one I knew as he has a limp. The idea of breakfasting out and asking people back is not an economical method from my point of view. For I alone should have but one thing whereas for visitors two courses are absolutely essential. Indeed about ten years ago five courses were strictly de rigueur.

Aubrey Rollo Mellor (1911)

Edward Cazalet (mt. 1956), riding Lochroe, jumping the last fence to win the Kim Muir Memorial Race at the Cheltenham Gold Festival in March 1958

One could say that, when I came up in October 1920, the new era in the University really began. Two outstanding matters created an unusual atmosphere. First of all the number of undergraduates was vastly inflated. Added to the normal intake of boys from the schools was the four-year backlog of those who had survived the war. The percentage of those who had survived the appalling slaughter of the war was small for a large section of that generation had been annihilated. Nevertheless, the actual number of undergraduates coming up was considerable. The result was that a large number could not be accommodated in college and had to live in lodgings. In my case I got one year in college and two at home, which at any rate in my case was not a good thing.

I took Greek for Mods and also for 'Divvers', a compulsory examination in Divinity, now abolished. By taking a Greek Gospel one somewhat shortened the examination. The examination involved a viva voce. I think an atheist could get out of this hardship by taking a large dose of Shakespeare.

In term time we had to dress properly, collar and tie, and at any rate for dinner we had to wear the wretched little gown. Plus fours were the fashion, but they were not allowed for dinner in Hall. This, I think, was partly responsible for the invention of

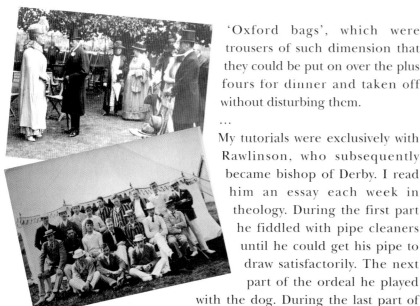

Visit of King George V and Queen Mary to Christ Church in 1925 as part of the quatercentennial celebrations, and the Bullingdon Club at the races

'Oxford bags', which were trousers of such dimension that they could be put on over the plus fours for dinner and taken off without disturbing them.

...

My tutorials were exclusively with Rawlinson, who subsequently became bishop of Derby. I read him an essay each week in theology. During the first part he fiddled with pipe cleaners until he could get his pipe to draw satisfactorily. The next part of the ordeal he played with the dog. During the last part of my essay his wife would appear and the tutorial would dissolve into an agreeable social occasion. Rawlinson would utter a few learned theological comments, indicate half a dozen theological treatises of which (being partially dyslectic, unheard of in those days) I usually managed to read one. Consequently the tutorial was agreeable and not entirely valueless to a future teacher of modern languages.

Oswald Shuffrey (1920)

Monday Oct 10th 1932

Dear Father

I've left my pen in my rooms. Hence the scrawl. I suppose you'd like to know something of what I'm going to do in the way of work. Well: I shall see my tutor for an hour every week – on Tuesdays. The books I'm doing are Aeschylus, Pindar and Catullus and Propertius; special subject Greek Lyric Poetry. B[arrington]-Ward let me choose just what I wanted; some other people I've spoken to – from other colleges – weren't allowed to, & rather envy me! Anyhow, the only one which is being lectured on this term is Aeschylus: by Miss K L Lorimer of Somerville (alias Highland Hilda), on Mon Wed & Fri at 12. I went to one today. Quite harmless. About 30 there, I should think – only 3 of 'em women. And if I get bored I shan't bother to attend this. B-Ward says I can have toothache on M W & F at 12.

26th January 1936

Dear Both of you;

Then that night the news came through at 6.0 that George's strength was diminishing. So Robin Zaehner and I went that night to a flick, in case the cinemas shut for the rest of the week. Actually we needn't have worried, as they shut for only one night. And it was a very bad film we got let in for. On coming back we heard that the reign would shortly be over; I listened to John Baldwin's wireless till the 12.0 one, when I decided that I should have to go and do some work. At twenty past twelve, however, Tom began tolling. The reason being quite obvious. It tolls, I understand, only on the death of (a) the reigning monarch (b) the heir apparent (c) the Dean. For George it had to toll 70 times; and at 30-second intervals. Tolling it at the ordinary four-or-five second intervals can't be too bad, as you've got the thing swinging; but for thirty-second intervals the wretched man must have to start it swinging again for each separate stroke. I should think the wretched porter must have been nearly dead himself at the end of it.

23rd February 1936

It appears that the new Professor of Greek – Dodds – has not been well received. He was Murray's choice, apparently; and Murray never dreamt that the appointment would make such a stir as it has made. Bowra and Denniston – both of Oxford – were joint favourites: it's said that when the appointment was made known Bowra put three bottles of hock in his pocket and called on Denniston to drink damnation to Dodds. Dodds conscientiously objected 1914–18: so Bowra has written a poem 'What did you do in the war, Doddy?' Dodds is automatically a Student of the House: so the House is more annoyed than anyone. Bobby Longden, asked if he'd met Dodds, said 'Yes, he has once contaminated my carpet.' Denys Page above all is extremely annoyed. Partly because Dodds once made a very tactless remark to him when he (Denys) was lecturing at Birmingham. Now it happened that on the day before the appointment was published Gilbert Murray's son Basil was fined pretty heavily (and unjustly) for some affair connected with a Fascist meeting in Oxford. So Denys, feeling revengeful, and knowing that Murray had got Dodds appointed but didn't know that he knew, wrote to Murray 'Basil yesterday, Dodds today. My heart grieves for you.'

Other happenings? A certain scholar of this college was found during the vac prizing the floorboards up; and when asked what he was doing said 'I want to get to the BBC'. He is now in a loony-bin.

William Spencer Barrett (deceased) (1932)

I unpacked my trunk and a box of crockery, boiled the kettle and made some tea. A little later, my scout, Humphreys, arrived and told me most of what I needed to know about the daily routine in College. He sold me a gown and a surplice which had belonged to one of his 'gentlemen who went down last year'. I was equipped; all I had to do now was to become fully-fledged as a member of the House. Humphreys was a great help to me; he didn't need to be told that I was rather out of my depth, but simply made the sort of suggestions which were appropriate from time to time. He was then about fifty, very square and stocky in build, with a round, humorous face, and very active, lively manner. He was one of the most senior scouts and had charge of twelve sets of rooms, four on the 'corkscrew' and eight on No-6 staircase. He strongly disapproved of wild behaviour, and had various ways of making his disapproval felt by the offenders. Persistent ill-doers generally moved elsewhere. He was no snob, but his favourite was undoubtedly Lord Lyell, a quiet, slender Etonian who was killed winning one of the first VCs of World War II. Humphreys was assisted by a junior scout and a boy. The latter, who held him in high regard, was, much later, in charge of the Hall meals and service at the House. He spoke of Humphreys as 'one of the old style of college servants', now presumably no longer extant. Certainly, there must be many, like myself, who had to find their way in strange territory, who owe much to the likes of Humphreys, splendid people of sterling character, often raised in hard conditions, maintaining a proud tradition of service which was the finest of all examples to those they served, many of whom would leave the college to carry on a tradition of service elsewhere, often

331 The Amateur Photographer May 19th, 1943

HOW WE MAKE OUR EXHIBITION PICTURES

No. DCXCVIII By A. and A. PALGRAVE-BROWN

Methods and Ideals of Well-known Pictorial Workers

From Information communicated to our Special Representative

We had our first cameras in our early schooldays, with which we merely recorded pictures of the holiday type, trying, however, to get as pleasing a result as possible. But it was not until 1937, at the age of 15, we began our own processing, and then realised the enormous scope of photography, not only as a means of recording happy moments, but pictorially, as an outlet for one's self-expression, where one's artistic urge and desire to create something individual could be satisfied.

Being chiefly interested in pictorial photography, our object is to try to secure, on the negative, a picture as sound in

The Great Staircase, Oxford. A. and A. Palgrave-Brown.

The Hall stairs and Canterbury Gate during the Second World War

overseas. *Autre temps, autres mœurs*; the climate of today does not produce such people and the world is a poorer place for it. I was fortunate to grow up in a world in which the concept was not regarded as being incompatible with 'doing your own thing' and I am grateful to Humphreys and many others who helped to shape my attitudes. Nearly all of them were regular ex-servicemen or had seen war service, and I can't help wondering whether there is some sort of lesson in that.

...

F.A. Lindemann, 'the Prof.' (later Lord Cherwell), who was an Alsatian by birth, nationalised British, became a legend during the First World War, when he worked out, on paper, a method of taking an aircraft out of a spin (then the cause of many pilot deaths) and proceeded to prove it in practice. An extremely wealthy man, he had studied and researched in Germany and elsewhere and retained many academic contacts in Europe and America. His contacts with undergraduates on the course were limited to his 12 o'clock lectures, twice a week, on 'The Kinetic Theory of Matter'. At about 11.45, the pale, tall, bowler-hatted figure would emerge from the chauffeur-driven Rolls and would spend a quarter of an hour walking through the research rooms, talking with Simon and a few intimates, then, punctually at 12 noon, would enter the theatre where he would

Above
Top to bottom: King George V and Queen Mary arriving in Tom Quad in 1925; R.H. Dundas's living room in 1960; a cartoon showing less than attentive students during a lecture in the cathedral

Right: Programme for the Royal Visit in 1925

lecture, interestingly but almost inaudibly, in a low voice, covering two blackboards with derivations of various formulae, relationships etc. The walls of the Clarendon were lined with blackboards, on which he would scribble ideas as they occurred to him. They were never rubbed off, except with his authority. Then, at 1 o'clock, he would be swept away in his Rolls to lunch, it was alleged, with some North Oxford hostess of Conservative persuasion.

Trevor Kerslake (1933)

Here on non-hunting days I 'sported my oak' and tried to concentrate on books. I studied French literature under the guidance of my modern languages tutor, Frank Taylor, who had lost a leg in the war and had a sensitive ear for the niceties of French pronunciation.

During my last two years I read for an Honours degree in History, but with so many distractions it was difficult to concentrate on the various books required. I enjoyed writing essays for my weekly tutorials, and I found that the dialogue between tutor and undergraduate was a stimulating experience. But although my tutors, of whom the seniors were J.C. Masterman and Noel Myres, were both patient and understanding, they felt anxious and uncomfortable. The gap between their standards and my performance was too great. In desperation the Senior Censor tried to stop me hunting by refusing a permit for me to drive my car, but to no purpose. Instead I drove to the meets in cars provided by my friends.

George Haig (1936)

Collie could start a physics theme, and finish it, but could not join it up in the middle. He worked at the Clarendon Laboratory and also at the Christ Church one. The latter dealt with radioactivity, so if he got contaminated there would be disaster at the Clarendon, and on arrival at the Christ Church one he would take off his trousers to put on his Christ Church ones. In between he would stand by the fishtail gas burners, which heated the lab, and warm his bottom at them.

The Christ Church lab was looked after by a lab assistant. It had a still to make distilled water: this had to be inspected regularly by Customs and Excise. The inspector would write in the record book 'still working' or 'still not working'. The lab would get untidier through the academic year but would all be put to rights in the long vacation. The lab man was in the RAMC Territorial Army so went off to war in September 1939 – who was to tidy up? I felt that this caused the lab to close. In Palestine in 1943 I went to see a soldier in hospital and happened to meet the lab man who was a sergeant there.

Fraser Scott (1937)

There was a formal interview presided over by the Dean and at least half a dozen members of the Governing Body. During the course of this somewhat formidable procedure I was asked what I saw as my future career following graduation. 'The Foreign Office', I replied, 'and if that falls down ... ', but I was unable to specify the alternative as my innocent response caused much donnish merriment, and at least broke the ice.

Christ Church Library was under the immediate supervision of Mr W.G. Hiscock, the

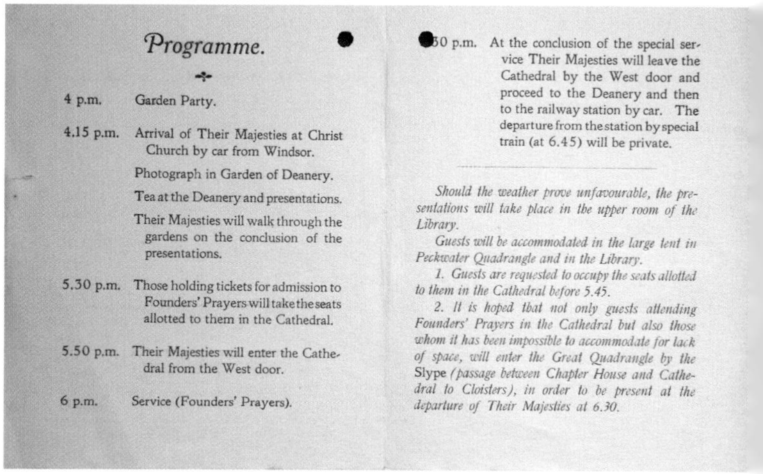
Programme.

4 p.m. Garden Party.

4.15 p.m. Arrival of Their Majesties at Christ Church by car from Windsor.

Photograph in Garden of Deanery.

Tea at the Deanery and presentations.

Their Majesties will walk through the gardens on the conclusion of the presentations.

5.30 p.m. Those holding tickets for admission to Founders' Prayers will take the seats allotted to them in the Cathedral.

5.50 p.m. Their Majesties will enter the Cathedral from the West door.

6 p.m. Service (Founders' Prayers).

[illegible]30 p.m. At the conclusion of the special service Their Majesties will leave the Cathedral by the West door and proceed to the Deanery and then to the railway station by car. The departure from the station by special train (at 6.45) will be private.

Should the weather prove unfavourable, the presentations will take place in the upper room of the Library.

Guests will be accommodated in the large tent in Peckwater Quadrangle and in the Library.

1. Guests are requested to occupy the seats allotted to them in the Cathedral before 5.45.

2. It is hoped that not only guests attending Founders' Prayers in the Cathedral but also those whom it has been impossible to accommodate for lack of space, will enter the Great Quadrangle by the Slype *(passage between Chapter House and Cathedral to Cloisters), in order to be present at the departure of Their Majesties at 6.30.*

Left: Christ Church beagles during the 1895/6 season; Right: Memorial bench for Sister Bronwen Huntley

assistant librarian, referred to by R. St. C. Talboys as 'the grim-faced man'. During the war I carried out fire-watching duties on a rota basis in the Library, which involved sleeping on a camp bed in or just off the Upper Library. Perched on the roof, and reached by a narrow staircase, was a sort of cupola but open to the sky and ample enough to accommodate two people standing. It was there on many a starlit night I watched bombers returning from raids on Germany, some limping home at low altitude towards the airfield then at Witney, north of Oxford.

Noel Myres (later to become Bodley's Librarian) tutored me for mediaeval history. Weekly sessions with him were an enjoyable, and indeed rewarding, experience. As I recall, I must have been taught by him for a term or two before he went off to a branch of the Ministry of Food as a temporary civil servant, and certainly after the war. Some years later, when dining at High Table, I asked him about his wartime experiences where it seemed he was in charge of the division responsible for the control of jam: 'I was assisted', he said, 'by three ladies, and I am sorry to say they were known as the jam tarts'.

My cryptographic work at GCHQ/GCB having folded up, I had obtained – with some difficulty – a 'Class B release' from the Ministry of Labour. In 1941, having reached the age of eighteen, I had formally enlisted as a Royal Fusilier but my call-up was deferred pending the completion of my university year (four terms in my case), and I assumed that my war service in the Foreign Office (at Bletchley Park and in London) nullified this commitment. Not so, since some time during the autumn of 1945 a military policeman turned up at Christ Church more or less accusing me of being absent without leave from the army. Fearful of my imminent arrest, I went to Dr A. S. Russell, the Senior Censor, who acted with great promptitude and averted this ignominy.

John Croft (1941)

1st Thursday in November 1941

The same week I had a Mr. Michael Flanders ill with a sore throat. He was most anxious to be fit to read some poetry at the Taylorian Institute on Saturday. He is a very attractive young man. He has a heart shaped head with rather long black hair and beautiful eyes. He himself looks like a poet and I rather suspect he is. He has a lovely soft voice and a charming manner. I heard he was far and away the best actor in Gordon Davies' production of 'The Ascent of F 6.'

March 5th 1942

I have just finished nursing Major Masterman. Sir Farquahar Buzzard called me to him. He is a mystery as he is not always here, and no-one seems to know when he is likely to come or go. Still there is a war on and one does not ask questions. Just now he has had severe influenza but I must not report it. I met his mother in the lodge today. She is a sweet person and very grateful for the treatment I gave her for her chilblains. It was just cod liver oil ointment.

Sister Huntley

Christ Church at War – A CHILDHOOD MEMORY

We were on holiday in Cornwall on the day the war broke out. The four children, Griselda (always known as Gelda), Paul, Patricia (equally always known as Pattice), and I, ages ranging from Gelda's ten to my six, were summoned by my father to listen to Neville Chamberlain's broadcast of 3 September 1939. The day, as I remember it, was sunny and warm, and my mother afterwards sat at her desk, combing her hair, doing her best to explain to me gloomily why we had to cut short our holiday forthwith and return to Oxford. My father, Dr N.P. Williams, was, as she explained, not only Lady Margaret Professor of Divinity but also Sub-Dean of Christ Church. As such, he had a particular responsibility for the protection of the cathedral from all possible catastrophes, real or, as it turned out to be, imaginary.

At the time, none of this made much sense to a six-year-old. We had lived a tranquil, if from time to time bizarre, childhood in the Priory House. True, we all knew that the house was haunted – Pattice had been particularly impressed by a sighting of the 'White Lady', and we were all familiar with the ghost of the beheaded Archbishop Wade wandering around Little Cloister with his head under his arm – but the Priory House garden in those days was peaceful and pleasant, we had a full complement of servants (including some rather fierce nannies) and there were friends – other canons' children, of course, but in particular the college porters and scouts, who were beyond praise indulgent in making sure that we were kept from harm, however badly we behaved.

Running over the roof-tops!

When we returned from our holiday in Cornwall, all had changed. My father, for no reason understandable to us, had had all the uncurtained windows in our home painted black and all the light bulbs changed to dark blue. At the best of times, Priory House, although undoubtedly beautiful and elegant, was for children dark and complicated. With the arrival of my father's black-out it now became something more sinister. Around every corner in the house – and there were many – a six-year-old could detect a potential menace. When thunder came, he had to run along the dark corridors, passing the cupboards in which he had happily played 'Sardines' before the war but which now concealed their own unspecified but ominous threat, until he could reach the haven of his mother's room. The 'White Lady' appeared again to Pattice with all sorts of warnings (but it was accepted, on the severest interrogation, that evidence for the apparition could not be relied on).

Furthermore, our Viennese cook, who was a great favourite with my mother because of her ability, from her previous career in Vienna, to mend my mother's underwear, inexplicably vanished. On enquiry, it turned out that she had been interned without any warning. That left my mother to do the cooking. So spectacularly bad was she at this that, after a humiliating incident with my father over who was to do the washing up, during which my mother threw a saucepan at him, my father demanded that our meals should henceforward be delivered from the college kitchen.

Then there were the 'evacuees'. Wartime conscription took its toll. The number of undergraduates diminished rapidly. The college had emptied almost overnight. Tom Quad became a desert to be navigated with care by a child going to school. But the empty places in Meadow Building were, over the winter of 1939–40, allotted to the influx of evacuees. It was not an easy migration. My mother and Mrs Lowe, the Dean's wife, were deputed to look after them, but they soon discovered that none of the evacuees had been properly baptised. My father was conscripted to do the business, and, refusing all applications for un-Christian names, duly baptised them, in serried ranks, with suitably canonical names.

Up till the summer of 1940 all passed peacefully. There were visits, of course, from uncles and cousins who were in the Army, but there was little sign of impending threats. With May 1940 everything changed. By the autumn, the air-raid sirens had started to sound at regular intervals. My father was an official 'Fire-watcher' and my mother, who had been a nurse in the east end of London in the First World War, ran a First Aid centre. Since the sirens usually went off at night, my father would emerge in his pyjamas – over which he put a suitably clerical suit and overcoat. He would then put on a tin hat and march off into the night. My mother, on the other hand, would put on a white overall – and also her tin hat – but would make sure that she was properly wearing her sable coat which was her – and our – pride and joy. She would then also march off into the night. We children were then escorted – not knowing whether we would ever see our parents again – down to the underground passage between the Chapter House and the Cathedral known as the 'Slipe'. There we would sit in anguish until the all clear was sounded.

In fact, although we could not know it, Oxford was never a target for German air attacks. But the protection of the cathedral had for us an unexpected benefit. Ladders were put up on the gables of the Priory House, leading to the cathedral roof, on to the roof of Hall, thence to Tom and, in the other direction, to the roof of the deanery and Kilcannon. The temptation was too much for the Williams children. We discovered a way out onto the Priory House roof through a window in the housemaid's cupboard. From there it was a simple matter to climb everywhere – onto every roof in Christ Church. We even formed a 'Williams Society', membership of which was confined to those of us who survived the climb half way up the fire ladder on the cathedral spire while the others held the ladder at the bottom. The roof, of course, was an ideal place from which to watch the spiral trails of the aerial dogfights in the distance.

As the menace of 1940 and 1941 grew less threatening, roof climbing took on a new dimension. Lawrence Lowe, the Dean's younger son, and I were constant companions. The roof was, again, our oyster. Nothing was beyond our capability. We could go over the roof of the cathedral, drop down into Canon Jenkins's garden and invite ourselves to tea with him. (But such was the state of his house and of himself that we had to take care that he did not, as he did on one occasion, drop his snuff into our tea.) From there, we could easily go through Alice's Green Door into the deanery garden for more tea with Mrs Lowe.

My father died in May 1943. We moved out of the Priory House to North Oxford. The rest of the Christ Church war thus passed me by. But there is one afterthought. When my mother left Priory House she – no doubt inadvertently – kept a bunch of keys. Then when I went up to the House as an undergraduate in 1951 she said, in an offhand way, that 'these might be of some use to you'. They turned out, of course, to be the keys of the gate from the Meadow to what was then called the College Garden and from there to the Priory House garden and into the house. As might be imagined, I could have hardly have been more popular with my friends.

Charles Williams (1951)

From Christ Church to the Coldstream

Robert Hamilton Dundas. From the Common Room album

The war had not yet destroyed all traces of the *ancien regime.* We were woken in the morning by an elderly scout, a wizened Dickensian figure, with cans of hot water for shaving. The bedrooms were icy, and only the prospect of cold shaving water forced us out of our warm beds. The sitting room was heated only by a small coal fire that we were not allowed to light before midday and took all day to warm the room. But there were baths – huge ones with plentiful hot water – across the quad, and our bedroom slippers crunched on the snow when we visited them. Before the war breakfast and lunch would have been served in our rooms, but that was now possible only for tea. So clutching little pots containing our sugar and butter rations, we mounted the great fan-vaulted staircase to get into Hall before the doors were shut on us at 8.45. There we ate under the serene gaze of the bishops and statesmen whose portraits covered the walls. Henry VIII glared down on us from above the High Table: Cardinal Wolsey prudently averted his gaze. The food did not measure up to the grandeur of the surroundings. The Steward was a retired soldier, and sardonic undergraduates who attended his military-history lectures suggested that he was so convinced of our imminent defeat that he did not think it worthwhile feeding us. So the temptation to have half an hour longer in bed and breakfast in a workers' café in the market was often irresistible.

My tutor was Keith Feiling, whose reputation rested on his beautifully written history of the Tory

Party. Gentle, shabby, wise, cocooned in books and tobacco smoke, he emanated learning and deepened my passion for the seventeenth century. 'It's a p-p pity you can't get up to the British Museum, Howard,' he would stammer, after listening patiently to my essay: 'You'd find some f-f-f-fascinating stuff in the Tanner Manuscripts about all that'. This may not have been particularly helpful, but it filled me with the determination to get to the British Museum sooner or later, which was probably a good thing. Political Thought was taught by the great medievalist Nowel Myres. As the poor man was doubling as a civil servant in the Ministry of Food during the day and could see me only in the evenings, he found it hard to stay awake during our tutorials, but he guided me skilfully through Aristotle. Hobbes spoke lucidly and wittily for himself; and no one could persuade me that Rousseau was anything more than romantic and dangerous nonsense. That it was important nonsense I learned from J.M. Thompson of Magdalen, a withered, saurian little man to whom I was farmed out for the French Revolution and Napoleon.

I was likewise farmed out to A.J.P. Taylor for nineteenth-century European history. Taylor was not yet the *enfant terrible* be was to become. The impression he gave was mainly one of efficiency. He lectured without a note, taking post on the dais in Magdalen Hall at five past the hour and concluding his last sentence as the clock struck. He listened alertly to my essays and commented on them point by point. The weekly hour I spent with him was exhilarating and fruitful, made all the more pleasant by the fact that he taught me in the summer term and I walked to his house at Holywell Ford down a chestnut avenue breaking into full blossom. That, I reckoned, was what Oxford was all about.

My Latin – then still quite properly regarded as an essential tool for historians – was execrable in spite of ten years' expensive teaching, and I had desultory tuition from Robin Dundas. Dundas was a 'character'; a shambling figure with a crumpled grey face, always wearing the same crumpled grey suit, cigarette eternally stuck to his lower lip, mainly notorious for his open interest in the sex life of his undergraduates, which he quite evidently wanted to share. In summer he frequented the nude bathing beach at Parson's Pleasure, eyeing speculatively any young man rash enough to be seen there. He was regarded by the undergraduates with a kind of affectionate disgust, and the main point in his favour was that he inhabited the rooms occupied sixty years earlier by Lewis Carroll and still furnished much as he had left them: in particular, the fireplace was surrounded by tiles depicting vaguely heraldic animals, the prototypes of the Gryphon and the Mock Turtle among other immortal beasts. These at least enabled us to change the subject when he asked us whether we masturbated, and if so, how often.

Very, very different was Tommy Armstrong the cathedral organist, a cherubic-faced, rather episcopal figure who also trained the Bach Choir. A very fine musician indeed, he combined total dedication to his craft with an encouraging openness to anyone, however young and inadequate, who wanted to practise it. I went to him for voice-tests that I happily passed. So I found myself singing Haydn's *Creation* in the Sheldonian Theatre, an experience in felicity surpassing even Sydney Smith's eating foie gras to the sound of trumpets. But even better things lay ahead. Shortage of male voices for the cathedral choir made Armstrong seek recruits among undergraduates; and since I was, or tried to be, a tenor, could sight-read adequately, and was prepared to return to Oxford, I spent the six winter months of 1941–2 as the cathedral's tenor, singing anything from Palestrina to Vaughan Williams. To listen to the choir had been joy enough: actually to sing in it was to dwell in the courts of the Lord.

I should also mention that I played under Armstrong's baton as an oboist in the Oxford orchestra. I suppose that I was a reasonably competent performer, but I was very surprised indeed to be visited one day by an Old Wellingtonian musician who was talent-spotting for the RAF orchestra. Would I be interested in joining the RAF, he asked, and training as an oboist? Since at that time I had little if any idea which Service I intended to join, beyond feeling rather unimaginatively that it would have to be the Army, the idea was not unappealing. I went to consult Feiling about it. He listened puffing his pipe, looking like a wise old owl. 'Y-yes, Howard', he said when I had finished. 'I-I can

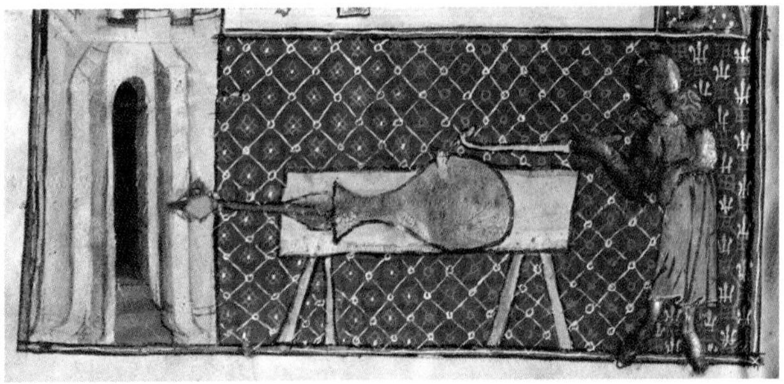

Said to be the earliest representation of a cannon, from a treatise on kingship presented to Edward III by Walter de Milimete in 1326. Library MS 92

see that it doesn't look a b-b bad idea But afterwards, when they ask you w-w-what you actually did during the war, and you said that you spent it p-p-playing the oboe.' I got the message and abandoned the idea on the spot. I doubt whether it would have made the slightest difference to my reputation if I had accepted: the odder the things people did during the war, the less it seemed to matter. But my career would certainly have taken a very different turn.

How we found time for any actual work Heaven alone knows, and the First that to my astonishment I was eventually awarded, I attributed to the indulgence of wartime examiners rather than to my own merits. It was as if we were determined to exhaust every experience that Oxford had to offer before war claimed us for its own. I acted with the OUDS – or rather its wartime stop-gap – in *Othello*, in which Michael Flanders and I provided grave senatorial foils as Brabantio and Lodovico to young stars whose names, alas, I no longer remember. I edited the student magazine *Cherwell*, which had been founded by my uncle George, where I was assisted by, among others, a serious young man called Geoffrey Rippon and the poet Sidney Keyes, some of whose best poems I had the honour of publishing and who would be dead within a year. And I became a regular speaker at the Union, usually from the cross-benches.

On top of all this was the OTC, membership of which was a necessary condition of the deferment of our military service. This occupied two afternoons a week and a full Sunday every month. I paraded in the narrow alley behind the town hall and marched to Christ Church Meadows where, like the army of Charles I three hundred years earlier, we practised our rudimentary military skills. On the lawns outside the Meadow Building we learned how to strip and reassemble the Bren Gun and went through the ritual of 'naming of parts'. We attacked assault courses, pulling ourselves across the Cherwell on fragile ropes. We were lectured on map-reading by Edmund Blunden, then a don at Merton; every inch a poet with wild hair and melancholy blue eyes, he wore a uniform that fitted nowhere. We were lectured on gas warfare by Captain Green, a solid officer from the Ox. and Bucks. We were lectured an tactics by a cheerful young subaltern in the Rifle Brigade, Jim Wilson later to become Lieut. General Sir James Wilson, KBE, MC. But the main figure in our lives was C.S.M. Reid, a tall Northumbrian in the Coldstream, who was all that a sergeant major should be: efficient, implacable, kindly, omniscient. The Adjutant was also a Coldstreamer, and school-girl like I swooned over his elegant black hat and the blinding flash of his buttons. When he suggested that I should join the Coldstream myself it seemed an excellent idea. The combination of elegance and efficiency was immensely appealing, and besides, their use of Figaro's aria 'Non più andrai' as their slow march seemed to indicate both civilization and wit.

I went up to London for my interview with the Regimental Lieutenant Colonel. Evelyn Waugh had not yet published *Put Out More Flags*, but his description there of a similar interview is exact. In the outer office huge guardsmen with hands like hams were pounding at antiquated typewriters. The inner office was furnished with Chippendale furniture and eighteenth-century prints. The Lieutenant Colonel, an immaculate figure smelling slightly of Trumper's Eucris, received me courteously, but learning that that I belonged neither to the Norfolk nor the Carlisle branch of the Howard family and that I neither hunted, fished nor shot, seemed a little puzzled. 'But why do you want to join the Coldstream?', he asked. 'Figaro' did not seem the appropriate answer under the circumstances. I stammered something about having always wanted to join the Regiment. This was neither true nor an answer to the question, but it was the correct reply. The Lieut. Colonel grunted approvingly. I was in. On the train back to Oxford I hummed happily:

Cherubino alla vittoria,
Alla gloria militar!

Extract fom Captain-Professor: A Life in War and Peace (Continuum Books. London, 2006)
Michael Howard (1941)

PHILOSOPHY AT CHRIST CHURCH

Peter Wardle,
Gilbert Ryle, 1967

If it were not for John Locke, and one or two other more recent figures, the title of this note could have been roughly equivalent to 'Snakes in Ireland'. Christ Church is, of course, by the far the grandest of colleges, emitting a vast profusion of prime ministers and archbishops of Canterbury. But it has neither produced nor employed many philosophers of note, with that one outstanding exception.

The first glimmer of Philosophy at Christ Church is evidenced by one Laurence Baker of All Souls being appointed a tutor in Philosophy at Cardinal College. Unsurprisingly, no more is known of him. Naturally Christ Church did not participate in the glories of late medieval philosophy from Grosseteste in the twelfth century to William of Ockham in the mid-fourteenth. From shortly after the time of Wycliffe to the beginning of the sixteenth century Philosophy seems to have been obliterated by the government's persecution of the Lollards.

With its proper foundation in 1547, the college was admirably placed to serve as a home for the watery English version of the Renaissance. That was not to be. There had been, at the beginning of the century, the lively group of 'Oxford reformers', of whom Thomas More and Colet were the principal ornaments. But we can hardly claim Thomas More retrospectively as a Christ Church man on the grounds that he was a member of Canterbury Hall. There seems to have been little going on intellectually in Elizabethan Oxford.

By the middle of the seventeenth century things were very different. There was an impressive group of mathematicians and scientists who went on to form the nucleus of the Royal Society after the Restoration. There were eminent medical men with

A.J. 'Freddy' Ayer. From the Common Room album

whom Locke studied. His chief interest until he was about fifty, and one of his main employments, was medicine. It was his valuable medical services to that somewhat shady political figure Lord Shaftesbury that secured him a role in the public life of his age and made it necessary for him shortly before the death of Charles II to make his way, like Shaftesbury, into apparently agreeable exile in Holland.

There can be no doubt that Locke is the most important Oxford, and therefore English, philosopher. In his massive and encyclopaedic *Essay* he covers most of what is now regarded as philosophy with some thoroughness and in a manner which is still wholly familiar today. In his *Treatises on Government* he, in effect, invented the political theory of liberty and representative government which established the political agenda of the Enlightenment and is the pervasive spirit of our national ideology. He had sensible things to say about education, economics and religious toleration. He was in some ways inspired by Descartes but he was much less silly. He would never have relied on that jack-in-the-box argument of Descartes that our clear and distinct beliefs are ratified by God. The *Essay* was a wild success, and was read in universities everywhere; indeed its triumph was assisted by an order from the heads of colleges that it should not be read by undergraduates.

We know that Locke's tutor was a worthy personage called Thomas Cole (1627–1697), who came to Christ Church in 1646 and was chucked out in 1660 for his non-conformist beliefs. The only other seventeenth-century philosopher to have been at Christ Church was the mystical occultist Robert Fludd. Somewhat Locke's senior, he cannot have had the slightest influence upon him.

The next person of note is Henry Aldrich (1647–1710), Dean from 1689 until his death. His most distinguished remains are architectural: Peckwater Quad in particular. Almost as long-lasting was his *Artis Logicae Compendium* of 1691, a totally unoriginal, frequently muddled textbook of elementary logic which dominated the teaching of the subject in Oxford for most of the next two centuries. A much cleverer man, Dean Mansel, produced a revised and enlarged edition in the 1800s. Aldrich was the impresario of the Christ Church wits whom he got to edit neglected classical works. One of them, Charles Boyle's *Letters of Phalaris*, was memorably and overwhelmingly torn to shreds by Richard Bentley.

The rest of the eighteenth century seems to have passed as quietly for philosophy in Oxford as for everything else. Such good philosophers as there were – and there were some – such as Joseph Butler, did not teach there. Christ Church has a rather wispy claim to Henry St John, Viscount Bolingbroke, who was awarded an honorary MA but probably took up philosophy when his appetites for drink and loose women were fading.

In the nineteenth century Christ Church supplied three supremely intelligent and well-educated prime ministers: Peel, Gladstone and Salisbury. Peel, at the first Schools examinations in 1808, took first classes in both classics and mathematics, but nothing of his philosophical formation is known. Ancient philosophy at least was part of the Greats curriculum from the beginning, but its teachers in Christ Church are not known to history. In general, Greats sat very loose to the many intellectual upheavals of the century. The only effect of the Oxford Movement was to propel the great E.B. Pusey into pure scholarship. The Idealist movement which preoccupied philosophical minds in Oxford in the last third of the century was at least as much Oxonian as Scottish, although many of its Balliol exponents were Scotsmen. Even in Edwardian and pre-1939 Oxford Christ Church took part only with the arrival from Queen's in 1925 of Ryle in the general flowering of philosophy in Britain that had begun in Cambridge at the beginning of the century. It was the brilliant versatility of Bertrand Russell and the obsessive lucidity of G.E. Moore, given further energy by the first Cambridge period of Wittgenstein's career. It may be that the rather timid and conservative Governing Body of the mid-1920s chose Ryle because his uncle was a bishop and he was willing to coach both. As things turned out Oxford philosophy was completely transformed from the constipated despotism of H.A. Pritchard and some cultivated residues of idealism in Joachim and Collingwood. Ryle was, to some extent, an ally of H.H. Price but his brew, as he might have put it, had the stronger flavour. Throughout the 1930s he produced a series of powerful papers leading up to the publication in 1949 of his splendid *Concept of Mind*.

As a tutor he nurtured a philosopher even more revolutionary in appearance – if not perhaps in fact – than himself: A.J. Ayer. His gloriously disruptive innovations culminated in *Language, Truth and Logic* in 1936, perhaps the most widely read work of Oxford philosophy since Locke's *Essay*. Ayer, although an Etonian, was not a typical Christ Church man. But he flourished there and the college was good to him, appointing him to a research lectureship when his shocking views were insufficiently assimilated for him to be given a job elsewhere.

Ryle left the college for Magdalen and a chair in 1945. The teaching of philosophy was left in the hands of the capable moral philosopher and Aristotelian, J.O. Urmson, and of the unhappy M.B. Foster, who eventually committed suicide. Before then, he had written a good book on the political philosophies of Plato and Hegel, and some interesting articles. It may be that there was a conflict in him between the Christian faith and the intellectual demands of philosophy. He was not good at being happy. Sending a letter praising the chef's dinner in Hall while protesting at the level of luxury which he was perhaps alone in discerning in it, he was mortified that no one else would sign it. Moving to Germany to succeed Sir Ernest Barker in some elevated role in the Control Commission, he found luxury even more rampant, with fleets of cars and servants. He returned to the relatively mild voluptuousness of Hall in Christ Church in the late, heavily rationed, 40s.

On the positive side, post-war Oxford produced one major philosopher (they have never heard of him in the United States) in Michael Dummett. He was an undergraduate from 1947 until going to All Souls in 1950, and ultimately to the chair of logic at New College. There was also a distinguished philosopher among the Students: David Pears. The story of philosophy in Christ Church is a matter of some bright light between long patches of shadow. But that is the story of philosophy in Oxford in general, only a little more intense, as one might reasonably expect of Christ Church.

Anthony Quinton (1943)

LAW AND LAWYERS

David Wynne, *E.H. Burn*, with the original E.H. Burn

The teaching of Law at the House over the last hundred years has been dominated by a small number of key personalities. An independent Honour School of Jurisprudence was founded at Oxford in 1870, and the first main law tutor at Christ Church was A.T. Carter (1895–1925), a very able man, described by Professor Harry Lawson (himself a lecturer for one year in 1925) in *The Oxford Law School* as a 'sinister and ambiguous figure'. His successor was S.N. Grant-Bailey (1927–54), whose methods were somewhat irregular and eccentric. The anecdotes about his conduct of tutorials (whether in a first-class compartment on the London train, or supine in college during the reading of the pupil's essay, and showing no sign of his hearing the words or not) are of sufficient frequency and similarity to persuade even the most sceptical jury to convict. But Grant-Bailey was skilful at furthering the careers of his pupils.

Edward Burn (1954–90), known to everyone as Teddy, established the law school on a more modern basis, with regular tutorials on the premises, reading lists, collection papers, and hospitality with Helen at 304 Woodstock Road. The highlight of the year was the Schools lunch. Other tutors gave black-tie dinners for their pupils after Schools in all-too-familiar college dining rooms. The Burns gave a relaxed lunch party in the most idyllic garden hidden away in busy North Oxford: smoked salmon sandwiches, strawberries, champagne – and (because

the timing was usually perfect) the Lords Test Match on television.

Edward Burn persuaded the Governing Body to add a second Student and introduced a system of weekenders who were drawn from old pupils who had achieved distinction in the BCL and the Schools and were starting on their careers at the Bar or as solicitors. He also reorganised the Christ Church Law Club on a less Olympian plane, and invited Assize judges, who used to dine at High Table during the Assize, and other High Court judges, to preside at moots in the Law Library, which was specially adaptable for the purpose. The judicial response was outstanding.

Edward Burn had become an Honorary Bencher of Lincoln's Inn in 1980. On his retirement in 1990 he handed the baton to John Cartwright, who had held the second Studentship since 1982 and who, with Edwin Simpson, carried on where Burn left off: a third Student was elected to replace the system of weekenders, and by increasing the number of postgraduates to read for the BCL and other law degrees. Significant changes in the profile of the law school in the House have therefore been made over the last half century.

House lawyers will think of the Law Library as their home. In the time of Grant-Bailey, there was (in the words of Lord Hobhouse (1951)– a 'wonderfully collegiate law library, then a book-furnished common room used for gossip and debate by law undergraduates'. The dual function – reading room and common room – was retained, but the priority reversed. In due course, Edward Burn changed the location of the Law Library from the bottom of Tom 4 to the premises vacated by the Treasurer and the Steward on the southern side of Tom Quad (spacious premises which opened up new possibilities for Law Library cricket). He then proceeded to fill it with complete sets of law reports: English, Commonwealth (Australian, Canadian and New Zealand), European and international; and periodicals, text books and legal reference works on a similar scale. The Library is open all hours and has achieved the reputation of being the best college law library in Oxford and elsewhere. The new Law Library was opened by Lord Justice Sachs on 26 June 1976, the refurbishment funded mainly by the generosity of the widow of President Roosevelt's adviser, Hugh Cox. Now, through the generosity of many of those who read law at Christ Church or were subsequently associated with its practice, it has been further redesigned, reequipped, and endowed to become a law library for the twenty-first century, and was reopened (by Edward Burn himself) on 8 May 2004 as the *Burn Law Library* – which gives a fitting context to the head by David Wynne, presented to the Law Library by his former pupils on Edward Burn's retirement in 1990. It also naturally contains a copy of the Festschrift that was presented to him by former pupils, colleagues and judges for his eightieth birthday.

Over the years, Christ Church has made a significant contribution to the Bench, through both law graduates and those who have read other degrees as undergraduates. Indeed, two of the most

David Wynne, *Quintin McGarel Hogg, Lord Hailsham*

significant judges in the development of private law in the seventeenth and eighteenth centuries – a formative period of the English common law – were both House men. In the seventeenth century Lord Nottingham was Lord Chancellor, and became known as the Father of Modern Equity. In the eighteenth century Lord Mansfield was Chief Justice of the King's Bench and was regarded by Lord Denning as one of our greatest judges. Mansfield's portrait hangs over the entrance to Hall. He can properly be regarded as the father of English commercial law – and many of his judgements on insurance law, maritime contracts and negotiable instruments are still cited today. In some respects, however, he was ahead of his time (which may be what endeared him to Lord Denning!). For example, he tried to bring into the common law the principle that a promise made in writing in accordance with mercantile custom is binding without consideration. But this went too far, and Mansfield was reversed by a Court led by Sir John Skynner, Lord Chief Baron of the Exchequer, also a House man, whose portrait by Gainsborough hangs on the north side of Hall. Mansfield was a Scot, but he appears in the University records as born at Bath. It appears that this is a mistranscription by an official who misheard the broad Scots voice announcing his home town (Perth). Throughout his life, Mansfield was a controversial, but principled, character. His protection of the rights of religious minorities caused some to think that he favoured both Dissenters and Roman Catholics – and his house in Bloomsbury Square was burnt down in the Gordon Riots in 1780.

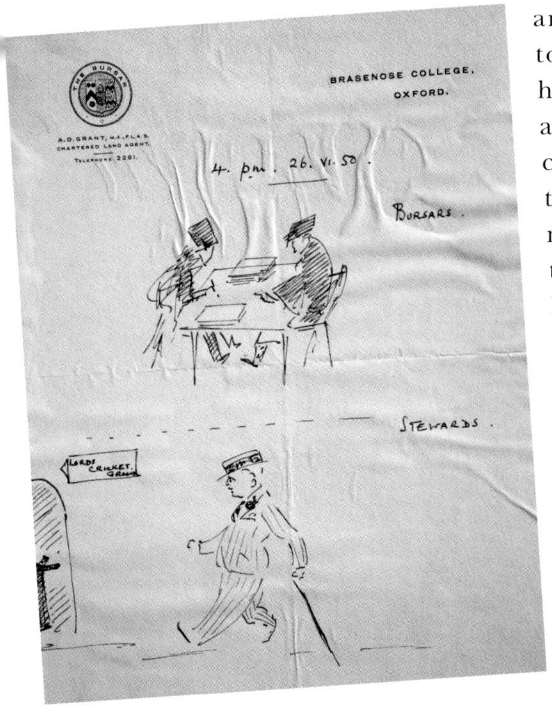

Cartoon from the Steward's photo album showing the bursars hard at work and the stewards off to Lords in the afternoon – not from Christ Church, of course!

In the modern era Christ Church has also provided three other Lord Chancellors, Selborne, Buckmaster, and Hailsham of St Marylebone (twice: his head, by David Wynne, is in the Law Library) and three Lords of Appeal in Ordinary, Greene, Jauncey of Tullichettle and Hobhouse of Woodborough. There have been one Master of the Rolls (Greene), nine judges in the Court of Appeal, and seventeen judges of the High Court (including Stable, who is regarded as one of the outstanding assize judges of the twentieth century; and Patten, Vice-Chancellor of the County Palatine of Lancaster, a former weekender), as well as at least ten judges of similar standing before 1875. In the Court of Appeal there have twice been two members of the House entitled to sit together (Cotton and Thesiger in the late nineteenth century, and Vaughan Williams and Phillimore in the early twentieth century), and once a trio (Sachs, Phillimore and Karminski in the mid-twentieth century).

We have also provided two Attorney-Generals; one Solicitor-General; a Master of the Queen's Bench Division; a Director of Public Prosecutions; a Chief Land Registrar who was responsible for the design of the Land Registry building in the south-eastern corner of Lincoln's Inn Fields, much admired by John Betjeman, and for giving impetus to the system of registered land at long last now prevalent in England and Wales; and the first President of the Caribbean Court.

Christ Church lawyers have entered all walks of life; as barristers; solicitors in large City firms as well as in small country practices; the Army, business and entrepreneurism; as Members of Parliament and the Cabinet; as ambassadors for Canada, India and Germany; as a Lord Mayor of London, as a Vice-Chancellor of Oxford University and as the Head of a Cambridge College.

John Cartwright and Edward Burn

DRAMA AND THE ARTS AT CHRIST CHURCH IN THE MID–TWENTIETH CENTURY

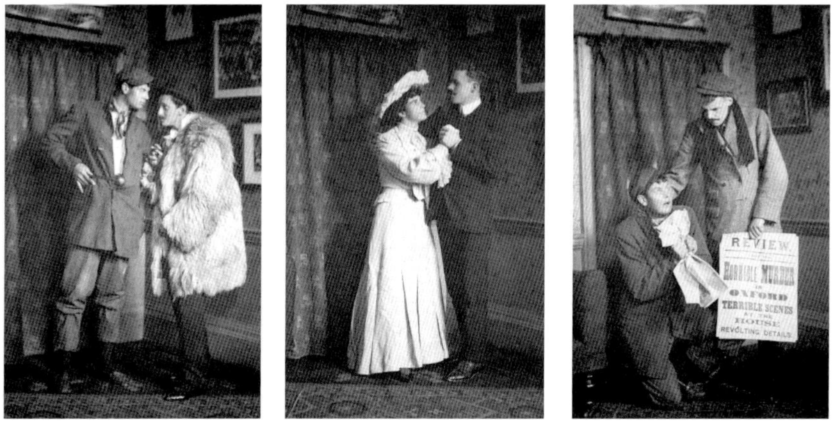

Full page:
D. Martin, *William Murray, Lord Mansfield*, circa 1770

Above:
Scenes from a mock trial for breach of promise enacted by members of the Cardinal Club in about 1900

The 1950s often get a poor press: ushered in by the post-war 'age of austerity', and ending with Supermac's 'never had it so good' years, the decade is most likely to evoke memories of grim military adventure (Korea), misadventure (Suez) or expected oblivion (the H-bomb). Nor do the 1950s get much credit for innovation in the arts. Nevertheless, changes *were* afoot, certainly in drama: when the decade opened Christopher Fry's verse plays (of which more later) were gently refreshing British audiences; by its close, alien invaders like Ionesco and Beckett had established a bridgehead, and the shock troops of John Osborne and the Angry Young Men were terrorising Aunt Edna and her friends all over the West End.

At the House, some, at least, of the arts flourished. The OU Poetry Society thrived, often under Christ Church leadership: 'the House has poets like other colleges have mice', commented *Isis* admiringly. Upriver, Oscar Mellor was painstakingly setting type on his Eynsham kitchen table for the eight-page 'Fantasy Press' pamphlets; and Anthony Thwaite and Adrian Mitchell (both 1952) were among the poets featured by him (their contemporary Alastair Elliot seems to have missed out, in this respect at least). The pamphlets sold for a shilling (5p) each.

Several Christ Church poets also found time to edit *Isis*, while Adrian Mitchell, now globally known as author and adaptor for the theatre, trod the boards himself in the Poetry Society's 1953 production of Eliot's *Murder in the Cathedral* (another play with Christ Church connections); the chorus was graced by the teenage actress Maggie Smith and the future literary biographer Ann Harrop (later Thwaite). More prosaically (literally), House men Howard Applin (1951) and 'Fred' Newman (1952) were among early editors of *Cherwell* in its new tabloid format.

There were devotees of the plastic arts, too, at the House. In mid-decade the Junior Common Room (JCR) Committee embarked on a programme of art purchase, concentrating on contemporary British painting. As with any undergraduate enterprise, where personnel and enthusiasms change every few months, this initiative seems to have flourished, then subsided.

Top Left: The 1960 production of *Murder in the Cathedral* showing (top) Piers Plowright playing Becket and Gavin Millar as the fourth tempter; and Bottom (left to right) Brian George, David Dimbleby, David Robson and Ferdie Mount

The Christ Church Dramatic Society, too, has its cycles. Before the Second World War, according to Freddie Madden (1935), it had gone through a quiet patch (not the last such: the 1981 *Annual Report* notes, 'The Dramatic Society entered *another* period of somnolence'). In summer 1940, however, the society had pulled off a notable coup with the first amateur production of *Murder in the Cathedral*, 'felicitously staged' in the cloisters, the author calling by to chat to the cast during rehearsals. The Society flouted Oxford protocol by hiring a female 'producer' ('director' in today's language), Frances Podmore, a third-year music undergraduate at the Society of Oxford Home Students; this could have been the first Oxford college production where male and female undergraduates acted together (Somerville undergraduate Iris Murdoch led the Chorus). Before this, dons' wives were roped in to play female roles in men's college plays; women's colleges made do with all-female casts.

The idea of a tradition-laden House putting a girl in charge of anything was plainly beyond the imaginings of the (anonymous) designer of the posters for the play, on each copy of which 'Francis' had to be converted to 'Frances' by hand. Defying dire news – Dunkirk, the fall of France – conscription, black-out and rationing, the production drew full houses and generally flattering reviews, especially for the original music, composed by Geoffrey Bush (Balliol) and performed to great effect on the cathedral organ by Ivor Keys (1938).

Reports of other 1940s productions are scanty. Towards the end of the war there was 'an enterprising and successful production' of Ibsen's *The Wild Duck* in the Library, and in autumn 1945 Shakespeare's *Henry VIII* was performed 'on a most ambitious scale' in Hall: ambitious indeed – the stage occupied nearly a quarter of the Hall..

In the 1953 *Report*, R.H. Dundas bemoaned the demise of 'the old Cardinals which read and wrote and acted plays . . . at their best, topical and irreverent and amusing; slightly "for men only" but not objectionably so'. His nostalgia was misplaced: the rest of the 1950s look something like a golden age of thespianism at the House. Productions in Oxford ranged from Shakespeare to Shaw, from Thurber's *The Male Animal* (1952) to Turgenev's *A Month in the Country* (1956), from Jonson's *The Alchemist* (1955) to *Murder in the Cathedral* again (1960).

The cloisters provided effective settings for historical dramas: Shaw's *St Joan* in 1952, Christopher Hassall's *The Player King* in 1953. Hassall's historical drama about Perkin Warbeck, although chosen to front the Edinburgh Festival the previous year, then extensively rewritten for Christ Church, was not universally popular with the cast. Subsequent productions of it are hard to trace; today Hassall is better remembered as librettist for Novello and Bliss and biographer of Rupert Brooke and Edward Marsh.

Although the 1960 *Murder* was staged in St Peter in the East (also used for the Poetry Society's 1953 production), the cloisters (where Richard Burton once famously drew blood, smiting the stonework to show just what a rogue and peasant slave he was) remained popular with the society (as did the cathedral gardens): in 1967 *Isis* thought that Tourneur's *The Revenger's Tragedy*, 'with its multiple rapes, murders, incest and lechery fits the mood of the place exactly'. Two years later the Society was performing Jean Anouilh's *The Lark* in the cathedral itself; the same venue saw a record-breaking, coffer-filling production of *Faustus* in 2003.

Other venues used in the 1950s included the central (but incommodious) Clarendon Press Institute in Walton Street, and the distant (and scarcely more welcoming) Marston Hall which – rather like Society records – seems to have vanished. By contrast, today's producers have the pick of municipally owned (but privately managed) Old Fire Station, the Burton Taylor Theatre (a grand name for a cramped loft conversion over the Playhouse) and several small but well-equipped college auditoria – alas, Christ Church not among them.

These reminiscences are necessarily partial: space would not permit mention of all those Drama Society performers who went on to distinguished careers in the media or related professions. Of three Christ Church actors who have played the Archbishop in Eliot's play, for instance, 1940's Thomas Becket, Gordon Davies (1938) took holy orders (a branch, surely, of the performing arts?), becoming both canon and professor; in 1955 Trevor Conway (1952), both took the lead and directed, then became a head teacher, vigorously promoting school and community drama into the twenty-first century; Piers Plowright (1958), prospered in broadcasting, where among other things, he produced the vastly popular BBC serial *Waggoner's Walk*.

Indeed, the programme of that, 1960, production is stuffed with familiar names, including those of the director, Giles Havergal (for many years director of the Glasgow Citizens' Theatre), David Dimbleby, Gavin Millar and Dominic Harrod.

In 1953, *Isis* published a supplement on Oxford student drama. One page had a photograph of an unnamed female undergraduate, seated in a field of wild flowers during a break from rehearsals for one of Oxford's many outdoor productions; the caption read simply 'Halcyon days'. And, aptly, Frances Podmore (now Rutherford) recalls a post-production party for the 1940 cast of *Murder in the Cathedral*, among the buttercups of Christ Church Meadow, linking it to Eliot's own lines, the First Tempter reminding Becket of happier times, when there were,

> *. . . . fluting in the meadows, viols in the hall,*
> *Laughter and apple blossom floating on the water.*

Fifteen years later, preparing the same play, Trevor Conway was an impressively stern taskmaster. After a particularly gruelling day of rehearsals, however, he allowed the cast an evening off and himself led a party punting on the Isis. By chance a choir (presumably 'town', since term had ended) was being gently poled up and down across the mouth of the Cherwell on a sort of pontoon, singing to beguile others on the water and in the Meadow. Again, Eliot provides a gloss: the Tempter hopes that Becket

> *. . . won't forget that evening on the river*
> *When the King, and you and I were all friends together?*
> *Friendship should be more than biting Time can sever.*

Chris Sladen (1953)

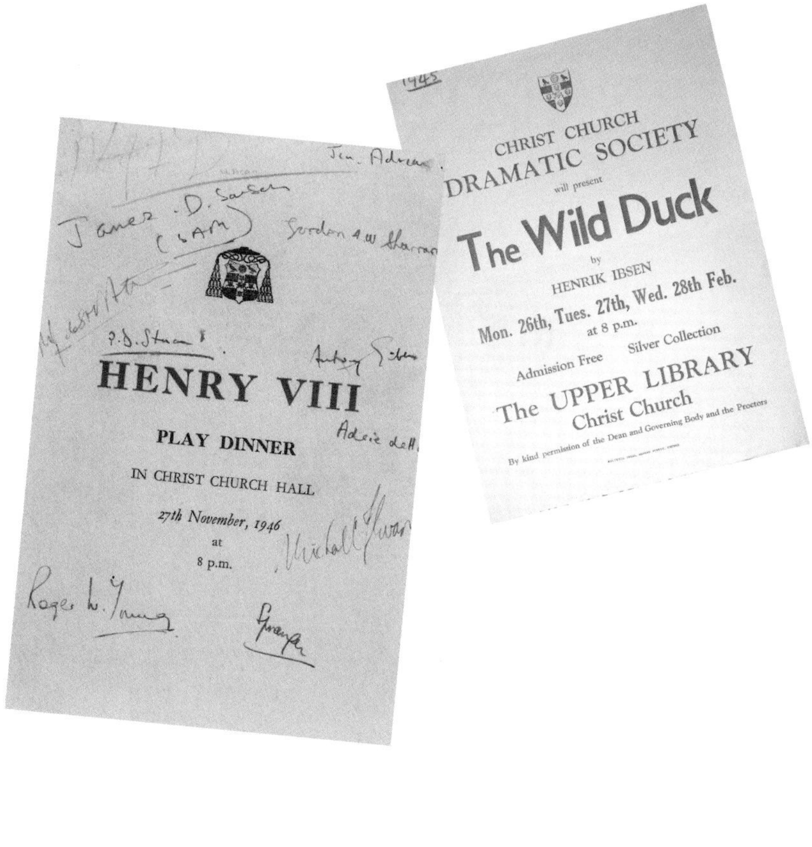

A signed programme from the 1946 production of *Henry VIII*, performed as part of the second quatercentennial celebration, and a flyer for Ibsen's *Wild Duck*, acted in the Upper Library in 1945

The Meadow Controversy

Good Brother Londiniensis: I go straight to the main matter: the long warre (longer than the warre of Troy) in which now, it seems, we have at last defeated those Road-hogs that would have driven a turnpike road through our Christ-church Meadow.

You must know that this Meadow, which they describe as a mere waste marsh, ripe for development, and we as an oasis of rustick peace in our urban Pandaemonium, is a great field, like your Hyde Park, betwixt Christ-church and the river, bounded by walks and trees (some of them exotique), which Christ-church, a rich coil., has always maintained at its own expense for the refreshment of all citizens of Oxon, except such as are of improper character, push hand-carts, or wear ragged or very dirty clothes: a proviso now (save in the matter of handcarts) lamentably disregarded. Some pragmaticall busybodies in the town have long clamoured for a road through this Meadow. They allege publickly that it would be a great relief to the High-street, drawing away the stink and noise and discharging it elsewhere; and they add (but privately, among themselves only) that it would also be a swipe in the eye to a rich proud college.

At this the Meadow colls. got together and Christ-church, as the most concerned, tweaked a string in the metropolis, and a debate was launched in the House of Peers, and many excellent speeches made, especially by the hereditary peers, most of whom had spent a brief time at Christ-church and

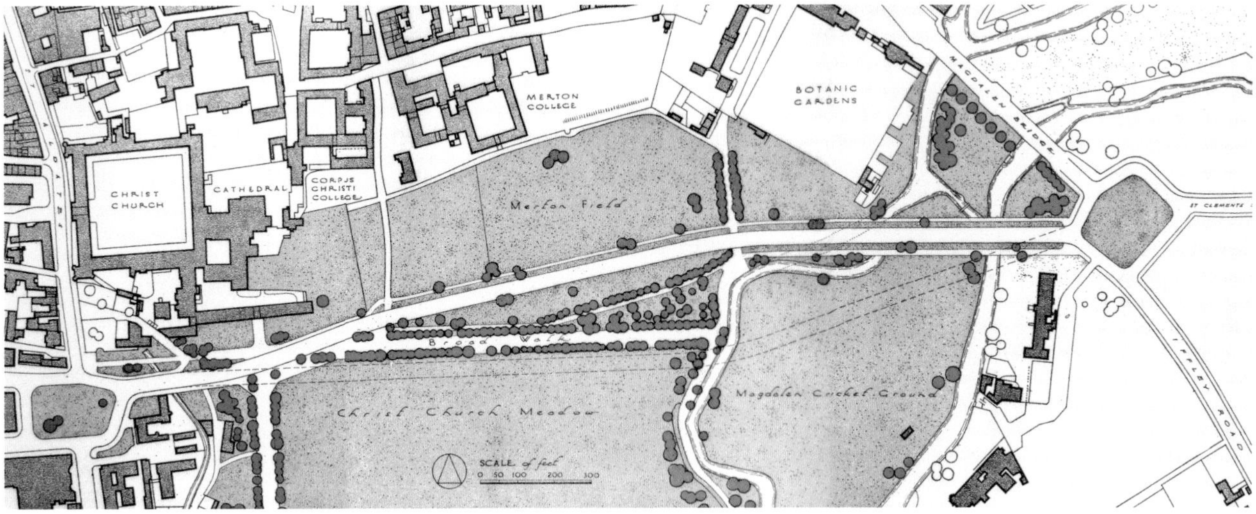

The proposed road across Christ Church Meadow. From Thomas Sharpe, *Oxford Replanned*, 1948

had kindly memories of the Meadow, in which they had breathed their unlicenced greyhounds, beagles, whippets, etc. (and perhaps tumbled a bird or two). But all came to nothing, the government peers fearing to risk their cor by defying what was called The Voice of People.

So the Road-hogs prevailed, and the government told the City to go on boldly and build their road.

For now it seemed that all was over, and nothing left for the friends of the Meadow but to keen over the desolation thereof. For the survayors began to measure the Meadow, this way and that, carving it up in their minds, and the contractors to sniff the spoils, and although good men protested, and totted up figures, and Sir Roy Harrod (the great oeconomist), with marvellous eloquence, urged them at least to sink their road underground, in a tunnel (so that they might all be drowned in it, at floodtime), yet the Road-hogs did but laugh at them, or pilloried them as enemies of Progress and of the People, and so cowed 'em into silence. And Christ-church in particular, for its gallantry and civick spirit, was lampooned, as if it were a crime to be rich, or to stand alone, guarding the interests of beauty and of the publick, against those Gadarene road-hogs who stampeded, grunting identicail grunts, down the broad way which leads to destruction. And even the best friends of that coll., great peers and cabinet counsellours, urged 'em to yield; for, said they, these are yielding times, 'tis best to be with it, to go with the herd; otherwise (besides the cost of it) we shall all be branded as heretiques, enemies of Progress, and of Master Warden Sparrow, and of the People.

Nevertheless, that great coll. was not deflected from its purpose but stood firm.They fee'd learned counsell, at huge expense, and fought inch by inch, and ensnared opposing learned counsell into long, labyrinthine disputations, so that all men marvelled at their virtuosity and the Publick Inquests became publick entertainments, like pantomimes or horse-races or raree shows; and thus they held out till the government of the city had changed, and of the country too, and new survays were made, and all the old summs were shown to be wrong, and a new arithmetique was brought in, and a new philosophy, and little by little the light dawned in men's minds, and the very survayors imployed by the city have now reported that a Meadow Road is not needed, nay is flat contrary to Scripture, Aristotle and right reason.

So you see, good broth Londiniensis, how virtue and sound sense can triumph, even in these degenerate days, if we do but stand fast till the epidemick folly passes, as it surely will.

'Mercurius Oxoniensis'

Top left & far left: Archimedes and the longhorn cattle herd, which were introduced onto the Meadow to improve it as grassland in 1987, and which rapidly became a very popular feature of Christ Church for both members and visitors

Top right: I made this small watercolour of the view from my meadows room in 1989. I balanced on the back of the sofa for an hour or two a day, over many weeks, trying to focus on the misty landscape. In those days I found paintings hard to finish, and this one was no exception, with the tones difficult to balance across the page. But I was pleased with the result and Christopher Butler persuaded me to sell it to him. I discovered to my horror that it has remained unglazed since then, balanced precariously on piles of books in his overflowing study. Perhaps this proves his reliable reputation in charge of the wine cellar, as the painting has never been washed off by a wobbly glass of red wine.

Catherine Story, (1987)

W.H. Auden and the House

Below:
John Haggis,
Wystan Hugh Auden,
1936

I was of course too young to be aware of Auden's existence when he was an undergraduate at the House in the 1920s, but got to know him well in Trinity Term 1960, his last term as Professor of Poetry. Ten years later he decided to leave the United States and retire to Oxford. After long negotiations with Christ Church he had been granted the tenancy of an attractive sixteenth-century stone cottage on the college's outskirts, known as the Brewhouse Cottage, where he spent part of the last year of his life and which is now known as the Auden Cottage.

Auden was above all else the author of some of the most beautiful and subtle lyric poems in the English language as well as of an oeuvre in verse and prose which puts him easily in the top rank of English writers of the twentieth century.

Not long after coming up in 1925 Auden decided, after two false starts, to read the Honours School of English Language and Literature. It was again not much to the credit of Christ Church that it then regarded English as an inferior discipline and did not appoint teachers of English to its tutorial body. But this had the lucky consequence that Auden had to be 'sent out' to Merton College to be taught his subject by Nevill Coghill. Coghill was a liberal-minded man of the greatest charm and intellectual distinction, an expert on Shakespeare and Chaucer, famed for his open-air Shakespeare productions in college gardens, who knew exactly how to turn a course of tutorials within a syllabus into a complete

The 'south' brewhouse, or Auden Cottage

literary education. Coghill and Auden were a revelation to each other and became friends for life. Wystan's weekly essays also enlivened, even *in absentia,* material brought by other pupils, who would read out, not the usual undergraduate plagiarisms but some brilliant nonsense, citing its final defence from the new authority: 'Well, that's what Wystan says anyway.' It was neither surprising nor important that he ended up with a third-class degree, indeed his contemporaries thought it 'grey' to get a second or even a first. A third was the fashionable thing to get and a third Auden got. On the other hand the breadth of his reading, his wit and cultivation, his wide sensitivity to influences and wide influence on others were immense on any showing. He always claimed that his normal reading speed, if he was to understand what he read, was never less than 100 pages per hour (though personally I never quite believed this). His friends had their futures summed up for them with absolute confidence: 'I know that you will be a poet' he told Stephen Spender, 'because you have such an infinite capacity for being humiliated. Art is born of humiliation.' Another close associate was his former school friend and future literary collaborator, the novelist Christopher Isherwood, who was also Wystan's lover on an intermittent and unromantic basis. Both were fascinated by the night-life of Berlin, then a Mecca for homosexuals, which they explored together after leaving Oxford in 1928. Wystan kept a diary there in 1929 (which is now in a New York library) and made a list, like Don Giovanni, of the names of the numerous boys he took up with. But Mr Right (as Wystan later at first called his principal lifelong beloved Chester Kallman), had not yet turned up and did not turn up until 1939 and in another country.

In 1956 it was chiefly the undergraduates who, though debarred from the vote, wanted him as Professor of Poetry. Placards demanding 'Auden for Prof' appeared all over Oxford. They wanted an already internationally famous poet, not an academic critic; his brilliance as a critic and essayist as well, however, meant that in fact they got both. During his tenure of the Chair of Poetry, Wystan was elected to an Honorary Studentship of Christ Church, which he regarded as an overwhelming honour. As a Student and as a former undergraduate he now had full dining and residential rights in the House. His professorship lasted for five years, ending in February 1961. He was required to give one lecture in each term, making fifteen in all, but by special dispensation he only came to Oxford during one term, the Trinity Term, in each year. He usually delivered his three lectures in May, which the University deemed equivalent to one per term for an academic year. This left him time for further voluntary teaching of the informal kind he most enjoyed. He would make it known that at such and such times he would be at a certain coffee house in the Cornmarket and that undergraduates or graduates would be welcome to come and discuss their poems or anything else with him. This system of impromptu seminars was notably successful. The Cadena became a well-known literary meeting point,

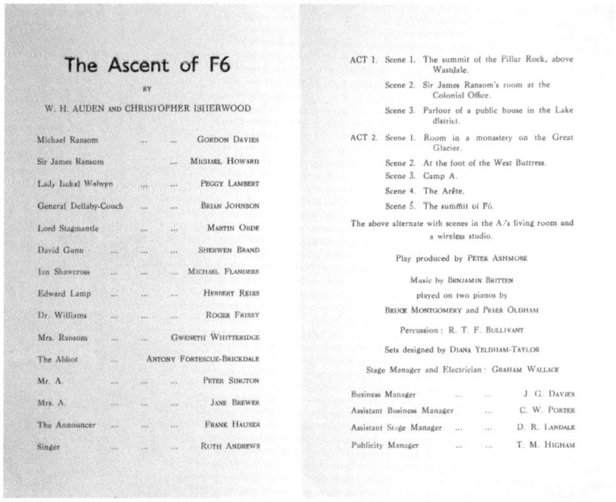

The Ascent of F6

BY

W. H. AUDEN AND CHRISTOPHER ISHERWOOD

Michael Ransom	Gordon Davies
Sir James Ransom ...	Michael Howard
Lady Isabel Welwyn	Peggy Lambert
General Dellaby-Couch	Brian Johnson
Lord Stagmantle	Martin Orde
David Gunn	Sherwen Brand
Ian Shawcross	Michael Flanders
Edward Lamp	Herbert Reiss
Dr. Williams	Roger Frisby
Mrs. Ransom	Gweneth Whitteridge
The Abbot ...	Antony Fortescue-Brickdale
Mr. A.	Peter Sington
Mrs. A.	Jane Brewer
The Announcer	Frank Hauser
Singer	Ruth Andrews

ACT 1. Scene 1. The summit of the Pillar Rock, above Wastdale.
Scene 2. Sir James Ransom's room at the Colonial Office.
Scene 3. Parlour of a public house in the Lake district.

ACT 2. Scene 1. Room in a monastery on the Great Glacier.
Scene 2. At the foot of the West Buttress.
Scene 3. Camp A.
Scene 4. The Arête.
Scene 5. The summit of F6.

The above alternate with scenes in the A.'s living room and a wireless studio.

Play produced by Peter Ashmore

Music by Benjamin Britten
played on two pianos by
Bruce Montgomery and Peter Oldham

Percussion: R. T. F. Bullivant

Sets designed by Diana Yeldham-Taylor

Stage Manager and Electrician: Graham Wallace

Business Manager	J. G. Davies
Assistant Business Manager ...	C. W. Porter
Assistant Stage Manager	D. R. Landale
Publicity Manager	T. M. Higham

Programme for *The Ascent of F6*, written by Auden and Christopher Isherwood, and performed in the Taylorian Institute in 1941

and the more gifted aspirants would also be invited to Auden's rooms in college. He would ask them to come at bizarre times such as 6.13, hoping no doubt to educate them as to his own obsessional conception of time. If the guest's lethally strong martini was not finished in time to enable Professor Auden to get to High Table with precise punctuality, it would be poured down the sink. This too was all part of the deal, as was the poet's famously lined face, which he himself would compare to a wedding cake left out in the rain, and of which Lord David Cecil was said to have remarked that if a fly were to walk across the Professor of Poetry's face it would break its leg. These were Auden's best days at Oxford. The plays he had written in collaboration with Isherwood (*The Dog Beneath the Skin* and *The Ascent of F6*) were produced locally with *éclat*, and he gave many poetry readings.

Wystan fleetingly contemplated settling in Iceland, his ancestral territory. Then, with a certain inevitability, Oxford was chosen as the homing-place, the nesting-place, where he might finally take refuge. It must be said that this choice was a mistaken one and the resulting social experiment, Auden's third Oxford period, was not a success. The Cadena seminars could not be repeated, if only because the Cadena no longer existed. As for the Christ Church SCR, what Auden was doing, after a lapse of many years which had in many ways Americanised him, was to reinject himself as a major world celebrity into a very English, very busy and rather conventional community of dons who were expected to listen to his risqué conversation and for the most part did not much enjoy it. Christ Church provided a safe environment, the audience and the food, to say nothing of the drink. This was not going to solve the essential problem of his personal isolation and could hardly be expected to. Auden needed above all else an intimate relationship – not necessarily sexual but intimate – and preferably with someone who could cook. Chester Kallman, his companion in New York, had provided this but now (except when they were staying in Austria in Auden's house at Kirchstetten) no longer did, and the worst consequence was that Wystan now found that he could no longer write as he had done in his mature years while he had been sustained by the magnetism of his principal human attachment. One should not put the matter in excessively grandiose terms, but the danger he must have sensed at this time was perhaps something like the loss or impairment of his genius, paralleled in a mysterious way to the loss or impairment of his nearness to Chester. The parallel had perhaps occurred to him twenty-five years earlier as he pondered his decision to stay on in the United States after the outbreak of war in Europe, the decision that exposed him to so much hostile questioning and to which he could never give a serious answer – far more questioning than the homosexuality he had never concealed. If total commitment to Chester brought him, as he believed, the total solution of his personal human problem, if his nearness to Chester was a marriage in this sense and if writing poetry was, so to speak, what his Maker, if he had one, required him to do, then the commands were equipollent: You are to bless what exists, you are to stay and give praise.

David Luke

Auden on the Stage

I first met Auden with another undergraduate, John Ryle, when we were invited to his rooms to interview him after he moved into Christ Church in 1972. The curtains were drawn to shut out the light. There were the famous carpet-slippers, the shuffling gait, those deep folds under the eyes, and a bottle of martini and a bottle of gin on the mantlepiece. We discovered you didn't get the gin in the cocktail until he knew you

better, but the interview contained one extraordinary story. He had tried LSD in his New York apartment, under suitable medical supervision, but, he assured us, it had no effect on him whatsoever. The only odd thing was that the paperboy came at completely the wrong time, and he never did that. I don't think Auden ever realised his sense of time had been completely altered by the drug.

His return had to be celebrated in some sort of student *hommage*, and I decided to direct a production of his 1935 play *The Dog Beneath the Skin*, written in collaboration with Isherwood. It is a political parody, and the major problem was that some of the political jokes were firmly planted in the 1930s. So I asked him if he would consider updating the more obscure references to something more understandable to a contemporary audience. His response, somewhat to my surprise and horror, was that I should do it. Isherwood's agreement was obtained, and I got to work, showing him a couple of the changes, but quickly realising he was quite content to leave it to me, the old renewed by the young.

There is also a cameo for a poet in the play, and the temptation was irresistible. A student actor of a suitable matching size took the part, and, like some KGB spy, shadowed the poet daily as Auden shuffled off to the café opposite Tom Tower for his morning coffee, learning all the mannerisms and the inflections of the voice, and remaining completely undetected. The resulting comic caricature was all too real, and the whole cast was wondering how Auden would take it. On the opening night he was sitting two seats down from me, and finally the figure of the Poet shambled on stage, cigarette lit, the sweep of his hand exactly mimicking Auden's gestures, and then that gravelly, slightly broken voice boomed from the stage. Everyone in our row sat tense. And then the voice – the real voice – issued, low but absolutely audible, resonant with pleasure: 'I think' – emphatic pause – 'that that is meant to be *me*'. It was the last of his plays he ever saw.

Mark Morris (1970)

A Memory of Auden

Leaning across the High Table, 'You didn't cross yourself', he said. They were Auden's first words to me. He thought a churchman ought to be a churchman in such matters. He was himself a churchman, and so I remember him in the months at Christ Church from October 1972 until he went off to Austria in April, 'our swallow in reverse' as one of the dons put it.

He was rather battered, rather tired, more sick, I suppose, than anyone knew. Oliver Sacks remarks, in Stephen Spender's posthumous tribute, on the sadness of his loss of a professional medical caretaker, but I do not take very seriously the talk of death wishes and drinking. He kept his routine of work, and he liked the routine (and was sorry at its diminishment) of port and conversation in the Common Room. You can make something neurotic of his 'ritualistic' obsession with time, but the amount it let him write in his lifetime remains, and he knew, no doubt, that time was not on his side. As I have said, he was fairly obviously tired, and not inappropriately the last line in Edward Mendelson's ordering of the *Collected Poems* comes out as 'Sleep, Big Baby, sleep your fill'

He had thought about death before, of course:
Give me a doctor, partridge-plump,
Short in the leg and broad in the rump,
An endomorph with gentle hands,
Who'll never make absurd demands
That I abandon all my vices,
Nor pull a long face in a crisis,
But with a twinkle in his eye
Will tell me that I have to die.

and in 'Talking to Myself':

Time, we both know, will decay You, and
already
I'm scared of our divorce: I've seen some
horrid ones.
Remember: when Le Bon Dieu says to You
Leave him!,
please, please, for His sake and mine, pay no
attention to my piteous
Don'ts but bugger off quickly.
But rather battered, yes, and rather tired –

Yet surely himself, and a little repetitively so: I can hear his very voice and very sentences as I read 'A Certain World' (the wedding present he promised me on the last evening, and he did not forget – and on the evening he was next signed in to dine, the returning migrant, we heard that he had died). He pitched the conversation to the person he was with: and so for the new canon of Christ Church it was the theological gambit, whether Grace at dinner, or the Purgatory game of placing incompatibles next to each other for the duration – who would go with Simone Weil?

He was always in the cathedral on Sunday morning at the eight o'clock Holy Communion (the only Book of Common Prayer celebration of the week, and he could not bear the new series of liturgies). He would have had the Mass in Latin ('which the dead share with us') – but he could say things to provoke. I see him coming in, in his carpet-slippers, as accurately as the celebrant on the stroke of cathedral time – 8.05, and he would shuffle out before the post-Communion prayer. I never celebrate in the Military Chapel without a thought of him in the front chair he always took. 'It was nice to have you yesterday', he said more than once: 'I cannot bear expression being put into the Mass.' I suppose that I administered his last Communion in the Church of England. It was Palm Sunday, 1973, and I picked up a bunch of palm branches for the distribution, and, without thinking, put a whole branch into his hand. He went out, with that viaticum, processionally, craggy, battered, before the post-communion prayers. 'He was one of a kind', the college carpenter said to me, noticing his books on the shelves he had come to see to, 'a real one-orf'.

A very human figure, then, and yet, as Hannah Arendt writes so sensitively in the Spender tribute ('an expert in the infinite varieties of unrequited love') something of a lonely one, despite his gift for friendship: and they were not the happiest days for him – Oxford noisier than he had ever thought to find it, and he had had to come back to England to have money stolen from his room, and perhaps the society of Senior Common Rooms had changed. It was a loaded moment when, on that October Saturday afternoon of his memorial service in the cathedral, they sang his and Benjamin Britten's 'Shepherd's Carol', which had been always part of Christ Church Christmas:

O lift your little pinkie, and touch the winter sky.
Love's all over the mountains where the
beautiful go to die
But my cuffs are soiled and fraying.
The kitchen clock is slow,
and over the Blue Waters the grass grew long ago.

Peter Walker

Memories of Christ Church 1945 to 1989

The baron of beef, prepared to celebrate the end of meat rationing in 1954

It's hard to recall the bareness of our post-war wardrobes. School clothing had been outworn, devoured by moths or consigned to 'salvage'; our 'Demob' clothing provided a bare minimum. So out came an array of service clothing, carefully preserved: British Warm overcoats, windproof jackets, naval sweaters, balaclava helmets. Most of us still had one or more woollen pullovers sent out to the fighting forces under various 'Comfort Fund' schemes. Many were fashioned from wool run down from previous garments, and some were ill made and poorly fitting: but anything that provided an extra layer was a boon.

The coal ration for each room was one bucket per day – barely enough to keep a fire going for a few hours in the evening – so the Great Freeze fostered togetherness. Syndicates were formed, providing one blazing fire shared between 24 people, and it became quite usual to see people wandering the corridors, bucket of coal in hand. (If a party was thrown it was not a matter of 'bring a bottle', but 'bring some coal'.)

Food was now more tightly rationed than in wartime: the meat ration was tiny and whale meat steak was an occasional luxury in Hall. Some interesting dietary supplements were discovered. Woolworths provided gull's egg sandwiches – a rare unrationed item.

The year 1946 was the four hundreth anniversary of the founding of Christ Church, marked on 24 October by a royal visit and dinner in Hall. 'The King, Visitor of Christ Church' was toasted in song – the old Cavalier song, 'Here's a Health unto his Majesty', and we let ourselves go on those final lines:

And he that will not drink his health
We'll wish him neither wit nor wealth –
Nor yet a rope to hang himself …

The windows rattled to the singing, much as they must have rattled three centuries earlier when Christ Church housed Charles I and his court during the Civil War. (By day Hugh Trevor-Roper, fresh from delving into the death of Hitler, filled the Hall with his lectures on the English Civil War.)

But perhaps my most memorable moment was fielding in the deep for Christ Church Warrigals under the lilac bushes at Wallingford and taking a catch on the boundary.

Geoff Tudor (1945)

When I arrived at the House in 1944, about thirty per cent of the undergraduates came from two schools, Eton and Westminster. Among them were some who were not just comfortably off, as I was, but rich. They gave the parties that the rest of us enjoyed – plenty of champagne, delicious food (game and salmon and such unheard-of goodies) despatched to Oxford from the family estates by parents harrowed by the depressing and wholly accurate accounts of the food in Hall. Many of these men had a vitality, charm and generosity of character that added to the life of the society but whose academic gifts would now alas make their admission unlikely, something which I myself am of an age and temperament to regret. A few were awful, and their exclusion would have been no loss.

By about 1946/7 more than half the undergraduate population had spent anything from one to six years in the armed forces, with all that that implies. Many of them were in their late twenties or older, married and with children. I myself, at the age of twenty-one, though I had never seen a gun fired in anger, had by 1947 commanded one of HM ships at sea, drunk my way in fleet wardrooms from Devonport to Manila, been thrown out of bars from Alexandria eastwards, and submitted to an exacting apprenticeship in the stews of Singapore.

I suffered only once, having been nabbed by a bulldog in the bar of the Randolph. The proctor (I forget who it was; perhaps Basil Mitchell of Worcester) fined me £5, which meant a week or two of poverty. The tale came to Gilbert Ryle's ears and a day or two later we bumped into each other outside Blackwell's. He took his pipe out of his mouth and said, 'Sorry to hear about your troubles at the Randolph. However, come into the King's Arms and I'll buy you a drink'.

Meetings of the JCR committee seemed to be permanently convulsed by endless debates about whether or not to take the *Daily Worker*.

Left: Robert Blake; Right: Jim Urmson

To have, as I did, a huge, elegantly panelled room with a charming view, and a separate bedroom almost as large, was luxury after the quarters I had been used to at school and in the RNVR. There was one, and only one, lavatory per staircase; unheated of course, and in February the question was on getting up first thing in the morning whether one's scout had got round to putting a kettle of hot water down it so as to disperse the ice. The other incentive to get up was the discomfort of shaving in cold water, and the hot water brought by one's scout for the purpose got cold very quickly.

I recall Jim Urmson with special tenderness. He was also a decisive intellectual influence. Insofar as I think of myself as a rational, sensible and balanced man it is because of him. His personal influence and conversation was important to me at a formative age.

Every year with the first burst of April sunshine Dundas would post a handwritten note on the board outside the JCR. It always read the same: 'There is a bed of purple-flowering *Iris reticulata* along the north wall of the garden which in the sun presents a notable sight and smell'. This was the sort of elbow-jogging for which one was very grateful.

Though I regret not having done Urmson and 'D' justice in Schools and, granted a rerun I'd like to do better, nevertheless I look back with a good conscience because I think my extramural time was

Above:
The hallway and stairs of Canon Claude Jenkins's rooms in 1959. Now the entrance to the Steward's Office and the Treasury
Right:
Unsigned, *Robert Cecil, marquess of Salisbury*, Prime Minister for three terms between 1885 and 1902

well spent: music, travel, conversation, friends and reading even if Tacitus, Thucydides and Aristotle did not figure as prominently there as they ought. The non-academic interests of my own circle were neither trivial nor frivolous, and I am convinced it was a good mixture (it was certainly an enjoyable, even a heady one) for someone intent on a career in commerce rather than academe.

Richard Law (1947)

I was fortunate to sit at the feet of Roy Harrod, who kept us duly humble with the aid of an intimidating photograph of Maynard Keynes he had on the mantelpiece. From Jim Urmson I learned not only philosophy but the value of a pipe as a tutor's aid; the need to light and relight it provided useful time to think how to sort out some muddled argument offered up by a pupil. But I must be wholly serious in extolling the memory of Robert Blake, Tutor in Politics. He had a slightly mischievous delight in the less uplifting episodes of political behaviour, but nothing diluted the top quality of his scholarship. As is well known, he went on to be Provost of Queen's, became a member of the House of Lords, and acquired a formidable reputation as a leading expert on the Constitution. It was Robert, I think, together with Charles Stuart and Hugh Trevor-Roper, who pleased us, and annoyed the rest of the University, by laying on a series of lectures entitled 'Eleven Christ Church Prime Ministers'.

Dick Sargent (1946)

From the first I loved it, its grandeur and its style. It had riches (though now I know that no Oxford college is so rich that it does not need a great deal more) and it used its riches well. In my first term the King and Queen dined in Hall. It was a memorable occasion. The Hall was crowded. We were all in *subfusc*. As the Royal party moved up the Hall, they were followed by the cathedral choir in their scarlet cassocks, singing madrigals, suitable pomp and circumstance for the foundation of Henry VIII. That was special but every night was a delight to this brash colonial. The lighted portraits looked down on us as a Scholar read the Grace, '*Nos miseri homines et egeni*' – not too *miseri* or *egeni* thought I. To be within 'the line of festal light in Christ Church Hall' was privilege indeed. In the cathedral too the choir was daily to be heard singing evensong, sounds of heaven.

The Big Freeze of 1947 tried us all, a baptism if not of fire. Coal was rationed, meagrely. Everything that could freeze froze. The lavatories froze, and the cisterns, and the water in my jug, and the towel on my rack. I had to put on my army balaclava and keep the blankets over my head all night. Rugger pitches were like concrete and play was impossible for weeks on end. So I sat in my room looking out over the snow-covered Meadow reading Plato, a happy time despite the cold. When the spring sprang, I sat reading in the Masters' Garden, then and now my favourite Oxford garden.

I bought my commoner's gown from a Porter for nine pence; it was an absurd thing, no more than a waistcoat in length, but I didn't care what I wore as long as it wasn't khaki.

Dining clubs were reborn, notably the Nondescripts and the Twenty Club. A number of dons played their part and the Steward, Col. D.V. Hill ('Hooky') gave his blessing. He was a connoisseur of wine and liked dinners. He had been a POW of the Japanese, having as a prelude to captivity had to take a detachment of troops to destroy the wine cellar at Government House in Singapore and so prevent the Japs getting drunk, no small irony for a man who had handled with tender loving care many a bottle of fine wine. (He was heard to say later on in the Senior Common Room: 'When I was a POW of the Japanese, I had time for reflection and after a great deal of serious reflection I came to the conclusion that claret is the best of wines'. By such means he had stopped the enemy getting him down.)

The real star was Canon Jenkins, a man of fascinating oddities such as clearing up the bits of toast left on High Table and secreting them in the sleeve of his gown; whether for himself or for birds or even for the goldfish in Mercury we knew not. His sermons, much enjoyed, regularly began 'In this eleven Viceroyed House ...' In the Great Freeze of 1947 he did not wait around in the chilly cathedral for the procession to form up, but with slick timing joined it just as it was beginning to go up the aisle, with as many layers of garments as he could manage; beneath his surplice and cassock his dressing gown was to be seen and beneath his trousers his pyjamas, on his feet his carpet-slippers, a man for all seasons, a wondrous eccentric. He lectured on a large range of subjects for hours on end, getting on to the subject, if not the point, with the aid of an alarm clock (or so I was told by a friend who went along to see what was what and when).

George Cawkwell (1946)

At first it seemed to me that Oxford's methods were antiquated: no attendance, no rote learning. Yet it appeared to give something to its students, a mode of thought which clarified their mind, made their vision larger and, above all, a caressing suavity of manner which came of a conviction that nothing matters except superiority. I understood that the key to this mystery is found in the operations of a person called the tutor. I had two tutors – a moral tutor, Sir Roy Harrod, who lived in Christ Church, and an academic tutor, Sir Hubert Henderson.

Nick Stacey and I were both Olympians, representing Great Britain and India in the sprints. The competition at Oxford was intense and we came out equally: I won the 100m and Nick the 200m. Roger Bannister awarded me a full Blue, the first Indian to get a Blue for athletics. There was great joy at Christ Church when I returned with the 100m trophy, the biggest of the cups, full three feet king size. Nondescripts threw a sumptuous dinner in my honour: fish, flesh and fowl, fine strong beer, gooseberry, rasberry and apricot pies. There was such a profusion that scarcely two of the fifteen ate of the same. Thirty-five years later, on retirement from UNESCO — Paris where I was chief of the Asia Section in the Education Sector, I met K.P.S. Menon at a dinner he gave in his family mansion in Trivandrum after he had retired as Foreign Secretary of India. 'Stevenson died just after I came down from Oxford', KPS said. I was stumped. Who was he talking about? I had last met

Eric Prabhaker winning the 100m final in 1949

Eric Gray.
From the Common Room album

KPS in Beijing when he was ambassador. But there was no Stevenson with him or me. 'Tell me one thing, Eric', KPS said when he saw me struggling with my memory. 'You must know Stevenson, the scout who served Meadows 3'.

I had been assigned a spacious set of rooms in Meadow building overlooking the Christ Church Meadows, with a distant view of the trees that bordered the river. 'I lived in Meadows 3.1 after you and Ambassador Menon, my father, before you', continued KPS, as we adjourned the conversation to the drawing-room. And it all came back to me and I remembered faithful Stevenson with great affection. To put Indians of any great promise in the same rooms, Meadows 3.1, over four decades shows a remarkable adherence to tradition. Christ Church, indeed, offered a most favourable environment to scholars from the erstwhile colonies, thereby strengthening the links in the Commonwealth.

Eric Prabhakar (1948)

On coming up I went to see Hugh Trevor-Roper who to my surprise asked me if I proposed to hunt. Not a factor that I had even considered, but I said I might and he then offered me his mare for which after several trials I paid £60.

Other delightful memories: Climbing in through J.I.M. Stewart's window to find a note on his desk asking those who entered by the window to please not disturb his papers if possible.

Thomas Baring (1948)

As we walked back from dinner, the Senior Censor, Eric Gray, envisaged the fun of trying to hole out in Mercury, decided that the tee should be in Peckwater and then challenged me to play the new hole! A few 'stiffeners' later and in pitch dark we were on the course allocating roles to the diners – markers, runners between Tom & Peck, torch-bearers etc. – and assessing the approach to the stroke. At that moment reality struck. The ball had to go straight over the irreplaceable sixteenth-century glass in the Library windows; teeing up any further to the right would involve the trajectory being too steep for the length of shot. Colonel 'Hooky' Hill, the Steward, who was also dining, had a nervous moment or two until he decided that any ensuing accident was adequately insured. Fortunately the choice of a five iron, allowing for the dinner jacket, and a high tee, produced the right elevation, and after two attempts, with the landing of the ball reported back by the markers and runners, the third shot resulted in a mighty splash and resounding cheers.

Peter Gardiner-Hill (1948)

The Peace Group later invited a speaker from another college to explain the Quaker understanding of pacifism. This meeting was on the second floor of Meadow Buildings, in a large room (as they were) overlooking the park. He had hardly got well into his topic when noises were heard from the stairs, a group stamping up to the chant WE WANT WAR! These were rowing men, we were told, who decided to form a War Group, after a visit to the Buttery, and to redeem the college's good name. Reaching the top they banged on the door. This being quite solid, those inside agreed on a no-open policy. Then lighted fireworks appeared under the door, and needed stamping on.

By now our visitor's contribution was rather lost to view. What should we do now, in the instant predicament? Most of the House men present favoured sitting tight: it was a good door and those silly fellows would tire of their fun, and need another drink. Our visitor disagreed: Come on, let's go out and give it to them! There are more of us. We can throw them down the stairs!

Humphrey Palmer (1949)

I was assigned to a young Christ Church man then at All Souls, Anthony Quinton (now Lord Quinton).

Quinton was smooth, stimulating and sparkling – and so voluble that I had difficulty getting a word in edgewise, an unusual and no doubt salutory experience for me.

The Oxford tutorial system in those days, with one-on-one hour-long sessions, was at its best unsurpassable, so much so that I felt it not worth while wasting time on lectures, unless they were actually at Christ Church. There were two exceptions to this: Isaiah Berlin and J.L. Austin, for both of whom I made the trek to the Examination Schools.

Oxford philosophy in those days was dominated by the school of linguistic analysis, with which I became fascinated, and of which Austin was the high priest – so much so that he cast a blight on many of his colleagues. It was in many ways an arid school, being concerned solely with the logical elucidation of every proposition, and its aridity was such that, although I was subsequently (much to my surprise) to get a first, largely on the basis of my philosophy papers, I had no wish to become a professional philosopher. But it did train its practitioners to think clearly and identify nonsense, however dressed up, which I subsequently found to be not a bad training for politics and government.

My politics tutors were, for political history Robert Blake, then Junior Censor (it was pleasing, incidentally, when forty years on I left politics and entered the House of Lords, that both my original Censors were already there), and for political institutions, Frank Pakenham (Lord Pakenham, subsequently the Earl of Longford).

Courteous, conscientious and kind, Frank Pakenham sometimes seemed to live in a world of his own (although when I came to know him in later life I discovered that this was largely, although not wholly, an affectation). Misunderstandings between us were not infrequent. One day in 1953, when I arrived at his rooms for my tutorial, he greeted me by saying 'Have you heard the good news? Stalin is dead'. Fearing (wrongly, as it turned out) that whoever might be Stalin's successor might turn the Cold War hot, I replied 'I'm not sure whether it is such good news'. Totally misunderstanding me, Frank piously replied 'Quite right: one should never rejoice at the death of a fellow man'.

Saturnine in appearance, discursive in speech, and intense in manner, I enjoyed having tutorials with Roy Harrod, even though I doubt if I greatly profited from the experience. That is partly because I was greatly distracted by his pipe-smoking problem. The problem was not that he insisted on smoking his pipe throughout the tutorial, as we sat by the coal fire in his rooms, but that the pipe kept going out. He would then suck on it noisily several times, in the vain hope of reviving it, then tap the dead tobacco out on the fire, then relight it (more sucking), and then it would soon go out again and the whole process would be repeated, preoccupying him almost as much as it distracted me.

The first wedding in the cathedral of two Christ Church under-graduates. Philip Lowe (mt 1980) and Sally Sutton (mt 1980) were married on 4 August 1984

Nevertheless, I did unfortunately imbibe from Roy the neo-Keynesian framework with its macroeconomic obsession and naive expansionism, from which only the passage of time and experience of the real world enabled me to emancipate myself.

Nigel Lawson (1951)

I was fortunate to come up to Oxford in the autumn of 1956: that year, 1956/7, we won the OUBC IVs and the Pazolt Cup (for weaker 1st IVs and for second IVs); the first Torpid made three bumps; and three House men rowed in the Oxford crew. 1957/8 turned out to be an even better year. Again, we won both the OUBC IVs and the Pazolt Cup. Again, three House men rowed in the Oxford crew. Again, we were expected to be the fastest crew in Eights and, this time, we did not disappoint. We broke the Oxford course record. On the first night of Eights, we bumped Merton, on the subsequent night, Queen's, and then rowed over comfortably for two nights to finish Head of the River for the first time since 1927.

It was, of course, important to follow tradition and to throw our cox, Philip Wetton, into the river. Philip, being a man of spirit, managed to take one of our number into the river with him. When they both climbed out, they took it upon themselves to extend the blessing of this christening to other members of the crew. In short order, seven dripping oarsmen and a cox stood on the raft – and suddenly realised that one member of the crew was not there. Rushing into the changing rooms, we found David Lloyd-Jacob stark naked; but, being well brought up, none of us had the nerve to carry him out in that state in front of our mothers in order to throw him into the river. Small surprise that he got a First!

Celebrations began with family and friends. The Senior Common Room gave us a champagne reception and dinner at High Table. We burnt a boat and drank too much. There was much to celebrate, given that it was thirty-one years since the House had been Head of the River; but for David Edwards and myself, there was an additional satisfaction. My father, William Rathbone (always known in the rowing world as Nono) and David's uncle, 'Sphinx' Edwards (both Blues) had rowed in the House Eights of 1925, 1926 and 1927. So for me, there was the satisfaction of knowing that Nono and I held four consecutive House Head of the River oars; and for David the same in partnership with his uncle.

The Buttery, looking through to the commemorative plaque to John Hammond, who funded its refurbishment in 1722

William Rathbone (1956)

Friday, February 15th, 1957.
'Cherwell' is quite the worst newspaper I have ever read; it is, so opinion runs, edited by and for homosexuals, and generally speaking the people who run it are the pasty-faced spotty individuals who go around in sweaters and green corduroy trousers accompanied by loose women. They drink coffee in 'La Roma', the Tackley and The Kemp and they are just about the end ….

Monday June 3rd, 1957.
I shall write a booklet on the subject: *Twenty Different Ways of Entering Ch Ch Without Going over the Garden Wall in Meadows Yard.* (This masterpiece, alas, never saw the light of day). I can think of about ten straight off: (1) Meadows, grating to Meadows bath and in (2) Rope to balcony of Meadows Building (3) Into Canon Cross' garden (the Priory Garden) and through his basement. This is no longer recommended – he used not to mind people coming through, provided they went through the basement, wiped their feet and shut the door behind them, but his aged father used to get frightened, thinking there were burglars. The canon himself knew better. It is of course child's play to get into the Meadows from either Merton, Rose Lane or St Cath's and then into the Masters' garden. The new iron gates have decoration which provides adequate footholds. (4) The Dean's garden has many possibilities. One can sink into a basement window of Canterbury Quad, or (5) go over the wall by Kilcanon or (6) through the Dean's house – though this is tricky as the Dean might be annoyed. Jenkins' [house] is not too easy either. One can get into the Dean's garden either from the Corpus car park or through the Cross' garden and the Cathedral graveyard. One might even be able to get into the cloisters through the graveyard door – I must see what can be done to pick the lock. If one can pick

locks, then (7) to come over the wall by Dr Lee's gallery gives access either to the iron doors leading to the Hall Staircase, or one can get into the SCR garden. To go through the SCR is risky as anyone may appear. There is a door leading straight through but I think it's locked and one has to go through the smoking room (8). The ninth way is to go through Dr Simpson's house, and this is facilitated by the fact that he has undergraduates staying there, but going through these Canons' houses demands care in case muddy feet get onto the carpet – very tactless. If one can get into the Archdeacon's garden one can go straight through his house but again this needs care; one may even get into the JCR windows: I forget whether they are barred or not. There is a way through the old stables and into Killcanon but I am not quite sure what it is. At any rate, I don't think it is very difficult. Peckwater lavatories also furnish a fair route. All these methods are practicable to a man with courage and soft shoes.

Simon Freebain-Smith (1955)

Christ Church 'University Challenge' team in 1965

But there was one occasion – there is a member of my club who claims to have witnessed the scene – when I climbed into college, using what I was advised was a safe route, from the Meadows by the gate from the Masters' Garden. It needs to be explained that I was at this brief moment rather a grand figure, a scholar, President of the Jowett (philosophy) Society, President of the JCR, President of the Union and seen as a candidate for All Souls (in which I failed entirely).

As I came over the wall into the Meadow Buildings Quad I was greeted in the full beam of a powerful torch wielded by the Head Porter, himself a most august figure, alike huge and venerable. Startled by my unexpected appearance amongst the ranks of the college's more usual suspects, he exclaimed in tones of mixed horror and reproof worthy of Lady Bracknell at her peak, 'Ohhhh, Mr Jayyyyy, Sirrrrrr'. I actually felt a tremor of shame pass through me at having provoked such moral pain in so noble a breast.

That was almost my last night in college; and it cost me a fine. But its effects marked me less than my first night in college, when the freshmen were summoned to the Junior Censor's rooms on Peck 9, where the Senior Censor, Charles Stuart, proceeded to confirm our various choices of Schools courses. When my turn came I blathered and havered, canvassing the rival merits of history and PPE, suggesting that perhaps a compromise – history for prelims, then PPE – might be best.

Charles scowled darkly at me and enquired what I wished to achieve at Oxford. 'Well', I said 'my ambition is to get a first'. The scowl became bleak and thunderous, the folds of the Censor's gown ever more copious as he sunk ever more deeply into his arm chair. 'In that case', he responded thinly 'I suggest that before you embark upon that long and stony road' – these words were extracted from him with apparently terrible pain and a hideous grimace – 'you first make up your mind what you wish to read and let me know by 9 am tomorrow'.

I was stunned, rushing up to my rooms – behind the parapet on Peck 9 – and wondering how on earth I was to decode so great a question in so short a time. I wrote down all the arguments for history – and all the arguments against it. Likewise for PPE. So what? I counted them up. The majority favoured History.

But what did that prove? What weight should be attached to each argument? What indeed was the nature of a decision? By what logical analysis, by what decision tree, could the matter be settled? Deductive reasoning seemed feeble in the face of such a choice. At last, at about 3 am I fell asleep, waking just in time to tumble downstairs and inform Stuart that I would definitely read PPE.

How this clear conclusion was reached I shall never know; but what I do know is that it had nothing whatever to do with any of the logic, formal or informal, which I studied for the next three years, indeed that it involved no conscious mental act at all. I had just slept on it; and then I knew. For the rest of my life that experience has guided me – and others whom I have advised – when ticklish decisions have had to be made.

Peter Jay (1957)

There were no half measures in [Alban Krailsheimer's] comments on my essays; he called a spade a spade. He asked me once at the end of a term if I was going straight home north to Nottinghamshire. 'Anything north of Watford is the North', he said. 'Yes', I replied, and asked if he intended going away too. His reply – 'No, my work starts when you've gone home'.

Rex Norman (1957)

Left to right: Charles Stuart, Alban Krailsheimer, Oscar Wood. From the Common Room album

I read PPE. My Philosophy tutor was the redoubtable Oscar Wood. When my one-to-one tutorial with him fell in the last slot in the day with no-one to follow, he used often very kindly to offer me a glass of sherry – which I invariably used to accept. He kept a pair of glass decanters on the sideboard at the far end of his room. My glass he used to pour out of the right hand decanter. His he used to pour out of the left hand decanter. One day, curiosity, helped by the sherry, got the better of me and I asked him what were his reasons. He replied that, as a logician, he was passionate about symmetry. He could not bear the level in the two decanters to be anything other than level with each other.

David Pitman (1957)

I came up to Christ Church in 1958 and the censors allocated me, by their own inexorable logic, rooms in Meadow Building, 9.11. It was a period of transition with undergraduates coming up already having done their national service, together with some of us like myself who had come direct from school. There was, nevertheless, a clear if lingering odour of 'Brideshead Revisited' still about the place. I discovered that Evelyn Waugh was visiting Oxford – no doubt to speak to some up-market Roman Catholic dining club – and accordingly wrote to him asking him if he could confirm that I was actually living in the rooms occupied by Sebastian. He was delightfully courteous, if vague, and admitted he was not quite certain which the rooms actually were, but was very happy, if it would please me, to agree they were indeed mine. For good measure he threw in the thought that it was scandalous that Latin and Theology were no longer a requirement for Prelims, and observed that this was yet a further step in Oxford of a long descent.

Timothy Hornsby (1958)

Every night a 'baby' concealed in swaddling clothes was transformed into a live piglet which scuttled around relieving itself in excitement outside this Meadow Building, and on some evenings the audience sat and watched under umbrellas (as shown in a contemporary *'Tatler'* magazine feature). There was even talk of live flamingos being used for the croquet game. This was an open-air joint production by Christ Church and Univ Dramatic Societies of *Alice in Wonderland* in the Meadow to celebrate the centenary of its publication in the summer of 1965. After its successful run in Oxford the production went on to the open-air Minack Theatre in Cornwall, and then to Rome's Teatro Goldoni.

It was instigated by Tim Mason (ChCh) who managed to keep control over this extraordinary production before going on to work at the Ballet Rambert. But the fantasy was conceived and directed with eccentric inspiration by the messianic bearded and cloaked figure of Adrian Benjamin who was then studying divinity at Wadham before training for holy orders at Cuddesdon.

Alice was played by the late Peter Ustinov's daughter Tamara (St Hilda's), who became a professional actress after Oxford, and whose famous father arrived by helicopter to see the show. In Rome the leading role was taken by Polly Toynbee, long before she became a journalist. There were also several other 'entiomorphic' Alices of varying heights who emerged from 'mirrors' in the set to enable her to change size. The narrator (Lewis Carroll) was portrayed by Nigel Rees (New College), now the celebrated writer and broadcaster.

The nervous twitching White Rabbit obsessed with time was played by the late Nick Loukes (ChCh), who then acted professionally for a short period before dying tragically young only a few years later. The brow-beaten King of Hearts was portrayed by Humphrey Hodgson (ChCh) and the Queen by the formidable Susan Solomon (Somerville), now a Professor of Hepatology and a distinguished barrister respectively.

Grinning broadly and imperiously as the Cheshire Cat, Alan Moses (Univ) prefigured his later elevation to become a High Court Judge. John Slater (Univ) as Bill the Lizard had to scale a long ladder each night up onto the thatched roof of the barn, and also had the daunting responsibility of controlling the piglets.

As the Mock-Turtle Dick Durden Smith(Merton), now a well-known professional actor, sang the mournful melody 'Beautiful Soup' with Bob Scott (Merton) as the Gryphon. Also playing the Old

The Mad Hatter's Tea Party, from the 1965 production of *Alice in Wonderland*

Man, Scott was President of OUDS, and later became Administrator of Manchester's Theatre 69 with Tom Courtenay, while the Young Man was David Wood (Worcester), now the celebrated children's playwright and director.

The hauntingly beautiful music was composed and conducted by Paul Drayton (Brasenose). Illuminated against the gathering dusk, the elegant setting by Colin Pocock (who later became a TV designer) was made up of interlinking white lattice 'mirror' frames of various heights to reveal the different size Alices. Beautiful gold and silver publicity posters, produced by Ernie Eban (Univ), were grabbed from notice boards to decorate college rooms as soon as they were put up.

My own involvement was as the March Hare in the tea party, with my fellow House man and good friend Rupert Jones-Parry as the Mad Hatter, and Dany Khosrovani (St Hilda's) as the Dormouse. At the end of the scene the long tea table covered in a huge cloth rose up and sped off stage courtesy of some energetic bodies underneath, as we threw plates, cups and saucers after it! I had an impressive head mask with long ears which further increased my substantial height of 6ft 4ins. One evening it fell off during the chase off-stage after the table. At the end of the show I went back onto the set to look for it, only to find a small child sitting clutching it in the front row, very unwilling to let go, and indeed to leave the dreamlike set. The production certainly seemed to capture the magic of Wonderland!

Ian Wyatt (1964)

The Head Porter was called Mister Hawker (one always called him 'Mister'). He was a man with a genial smile, an avuncular manner, and a reassuring Oxfordshire brogue. But an absolute stickler for the rules. If an undergraduate was not back in college when the gates shut at 12.20 am, a meeting with the Senior or Junior Censor next morning was inevitable. Mister Hawker always wore a bowler hat, a suit, a pullover and a tie sported over his pullover.

At least one junior porter was on patrol throughout the night. The most memorable was 'Mitch', who was small, irascible and ancient. My rooms (a relatively palatial sitting room with a pretty large separate bedroom on Peck 9) were on the ground floor almost in the middle of the college, and I went to bed late. Mitch would drop in most nights he was on duty. He would spend an hour or more demolishing my bottle of college port, comparing the present unfavourably with the past. He would bemoan the fact that most of the undergraduates at Christ Church were now untitled, poor and only had mediocre port. Not a tactful guest.

My scout was so scandalised by the state of my shirts that he suggested that his wife wash and iron them for me. We agreed a mutually acceptable price of 6d, now 2.5p. I also remember that he used to put up somewhat idiosyncratically expressed and spelt messages at the entrance to the staircase. Once, we were informed that 'Mice have come into residents' and that we should accordingly not leave 'crumms lying about'.

When my son Max came up thirty-five years after me, the position was very different. The college was open twenty-four hours a day. His staircase shared a woman cleaner with a number of other staircases. He hardly ever saw her, as, like his father, he was not an early riser.

David Neuberger (1966)

I have no doubt that the college environs had been afforded special attention ahead of this event. In Tom Quad, as elsewhere, not a single blade of grass would have gone untrimmed in anticipation of Her Majesty's visit and the college looked its very best as a result, yet somewhat churlishly her arrival at Tom Gate was heralded by a drenching cloud-burst.

Members of the House, who had collectively been exhorted to assemble and 'mill about' in full academic garb (as per normal?!), sensibly enough sought shelter for themselves in the staircases and under archways all through the college.

Mercifully the weather conditions improved, allowing them to re-emerge just as Her Majesty set out to cross Tom Quad, enquiring as she did so of one undergraduate: 'And how long have you been here?' Her expectation was to be advised that he was 'in his first year' or that he 'came up in '67', but in the event nerves almost certainly prompted the apocryphal response – 'since the rain stopped, Ma'am'.

Peter Rooley (1966)

For a certain generation of us – the 1950s to the 1980s? – the scholarship and interview system are an indelible part of the whole Oxford experience. This chapter and method of selection have probably gone forever. The essence of the exercise was speed: the scholarship exams, sat at schools all over the country in the last week of November, the wait to be called for interview, the interviews themselves in the second or third week of December, and then the agonising suspense, all the more acute because the whole system essentially had to be wrapped up by Christmas.

We arrived in freezing temperatures at lunchtime, the ice thick on Mercury and the sluggish fish hardly visible below. Found my room in Blue Boar, and the luxury of central heating. Then off to scour the notice boards which, we'd had drummed into us, would be the sole means of communication for the whole interview period in Oxford. Identified the English list. Interviews in Dr J.I.M. Stewart's rooms, Meadow Building, at the following times. Counted the names. Thirty of us for the ten available places. Located my name. Last on this evening at 8.45 pm. The lateness of the hour and size of the list seemed to bring home dramatically the pressure and immediacy of the whole process. No time to waste, it seemed to say. This is for real.

I can't think about the questions, let alone the food, only about the looming 8.45 appointment. Dinner finishes at 8.00 pm, and the predicament of what to do now. I'd already established where Meadow Building was, and Dr Stewart's rooms on the ground floor, half way along. Decide 8.15 is a safe time to turn up, and a couple of turns round Tom Quad in the icy night air help to while away the time, if not to calm the nerves. When I arrive, I can hear voices inside. What do I do now? Knock? Announce my presence? Wait? Timidity wins, and I wait, walking up and down the flags in front of the towering Victorian building. 8.25. 8.30. 8.35. Exquisite dilemma. Should I have knocked? Are they waiting for me? Have I fallen at the first fence? Rising feelings of panic, when suddenly the door opens, and out comes a young candidate in spats, closely followed by a cheerful, bespectacled man, calling out 'Mr Shaw?' Thank heavens I didn't knock. A sideways glance at the spats – I'm in school uniform, the only relatively smart clothes I possessed at that time – and we're in.

In to a dark, book-lined study, shelves from floor to ceiling, a couple of small lamps giving what little illumination there was. A coal fire blazing away gives the room a probably misleadingly cosy atmosphere. The bespectacled man introduces himself as Richard Hamer. Anglo-Saxon, Medieval and something else I missed. Behind the large desk is a small elderly man in a thick three-piece suit and half-moon glasses. He's introduced as Dr Stewart, Literature. There's a third shadowy figure somewhere at the back of the room, much younger than the other two, but also wearing glasses. This is Mr Butler, I'm told, also Literature. 'But much more up to date than me!' declares Dr Stewart. They all laugh, but deciding it might be pretentious to join in, I manage a cough instead. They gesture me to a chair by the fire.

Left: J.I.M. Stewart; right: David Luke. From the Common Room album

This isn't at all what I imagined. I wasn't expecting three interviewers, I didn't think it would be at night, I thought I'd be face to face with my interrogators at least ... Oh for heaven's sake, be honest and admit you hadn't got a clue what to expect. The voyage into the unknown starts here, chum.

'Right! Let's have a little look at your papers, shall we?' I'm horrified to see my childish loopy handwriting all over his desk. 'Let's start with the Authors Paper, shall we? Questions on Chaucer – you enjoyed that one didn't you, Mr Hamer?' No pause to determine whether Mr Hamer had indeed enjoyed it or been bored rigid. ...'Two essays on Hardy. Yes, you obviously like the chap, don't you?' Then I remember that Stewart's written a book on Hardy and had put him in first to bat in *Eight Modern Authors*, his volume of the *Oxford History of English Literature*. Perhaps a double dose wasn't such a *faux pas*? I manage a nervous glance upwards and, seeing him grinning at me over his half-moon glasses, start to relax.

'The sheer awkwardness of much of Hardy's prosody is the guarantee of its sincerity ... 'What on earth does that mean' Dr Stewart enquires archly. I think I can explain it, and explain away the pomposity of the style. He seems satisfied. But then he darts into the script again. 'The flatness of the morally good characters is only matched by their banality'. No point in defending the indefensible, and I run up the white flag immediately. I'm sorry, I confess, but I haven't a clue what I meant by that. Well, that makes two of us, ripostes the Great Man. 'Three of us' from the young man in the shadows. 'Mr Hamer?' 'Sorry, not my period', and everyone's laughing. This is all turning out a lot easier than I imagined.

...

Then a knock at the Upper Sixth form room door. Shaw to see the Headmaster immediately. Blimey – what have I done now? Downstairs in some trepidation. Knock at Canon Whitfield's door, and wait for the traffic lights to signal 'Come In'. As frightening as ever. 'Your mother has just telephoned, Shaw. Letter from Oxford arrived second post.' Everything's swimming. Rush to find my English teacher. 1.55 pm, five minutes of lunchtime left. Somehow blurt out the news. 'You're a very lucky boy!' he says. For a split second, I misunderstand him, imagining he was implying some fluke or serendipity. But the warmth of his handshake shows me I've got it wrong. He means I'm the luckiest person alive to have this prize in front of me.

I knew then that he was right, and thirty-five years later, I know it more assuredly than ever.

Paul Shaw (1969)

In my final year (1974) I stayed in a basement room in college premises across the road in St Aldate's. I was plagued by slugs and mice, and once managed to catch a live mouse. Rather than killing it, I somehow managed to get it into a desert boot with the plan of releasing it in Christ Church Meadow. I was proceeding through Tom Quad with said live mouse in desert boot when I met my tutor, David Luke, who seemed very taken with the idea of mice. After a rather gruesome description of his methods of mouse disposal in his cottage in the Scottish Borders (quite worthy of Roald Dahl, to whose work David first introduced me – David's tutorials were wonderfully irrelevant!), he then began the first of many excursuses on the role of mice in German literature. Tutorial after tutorial I would arrive to hear some new take on this ever-expanding area of David's new research interest.

Bill Gray (1971)

Mr Dean, my Lords, ladies, and gentlemen – When we came up to Christ Church in the late 1970s, the dons may have included some of the most advanced thinkers of the day, but I'm sure you'll agree that the undergraduate culture, by and large, was still in a state of heroic denial about most of the previous century of British social history. My first awed impression of life at Christ Church, during freshers' week, was of a great, dark place where in the evenings there were always lots of fine, strapping, well-bred young men around in immaculate evening dress, companionably and fraternally vomiting over each other; and every upstairs window in Peckwater always seemed to have a sofa flying out of it just as I was walking past. There were some concessions to the present, it's true: as well as its beagles (may God preserve them), the college boasted its very own angry, hard-core, disaffected punk rock band, whose very name proclaimed a kind of alienated street credibility which no mere Sex Pistol could hope to match – I refer, of course, to Tom and the Quads. But, on the whole, the ambience of the place spoke as much of the 1870s as it did of the 1970s, with a strong dash of the medieval thrown in. I'm sure I'm not the only person here who had the odd experience of going with his children not long ago to see the first Harry Potter film – the tale of a boy's arrival at a vast, bizarre, archaic academy, part boarding school and part castle – and recognising the Hall staircase at several key moments. The choice of location didn't surprise me; what surprised me was how accurate and unsensational the film was about it, offering an almost documentary-style depiction of the experience of coming to Christ Church in the seventies.

By 1981, like Hogwarts, Christ Church too had begun to admit clever nice-looking girls from the Dragon School, and from elsewhere too. Those of us who were here in Michaelmas 1980 had the privilege of observing at close quarters a little anthropological miracle. Overnight, the sofas stopped falling, and the puking at least became more discreet. Furthermore, the shower below Tom 3, where the rugby team had since time immemorial unmuddied themselves in unembarrassed bachelor splendour, would never be the same again – for one of the first female students admitted to read English, who was very keen on drama, decided that one of the long deep baths in cubicles right next to that shower would be the perfect place to rehearse the role of Cleopatra. And she rehearsed it pretty thoroughly at that. I lived on that staircase, and I was studying Shakespeare at the time, and I'll tell you one salient thing about *Antony and Cleopatra*: it isn't a one-woman show. The sound effects alone were enough to bring a blush to the cheeks of the toughest quarterback. But thus was Christ Church belatedly made safe for Beauty, Culture, and Modernity.

Members of other colleges – and I name no names – sometimes complain that Christ Church is too big, but of course that's the whole point. The House, like its founder, is in all things reassuringly massive. An enormous compound of institutional momentum and institutional inertia, part liner and part iceberg, it continues to surge unstoppably onwards from the Renaissance towards the future. It is far too grand and complicated for even as great a reform as the admission of women to make more than the most superficial impression on its character or to be more than the most minor redefinition of its great purposes, far too long-lived and widely connected for our time here to have been more than a tiny fraction of its mighty presence in the wider world. Let us just give thanks that it is still here, and that tonight we are here too, and for one good reason. However thoroughly our personal memories of undergraduate life may partake of the ridiculous, this is the one human institution I've ever known that definitely partakes of the sublime. Christ Church is in the end the place where, if nowhere else, all our lives have been touched by magnificence. If you will rise: my Lords, ladies and gentlemen I give you – The House.

Michael Dobson (1979)

Hogwart's School of Witchcraft and Wizardry: Christ Church transfigured!

For a young research student wishing to explore Christ Church's great seventeenth-century library of string music, and who also wished to continue performing seriously, the House was the logical choice. I had been out of the country for several years and so my knowledge of the actual 'student experience' for musicians was scant at best. Yet like so many applicants before me, Christ Church was associated with blue riband, pioneering performances and recordings under Simon Preston, Francis Grier and Stephen Darlington. Reputation, pure instinct and the wonderfully reassuring graduates' tutor, Peter Parsons, was more than enough.

Christ Church breeds a kind of quiet confidence in its musicians as an establishment answerable largely to itself. I suppose, in purely practical terms, a large college (in Oxford musical terms, a choral foundation) can claim to offer more stimulation and activity for its members. Even for someone who was told that he wouldn't be asked to deputise in the choir 'short of the Black Death' (Darlington to me, 1985), the Christ Church sound – open-throated and rich – resonated vicariously for all college musicians in one way or another. I won't say I practised the trumpet better but I certainly knew I had something to match up to. During that time, performing with the choir for the occasional broadcast, CD, service or concert provided some welcome professional experience, alongside a degree where the performance of music was regarded a necessity only *in extremis*.

Christ Church musicians had long discovered that the most congenial environment for their sober extra-curricular deliberations was the Old Tom hostelry across St Aldate's. Such evenings often witnessed a landlord so overcome with a fascination for the finer points of *musica ficta* in late fifteenth-century polyphony that he was prepared to lock the door and draw the curtains for fear of unwelcome plagiarisers from New College or Magdalen. In truth, these post-prandial ales were merely overtures for a procession to one's rooms where the merry throng would conduct Karajan's Bruckner symphonies, to the very occasional accompaniment of a fire extinguisher.

A hidden corner of the Library, known as Hyp.

It seems like yesterday that our unerringly helpful librarian, John Wing, would trustingly hand me the key to the little room just beyond the Upper Library and I would pore over a Gibbons manuscript. After that, one would invariably be involved in a rehearsal. Again, the large college – which happens to have a cathedral as its chapel – has many advantages, not least that outrageous and youthfully ambitious ideas generated in Hall can be practically undertaken without the prospect of terminal embarrassment: trumpet and organ concerts with the organ scholar, Iain Simcock, of Bach's Flute Suite (!), a 'Jauchzet Gott' with Susan Gritton under Laurence Cummings and various challenging Stefan Asbury events. Many Oxford concerts are legendarily ad hoc ('a celebration of amateurism', as someone famously wrote), but student collaborations within Christ Church occasionally yielded a quality of event which merited critical scrutiny among the best, no doubt encouraged by Stephen Darlington's view that there should be a limit to the ricochet of split notes heard in college.

We happened to have a pretty decent brass quintet – and we played a few concerts in the cathedral – but it is always the nightmare one remembers. As the first trumpet, it was coming in early during a Gabrieli canzone: similar to disembarking a button-lift on the slopes, once you've gone you've gone. I'll never forget that disoriented cornetto filigree, not badly executed but worthlessly floundering alongside the static and austere trombone and tuba fifths. They were the only ones surviving intact as the others had been dragged down with me ... and then the disbelieving silhouette of Dr Darlington under the organ. Telling him it was just the encore didn't help. I've taken better care to count my rests ever since.

Jonathan Freeman-Attwood (1985)

I have so many wonderful memories of Christ Church, some of which reached my grandfather, while others did not. Staying up all night writing essays in Blue Boar, then running to tutorials in my slippers as the clock chimed ten. Dressing for bad taste parties where we danced on Peck window sills, whether anyone came or not. Dark nights in the Undercroft, drinking Newcastle Brown. (Why? I haven't touched the stuff since.) Playing left wing for the Christ Church women's football team and scoring the equaliser in the Cuppers final. Reading out my History essays to W.E.S. Thomas and being told 'Bravo!'. The illicit thrill of waking up on Sunday mornings to see who'd sabotaged Mercury this time – I particularly remember him resplendent in a tartan tie.

And, even now, when I imagine peace, I think of quiet mornings in the Library, when only pages stirred. Christ Church gave me many firsts; it was where I first learned to do my own washing; where I first fell in love – *and* had my heart broken – and where I smoked my first (and last) cigar! And of course, it was where I first learned to live without seeing my grandfather every day. And yet, my strongest Christ Church memory is of him. His face a mixture of horror and pride as he lugged to my room a trolley full of my unnecessarily copious belongings at the start of each term. The joy, each week, of his letters in my pigeon hole. (I still have them all.) And the frantic snapping of his camera in front of every Christ Church landmark imaginable on the day of graduation where he wore a smile that split his face.

Christ Church gives much to its students. Throughout my life, I have felt the confidence it gave me to have made it there and to have achieved there, behind everything I have done since. But not everyone who loves Christ Church is a former student and I thought it was worth remembering the parents and grandparents for whom it has also been a source of much happiness and pride. I was working as a magazine editor in New York when my grandfather wrote to me for the last time. It was a tired but contented letter from someone who knew he had lived a good life which was now reaching its end. In it he wrote something which he had never verbalised but which I had always known: 'You have given me so much joy'.

I know that when he wrote those words, he would have been thinking mainly of Christ Church. It was his unlikely dream for me and I will always be grateful that it did not let him down.

Liz Nice (1989)

THE CENSORS

A View from the Censors' Office

Is there more to the Censors than their curious title? A junior member might pass through the House without much contact with the Senior Censor (or Censor *Moralis Philosophiae* as we ought to describe him), but they will have a dull time if they do not visit the Junior Censor (or Censor *Naturalis Philosophiae* as we ought to describe her) once or twice. So far as the dons are concerned – perhaps a point of view more theoretical than real – no 'party' (precisely defined to the academic mind as any gathering, spontaneous or wilful, of eight or more) takes place within the curtilage without the Junior Censor's specific permission. Such prior consent is obtained, during particular hours – on Fridays there can be a queue – from the poky little office at the top of Tom 8 (no longer the palatial splendour of Peck 9, long since converted into the Development Office) where the young face a short grilling about timings and intentions, or the probable load-bearing capacity of this or that college room.

Those who make poor use of their time at the House risk meeting the Junior Censor, whose job it is to ensure appropriate behaviour generally among junior members, a good deal. (Such work is done by 'deans' in other colleges, so the need for a distinct title in Christ Church is clear.) This can have its entertaining moments for the mid-career academic at the top of the stairs. What is the right thing to do with someone who denies any knowledge of the cigar burns in their bedroom carpet? Could it really have been the

Dean Cyril Jackson and Censor James Webber. Drawn, etched and published by Robert Dighton, 1807

scout? Can folding bicycles be kept in junior members' rooms, or must they take up space in the bike-sheds? What about a folding bicycle with an engine? How should one deal with the graduate who claims to have kicked a porter's car 'on principle' – the principle proving, upon examination, to be 'environmentalism'? It was Peter Oppenheimer, apparently, who introduced the sturdy approach to duckings in Mercury of fining both thrower *and throwee* – based, no doubt, on the insight that it will have been six of one and half a dozen of the other. The principle remains to be tested before a court of human rights, when perhaps the moot point of what is to be done if someone simply jumps might conveniently also be considered – fined twice, or not at all?

There is guidance on the proper approach to matters disciplinary available from ex-censors, and old members appear surprisingly willing to share what was done to them in the past. A peer of the realm told me at High Table recently of the occasion when he had badly hurt his leg crashing his cherished car in the late 50s – a vehicle which he had no permission from the censors to be keeping in Oxford at all. Teddy Burn was the Censor of the day, who, after ruminating for a while as to an appropriate punishment, resolved only that, whilst the leg healed, its owner could park in Tom Quad. Perhaps that story should set the standard. Whatever mischief the young throw at you may best be met with disarming kindness. Of course there are those, from time to time, who require firmer handling, but our maturing young seem often to learn more from general example than from particular censure.

Junior Censors mature into Senior Censors, who act as a senior tutor might in another college, chairing meetings of the tutors, considering the plight of undergraduates struggling with their academic work, drafting responses to the latest government or University initiative on the admissions process, or institutional governance, or academic strategy – or car parking. But there is perhaps rather more to the job in Christ Church than that suggests. The Dean has a cathedral to run as well as a college, and it seems part of the Censors' role not only to assist generally with the latter but also to ensure smooth communication with the former.

It is perhaps here that any remaining mystery of the Censorship lies: in the institutional uncertainty whether to forget or cherish an ancient feud. It is recalled discreetly, at an annual dinner, when the censors invite the Students to reminisce upon ancient battles – won and lost – between their predecessors and the canons. Christ Church had Canons and Censors from the start, the title of Censor alluding to the magistrates in ancient Rome, responsible for the census of the citizens and the supervision of public morals. (At least Dr Belinda Jack and I are not still expected to carry out a census.) But the censors' lot, along with that of the Students in general, was a sorry one for more than 300 years. They were excluded from the Governing Body (unlike the Fellows of other colleges), which in Christ Church consisted of the Dean and canons alone. The censors' role in the educational work of the House was always clear. They lectured to the bachelors, moderated at disputations, questioned the scholars; and, with the Dean and the lecturer in Rhetoric, heard themes in Hall. But their powers remained necessarily limited by their exclusion from the Governing Body.

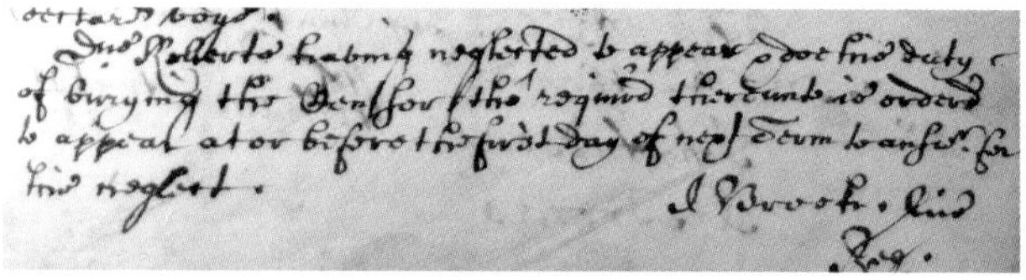

Left:
An extract from the Chapter Books, dated Christmas 1711, recording the admonition of Thomas Roberts (mt. 1707) for failing to 'bury the Censor'

Reform was not rushed, but after the 300 years had passed the exclusion of the Students from institutional governance was finally addressed, with the Censors at the heart of the unavoidable power struggle. It was a Censor, Thomas Prout, who summoned a meeting of the Senior Students of the Old Foundation, on Saturday 11 February 1865, to consider their plight. Not only were they excluded from the Governing Body, they had not until recently even been allowed to dine at High Table, which was reserved for noblemen. Meanwhile, the Canons received a stipend of, on average, £1,500 per year, whilst the Regius Professor of Greek still received the £40 provided by its original endowment. As the present occupant of that chair – or even his immediate predecessor – might say: something had to give.

Dodgson was present amongst the eighteen who resolved that day upon 'the admission of the Students into the Corporation of The House, with a due share of the administration of the revenues and in the governance of the same, and also the possession of such other rights and privileges as commonly attach to the Fellows of other Colleges'. It took two more years to be achieved, but it was done. The Christ Church Oxford Act of 1867 created the collaborative foundation we now know, where Dean, canons and Students unite in a Governing Body on all matters save those exclusively diocesan in character.

The annual Censors' Dinner survives ('one of the more searching tests of after-dinner oratory in Oxford', according to Bill and Mason, *Christ Church and Reform 1850 to 1867*); and appears really to have had its origins in an ancient practice known as 'burying the Censor'. As the censors neared the end of their year of office, the fiction that they then 'died' was commemorated with an appropriate ceremonial 'burial'. The Subdean appointed four bachelor students to dispute in Hall during the dying days of Michaelmas Term. By the eighteenth-century, the exercise had become an occasion for the delivery of speeches of compliment to the censors, to which the Senior Censor responded with a Latin oration commenting on the events of his year of office. Failure by the bachelors to 'bury the Censor' satisfactorily incurred the wrath of the Chapter. In 1790 J.F. Edgar was rusticated for a year because of the 'indecent and improper manner in which he performed the exercise'. But the Censor had to mind his step too. In 1768 Francis Atterbury (not to be confused with the earlier person of the same name, the only Dean of Christ Church – thus far – to be convicted of high treason) appeared to make critical remarks about the Visitor, and only escaped censure from the Chapter by muttering his delivery – and by burning his speech immediately afterwards.

Accordingly, the Censors' Dinner has its earliest origins in an occasion celebrated equally by Dean, Canons and Students alike, and it remains so today. This year, the occasion fell pleasingly on Saturday 11 February, and the company was invigorated by the most welcome presence of Dr Rowan Williams – now an Honorary Student of course, but a former canon and Lady Margaret Professor of Divinity. The censors perhaps have a wider role therefore than simply superintending the conduct of junior members: they may also assist in tying the strands of our complex House together. The still grand Senior Censor's office (situated directly beneath the Junior Censor's poky one, and immediately above the war memorials at the entrance to the cathedral) remains at the heart of Christ Church. From there, the Senior Censor can see Tom Tower and its clock as he writes; and, should he walk to the window, survey all that is taking place in Tom Quad below. Incomparably the best view in Oxford.

Edwin Simpson, Censor *Moralis Philosophiae*

Twentieth-Century Architecture

Blue Boar Quad. Designed by Powell & Moya, and opened by the Queen in 1968

With buildings ranging from the twelfth to the twentieth centuries, Christ Church can be regarded as a built museum of the history of architecture. Both ecclesiastical and vernacular styles sit side by side, but what dominates is that more specialised 'collegiate' type, staircases providing accommodation for students and senior members alike, plus all the necessary supporting accommodation: the Library, the treasury, lecture theatres, scouts' pantries and so on. Yet despite this rich mix there is a sense of worn homogeneity about the feel of the place unless, of course, you find your way to Christ Church's backyard where you are gradually introduced to Blue Boar Quad (1968), often regarded as architecturally distinct from the rest of the place, to put it at its most polite.

But that sense of architectural harmony elsewhere in Christ Church is in part deceptive. The cathedral, cloisters and former refectory of the priory (later Old Library) date from the twelfth to the sixteenth centuries, and Tom Quad was built over a period spanning two centuries; Killcanon is seventeenth, Peckwater eighteenth (earlier buildings were completely demolished to make way for it) and Meadow Buildings were completed in 1863. Built across the centuries, it is clear that careful consideration went into each new addition, although both Peck and Meadows do seem to give off what could be construed as a certain arrogant competitiveness.

Blue Boar Quad and the Picture Gallery (1968) are, arguably, Christ Church buildings at their most discreet and subtle. The architects for both were Powell and Moya, and in a fascinating contemporary article by Powell, 'New Grafted on the Old', he draws our attention to the constraints imposed by both sites, and to the effects of these restrictions on the design processes which produced the two buildings:

> *We might feel that a love affair with such pervading beauty (the University, one of the greatest and most consistent monuments to Medieval and Renaissance architecture) must*

inhibit today's architect when he is called upon to interfere with something so fragile and vulnerable … Yet this may not be so. Sympathy with the scale and character of a beautiful and historic scene must act as an inspiration, yet it properly narrows the range of the architect's decisions. In the end surroundings and client's needs seem to act upon one another to tell him what the inevitable design must be.

The long narrow site, the old wall which forms the northern curtilage of Christ Church, the need to respect the scale of Tom Quad, on which the upper stories of Blue Boar look out, the requirement for materials that are sympathetic to the colours and textures in neighbouring buildings, the type and variety of accommodation specified in the brief: all these have dictated a building which is not grandiose and imposing but subtle, practical and modest. It is also wonderfully sculptural and rhythmical, aspects of the building that are particularly influential in the decision of the Secretary of State for Culture, Media and Sport to list Blue Boar as a Grade II* building. Traditions of use have also been attended to: there are four 'staircases', and undergraduates and senior members live and work alongside one another: the young inspired perhaps by tutors' industry, the tutors reminded of the energy and creative experimentation of youth. Rooms have two doors, an inner and an outer, adding privacy and acoustic insulation, but also allowing for the tradition of 'sporting one's oak'. The only dramatic departure from tradition are the large windows, one of the inspiring powers which modern engineering techniques allow. Likewise the design of the Picture Gallery, surely one of the most modest, yet dynamic modern buildings in Oxford, is dictated largely by the daunting constraints of its site. You enter via Canterbury Quad and descend into a semi-basement, yet one which is brightly lit and airy thanks to the glazed corridor which looks out onto an inner courtyard so typical of the Oxbridge college as a type. From here you can turn into the differently sized spaces of the gallery, some of which allow one to look at larger canvases from a distance, while others invite one closer to examine smaller works. It is all carefully thought through and one's engagement with the artworks is, arguably, more subtly controlled than at the Ashmolean, for example, where the visitor's engagement with the viewing process is unmodulated.

Top:
Liddell Building. Designed by Maguire & Co., and opened in 1991 as a shared residence with Corpus Christi College
Bottom:
St Aldate's Quad, designed by the Architects Design Partnership in 1987

Christ Church's buildings by Powell and Moya are its most distinguished twentieth-century additions. Later came St Aldate's Quad (Architects Design Partnership, 1987) mostly for graduate students, less dramatic perhaps but functional and discreet: the historic façade onto St Aldate's was, in the end, saved. The Liddell Building (Maguire and Co., 1991), on the edge of the Sports Ground on the Iffley Road, was a joint project with Corpus Christi, and houses mostly finalists. Unlike the sites which Powell and Moya had to work in, here the space was open and the resulting buildings are likewise plainer and more regular.

What Christ Church's twentieth-century buildings cannot yet offer is the extra dimension of history, that erosion of centuries of rain and sun, and of generations of students who have pushed past and rubbed against them. But that will come.

Belinda Jack

Christ Church 1957–2005

Half a century ago the House was another country. They did things differently then. How differently was particularly striking for a newcomer from Cromwellian Cambridge who shared his teaching with Magdalen College. My college at Cambridge had been King's, which its detractors called the nearest thing Cambridge had to Oxford. The description was only partly valid. It certainly had a strong literary-aesthetic bias. Its Fellows in my time there included E.M. Forster and George Rylands. I only just failed to coincide with Maynard Keynes. It boasted its stunning choir. In fact the college was more Bloomsbury than Cromwell, though it is worth remembering how much of Bloomsbury was descended from Victorian Evangelicals. King's was militantly informal. Lunch, though not dinner, was taken communally. Everyone, from the Senior Tutor to the rawest freshman, was on first-name terms. In the absence of any other experience I came to assume that this was the academic norm. When I moved to Christ Church I was discomfited by being addressed as 'sir', as if I were a prep-school beak. This no longer happens, but I still find it a great barrier, when teaching on the Continent, that beardless youths and barely post-pubertal maidens expect to be addressed as 'Sie', 'vous' or 'Lei'. What was most impressive about King's was its intellectual competitiveness. The greatest compliment one undergraduate could bestow on another was that he was 'brilliant'.

The House was not quite like that, Magdalen a little closer to it. The House, like Oxford in general, was worldly. All those prime ministers. All those viceroys. It looked to London and to country houses, not the Fens. It kept beagles. It had membership of the Frilford Heath golf club. It contained that most worldly of institutions, a cathedral. It had something of a club about it. After my first night at High Table I was asked whether I played bridge. I had the sense to say no. It was a conscientious teaching college, but rather lax about whom it admitted. Pre-UCCA the procedures were distinctly untransparent, at least in the subjects I was concerned with. Indeed the entire constitution of the place was obscure, for all the statutes and bye-laws, since many of the decisions were made by a senate of ex-Censors. There was no compulsion, indeed little incentive to publish. The best undergraduates were outstanding, the average was not bad, but the tail was long. That was one of the differences with Magdalen, where for the first five years I did half my teaching. There were other differences which, counter-intuitively, put the House in quite a good light. Magdalen was rather hierarchical. One processed, and sat at High Table, in strict order of seniority. At the House one shambled in any old how, in accordance with the internal democracy of the upper classes. Once you were in, you were in. I liked that. There was a good side to the clubbiness, too. Christ Church dons were very hospitable to a newly arrived, initially unmarried colleague. I was grateful for that.

Dave Coles, sporting the Cardinal's regalia, with Archimedes. By Jim Godfrey

It would be wrong to suggest that the House, even then, was an intellectual desert – certainly not in the sciences. Its reputation was also high in law, classics and philosophy. It is rather that the achievement was patchy. Pushing back the frontiers of knowledge was *an* objective, not *the* objective of the institution. The stages by which reform came, incremental but cumulatively decisive, are not easy to remember. As the pre-war generation of dons retired, they were replaced by more meritocratically oriented and internationally minded successors. The beagles were privatised some time in the 1970s. Admissions became more professional, and it is now twenty-five years since the existence of the second sex was formally embraced. In 1984 at the freshers' dinner in my last year as a Tutor a girl sitting next to me asked me whether it was true that the House 'had once been for boys only'. I was appalled by her ignorance of social history, gratified that the battlements so recently stormed had so thoroughly crumbled into oblivion.

Peter Pulzer

Living in Christ Church

What struck me most about living in Christ Church as a canon for six years was how like living in a small village it felt. Those of us who lived there throughout the year naturally saw that bit more of staff, especially those who also lived on or around the premises; we experienced the place twenty-four hours a day and seven days a week; we were there over Christmas. Friendships formed over the routine business of sharing the territory.

Our first child was born just over a year after we moved to Christ Church and lived for her first four and a half years in Priory House; so quite a lot of our perception of Christ Church was connected with her growing up. Despite the fact that the passages from Tom Quad to Priory House are not exactly designed for prams or pushchairs, it was a good environment for a small child because – the village thing again – everyone she was likely to meet around the House was likely to know her, from the maintenance staff to the custodians and vergers. And sometimes this could mean some very unexpected and exotic treats. We were all specially fond of Dave Coles and his family; and my most vivid recollection is of an afternoon when, at the end of a walk with my daughter in the Meadows, Dave invited us into the barn to visit the barn owl chicks he was rearing. I remember scrambling up a shaky ladder, holding Rhiannon very tightly, to see the fierce-eyed little scraps being lovingly fed by Dave with chopped mice. Not what everyone associates with Christ Church, perhaps, but for us as a family a characteristic memory.

I mentioned Christmas; and I suppose all the members of the Chapter at that time will recall the distinctive pleasure of being locked in after the end of the morning service. Tom Gate was closed and we were 'thrown upon each others' company', as an earlier generation would have put it. There was always a very substantial party at the Archdeacon's Lodgings – Frank and Poppy Weston's hospitality was legendary. There were walks in a deserted Meadow. Sometimes one or two of the Chapter families shared Christmas dinner or at least tea.

I hadn't, to be honest, expected Christ Church to feel quite so homely. A year there as a graduate student in the early Seventies hadn't always felt comfortable or relaxed (despite my enthusiastic involvement in an extravagantly inventive production of a medieval play of the Last Judgement, staged – complete with Last Trumpet and a massive papier-mâché Hellmouth – in the then unoccupied Chapter House), and the prospect of returning felt a little uncertain at first. The welcome we had from Eric and

Rachel Heaton set the tone for the coming years, though; we were immediately treated like extended family and swept into a warm and busy round of shared life and labour. John Norsworthy, then Cathedral Registrar, living in Auden's Cottage, was a family friend already, and provided constant support, meals, drinks and company. Eric and John are probably the figures who stand out most for me from those years, and we still miss them grievously. Sometimes you need a father figure or two; and, professional relationships apart, both men were wonderfully equipped both to encourage and to deflate younger colleagues.

In appropriately scriptural phrase, the time would fail me to tell of other domestic recollections – the Herculaean and largely unsuccessful struggle to tame the Priory House garden, unkindly compared (and in print too) by a colleague (you know who you are) to the state of the writer's beard ... Or how one of our cats became an honorary member of the JCR at Corpus. But it is a pleasure to pay even a brief tribute to a place where we experienced some of the most uncomplicatedly happy years of our married life. It was a joy to be part of a Chapter all of whom we regarded as utterly trusted and loved friends, a joy to have the cathedral's worship and music on the doorstep day by day; but simply a joy to have the unique experience of living in this extraordinary village (with, yes, predictably, its Alice in Wonderland elements at times). We had the privilege of knowing the House as a home.

Rowan Williams

'Going Mixed'

WOMEN AT CHRIST CHURCH

The first women to matriculate from Christ Church, 1980:
BACK ROW (from left to right) Sally Sutton; Louise Chadwick; Jacqueline Butcher; Helen Brace; Penny Challoner (first woman JRF); Pamela Jones; Fiona Rice; Gaynor Williams; Henrietta Podd; Carolyn Morley; Judith Pallot (first woman official student); Susan Finlayson; Mary Mitchison; Josephine Taylor; Katherine Wall
FRONT ROW (from left to right) Isobel Walder; Michele Totah; Alice Lumsden; Tania Brisby; Rachel Smyth-Osbourne; Katherine Paul; Sarah Dodgson; Annabel Freyberg; Nadine Artesani

For the first four hundred and fifty-two years of its existence, the history of Christ Church was the history of men. From 1 October 1978, when a lone female research lecturer (junior research Fellow) became a member of the college, it was the history of women as well. The path to the momentous Governing Body decision of 9 March 1977, by a vote of thirty-one to six, 'that Studentships and Lectureships be open to competition without discrimination of sex' was less smooth than the balance of votes would suggest. And it was to be another twenty months before this decision was extended to the junior membership.

From the moment of the introduction of the Sex Discrimination Act in 1975, it had been obvious that, like other all-male colleges in Oxford, Christ Church would eventually have to 'go mixed', but Governing Body's preference was for this change to take place slowly. Fortunately for the women who came up in the early 1980s, but unfortunately for those who regretted the change, the gradualist option proved to be untenable; during an intense year of bargaining, and of deals struck and promises broken, Oxford in 1977 edged its way toward the logical, and only fair, outcome of its decision in 1920 to end its centuries-long discrimination against women taking degrees in the University, dragging Christ Church along with it. The process had begun with an experiment embarked upon in 1972 to allow five all-male colleges (Brasenose, Wadham, Hertford, Jesus and St Catharine's) together to admit one hundred women. In 1977, when the experiment came up for review by Congregation, the apparent consensus was that there should be an 'orderly progression' of colleges following suit. Another group of five to seven colleges would admit women in 1979 and this would be followed 'some years later', and not before 1983, by another similarly sized group. Christ Church was not among the colleges clamouring for change, preferring, instead, 'to exercise restraint' on the question of co-residence. But the actions of other

colleges were to frustrate the House's attempt to restrain itself. At the first meeting of Governing Body in Hilary Term, the Senior Censor had to inform members that seven colleges were already in the process of changing their Statutes to admit women at all levels, two were likely to embark on the process at the end of term, and another two were discussing changes. The decision of the 9 March Governing Body to open competition for senior posts to women was taken against the background of a disintegrating consensus in the wider community to move forward in an orderly way. Having already decided to admit women at the senior levels (Governing Body had already agreed to do this 'in principle' for research lecturers the previous year), the discussion in Governing Body now focused on how to manage change in such a way as to protect the college from being bounced into taking women junior members before it was ready. A recommendation from the Senior Censor to delete Statute 1.2, which confined membership of the House to men, and to rely on the by-laws to extend membership to women for different categories as need arose, did not win support. Instead, Governing Body opted to amend the statute to allow both men and women to become senior members of the House but to make any proposal to extend membership to further categories subject to a two-thirds majority vote. This, it was argued, would defend the college better from further outside interference than relying on the by-laws, whilst obviating the necessity of repeated applications to the Privy Council. It took one more meeting and further legal advice before Governing Body was ready to vote on the statute change, which it did at a specially summoned meeting on 25 May 1977.

From the May Governing Body on, the issue for Christ Church was how firmly it was going to adhere to its earlier decisions on an appropriate time-scale for extending junior membership of the college to women. The arguments marshalled for holding the line at 1983 have a hollow ring thirty years on. The concern for the impact of change on the women's colleges, even if not sincerely held by all who expressed it, had some justification, but more obviously contrived was the doubt that there were sufficient 'suitably qualified women' to fill the places that would be on offer (was the secondary education girls were receiving in the 1970s so much inferior to that of today?) or the fear that women would be 'spread too thinly' among the colleges (the historical record does not make clear whether it was the impact on women or men that was uppermost in people's minds in this objection).

As the academic year drew to a close, Christ Church was among seven men's colleges and four women's that had not yet voiced the intention of going mixed. Christ Church continued to 'hold firm' through the first half of the next academic year, Governing Body rejecting a proposal by one member in Michaelmas Term that it express its intention of admitting women undergraduates to Christ Church in 1980. However, by the end of Hilary Term the pressure for change sooner rather than later had built up among a substantial majority of tutors and enough for the Senior Censor to feel sufficiently confident to announce that the admission of women as undergraduates would be placed on Governing Body's agenda for Michaelmas Term of the next academic year. The outcome of the vote when it finally came in November was a foregone conclusion, although, bearing in mind the two-thirds majority needed, it was a comfortable, rather than landslide, victory. It is difficult to judge thirty years on whether Christ Church's foot-dragging was the product of a collective caution or was motivated by a less forgivable form of conservatism. Happily, the answer to this question is only of historical interest today and there are plenty of areas where, far from bringing up the rear, Christ Church is at the forefront of change for the better in education and learning. It may be that there are still people around who believe that the admission of women did not bring any benefits to the House, but what is certain is that the change has been to the benefit of the women, now numbering more than a thousand, who have been allowed, like the generations of men before them, to make Christ Church part of their lives.

Judith Pallot

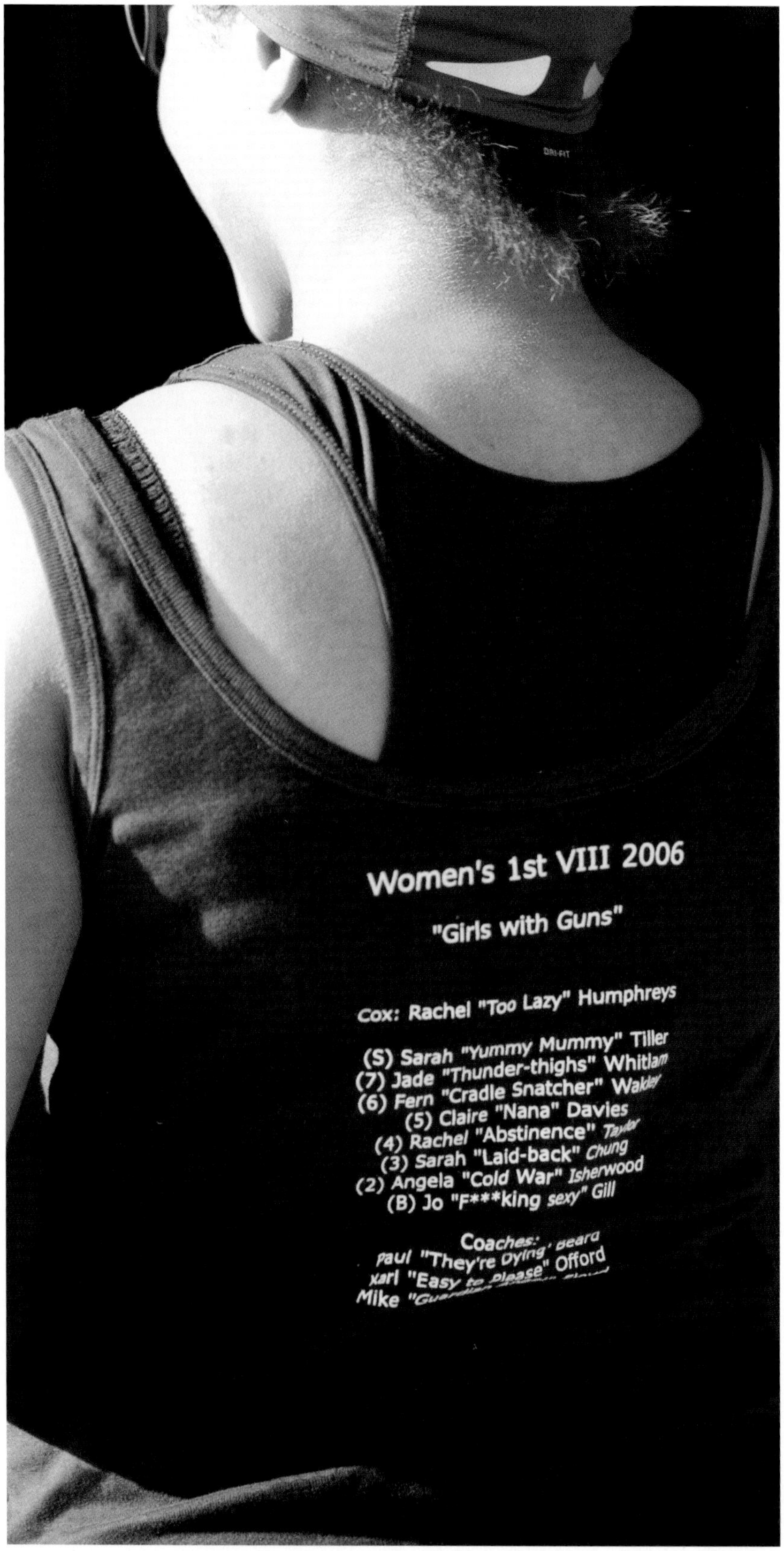

THE FUTURE

The past of the House is a foreign country where they do things differently, wreathed in mist from the Meadow. The future is simple for there we cannot be contradicted.

The glory of Christ Church will continue to stem naturally from its way of gathering together people of all sorts, at different stages of their lives who labour in all manner of disciplines. There will be a continuing shift away from a culture designed largely for men and for unmarried men at that. Port will wither on the vine. The mix will include more women senior members, a proportion to be increased by the appointment of the next dean. To this mixture will be added some of the many researchers who contribute to the lively work of Oxford and currently do not have a college home. Yet the most important factor will remain the mingling life: the light in the economist's eyes sparring with, or listening to, the physicist or the ancient historian. What is more, at a junior and senior level, all have to unite and have a shot at running the place, whether the task be a summer play or the finances.

The past is distinguished by characters and events woven into the majestic fabric. Dean Liddell was not amused when '... not very long after I took possession, a kettle charged with gunpowder was found fastened to the handle of my front door with a match inserted in the spout ...' Such happenings will continue according to the spirit of the age and give the place distinctiveness. It is hard to put a finger on what makes the House unique, but one clear feature is the cathedral, embedded in its history, geography and future. The cathedral's role may change more rapidly than the rest of Christ Church for it is well placed to diversify and flourish in an age of less established, more disparate religion, providing a sacred space, the neutrality and use of which is blessed by God and attractive to people of all religions and none. Visitors will pour in and ask questions such as 'Are you open on Christmas day?' or 'Where are the dungeons?', giving opportunities for welcome and interpretation. Its role as a centre of Christian prayer and worship and as the college chapel will not change, yet around that core the cathedral will take more risks in worship, art, music and in its relations with people of faiths other than the Christian. Its independence from some of the developments affecting the Church at large will continue to be a privilege to be enjoyed and put to imaginative use. The cathedral will be one of the ways in which the House is kept firmly open to the world.

The cathedral is part of the mysterious evolution of the place, with its endless surprises. Monastic origins from long before will continue to be apparent in our democratic form of government. In the University at large, the role of each self-governing college will ever be to cut the whole up into digestible pieces, to teach, support research and furnish a home. The mythology of student life, and of don life too, underestimates the degree to which sustained

Dean Christopher Lewis, in the Gallery Garden

academic work is tough to do and requires a sustaining house.

Oxford is at root a federation of happily autonomous bodies and it is unthinkable that the Botanic Gardens, the University Press, the Business School or the colleges will not keep robust identities – the colleges most of all because they are admired everywhere, except in their own country. Despite the perceptions of the outside world, they will change as they always have done, often rapidly; in this respect the architecture deceives although it, of course, has altered and grown too.

In the University and elsewhere, the corporate centrism of the early twenty-first century will pass, for people will see that to gather power and govern hierarchically (while, of course, proclaiming the beauties of subsidiarity) damages morale and inhibits lateral thinking. Just by the way, it is said that lateral thinking was invented at Christ Church when Edward de Bono had invited two girls to a dance and each had to know that she was the only one. In the rosy future such sexist illustrations will not be necessary because, since 1980, a girl could ask two boys. Back to the point: the University as a whole is too large a body to which to belong with stout loyalty; power will be shared with the places where affections lie. What is more, a decentralised organisation contains balances and checks, often seen as curbing progress, but better viewed as a means for scrutiny and ensuring proper pacing. Marconi was lost in a day.

The House will become ever more self-sufficient. Dependence on endowments will increase and the money, property and land will have to be managed with imaginative care. If the endowment, bolstered with help from old members and others, does not prove to be sufficient, then the size and shape of the whole will be reviewed. There is a significant calculation to be made simply by dividing the endowment by the number of people (and buildings) sustained by it. On that basis, the House is not especially prosperous. In the future the link between independence of thought and self-sufficiency will become increasingly apparent.

In spite of pressure to the contrary, numbers may therefore stay steady or decline. We can take a leaf out of Princeton's book: small, beautiful and 'excellent'. At its present size, Christ Church can know and look after members to a reasonable but not intrusive degree. With housing as it will be in Oxford, we will need to continue to accommodate all undergraduates who wish to live in. As to graduates, an increasing number will need rooms provided by the college.

Some of the new funding will be for specific research projects. In fact there will be more research done with the college's support, signalling diversification. In the past, places like the Lee Building in Schools Quad were intended to further special programmes, in its case first an anatomy demonstration hall of beauty and scientific usefulness and subsequently an effective chemistry laboratory. To see all such activity as moving out of the House would be a mistake. There will be a number of institutes allied to the college, some in the form of the new 'centres' which Oxford attracts, almost all of which cross traditional disciplinary boundaries. Another aspect of this variety will be the conferences which will become part of the life of the place rather than an intrusion.

The graduate body and that of Students is already international. They will become more so and will be joined in this development by the undergraduates. Although undergraduates will continue to study predominantly in their native countries, they will increasingly look at possibilities all over the world. As Oxford admits on merit and potential, the number from abroad is likely to rise. The change will be seen as an attempt by Oxford to generate income, but as the greatest number will come from Europe, there will be a high demand for bursaries. The House will make the adjustments necessary to flourish in an international market. Although firmly part of the University of Oxford, there will be opportunities for affiliations with universities abroad.

Once Oxford can charge reasonable fees and so be able to give much larger bursaries, dons will be paid more. The drain of brains abroad is much exaggerated, but this rise in pay will be a matter of simple justice. There will be broad appraisal of the work of everyone, consistent with academic freedom. The close attachment of senior members to the House will remain, as will an obligation to take part in its administration. Decision-making will be swifter, but not so fast as to swamp the intelligence of the participants. The Senior Common Room will remain physically a place in which to read the *New Yorker* in peace and generally one of the least formal and most liberal in Oxford. The fact that the walls will continue to be scattered with viceroys of India will not detract from appropriate conviviality; indeed it may be that the viceroys have an enabling role. An informal style strengthened by glorious surroundings will remain the distinguishing feature of the House.

The central aim will ever be that of educating members to take responsibility in life as public people, complemented by a firm commitment to research. If there is a disappointment at the time of writing, it is that undergraduates home in on a somewhat narrow range of roles and that, having had three or so years to sharpen their critical faculties, few have an obvious passion for changing the world. Of course such enthusiasm may come later; in the future, I hope it will come sooner. Yet what the House will send out, whatever the year and whatever the subject studied, is people who have aptitude honed in the process of assimilating an excess of material to meet a deadline, then drawing the most reasonable conclusions possible in the circumstances. That is a fair description of the educational method and also of the lot which falls to many of us every day. So Christ Church has a firm place in the future. It will remain as life-changing an experience for the next 500 years as it has for the last.

Christopher Lewis

List of Contributors

We would like to thank the following people whose written contributions are included in the Portrait of the House.

Mr Christopher Baker
Assistant Curator of the Picture Gallery, 1997–2003
Lieutenant-Colonel Thomas Baring
Self–employed Arts Consultant
Mr William Spencer Barrett (decd)
Lecturer 1938; Tutor in Classics at Keble College 1939–81;
Reader in Greek Literature at the OU, 1966–81
Dr Mishtooni Bose
Christopher Tower Student in Medieval Poetry in English
Mr Edward Burn
Emeritus Student, and Tutor in Law, 1955–90
Professor Christopher Butler
Student, and Tutor in English
Mr John Cartwright
Student, and Tutor in Law and Reader in the Laws of Contract
Mr George Cawkwell
Emeritus Fellow of University College, Oxford
Mr John Croft CBE
Head Home Office Research Unit, 1972–81 (retired); painter
Mrs Judith Curthoys
College and Cathedral Archivist
Dr Mark Curthoys
Archivist (1991), and Research Editor, *Oxford Dictionary of National Biography* since 1993
Dr Stephen Darlington
Student, Organist and Tutor in Music
Professor Roger Davies
Student, and Philip Wetton Professor of Astrophysics
Professor Michael Dobson
Professor of Shakespeare Studies, Birkbeck College,
University of London
The Very Revd John Drury
Honorary Student, Dean of Christ Church, 1991–2003
Mr Simon Freebairn-Smith
Principal Teacher of Classics (retired)
Professor Jonathan Freeman-Attwood
Vice-Principal, Royal Academy of Music

Mr Peter Gardiner-Hill
Founder & President, Penna Executive Coaching (retired)
Dr Mark Girouard
Honorary Student, architectural historian and
Slade Professor of Fine Art, 1975–1976
Mr Jim Godfrey
Canons' Verger
Mr Howard Goodall
Composer and broadcaster
Dr Bill Gray
Senior Lecturer in English, University College, Chichester
Dr Anthony Grenville
Lecturer in German (retired)
Dr Martin Grossel
Student, Lecturer in Organic Chemistry, and Curator of Common Room
The Right Hon the Earl Haig OBE
Painter
Dr Christopher Haigh
Student, and Tutor in Modern History
Mr John Harris
Steward of Christ Church
Dr David Hine
Student, and Tutor in Politics
Miss Fiona Holdsworth
Editor of Christ Church Association News and formerly
European Communications Director for ACNielsen
Mr Timothy Hornsby
Research Lecturer 1964; Senior Civil Servant predominantly
in rural affairs
Professor Sir Michael Howard
Honorary Student, and Regius Professor of Modern History, 1980–1989
Sister Huntley (decd)
First college nurse
Dr Belinda Jack
Student, and Tutor in French and Junior Censor
Mr Peter Jay
Formerly Her Majesty's Ambassador to Washington (retired)

Dr Paul Kent
Emeritus Student, Tutor in Chemistry, 1955–72, and Censor of Degrees
Mr Trevor Kerslake
A Guinness Son & Co Ltd (retired)
Mr Richard Law MBE
Governor of the British Institute of Florence until 2001; Banker, Euromed Group (retired). Writer on opera.
The Right Hon Lord Lawson of Blaby
Honorary Student and Chancellor of the Exchequer, 1983–1989
The Very Revd Christopher Lewis
Dean of Christ Church
Dr David Luke (decd)
Student, and Tutor in Modern Languages, 1960–8
Dr John Mason
Emeritus Student, and Tutor in Modern History, 1957–87
Professor Colin Matthew (decd)
Lecturer in Gladstone Studies 1970, Gladstone Student 1974; Tutor in Modern History at St Hugh's 1978. Editor, *Oxford Dictionary of National Biography*
Professor Henry Mayr-Harting
Regius Professor Emeritus of Ecclesiastical History
Mrs Janet McMullin
Assistant Librarian, Christ Church
Ms Jan Morris CBE
Honorary Student and travel writer
Mr Mark Morris
Artistic director, KidsOp, Canada; academic, and opera librettist
Mr Tom Morris
Producer, BBC
The Right Hon Sir David Neuberger
Lord Justice of Appeal
Miss Liz Nice
Journalism Lecturer, University of Sheffield
Mr Rex Norman
Headmaster (retired); Christ Church Cathedral steward
Mr Peter Oppenheimer
Student, and President of the Oxford Centre for Hebrew and Jewish Studies
Dr Judith Pallot
Student, and Tutor in Geography
Mr Humphrey Palmer
Professor of Philosophy, Cardiff University (retired)
Professor Gerald Parkhouse
Corning Glass Professor of International Business, Elmira College
Professor Peter Parsons
Emeritus Student, and Regius Professor of Greek, 1989-2003
His Honour Judge (David) Pitman
Circuit Judge (retired)
Mr Eric Prabhakar
Represented India in the 1948 Olympic Games. Administrative Executive, UNESCO from 1970 (retired)
Professor Peter Pulzer
Emeritus Student, Tutor in Politics, 1962–84; Gladstone Professor of Government and Public Administration, All Souls College, 1984–96

The Right Hon Lord Quinton
President of Trinity College, Oxford, 1978–1987
Mr William (Bill) Rathbone
Director and Chief Executive, Royal United Kingdom Beneficent Association and Universal Beneficent Association, 1988–2001 (retired)
Mr Peter Rooley
Personnel manager and PR consultant
Mr Francis Russell
Deputy Chairman, Christie, Manson & Woods Ltd
Mr Dick Sargent
Economist
Mr Timothy Schroder
Freelance lecturer and Consultant Curator at the Victoria & Albert Museum
Brigadier Fraser Scott
Commander of the 94th regiment, Royal Artillery (retired)
Revd Paul Shaw
Priest, St Luke the Physician, Wirral (retired)
Mr Oswald Shuffrey
Schoolmaster (retired)
Mr Edwin Simpson
Student, Tutor in Law and Senior Censor
Mr Christopher Sladen
Civil Servant (retired)
Ms Jacqueline Thalmann
Curator of the Picture Gallery
Dr Ron Truman
Emeritus Student, and Tutor in Modern Languages, 1964–2001
Mr Geoff Tudor
Lecturer in History, Dartmouth RNC. Competed in the 1948 Olympics in the 3000m steeplechase
The Right Revd Peter Walker
Bishop of Dorchester and Canon of Christ Church, 1972–77; Bishop of Ely, 1977–89
The Right Hon Lord Williams of Elvel CBE
Cricket blue, banker, and deputy leader of the Labour Party in the House of Lords
Dr Rowan Williams
Most Revd and Right Hon The Lord Archbishop of Canterbury, and Honorary Student.
Dr Jonathan Wright
Peter Pulzer Student, and Tutor in Politics
Mr Ian Wyatt
Executive Producer, TV Directors' Training, BBC
Dr Brian Young
Student, and Tutor in Modern History

We would also like to thank The Hon John Jolliffe (1953) who, as contributing editor, had particular responsibilities for the 1930s, 1940s and 1950s.

List of Subscribers

Michael Abbott	1972
Prof. John A.S. Abecasis-Phillips	1955
Lord Aberdare	1965
Dr John Ackers	1960
David Acland CBE DL	1949
Rev'd Dr R.J.P. Acworth	1949
Jane Adams (née Bray)	1988
James D.S. Adams	1985
James Agnew	1976
Rami Aharoni	1977
So Won Silas and	
Jacqueline Ahn	1995
John Aird	1958
Hamish Aird	1961
E.J.C. Album	1956
Sylvia de Bertodano	1987
C.A. Alikhani	
James Allan	1953
Graham Allatt	1967
Sarah Allatt	1996
Kerry Allerton	1995
Tessa Allingham (née Fox)	1985
John A. Allsop	1956
Dr Gerhard Altmann	1995
Dr David L. Amarnek	
C.J. Ames	1972
Mark Amory	1962
Zarathustra Jal Amrolia	1983
Professor B. Anagnostopoulos	1947
John Kinlock Anderson	1946
William F.T. Anderson	1953
Liz Andrews and John Caughey	
Professor Jay Appleton	1938
M.R. Armond	1980
R.J. Jarrett	1955
Dr Jason Arvis	
Dr Joanna Ashbourn	1988
M.H. Ashton	1967
Richard S. Ashworth	1961
Dr Ivon Asquith	1965
The Hon. Nicholas Assheton	
CVO	1954
Dr Nigel Aston	1979
Claire Athis-Edwards	1987
R. Attfield	1960
Stephen Ayre	1996
William Bacon	1947
B.E. Badcock	1989
Roger S. Bagnall	1995
Nicholas Bagshawe	1964
Dr Val Ballard	1991
Ranjit Banerji	1951
Lawrence Banks	1958
C.H. Barber	1946
T.M. Baring	1948
Susan and David Barker	
Peter Barnes	1953
Dr J.E.G. Barnett	1957
Dugald Barr	1961
Rachel Barrett (née Sparrow)	1983
David Barron	1966
Paul Barrow	1985
Prof. Robin Barrow FRSC	1963
Philip Bartle QC	1971
Jonathan E. Barton	2000
J.K. Batey	1964
Michael Beaumont	1958
Tim Beaumont	1949
Martin J. Beaver	1953
Lauren Becker	2000
Michael J. Bell	1969
David Bell	1979
Simon Nihal Bell	1986
Anthony Benn	1931
James Benn	1970
John A. Bennett	1963
Simon Bennett	1982
His Most Eminent Highness Fra	
Andrew Bertie	1951
Emma Bevan	1995
Dolin Dwijen Bhagawati	2001
Bishop John Bickersteth	1946
Thomas Biggins	1987
Brendan Biggs	1996
Kate Bingham	1983
David Binsted	1973
Robert Binyon	1969
Robin Birch CB DL	1957
John N. Birch	1960
Tim Birchall	1985
Mark Bisset	1985
Richard J. Bisson	1979
Thomas N. Bisson	2004
S.N. Blair Harris	
E.A. Blair Plimmer	
Graham Blair Williams	1947
C.G. Bland	1968
Sonja Bland	2004
Anthony Blood	1948
Philip Bodman	1979
M.A. and A.J. Bogod	1948
Tony Bolt	1943
Alastair J. Bonar	1958
Andrew D. Bond	1993
J.R. Bonham	1977
Miss Elizabeth A. Bonnice	2007
Gordon W. Bonsall	1952
Emily Boon	2002
W.J.G. Boot	1954
Christopher Bostock OBE	1942
Anthony J. Boucher	
Mrs Alexandra Bould	
(née Hewitt)	1989
Prof. D. Boulter	1944
Professor J. Bowman	1942
Harriet Boyd	2005
Dr L.L. Boyle	1960
Anthony Bradford	1955
Neil Bradford	1991
Simon Bradley	1984
Geoffrey Breeze	1967
Peter Brimacombe	1990
Sir Theodore Brinckman Bt	1950
John Brisby Esq. QC	1974
Peter Brockman	1955
Jaqueline Broers	1998
Sir Rupert Bromley	1956
Spencer T. Brooke	1958
Professor John Brookfield	1973
F. David Brooks	1952
Gavin Brown	1943
K.C. Brown	1975
Dr Karen E. Brown	1987
Andrew Brown	1985
(Canon) Wilfrid Browning	1937
Keith Bruce-Smith	1972
Martin Warwick Bryant	1972
Stephen Bubb JP MA	1972
Dr D.F. Buck	1970
Mr Nick Buckland	1963
Clare Buckley	2002
Mr Stephen N. Burbridge CB	1955
Dr H.H. Burchnall	1938
Christopher Burgess	2003
Edward H. Burn	1954
M.T. Burnyeat	1977
David Burton	1975
C.M. Bury	1992
Barry Cahill	1977
Ian Cairns	1953
Mr Michael J. Calder	1953
Ariadne Calvo-Platero	1982
Donald Cameron of Lochiel	1965
Sir Ilay Campbell Bt	1948
Alain Camu	1952
Robin Cannon	1972
Gerald J. Cardinale	1989
Simon H.D. Carey	1949
John H. Carr	1941
David Cartwright	1978
Ralph Carver	1957
Paul Castle	1981
David P.J. Cater	1977
G.L. Cawkwell	1946
Edward Cazalet	1956
Chak Ming Chan	2006
Sir Jeremy Chance Bt	1944
Eugene Chang	1970
Mr and Mrs R. Chapman	
Luke Chappell	1986
Elizabeth Chapple	2005
A.P. Charters	1991
Stephen Chater	1974
William Cheng	1948
Mr Roger Cherry	1955
Paul G. Chesson	1986
V.K. Chew	1933
Rhian Chilcott	1989
Dr Roman Cholij	1991
Charles W. Clark	1999
R.C. Chwoles Villers	1970
Anna Maria Clarke	
(née Vella-Briffa)	1992
Jane Clarke	1990
Christopher Claxton Stevens	1971
Jeremy Clayton	1975
John Clennett	1977
John G. Cleworth	1968
Kieran Clifford	1989
Edward Clive (Lennox Boyd)	1986
A.D.P. Clover	1959
Anthony Clover	1959
Francis Clube	1978
R.M. Coates Esq.	1993
Caroline Cohen	2004
James Collier	1976

LIST OF SUBSCRIBERS

R.A.H. Collinge 1943
Rebecca Collins 1997
Rory Collins 1970
Alison Colls 1994
Albert Connolly 1953
George X. Constantinidi 1948
Trevor Conway 1951
Commander K. Cook 1978
Rachel Cook 2003
Nigel J. Cooper 1961
Michael V. Cooper 1983
Jim Cooper 1969
Sarah J. Cooper 2002
Dr Frank Copplestone 1990
Simon Cornelius 1979
Dr Eimear Cotter 1997
Dr Philip Cowdall 1991
Stuart H. Cowper 1989
A.K. Crackett 1966
Michael Craddock 1954
Anthony L.T. Cragg 1974
Dr Harry Craig 1949
Martin Crane 1969
Mr Tim Crapper 1984
I.P.G. Creasey 1975
Jonathan Cree 1967
Dr D.J. Crennell 1957
Paul Crisell 1989
John Croft CBE 1941
Patrick Cronin 1958
Tony Crooks 1983
Peter A. Cross 1963
Anthony Crossland 1957
Amy Alexandra Crossley 2001
Helen Crossley 1995
Jonathan Crossman MBE 1965
David Crowe 1958
Robert Crowe 1974
David Crowley 1953
Humphry Crum Ewing 1955
Peter Culver 1981
The Rev'd Canon
William Cummings 1957
Vicky Cunningham 1987
Lyndon da Cruz 1990
Douglas Dales 1971
Earl of Dalkeith 1972
Russell M. Dallen, Jr 1988
Sophie Daly 2004
J.M. Anthony Danby 1947
B.A. Daniels 1972
John A. Darragh 1973
Paul N. Davey 1977
Hilary Davidson 1993
Michael Davie 1980
Jonathan Davies 1980
Martin Davies 1952
Dr Benjamin Davies 1991
Dr Ashley Davies
John R.M. Davies 1960
Hugh Davies 1964
Michael H. Davis 1959
Dr T.H.P.A. Davies 1962
Alan Dawes 1946
Bill and Rose Day
Keith Day 1978
Mark F. van Coeverden de Groot 1986
Professor Nicholas de Lange 1962
Florence de Maré 2003
Louise de Muscote-Cholij 1993
Mark de Rond 1996
Jaroslav Dedek 1961
Conrad Dehn QC 1945
Eric Descheemaeker 2001

Alan Detheridge 1966
R.H. Dickinson 1954
William Wolfgang Dieneman 1947
Mijanou Caroline Dilks 2004
David Dimbleby 1958
Professor Michael Dobson 1979
Sir Richard Doll (Decd) 1969
Theodore Doll 1966
Anna-Silvia Dooley
(née Fattorini) 1988
T.L. Dowie 1972
John Downey MD DPhil 1960
C.V. de P. Doyle 1986
Mohsin Drabu 2001
Sara Draper (née Teague) 1989
Peter L. Duffett 1960
Sir Robert Dunbar Bt 1976
Ben Duncan 1950
Joel Dupont 1961
Viscount Dupplin 1981
Mark Dyer 1949
Sara Dyson 1986
Anthony J. Earl 1986
Mr E. Earlam 2002
Mrs V. Earle
Matthew Eastmond 1992
The Hon. Ronald Eden 1951
John C. Edwards 1972
Jonathan Edwards 2002
Lord Egremont 1967
Jeffrey Tevebaugh Ehmsen 2001
Ray Eitel-Porter 1981
Dr John Elder 1993
Alan Christopher Elliot 1955
John A. Ellison 1950
Chris Elliss 1981
Graham F. Elms 1970
Mark Elsner and Christine E. 1994
Charles Emmerson 1996
Katie Ernest (née Mercer) 1984
Martin J. Evans 1980
Laura Evans (née Pamplin) 1985
Matthew D. Evans 1995
Richard Everest 1958
Charles R. Ewald 1979
Dr Gregory Ezra 1976
G.B. Fairbairn 1948
John S. Faulder 1948
Fred Fearn 1975
Professor N.R. Feldman 1992
Wendell Fenton 1961
Eric Fergusson 1999
C.H. Fernando 1953
Sarah Brown Ferrario, MPhil 1996
Ronald Findlay 1937
Robin Finlay 1958
Rosemary Finnon 1993
M.J. Firth 1977
Simon Firth 1983
Donald Fisher CBE 1949
Sarah Flaherty 2003
Mr T.L. Flaxman 1994
Catherine Fleming 1995
C. Trevor Fletcher 1946
John A. Fletcher 1964
Mr S. Flunder 1971
John Foad 1957
Geoffrey M.T. Foley 1965
F.V. Ford 1960
Brian W. Forgham 1948
James Forrest 1962
Paul Forte 1982
Fiona J. Foster 1984
Liz Fox 2000

Stephen Foxall 1980
Giles R. Frampton 1976
Sarah Francis 1984
R.M. Franklin 1963
Mr I.G.K. Fraser 1957
Simon Freebairn-Smith 1955
Robert J. Freeman 1956
Professor Jonathan
Freeman-Attwood 1985
Ashley Paul French 2003
Nicholas Fridd 1971
Myles Frisby 1962
Sophie Fuller 2001
Tom Fuller 1946
Louis Lik Chim Fung 1986
Stephen Furness 1968
Robert Galloway 1977
Peter Gardiner-Hill 1948
Barrie Gardner 1962
John Gaynor 1954
Tom Gentleman 1999
Brian George 1959
P.N. Gerrard 1948
Emma Ghosh (née Collins) 1994
Alan Gibbs 1971
M.E.H. Gibbs 1950
Roger Gibbs 1958
Ian Gibson 1969
Guy Gibson 1966
Jessica Gibson 2002
Mr David G. Gidney 1970
Anthony Gilbert 1984
Mr David A. Gilkes 1956
David W.J. Gillespie 1960
Robert W. Ginty 1971
Mitchell M. Gitin 1960
Sir William Gladstone Bt KG 1946
J. Francis Gladstone 1960
Anthony Gladstone-Thompson 1962
M.A. Glasby 1968
Ben Glassman 2002
Michael Glenn 1991
Neil Glenn 1987
Miss Emma Godfrey 1990
Jeremy Goford 1963
Dr Peter Gold 1963
Mr Kenneth Goldsbrough 1977
Hugh Goodfellow 1988
Mr and Mrs R. Goodstone
Graham Gordon 1945
Ned Gould 2003
George Goulding 1970
Neil Graham 1988
Dr Roger Grant 1957
D.L. Grant 1957
Hamish Grant 1992
J.B. Grant 1970
William Nelson Gray 1971
Bob Green 1964
Brian Green 1953
Dr D.J. Greenland FRS 1948
David Greetham 1960
Francis Grenfell 1958
Father Philip Griffin 1983
Stephen L. Griffith 1967
Gareth Griffiths 1986
Graham Grist 1965
Matthew Gromada 2001
Brian Grumbridge 1966
John R. Grundon 1951
William Guast 2005
Arnold Guetta 1943
Azmina Gulamhusein 2000
Natalia Gurushina 1990

Erlend Haaskjold 2004
Jo Ann Hackett 1996
The Right Hon the
Earl Haig OBE 1936
The Earl of Halifax 1963
Peter Hall 1977
Douglas Hall 1991
Julian Hall 1957
Damien Hall 1992
R. Halvorsen 1980
Bryce Hamblin 1969
Dr Saeed Hamid-Khani 1996
F.R.O. de C. Hamilton 1958
Dr Laura Hamilton 1998
Ben Hanbury 1948
Dr Michael Hand 1997
Jonathan Hand 1986
Neil Handley 1991
Robert Hanrott 1959
James V. Hansford 1976
Emily C.E. Hanson 2003
Roger Hardiman 1960
Julian Hardwick 1983
Norman Hardyman 1948
Aidan R.J. Hargitt 2001
Dr A.H. Harker 1970
Tim Harlow 1978
Barry James Harmer 1965
Dr Phillip T. Harries 1965
Anthony M. Harris 1954
Joanne Harris 1998
Dr Edward L. Harrison 1947
B.L.E. Harrison 1962
Mr Robert N. Harrison 1943
Victoria Harrison 2005
Dominick Harrod 1959
Stephen Harrow 1991
Miss Samantha Harthen 2001
Helen Louise Hartwell 2000
Sonia Jane Hartwell 1994
Sir James Harvie-Watt Bt 1959
Christopher Harwood 1949
Brian R. Hawtin 1964
Sidney Hayes 1946
Garth Haythornthwaite 1956
Ben Haywood Smith 1975
Dr Ronald J. Heal DPhil 1999
Peter Hearn 1970
Nicholas Heath 1975
David Heaton OBE 1946
David Heimann 1955
Jonathan Hellewell JP 1991
Sarah Henderson
(née Johnstone) 1988
Robin Herbert 1954
Thomas Hesse 1986
Alison Hill 2004
Paul Hill 1967
Prince Abbas Hilmi 1961
Dr C.N.H. Hitchings 1993
Andrew J.A. Hobson 1956
James Matthew David Holden 2002
Ron Holding 1969
John Holland 1958
Tom Holme 1977
David Holmes 1953
A.M. Holroyd 1956
J.K. Holroyd LVO 1944
Robert Holroyd 1981
Oliver Holt 1985
Michael Honeybone 1959
Simon John Hood 1995
A.M. Hook 1962
Lord Alexander Hope 1989

Professor Anthony G. Hopwood 1997
Sarah Hordern 1991
Sir Peter Hordern PC 1949
The Very Rev'd Timothy
(Michael) Horner OSB MBE 1938
Timothy Hornsby 1958
Toby Horton 1965
Michael Housden 1978
Dr Bob Hoyle 1983
David Hudd 1977
Clifton Hughes 1964
David A. Hughes 1996
Nicholas Hughes 1973
Martin Humphries 1991
Philip Hunt 1979
Richard Hurst 1975
Graham Hurst 1945
Sam Hutchings 2000
Steve Hutchinson 1973
Matthew Hutton 1971
John Hyde 1954
Yasser Idilby 1951
Tony Insall LVO 1968
Grace Ireland 2003
Nicholas Ireson 2004
Carole Irvine 1996
Thomas P. Izod 1966
Mr Ian Jackson 1965
Charis R. Jackson 1994
Mark Jackson-Stops 1968
Sir Francis Jacobs 1957
Dr Roger J.B. Jakeman 1979
Michael James 1970
Eric Janssen 1953
Very Rev'd Robert Jeffery
Sub-Deacon and Canon 1996-2002
Kate Jillings 1998
J.A.A. Johnson 1976
Cleveland Johnson 1978
Dr Nichola Johnson 1993
David V. Jones 1977
Garry Jones 1964
Catherine A. Jones 2003
Gareth Jones 1996
Lyndon Jones 1977
M.C. Jones-Mortimer 1959
Mike Jordan 1985
Dr Miriam Ruth Jorgensen 1987
Steven F. Joseph 1974
David S. Joyner 1981
Juliane Kaden 2001
Brigadier Antony Karslake 1951
J.T. Katz and K. Volk 1991
Maya Kaushik 2004
Dr Thomas Kern 1995
Dr Milo Keynes 1962
C.G. Kemp 1972
V.G. Kendall 1950
John Kerby 1961
Arthur Kincaid 1966
Peter Kincaid 1971
Rev'd David King 1960
Professor W.J. Torrance Kirby 1979
Patrick Kivlin 1971
T. Bryan Knight 1953
Chris J. Knights 1961
Dr Kristine Krug 1991
Peter A. Kyle 1963
John J. Lake 1961
Dr Donald J. Lane 1953
Nicholas D.J. Lane 1957
A.J. Larner 1984
Mr Michael Latham 1956
Joseph Lau 1999
Richard Law 1947

Dr Tony Law 1965
James Lawry 1989
Matthew C. Le Merle 1981
Dr Russell Leather 1942
J.M. Lee 1986
Adam Lee 1960
Edwin A.M. Lee 1995
James Carloss Legge 1993
Michael Legge 1962
Rupert Legge 1969
Brian Leigh-Bramwell 1970
Mr David R Leighton 1951
Paul Lettow 1999
Brian G. Levy 1958
Ogden N. Lewis 1965
Meredith E. Lewis 2001
Dr P.A. Lewis 1993
J.G. Lewis-Anthony 1998
David V. Lidderdale 1951
Martin J.D. Light 1962
David Limb (in memoriam) 1979
Francis W. Lindsay 1943
Kimberley Littlemore
(née Jenkins) 1985
Zoya T. Loeb (née Todorovic) 1997
James M. Long 1974
Sara L. Longworth 1981
Carl Arthur Lu 1979
Nigel Lovett 1964
Christopher Lowe 1949
Rev'd Nicholas Luckett 1962
Professor Jack A. Lucy 1949
Sir Nicholas W. Lyell 1959
Alexander Lyell 2000
Frederick Lyons 1968
Anthony Machin 1955
Floyd MacNeile-Dixon 1957
Pat Maconchy 1936
Tom Madden 1939
Ian Maddison 1963
Eric Madre 2004
Sharon Maxwell Magnus 1981
Charles W. Mahoney 1987
J.S.K. Mainwaring 1958
Saman Majd 1974
Constantine Mano 1956
Martin Mansergh 1966
Daniel Mansfield 1989
Lawrence Wayne Markert 1976
Stephen Marnham 1964
John C. Marsden 1966
Richard Marsh 1981
Quentin Marshall 1992
Dr Andrew C.R. Martin 1982
Dr W. Mather Mason 1965
Michael Matantos 1968
Alastair Mathewson 1979
R.A. Mathias 1963
Dominic Mathon 1991
Dr K.R.K. Matthews 1982
Sir Robin Maxwell-Hyslop 1951
Dr W.D. May 1941
Jenny Mayhew 2003
Andrew A. McAleer 1980
Anne McCabe 1993
Warwick A.M. McDonald 1997
Arundel McDougall 1972
Douglas McDougall 1962
Barry McFadzean 1957
Dan McGurk 1949
Dr Chistopher A. McIntosh 1962
Matthew McKaig 1983
J. Bryce McLeod 1950
Declan McLoughlin 1960
Don H. McLucas Jr 1962

Alan Meacock 1946
H.S. Mellor 1957
"Cim" Mellor 1941
K.R.N. Menon 1954
Bhaskar Menon 1953
Andrew C. Menzies 1961
Geoffrey E. Merrick MC 1946
Cristian Micheletti 1992
John P. Miller 1958
Terry Mills 1963
Nigel Mills 1976
Thomas J.W. Milner 2004
Charles Mindenhall 1990
Rev'd Desmond Minty 1944
F.P. Mitchell 1940
John C.W. Mitchell 1957
Simon Mitchell 1959
F.P.W. Mitchell 1940
Ana Mitric 1992
Sir Nigel Mobbs (Decd) 1956
John Mole 1964
Philip Monbiot 1965
Martin A. Monroe 1997
Richard M. Moore 1977
Jonathon Moore 1998
The Rev'd Michael J. Moreton 1946
Ian Eversfield Morgan 1962
Alexandra Morgan
(née Henderson) 1981
Philip Morgan-Klein
Lewis Morgan-Klein 2004
Mitsue Morita 2002
Michael Moritz 1973
Gerard Morris 1987
N.G.U. Morris 1959
Dr Peter J.T. Morris 1974
Roger Morris 1966
David N. Morrison 1960
Romilly Moses 2004
Mr and Mrs A.G. Moses
Simon Mosley 1948
Antony Moss and Lois Moss 1992
Professor Peter Mudford 1957
Peter C. Muller 1985
Canon Peter Mullins 1979
R.C. Munns 1972
R.A. Murley 1975
David Murray 1996
Dr Andrew Murray 1996
A.J. Myers QC 1971
Julian Naden Robinson 2005
Dr Heather Lucy Elizabeth
Neilson 1986
Liam Neilson 1995
David G.H. Nelson OBE 1953
James Neuberger 1968
Rt Hon. Lord
Justice Neuberger 1966
Mrs Shirley S. Newton
Alex Nicholas 1998
Clare Nicholls 1988
David Nicholson 1962
Matt Nicol 1978
Yasou Noguchi 1961
Nicholas Nops 1968
Rex Norman 1957
Hugh D. Norton-Amor 1975
Robert W. Nowak 1989
Simon Nurick 1952
Anthony Gordon O'Brien 1969
Aidan O'Byrne 1990
Allegra O'Cock 2004
Collette and Pat O'Connor
Philip A.R. Oetker 1993
Mrs Susan Ogonovsky

Asayo Ohyori 2000
Michael J. Oldfield 1963
Terence O'Leary 1969
Dr Edward Olleson 1963
Derek Ong 1993
Susan Orchard 1984
Richard Orgill 1971
S. Osborn 1992
Neville N. Osborne 1984
Clive Osborne 1974
Mr and Mrs J.H. Ovens
Kelly Tania Page 1993
Marcus Pakenham 1979
Alan Palgrave-Brown 1941
Hon. Henry Palmer 1960
Emily Parfitt 2004
Mr C.R.W. Parish 1968
Daisy Parish 1991
Luke P.I. Parker 2004
Victoria Parker 2001
David I. Parker 1974
Jonathan Parry 1992
Dr Graham Pascoe 1968
Andrew Paterson 1969
William Pattisson 1982
David Peake 1955
Augur Pearce 1975
Mr Martin Pearson 1961
J.H. Peltzer 1999
James Pennefather 1993
Michael Perceval 1953
R.A. Percy 1965
Algernon Percy 1987
Mark Perfect OBE 1973
Steven B. Pfeiffer 1969
J.E. Philpott 1990
William J. Philpott 1983
G.J. Pickering 1968
Christopher Pike 1962
Nick Pike 2002
Colin Pilbeam 1980
M. Azariah Pinney 1954
David Christian Pitman 1957
Nick Pitts-Tucker 1968
Richard Platts 1954
Ian Plenderleith 1961
Corinne Pluchino 1991
Gerald Porter 1964
Roque F. Portugal 1989
Mike Poulton 1953
Stephen Power 1987
Eric Prabhakar 1948
Peter Preece 1963
Christopher Prentice 1973
Professor J. Prescott 1950
Nick Prest 1971
P.K. Preston 1935
Lydia F. Prieg 2004
Dr John A. Prince 1960
Richard Pringle Benthall 1986
Mr Simon Prior-Palmer 1970
Paolo Quattrone 2003
Fabienne Queyrane 1995
Lord Quinton 1943
James Radcliffe 1958
Alastair Ramsay 1986
William Rathbone 1956
Dr Khanta Ratnavel 1960
Mr Timothy Rawe 1975
John Raymond 1965
Nicola Read (née Weller) 1988
Gerald Reading 1953
John H. Redding
Christopher Redfern 1963
William Reece Smith, Jr 1949

T.B. Rees 1957
Leila Rees 1995
Mr Edward J. Reid 1994
Dr John. B. Reid 1962
Dr P.G.E. Reid 1962
John Reilly 1981
Professor Tore Rem 1998
C.P. Rentoul 1961
Miss C.L. Rhodes 1992
James Rice 1976
Mr Michael D. Rice 1974
Hugh Richardson
Nigel Riches 1970
Robert F. Riding 1959
Sarah Rimer 1996
Wolf-Georg Ringe 2003
Hamish M.J. Ritchie 1961
Edward Hugh Roach 1939
Rachel Roads (née Chesworth) 1986
Andrew Robinson 1990
Dr Duncan Robertson 1998
Chris Robinson 1972
Lucy Robinson 2005
Samuel D. Robinson 1991
Alexander Joseph Robinson 2002
Frank Robson 1958
Max Roessler 1975
Helen Louise Rogers 1993
Sara Rogers 1990
Robert Ronus 1961
Alison Ross 1996
Ian Ross 1969
Vicky Ross 2003
Michael Rowe 1990
Tamsin L. Rowe 2001
Sarah Rowland-Jones 1997
Geoff Ruddell 1989
Charles Runge 1964
Philip Rush 1973
Anwar Saifullah-Khan 1967
Kirsten and William Sampson 1997 and 1999
Carla Samuels 1992
Hugh Sassoon 1949
A.P. Saunders 1973
Dr Kate Saunders 2000
Paul Sauvary 1971
Robin Sawers 1953
David Robertson Sawyier 1972
Alexander Schmitt 2002
Catherine Schneider (née Ibbotson) 1988
Stephen Schneider 1988
Tim Schneider 1985
Santiago Schnell 2001
Timothy Schroder 1972
Anthony Schur 1958
Wolfgang Schwerdtle 1991
Simon Scott 1983
(Brigadier) Fraser Scott 1937
Sir Anthony Scott Bt 1955
See Weng Keong, Irwin 2001
Jeremy Seigal 1978
G.N. Selbie 1964
Alan M. Senior 1962
Julien Sevaux 1989
Nicola Shackleton 1981
Michael Sharp 1996
David Shasha 1974
Mr Graham J. Shaw 1964
Dr Dennis F. Shaw CBE 1942
Professor Alan Shaw 1938
Nigel Sheffield 1951
Maria Sherwood-Smith 1990

James Shirras 1976
G. Oswald Shuffrey 1920
Mrs Naz Sienkiewicz
Rupert Simons 2000
David Simpson 1959
Guy Slatter 1955
Bruce Smith 1958
Garth A. Smith 2005
J.D. Smith 1996
Dr Michael Smith 1955
Patrick Smith 1997
Helen Smith 1989
Dr Timothy W. Smith 1986
Andrew Snowdon 1971
Dr R.A. Sochynsky 1976
Greville Sockett 1955
Prof. J.A. Soggin 1991
David Warin Solomons 1972
Kahlil D. Somauroo 1998
Dr D.B. Southern 1965
Heather J. Southwell (née Foley) 1995
B.H.G. Sparrow 1939
Charles Sparrow 1981
Hattie Spence 1997
James Spicer 1983
James A. Spooner 1952
Kathryn Staley 1998
J.E. Stanfield 1952
Dr Christopher Rowland Staniforth MA MBRS MRCGP DCH 1979
Michael Stannard 1948
Dr J.M. Stansbie 1960
Rob Staplin 1994
Sir John Starkey Bt 1958
Arabella Steel 1984
James Steel 1978
Ian Steer 1972
Benjamin James Stephens 1998
James Stephens 1988
Philip Stephens 1960
Karl Sternberg 1988
Gordon Stevens 1943
John A. Stewart 1987
Stephen Stewart 1990
Michael Stewart 1964
David Stone 1994
Dr Brian R. Stonebridge 1958
J.S. Story 1935
John Story 1935
C.M. Strong 1957
Mr. Nick Stroud 1979
P.D. Stuart 1938
Andrew Studdert-Kennedy 1977
The Rev'd Dr Richard Sturch 1954
Dr Carol Sullivan 1981
Michael Sutton 1961
Dr Michael W. Sweet-Escott 1941
Lt Col J.F.P. Swift MBE R. Welsh 1985
Helena Sykes 2000
Robert Sykes 1968
Timothy Symons 1990
Nicola Emma Talbot 1993
Michael H. Tarrant 1975
David Tate 1959
Geoffrey Tattersall 1966
Victoria Tattersall 1997
Dr Justin Taylor 1993
Gerald Tedder 1954
John Temple 1955
Jonathan R. Tetsill PhD 1987
Helen Thomas 1998
Daniel Thomières 1973
Mr Ian J.A. Thompson 1993

Nicolas Thompson 1946
Rev'd Dr J.D. Thompson 1965
Paul Thomson 1996
Sarah Tiller 2004
The Venerable John Tiller 1957
Patrick Tobin 1960
Roland Todd 1979
Claire Townsend 1998
Dr C.G. Townsend 1989
C.J. Train 1951
Graham Trasler 1962
Jon Treers 1996
William Trower QC 1978
Charles E. Tucker 1961
H.J.M. Tucker 1950
Geoffrey Tudor 1945
Richard Tydeman 2002
S.P. Tytherleigh 1977
John O.T. Underwood 1931
W.E.B. Usher 1951
Nikhil Vadgama 2003
Rev'd A.S. Valle 1936
Dr Anton Van Dellen 1997
George H. Van Kooten 1995
Michael Vaughan-Lee 1962
Frank Versaci 1957
Dale Vesser 1954
Giles Vicat 1976
Emma Vickery 1991
Robert Vilain 1983
Clive Vinall 1964
Charlie Vincent 2000
Rudolf Wachter 1987
Dr Geoffrey A. Wagner 1939
Edward Wakeling 1981
Mr Derick Walker 1976
Nicholas Walker 1973
Richard Walker 1959
Alan Gordon Walker
Michael Walker 1957
Nicholas Walker 1973
Thomas G. Walker 1997
R.M.T. Walker-Brash 1939
R.P. Walther 1962
Dr Milton Wan 1980
Hon. Peter Ward 1947
Andrew Warner 1974
Andrew J. Warner 2001
Sir Henry Warner Bt 1940
S.A. Watson 1962
John Watson Wemyss 1947
Dr A.A. Watt 2003
Christopher H. Weeks 1958
Herbert D. Weintraub 1952
Sarah Wells (née Sturch) 1988
William Wells 1976
Colin P.N. West 1980
Mr Christopher W. Westall 1960
Rob Westcott 1955
Jeremy Western 1970
Charles Whateley 1973
Dr A. Gordon Wheeler 1962
Stephen Wheeler 1982
D.W.R. Whicker 1957
Clive L.S. Whitcher 1966
Robert Whitcombe 1974
Colin A.H. White 1957
Maria-Cristina White 1990
Andrew J. Whitehouse 1995
David S. Whitelegge 1949
Gregg Whiting 1992
E.Y. Whittle 1943
Donald Whitton (Decd) 1949
Dr Charles Wickham-Jones 1945

Michael Wilkinson 1954
P.M. Wilkinson 1977
Dr A.P. Wilkinson 1984
George T.N. Wilkinson 1972
Jeremy Willder 1958
Andrew R. Williams 1969
B.V. Williams 1950
Dr D. Bryn Williams 1956
Dafydd Williams 1978
David J. Williams 1949
Gareth Williams 1998
Jeremy Williams 2000
Terry Williams 1975
Richard Williams-Ellis 1953
Dr Stefan Willitsch 2004
Brian J. Wilson 1950
G.A. Wilson 1942
Mr John A.W. Wilson 1961
H.J.R. Wing 1954
Michael Wingfield Digby 1959
Stephan B. Winkler 1998
Charles Winnifrith CB 1954
Tim Winstanley 1977
Buster Winter 1976
David Witton-Davies 1967
Tim and Sarah Wolfenden 1984 and 1988
Mark Woloshyn 1973
Alistair James Wong 2003
Prairie Yuen Ying Wong 1994
John Wood 1967
Sir Martin Wood 1957
Oscar Wood 2005
P.W.J. Wood 1943
James Woodford 1955
J. Woodhouse 1958
Ellison Murray Woods 1936
Victor L. Woodford 1943
Geoffrey A. Woodward 1944
T.W. Woolerton 2004
D.A. Wright 1980
John D. Wright 1968
Mike Wright 1979
Miles F.M. Wright 1963
P.B. Wright 1954
Ian Wyatt 1964
Mr J.G. Wyatt 1957
Dr Jennifer Yee 2005
Roger Young 1946
Richard Youngman 1978
Colin Youngs 1969
Major Archie Yuill JP 1940
Christopher Zeal 1977
Marke Zervudachi 1949

Index of Names

Names of Contributors can be found on page 204

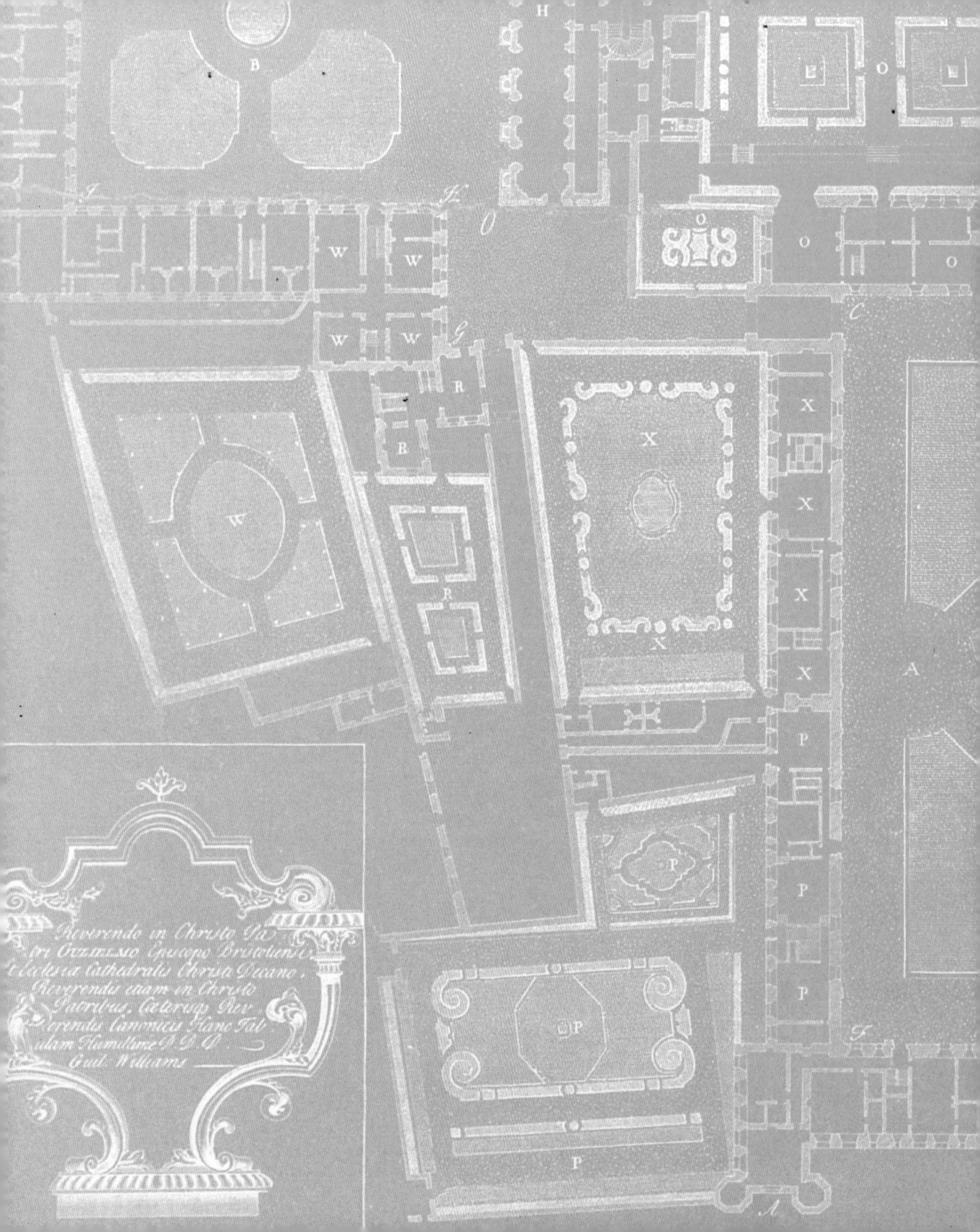
Reverendo in Christo Pa
tri Gulielmo Episcopo Bristoliensi
Ecclesiæ Cathedralis Christi Decano,
Reverendis etiam in Christo
Patribus, Cæterisq; Rev
erendis Canonicis Hanc Tab
ulam Humillime D.D.D.
Gul. Williams